THE HISTORY OF ANCIENT INI

Vol. 1

THE HISTORY
OF
ANCIENT INDIA

Vol. 1

R. C. Dutt

BHARATIYA KALA PRAKASHAN
DELHI (INDIA)

First Published : 1914
Revised Edition : 2009
Revised Edition : 2024

Published by C.P. Gautam *for*
BHARATIYA KALA PRAKASHAN
3480/1, Ground Floor, Narang Colony,
Tri Nagar, Delhi - 110035,
Phone No. : 011 71522860, 9811642997, 8595139625,
E-mail : info@bkpbooks.com; sales.bkpbooks@gmail.com
Website: www.bkpbooks.com

ISBN : 978-81-8090-234-5 (2 Vol. Set) HB

Laser Type Setting
Creative Graphics

Printed by :
G.S. Offset Printers
Delhi

CONTENTS

Chapter *Page No.*

Preface ix

Introduction—Epochs and Dates xxix

BOOK-I

VEDIC PERIOD, B.C. 2000 to 1400

1. Immigration of the Indo-Āryans--Their Literature 1
2. Agriculture, Pasture, and Commerce 9
3. Food, Clothing, and the Arts of Peace 16
4. Wars and Dissensions 23
5. Social and Domestic Life : The Position of Women 35
6. Vedic Religion 49
7. Vedic Ṛṣis 71

BOOK-II

EPIC PERIOD, B.C. 1400 to 1000

1. Literature of the Period 85
2. Kurus and Pāñcālas 98
3. Videhas, Kosalas, and Kāsis 112
4. Belt of Non-Āryan Tribes 124
5. Caste 130
6. Position of Women 143
7. Law, Astronomy and the Progress of Learning 154
8. The Sacrificial Rites and Legends of the Brāhmaṇas 160
9. The Religious and Philosophical Speculations of the Upaniṣads 171

BOOK-III

RATIONALISTIC PERIOD, B.C. 1000 to B. C. 242

1. Literature of the Period 185
2. Expansion of the Hindus and the Rise of Magadha 196
3. Administration 209
4. Laws 218
5. Caste 233
6. Agriculture and Arts 243
7. Woman The Position of Social Life 247
8. Domestic Ceremonies and Gṛhya Rites 261
9. Geometry, Grammar, and the Progress of Learning 273
10. Agnostic Sāṅkhya and the Theistic Yoga Philosophy 280
11. Nyāya or Logic and Vaiśeṣika orAtomic Philosophy 293
12. The two Mīmāṁsā Schools or Orthodox Philosophy. 299
13. Buddhist Sacred Literature 309
14. Life of Gautama Buddha 223
15. Doctrines of Gautama Buddha 344
16. Moral Precepts of Gautama Buddha 365
17. Buddhist Monastic Order 375
18. History of Buddhism 385
19. Budhism and Jainism 402
20. Buddhism and Christianity 411

BOOK-IV

BUDDHIST PERIOD, B.C. 242 to A.D. 500

1. Aśoka the Great and his Edicts 425
2. Language and Alphabet 447
3. The Kings of Magadha 454
4. Kashmir and Gujrat 467
5. Gupta Kings 475
6. Fa Hian's Account of India 482
7. Houen Tsang's Accound of India 490

8. Buddhist Architecture and Sculpture 513
9. Social Manners : Caste 530
10. Domestic Life : The Position of Women 544
11. Civil and Military Administration 551
12. Laws 558
13. Astronomy and the Progress of Learning 572

BOOK-V

PAURĀṆIK PERIOD, A.D. 500 to A.D. 1194

1. Vikramāditya the Great and his Successors 581
2. The Valabhis and the Rajputs 593
3. Bengal and Orissa 601
4. Kashmir and Southern India 612
5. Religion and Religious Literature 624
6. Caste 647
7. Domestic and Social Life : The Position of Women 660
8. Hindu and Jaina Sculpture ... 672
9. Astronomy and Mathematics 690
10. Medicine Chapter 696
11. Drama... 706
12. Poetry...... 731
13. Fiction 746
14. Early Paurāṇik Gvilisation 752
15. Later Paurāṇik Gvilisation 765
Index 782

PREFACE

"If I were asked," says Professor Max Müller, "what I consider the most important discovery which has been made during the Nineteenth Century with respect to the ancient history of mankind, I should answer by the following short line :—

Sanskrit, DYAUSH Pitar= Greek, ΖΕΥΣΠΑΤΗΡ (ZEUS PATER)—Latin, JUPITER = Old Norse, TYR."

And certainly, the discoveries which have been made by European scholars within the last hundred years, with the help of the old Āryan language preserved in India, form one of the most brilliant chapters in the history of the advancement of human knowledge. It is not my intention to give a sketch of that history here ; but a few facts which relate specially to Indian Antiquities may be considered interesting.

It is about a century since Sir William Jones, startled the scholars of Europe by his translation of Śakuntalā, "one of the greatest curiosities," as he said in his preface, "that the literature of Asia has yet brought to light," and one of the tenderest and most beautiful creations of human imagination produced in any age or country. The attention of European literary men was roused to the value and beauty of Sanskrit literature ; and the greatest literary genius of the modern age has recorded his appreciation of the Hindu dramatic piece in lines which have been often quoted, in original and in translation :—

> Would'st thou the life's young blossoms and the fruits of its decline,
>
> And all by which the soul is pleased, enraptured, feasted, fed,— Would'st thou the earth and heaven itself in one sweet name combine?

I name thee, O Śakuntalā. and all at once is said."

—*Goethe.*

Sir William Jones translated Manu, founded the Asiatic Society of Bengal, and lived to continue his researches into the store-house of Sanskrit literature, and acheived valuable results : but he did not live to find what he sought, ~ a clue to India's "ancient history without any mixture of fable." For his enthusiastic labours were mostly confined to the later Sanskrit literature,—the literature of the Post-Buddhist Era ; and he paid little heed to the mine of wealth that lay beyond.

Colebrooke followed in the footstep's of Sir William Jones. He was a mathematician, and was the most careful and accurate Sanskrit scholar that England has ever produced. Ancient Sanskrit literature concealed nothing from his eyes. He gave a careful and accurate account of Hindu Philosophy, wrote on Hindu Algebra and Mathematics, and, in 1805, he first made Europeans acquainted with the oldest work of the Hindu and of the Āryan world, *viz.*, the Vedas. Colebrooke, however, failed to grasp the importance of the discovery he had made, and declared that the study of the Vedas "would hardly reward the labour of the reader much less that of the translator."

Dr. H. H. Wilson followed in the footsteps of Colebrooke ; and although he translated the Ṛg Veda Saṁhitā into English, his labours were mostly confined to later Sanskrit literature. He translated into elegant English the best dramatic works in Sanskrit, as well as the beautiful poem of Kālidāsa, called "Meghadūta." He also translated the Viṣṇu Purāṇa, and laboured to adjust the history of the later Hindu period, and settled many points on a satisfactory basis.

In the meantime; a great genius had arisen in France. The history of oriental scholarship contains no brighter name than that of Burnouf. He traced the connection between the Zend and the Vedic Sanskrit, and framed a Comparative Grammar for his own use before German scholars had written on Comparative Grammar. By such means he deciphered the Zend language and scriptures, elucidated the Ṛg Veda, and shewed its true position in the history of Āryan nations. Versatile as he was profound, he also deciphered the Cuneiform inscriptions of Assyria, and thus earned for him self an undying fame in Europe. And further, in his Introduction to Buddhism, he gave the first philosophical and intelligible account of that great religion. His lessons created a deep sensation in Europe during nearly a quarter of a century (1829 to 1852), and left a lasting impression on the minds of admiring and enthusiastic pupils in Paris, some of whom, like Roth and Max Müller, lived to be the profoundest Vedic scholars of our age.

German scholars, in the meantime, had commenced their labours; and when once they began work in this[1] line, they soon excelled and even dusted all other labourers in the field of Indian Antiquities ! Rosen, the contemporary and friend of Raja Ram Mohan Roy, published the first Aṣṭaka of the Ṛg Veda, with a Latin translation, but his untimely death prevented the further progress of the work.

But the most eminent German scholars of the day set before themselves a higher task; and the industry, perseverence, and genius of men like Bopp, Grimm, and Humboldt soon achieved a result which ranks as one of the noblest and most brilliant discoveries of the century. They marked and traced the connection among all the Indo-European languages—the Sanskrit. the Zend. the Greek, the Latin. the Slav, the Tuton, and the Celtic—they demonstrated all these languages to be the offshoots of the same original stock, and they even discovered the laws under which words were transformed in passing from one language to another. Classical scholars of the day, who believed that all civilization and culture began with the Greek and the Latin, at first smiled and ridiculed, then stood aghast, and ultimately gave way with considerable chagrin and anger to the irresistible march of Truth !

The desire to elucidate ancient Hindu literature and history deepened among scholars as they became more thoroughly alive to the value of Sanskrit. Roth, one of the profoundest Vedic scholars of the century, produced his edition of Yāska with his most valuable notes, and later on he published, with Whitney, an edition of the Atharva Veda, and completed, with Boehtlingk, the most accurate and comprehensive Sanskrit Dictionary yet written. Lassen published his profound work, Indische Alterthumskunde, displaying a deep learning and accurate scholarship which has seldom been excelled. Weber published the White Yajur Veda with its Brāhmaṇa and Sūtras, elucidated many obscure points of Ancient Hindu History in his Indische Studien, and gave the first clear and comprehensive account of Sanskrit literature in his History of Indian Literature. Benfey published a most valuable edition of the Sāma Veda, of which an edition, with translation, had been published by Stevenson and Wilson before. And Muir collected the most suggestive and historically-valuable texts from Sanskrit literature, in five volumes, which are a monument of his industry and learning.

And lastly, Professor Max Müller mapped out the whole of the ancient Sanskrit literature chronologically in 1859 in his great work on the object.

More valuable to Hindus than this great work-- more valuable than the learned Professor's numerous works and contributions on Language, Religion, and Mythology--is his magnificent edition of the Ṛg Veda Saṁhitā, with Sāyaṇa's Commentary. The work was hailed in India with gratitude and joy; it opened to Hindu students generally the great and ancient volume, which had hitherto remained sealed with seven seals to all but a very few scholars; and it awakened in them a historical interest in the past--a desire to enquire into their ancient history and ancient faith from original sources.

Jones and Colebrooke and Wilson had worthy successors in India, but none more distinguished than James Prinsep. The inscriptions of Aśoka on pillars and rocks all over India had remained unintelligible for over a thousand years., and had defied the skill of Sir William Jones and his successors. James Prinsep, then Secretary to the Asiatic Society, deciphered these inscriptions, and a flood of light was thus thrown on Buddhist antiquities and post-Buddhist history. Prinsep was also the first to deal, in a scholar-like way, with the coins of the post-Buddhist kings found all over Western India. He has been followed by able scholars. Dr. Haug edited and translated the Aitareya Brāhmaṇa, and elucidated the history of the Parsīs ; Dr. Burnell wrote on South Indian Paleography ; Dr. Bühler has ably dealt with the ancient legal literature ; and Dr. Thibaut has, in late years, discovered ancient Hindu Geometry.

Among my countrymen, the great reformers, Raja Ram Mohan Roy and Dayanand Sarasvati, turned their attention to ancient Sanskrit literature. The first translated a number of Upaniṣads into English, and the latter published a translation of the Ṛg Veda Saṁhitā in Hindi. Sir Raja Radha Kanta Dev cultivated Sanskrit learning, and published a comprehensive and excellent dictionary entitled the Śabdakalpadruma. Dr. Bhao Daji and Professor Bhandarkar, Dr. K. M. Banerjea and Dr. Rajendra Lala Mitra have, by their varied and valuable contributions, taken their fair share of work in the field of antiquities. My esteemed friend, Pandit Satya Vrata Sāma Sramin has published an excellent edition of the Sāma Veda with Sāyaṇa's Commentary and an edition of the White Yajur Veda with Mahīdhara's Commentary, and is now engaged in a learned edition of Yāska's Nirukta, and lastly, my learned friend, Mr. Anand Ram Borooah,[1] of the Bengal Civil Service, has published a handy and excellent English-Sanskrit Dictionary, and is now engaged in a Sanskrit Grammar of formidable size and erudition !

General Cunningham's labours in archaeology and in the elucidation of Ancient Indian Geography are invaluable: and Burgess and Fergusson have treated on Indian Architecture.

---

1. Since the above lines were written, the author has received the sad intelligence of the death of the talented scholar. His untimely death is a loss to Sanskrit scholarship in this country, which will not be easily remedied. To the present writer, the sorrow is of a personal nature, as he enjoyed the friendship of the deceased for twenty years and more,— since the old College-days in this country and in England.

Fergusson's work on the subject is accepted as the standard work.

In Europe, Dr. Fausböll may be said to be the founder of Pāli scholarship, and edited the Dhammapada so far back as 1855, and has since edited the Jātaka Tales. Dr. Oldenberg has edited the Vinaya texts ; and these scholars, as well as Rhys Davids and Max Müller, have now given us an English translation of the most important portions of the Buddhist Scriptures in the invaluable series of Sacred Books or the East.

I wish to say a word about this series, because I am, in a special degree, indebted to it. Professor Max Müller, who has, by his lifelong labours, done more than any living scholar to elucidate ancient Hindu literature and history, has how conceived the noble idea of enabling English readers to go to the fountain-source, and consult oriental works in a series of faithful translations. More than thirty volumes, translated from the Sanskrit Chinese, Zend, Pahlavi, Pāli, Arabic etc., have already been published, and more volumes are expected. I take this opportunity to own my great indebtedness to the volumes of this series which relate to Indian History. I have freely quoted from them,—allowing myself the liberty of a verbal alteration here and there; and I have seldom thought it necessary to consult those original Sanskrit works which have been translated in this faithful and valuably series.

And this brings me to the subject of the present work, about which I wish to say a few words. I have often asked myself: Is it possible, with the help that is now available, to write, in a handy work, a clear, historical account of the Civilization of Ancient India, based on ancient Sanskrit literature, and written in a sufficiently popular manner to be acceptable to the general reader ? I never doubted the possibility of such a work; but I have often wished—even when engaged in this task— that it had been undertaken by an abler scholar, and by one who could devote his attention and time more exclusively to it than I could possibly do.

Scholars who have devoted their lifetime to the study of Indian antiquities, and who have brought out rich ores from that inexhaustible mine, seem however to have little time or little inclination, to coin the metal for the every-day use of the general public. That unambitious task must, therefore, devolve on humbler labourers.

That there is need for such a popular work will not be denied. The Hindu student's knowledge of Indian History practically begins with the date of the Mahommedan Conquest—the Hindu period is almost a blank to him. The school-boy who knows all about the twelve invasions of Mahmud, knows little of the first invasions and wars of the Āryans, who conquered and settled in the Punjab three thousand years before the Sultan of Ghuzni. He has read of Shahab-ud-din Muhammad Ghori's conquest of Delhi and Kanouj, But has scarcely any historical knowledge of the ancient kingdoms of the Kurus and the Pāñcālas in the same tract of country. He knows what emperor reigned in Delhi when Sivaji lived and fought, but scarcely knows of the king who ruled in Magadha when Gautama Buddha lived and preached. He is familiar with the history of Ahmadnagar, Bijapore, and Golkonda, but has scarcely heard of the Andhras, the Guptas and the Chalukyas. He knows exactly the date of Nadir Shah's invasion of India, but scarcely knows, within five centuries, the date when the Śakas invaded India, and were repelled by Vikramāditya the Great. He knows more of the dates of Ferdusi and Ferishta than of Āryabhaṭṭa or Bhavabhūti, and can tell who built the Taj Mahal without having the fainest notion when the topes of Sanchi, the caves of Karli and Ajanta, the temples of Ellora, Bhuvanesvara, and Jagannatha were built.

And yet, such things should not be. For the Hindu student the history of the Hindu period should not be a blank, nor a confused jumble of historic and legendary names, religious parables, and Epic and Paurāṇik myths, No study has so potent an influence in forming a nation's mind and a nation's character as a critical and careful study of its past history. And it is by such study alone that an unreasoning and superstitious worship of the past is replaced by a legitimate and manly admiration.

It almost seems an irony of fate that the past should be considered a bank in a country where ancient sages have handed down traditions and elaborate compositions through thousands of years, and where generation after generation has preserved the heritage by a feat of memory which is considered a miracle in modern days! In vain must the thousands of ancient Hindu students and scholars have toiled to preserve these works, if the works give us no clue to a general outline History of Ancient India. And in vain, too, must eminent European scholars and antiquarians have worked during the last hundred years, if it be still impossible to put together the results of their learned researches in the shape of a connected history which will be intelligible to the general reader and the ordinary student.

Happily this is no longer impossible. And although many portions of Indian History are still obscure, although many questions of detail are still subjects of controversy, to construct a general history of the Hindu Period is no longer a hopeless task. And, however unfit I feel myself to accomplish this task, I nevertheless venture to make a commencement, in the hope that abler scholars will pardon my shortcomings, rectify my inevitable errors, and perform skilfully and well, what I may do clumsily or leave undone.

In undertaking this great work, I must, once for all, disclaim any intention to make any new discoveries, or to extend in any way the limits of oriental scholarship and research. My limited knowledge of the subject precludes the possibility of such a pretention being advanced, and the limits of the present work make it impossible that any such results should be achieved. I have simply tried to string together, in a methodical order, the results of the labours of abler scholars, in order to produce a readable work for the general reader. If, in the fulfilment of this design, I have been sometimes betrayed into conjectures and suppositions, I can only ask my readers to accept them as such— not as historical discoveries.

Ten years ago I collected and arranged the materials then available to me, with a view to write a little school-book in my own vernacular; and the little work has since been accepted as a text-book in many schools in Bengal. Since that time I have continued my work in this line, as far as my time permitted ; and when, three years ago, I was enabled, by the generosity of the Government of Bengal, to place a complete Bengali translation of the Ṛg Veda Saṁhitā before my countrymen, I felt more than ever impelled to re-arrange the historical materials furnished by our ancient literature in a permanent form. In pursuance of this object, I published some papers, from time to time, in the *Calcutta Review;* and these papers, together with all other materials which I have collected, have been embodied and arranged in the present work.

The method on which this work has been written is very simple. My principal object has been to furnish the general reader with a practical and handy work on the Ancient History of India—not to compose an elaborate work of discussions on Indian Antiquities. To study clearness and conciseness on a subject like this was not however an easy task. Every chapter in the present work deals with matters about which long researches have been made, and various opinions have been recorded, I would have afforded some satisfaction to me to have given the reader the history of every controversy, the account of every antiquarian discovery, and the *pros* and *cons* of every opinion advanced. But I could not yield to this temptation without increasing the work to three or four times its present humble size, and thus sacrificing the very object with which it is written. To carry out my primary object, I have avoided every needless controversy and discussion, and I have tried to explain, as clearly, concisely, and distinctly as I was able, each succeeding phase of Hindu civilization and Hindu life in ancient times.

But while conciseness has been the main object of the present work, I have also endeavoured to tell my story so that it may leave some distinct memories on my readers after they have closed the work. For this reason, I have avoided details as far as possible, and tried to develop, fully and clearly, the leading facts and features of each succeeding age. Repetition has not been avoided, where such repetition seemed necessary to impress on my readers the cardinal facts—the salient features of the story of Hindu civilization.

The very copious extracts which I have given (in translation) from Sanskrit works may, at first sight, seem to be inconsistent with my desire for conciseness. Such extracts, however, have been advisedly given. In the first place, on a subject where there is so much room for difference in opinion, it is of the highest importance to furnish the reader with the text on which my conclusions are based, to enable him to form his own judgment and to rectify any mistakes if my conclusions are erroneous. In the second place, it is a gain in the cause of historical knowledge to familiarize the reader with the texts of our ancient authors. It is scarcely to be hoped that the busy student will spend much of his time in reading the ancient and abstruse works in the original or even in learned translations, and the historian who seeks to familiarize his readers with some portions at least of these ancient works, adds in so far to the accurate knowledge of his readers on this subject. And lastly, it has been well said, that thought is language, and language is thought. And if it be the intention of the historian to convey an idea of ancient thought—of what the ancient Hindus felt and believed—he cannot do this better than by quoting the words by which that ancient people expressed themselves. Such brief extracts very often give the modern reader a far more realistic and intimate knowledge of ancient Hindu society and manners and ways of thinking than any account that I had give at twice the length. And it is because I have desired the modern reader to enter into the spiral and the inner life of the ancient Hindus, that I have tried to bring the old composers of Hymns and Upaniṣads face to face with the reader, and allowed them to speak for themselves. Such an intimate grasp of the inner life and feelings of the ancients is the very kernel of true historical knowledge, and I have felt it a Hopeless task to impart this knowledge more accurately or more concisely than in the words of the ancients. It is for this reason mainly, and consistently with thy anxiety to be concise, that I have quoted copiously from ancient works.

In conclusion, I have to crave the indulgence of the reader for the many deficiencies which he will, no doubt, find in the present work, written in moments stolen from official work, and in places where a decent library was never available. Such claim to indulgence is seldom admitted, and the reader very pertinently enquires why a writer should ever undertake a work for which he was not in every way fully equipped. Nevertheless, I mention the circumstances, as they may explain, if they cannot justify, the shortcomings of the work. The time of the present writer is not his own, and the charge of a Bengal District with an area of over six thousand square miles and a population of over three millions, leaves little leisure for other work. To arrange my materials, under these circumstances, has been an arduous task, and I can only ask the indulgent consideration of my readers for any errors and defects which may have crept into this work.

VOL. II–RATIONALISTIC AGE

A Great work has been recently completed. An English translation of the Ṛg Veda Saṁhitā, which was commenced by Dr. H. H. Wilson many years ago, has lately been brought to completion by Professor E. B. Cowell of Cambridge, and Mr. W. F. Webster. I only regret I had not the advantage of consulting the last portions of this work before my chapters on the *Vedic Age* passed through the press.

Dr. Wilson's translation is based, as is well known, mainly on Sāyaṇa's interpretation of the Veda. Sāyaṇa has his mistakes, but is invaluable in spite of them, and no translator can afford to overlook or to neglect the traditional Hindu interpretation of the ancient Hindu work. The most recent as well as the most scholarlike translation of the Ṛg Veda is the German translation of Ludwig; and his translation comes closer to Sāyaṇa than many previous attempts to translate the Veda into European languages.

The literature of the second or *Epic Age* has not received the same degree of attention as the Veda. With regard to the Epics themselves, it will probably ever remain a hopeless task to separate the portions which are genuine and ancient from those which are later additions. The whole of the Mahābhārata and the Rāmāyaṇa, as we find them now, has been recast in modern Sanskrit, and language therefore is no indication as to the dates of the different portions. Nevertheless, patient criticism and a careful comparison with the contemporaneous literature of the Epic or Brāhmaṇa Period can effect much. And it is possible by such means to point to many details in the History, the Geography, the Religious beliefs, and the Social customs narrated in the Epics, which are undoubtedly of an ancient age.

Many of the Brāhmaṇas and Āraṇyakas have been edited, and some have been translated. The old and genuine Upaniṣ ads have been several times published in India with vernacular translations, and since the days of Raja Ram Mohan Roy, several of them have been translated into European languages from the original Sanskrit. Professor Max Müller's translation of them in a collected form is the latest—and will be useful to English readers.

The third, or *Rationalistic Age,* forms the subject of the present volume. For an account of the Hindu life and social manners of this period, the Dharma Śāstras and the Greek accounts of India should be read together. In the Dharma Śāstras we see the ancient Hindus as they saw themselves, in the Greek accounts we see them as others saw them. In the former the Hindus paint themselves, in the latter they are painted by civilized and careful and friendly foreigners. There is a close resemblance between the two pictures—and a comparison of them gives us a correct and very favourable idea of the ancient Hindus, their manners, and their civilization.

Hindu Philosophy, properly so-rcalled, is to be found in the Mental Philosophy of Kapila and the Logic of Gautama. The former has received much attention in Europe, and some of the latest systems of German and French Philosophy are a reproduction, in a more elaborate form, of the Sāṅkhya Philosophy of Ancient India. Hindu Logic has not received the same attention from scholars, and there is room for researches on this subject. It is to be hoped that the want will be soon supplied, and that duly qualified scholars will give us a thorough exposition of Hindu logic, based on the ancient text and commentaries.

My account of Buddhism has been condensed as far as possible—but nevertheless fills a good portion of the present volume. It is essential, however, to grasp the principles of the religion, in order to comprehend the history of India during eight centuries, during which Buddhism was the prevailing religion of India. It is still the prevailing religion of Asia, and recent researches disclose to us its intimate connexion with the religion of Europe. In treating this subject, I have followed the same method as in the other portions of my work, and have furnished my readers with copious extracts from the texts on which my conclusions are based.

In conclusion, it is my pleasing duty to acknowledge the help which I received, while this second volume was passing through the press, from my esteemed friends, Mr. G. A. Grierson. of the Bengal Civil Service, and Pundit Hara Prasad Sastri, M.A., Librarian to the Bengal Government. As labourers in the field of Indian antiquities, both these scholars are doing useful and valuable work, and they have kindly and cordially rendered help to a fellow-labourer in the same field. I am indebted to them for many valuable hints and much useful information.

One, more honored name I may be permitted to add. My

sincere acknowledgments are due to Sir Steuart Bayley for the great interest he has evinced in my unambitious little work, and for the very kind and favourable reception with which he has honored the first volume.

VOL. III—BUDDHIST AND PAURĀṆIK AGES

It is with mingled feelings of pleasure and unfeigned diffidence that I now place this completed work before the public. The great task of compiling for the first time a connected and clear history of the Ancient Hindus requires greater leisure and more extensive reading than I can lay claim to. Years of study, often interrupted, enabled me however to grasp the leading facts, and during the last three years I have worked continuously in moments spared from official duties to arrange these facts in their present shape. The first chapters on the Vedic Age were commenced in April 1887, the last chapters on the Paurāṇik Age have been revised in March 1890. The work, such as it is, is now placed in the hands of my indulgent countrymen for whom it has been written.

The reception which my countrymen have given to the earlier volumes has surpassed my most sanguine expectations. The entire edition of a thousand copies has been nearly exhausted before the third volume is out, and a second edition has been called for, and will be shortly taken in hand. More gratifying to me were the requests which were made to me, and which have been gladly acceded to, for permission to translate the work into the vernaculars of Bombay, Madras, and the North-Western Provinces. And equally encouraging to me were the numerous enquiries, congratulations and expressions of sympathy which I have received from all parts of India testifying to the interest which has been taken in this somewhat novel venture. I am too keenly aware of the imperfections of my rude attempt, to ascribe the success of the work to its merits ; and I can only suppose therefore that the demand for a readable handbook of this nature was so great among my countrymen, that they have consented to accept the article even from such a clumsy workman as myself.

I take this opportunity also to thankfully acknowledge the valued opinions, notices and reviews with which many scholars in this country and in Europe have honored this work. A popular work of this nature can scarcely be acceptable to scholars who have devoted their lifetime to all the minutiae of Indian antiquities, and I feel therefore all the more grateful for the cordial and favourable acceptance (too favourable for its merits), which it has received at their hands. My sincere acknowledgments are due to Doctors Roth, Weber, Max Müller, and several other scholars.

Of greater value to me than these favourable notices are the criticisms of some of these scholars on certain portions of my work, and it is due to my readers that I should indicate the main points on which my views have not always received assent. It is necessary to do this, if only to guard my readers from accepting my conclusion in all cases, and to induce them to form their own judgments on the facts.

Scholars belonging to the orthodox section of my countrymen have not always accepted my account of Vedic civilization. Life in the Vedic Age, they hold, was more "spiritual," more pious and contemplative in its tone and character, and they are scarcely prepared to accept my account of the rude self-assertion and boisterous greed for conquests of the Vedic warriors. On the other hand, some, European scholars think that I have represented Vedic civilization in too favourable a light. M. Barth, who did me the honour of favourably noticing in Paris my chapters on the Vedic Period, when they first appeared in the *Calcutta Review,* expressed his opinion that my account should be accepted with some degree of caution. And Dr. Kern, who has published a favourable review of the first volume of the present work in a Dutch journal, states that opinion is divided as to the character of the Vedic civilization. Some scholars delight in describing all that was robust and manly and straightforward in the character of the Vedic Hindus, while others pourtray their coarseness and imperfections. Dr. Kern is of opinion that I have adhered to the first school of opinion, but that the truth lies midway.

I am not aware that I have tried to keep back the robust rudeness—coarseness, if you like—of the civilization of the Vedic Age., But I confess, that like most modern Hindus, subject to all the drawbacks of a later and more artificial civilization, I feel a warm appreciation for the manly freedom of ancient Hindu civilization and life. I have sought to pourtray this prominently in my account of the Vedic Period; and in my description of later ages, I have not hesitated to point out, emphatically and repeatedly, how much we lack in all that was healthy and free, unrestricted, and life-giving in the ancient Hindu institutions and social rules. It is a truth which we Hindus need bear in mind.

Coming now to the Epic Age, scholars are generally agreed that the caste system of India first took its rise in this period. But here again we should ever remember that caste rules, with all their potential evils, served in this early period as a sort of moral code for the Āryan Hindus, and tended to unite them by classing them in three great sections, with sanction for inter-caste marriage and religious instruction for all. The caste-system of the Epic Period was no more like the system of to-day than the Feudal institutions of the middle ages, which hadc their object and their use, were like the baronial oppression of the 18th century in France. As it was neither possible nor desirable under changed circumstances to restore the old institution of the middle ages, the living nations of Europe swept away its debased and oppressive substitute which flourished down to the last century.

In the second volume of the present work I have treated of the Rationalistic Period, and of the rise of Buddhism which took place in this period. My appreciation of Buddhism has been criticised, and many friendly critics have reminded me that Buddhist precepts, literally obeyed, would not hold the world together, but would lead nations to subjection, to inaction, and to beggary. This is not the place to enter into a controversy on the subject, but I may be permitted to point out that a religion cannot be criticised in this spirit, and that the teachings of the pure-souled Jesus have not been thus criticised. He, too, recommended a relinquishment of the world, and unresisting submission to wrongs and injuries, but neither, he nor Gautama intended that men should cease to be men. Religion holds before us great models and perfect—ideals of virtues, like charity, love and unselfishness ; and these ideals, conveyed in precepts or commandments, legends or parables, have their effect on our moral nature and on our actions in our eternal and selfish struggle in this world. Let us be candid then, and concede that Gautama's ideals were lofty and holy ; that his message of the equality of men, proclaimed to the caste-stricken people of India, was large-hearted and benevolent ; and that his religion, which imparts moral lessons to a third of the world's population, is beautiful and great.

On another and a more delicate point, I expected my position would be assailed. My account of the historical connection between Buddhism and the rise of Christianity has been questioned. But enough, I hold, has been discovered to prove that connexion, and we can afford calmly to await the result of future researches. I do not hesitate to maintain, though few Christian writers will agree with me, that the world owes to India that higher system of ethics and noble code of morality which distinguish the modern religion from the religions of the ancient world.

In the present volume I have treated of the Buddhist and the Paurāṇik Age. The edicts of Aśoka have thrown a flood of light on his administration and his times and numerous other inscriptions, which have been read, elucidate many facts relating to the regal dynasties of the different provinces of India. But for an account of the people, their customs, laws and manners, we must turn to the code of Manu and to the account of the Chinese travellers. When we have compared these two records, we know how the Hindus saw themselves and how they were seen by others.

The Paurāṇik Age opens with the sixth century A.D., when there was a renaissance in literature, science and religion. This opinion which is now held by most scholars is not, however, acceded to by all. My kind critic Dr. Bühler has pointed out that the Kāvya literature flourished during the early centuries of the Christian Era; that Chandragupta II and his father Samudra-gupta of the Gupta dynasty were celebrated patrons of poetry and learning in the 5th and 4th centuries A.D.; and that it cannot therefore be asserted that there was a renaissance in Sanskrit literature in the 6th century A.D.

I have in the present volume admitted all the facts kindly pointed out by my learned critic, but I demur to his conclusion. Kāvya literature no doubt had its commencement in the 4th and 5th centuries of the Christian Era, just as modern English poetry had its commencement with Chaucer and Gower. But nevertheless, the 6th century A.D., which I take to be the era of Vikramāditya and Kālidāsa, marked a real revival and renaissance of Sanskrit literature, as the age of Elizabeth and Shakespeare marked a real revival of English literature. It was the commencement of a new epoch, marked by an upheaval of the national mind.

In order properly to comprehend the subsequent history of the national mind in the Paurāṇik Age, we must compare the Dharma Śāstras and the Paurāṇik literature with the account of the Hindus from the discriminating and friendly pen of Alberuni. This I have attempted to do specially in the two closing chapters of the work, and the impression which is left on the mind is one of sadness. An unhealthy superstition and social system warped the national mind and paralyzed the national vigour. Worshippers were divorced from religious learning, warriors were divided from the people, professions and sects were disunited for ever and enfeebled. Men were subjected to unmeaning restrictions and hurtful rules; women were encouraged to perish on the pyre. A monopoly of knowledge was established, social and religious freedom was extinguished, and the lamp of national life was quenched with the light of freedom and of knowledge. The Hindu who can deservedly boast of the religion of the Upaniṣads and the ethics of Gautama Buddha, owes it to Truth and to History to confess to the degeneracy of later times. I have not sought to suppress this sadder portion of our national story; rather have I tried to tell it fully and impressively, so that we may flow learn to turn to a brighter page of our national existence. If the present work contributes in any degree towards this result, if it helps us to sink our social disunion, to cast asunder hurtful restrictions, and to turn towards that unpolluted stream of life-giving religion, morality and knowledge which are our birthright, my labours, humble and unworthy as they are, have not been altogether in vain.

—R. C. DUTT

INTRODUCTION
EPOCHS AND DATES

The History of Ancient India is a history of thirty centuries of human culture and progress. It divides itself into several distinct periods, each of which, for length of years, will compare with the entire history of many a modern people.

Other nations claim an equal or even a higher antiquity than the Hindus. The Egyptians have records on their everlasting monuments of a civilization which goes beyond three thousand years before Christ. Assyrian scholars have claimed an equally remote antiquity for the Shumiro-Accadian civilization of Chaldea, which is said to have flourished over a thousand years before Nineveh and Babylon were founded. The Chinese, too, have a history which dates from about 2,400 B.C. For India, modern scholars have not claimed a higher antiquity than 2,000 B. C, though future researches may require an extension of this date.

But there is a difference between the records of the Hindus and the records of other nations. The hieroglyphic records of the ancient Egyptians yield little information beyond the names of kings and pyramid-builders, and accounts of dynasties and wars. The cuneiform inscriptions of Assyria and Babylon tell us much the same story. And even ancient Chinese records shed little light on the gradual progress of human culture and civilization.

Ancient Hindu works are of a different character. If they are defective in some respects, as they undoubtedly are, they are defective as accounts of dynasties, of wars, of so-called historical incidents. On the other hand, they give us a full, connected, and clear account of the advancement of civilization, of the progress of the human mind, such as we shall seek for in vain among the records of any other equally ancient nation. The literature of each period is a perfect picture—a photograph, if we may so call it— of the Hindu civilization of that period. And the works of successive periods form a complete history of Hindu civilization for over three thousand years, so full, so clear, that he who runs may read.

Inscriptions on stone and writings on papyri are recorded with a design to commemorate passing events. The songs and hymns and philosophical and religious effusions of a people are an unconscious and true reflection of its civilization and its thought. The earliest effusions of the Hindus were not recorded in writing—they are, therefore, full and unrestricted— they are a natural and true expression of the nation's thoughts and feelings. They were preserved, not on stone, but in the faithful memory of the people, who landed down the great heritage from century to century with a scrupulous exactitude which, in modern days, would be considered a miracle.

Scholars who have studied the Vedic hymns, historically, are aware that the materials they afford for constructing a history of civilization, are fuller and truer than any accounts which could have been recorded on stone or papyri. And those who have pursued Hindu literature through the different periods of Hindu history, are equally aware that it forms a complete and comprehensive story of the progress and gradual modifications of Hindu civilization, thought and religion for over three thousand years. And the philosophical historian of human civilization need not be a Hindu to think that the Hindus have preserved the fullest, the clearest, and the truest materials for his work.

We wish not to be misunderstood. We have made the foregoing remarks simply with a view to remove the very common and very erroneous impression that Ancient India has no history worth studying, no connected and reliable chronicle of the past which would be interesting or instructive to the modern reader.

Ancient India has a connected story to tell, and so far from being uninteresting, its special feature is its intense attractiveness. We read in that ancient story how a gifted Āryan people, separated by circumstances from the outside world, worked out their civilization amidst natural and climatic conditions which were peculiarity favourable. We note their intellectual discoveries age after age; we watch their religious progress and developments through successive centuries; we mark their political career, as they gradually expand over India and found new kingdoms and dynasties; we observe their struggles against priestly domination, their successes and their failures; we study with interest their great social and religious revolutions and their far-reaching consequences. And this great story of a nation's intellectual life—more thrilling in its interest than any tale which Shaharzadi told—is nowhere broken and nowhere disconnected. The great causes which led to great social and religious changes are manifest to the reader, and he follows the gradual development of Hindu civilization through thirty centuries without a break or interruption.

The very shortcomings of Hindu civilization, as compared with the younger civilization of Greece or Rome, have their lessons for the modern reader. The story of our successes is not more instructive than the story of our failures. The hymns of Viśvāmitra, the philosophy of Kapila and the poetry of Kālidāsa have no higher lessons for the modern reader than the deep causes which led to the decadence of our political life and the ascendancy of priests. The story of the religious rising of the people under the leadership of Gautama Buddha is not more instructive than the causes which account for the absence of any political rising among the people, the absence of any efforts after popular freedom. And the great heights to which the genius of Brāhmans and Kṣatriyas soared in the infancy of the world's intellectual life are not more suggestive and not more instructive than the absence of genius in the people as large in their ordinary pursuits and trades—in mechanical inventions and maritime discoveries, in sculpture, architecture and arts, in manifestations of popular life and the assertion of popular power.

The history of the intellectual and religious life of the ancient Hindus is matchless in its continuity, its fullness, and its philosophical truth. But the historian who only paints the current of that intellectual life performs half his duty. There is another and a sadder portion of Hindu history—and it is necessary that this portion of the story, too, should be faithfully told. We have said before that the history of Ancient India divides itself into several distinct and long periods or epochs. Each of these periods has a distinct literature, and each has a civilization peculiar to it, which modified itself into the civilization of the next period under the operation of great political and social causes. It is desirable that we should, at the outset, give a brief account of these historical epochs and the great historical events by which they are marked. Such an outline-account of the different periods will make our readers acquainted with the plan and scope of this work, and will probably help them to grasp more effectually the details of each period when we come to treat them more fully. We begin with the earliest period, viz., that of Āryan settlements in the Punjab. The hymns of the Ṛg Veda furnish us with the materials for a history of this period.

FIRST EPOCH

In this priceless volume, we find the Hindu Āryans as conquerors and settlers on the banks of the Indus and its five branches; and India beyond the Sutlej was almost unknown to them. They came as a conquering race, full of the self-assertion and vigour of a young national life with a strong love of action and a capacity for active enjoyments. They were, in this respect, far removed from the contemplative and passive Hindus of later days; they rejoiced in wealth and cattle and pasture-fields; and they carved out, with their strong right arm, new possessions and realms from the aborigines of the soil, who vainly struggled to maintain their own against the invincible conquerors. Thus, the period was one of wars and conquests against the aborigines; and the Āryan victors triumphantly boast of their conquests in their hymns, and implore their gods to bestow on them wealth and new possessions, and to destroy the barbarians. Whatever was bright and cheerful and glorious in the aspects of nature struck the Āryans with admiration and gladness, and such manifestations of nature were worshipped and invoked as gods.

It is needless to say that the entire body of Āryans was then a united community, and the only distinction of castes was between the Āryans and the aborigines. Even the distinction between professions was not very marked; and the sturdy lord of many acres, who ploughed his fields and owned large herds in times of peace, went out to defend his village or plunder the aborigines in times of war, and often composed spirited hymns to the martial god Indra in his hours of devotion. There were no temples and no idols; each patriarch of a family lighted the sacrificial fire in his own hearth, and offered milk and rice offerings; or animals, or libations of the Soma juice to the fire, and invoked the "bright" gods for blessings, and health, and wealth for himself and his children. Chiefs of tribes were kings, and had their priests to perform sacrifices and utter the hymns for them; but there was no priestly caste, and no royal caste. The people were free, enjoying the freedom which belongs to vigorous pastoral and agricultural tribes.

What is the date of this period of Āryan settlements in the Punjab ? Colebrooke, who was the first discoverer of the Vedas for European readers, fixed the fourteenth century as the date when they were finally compiled and arranged. And as all scholars allow five or six centuries for the expansion of the Āryans along the Indus and its five tributaries, we may fix the dates of the first period at 2,000 to 1,400 B.C. Professor Max Müller, in his latest works, allows 1,500 B.C. as the date when the Vedas, such as we now have them, were composed, or 1,500 to 1,000 B.C. as the period when they were composed and finally arranged. In another work he states : "Four thousand years ago (or it may be earlier) the Āryans, who had travelled southwards to the rivers of the Punjab called him Dyauṣ Pita or Heavenly Father."

Professor Weber allows a thousand years for the "occupying, subjecting to complete cultivation, and Brahmanising the immense tract of land" from the Indus to the Granduck. With this argument we agree; but the Professor is wrong when he fixes 500 B.C. as the time when the Hindus settled on the Gunduck. We will shew that they founded the kingdom of the Videhas by that river about 1,000 B.C., and the Āryans must have first crossed the Indus about 2,000 B.C.

Professor Whitney gives 2,000 to 1,500 B.C. for the Ṛg Veda hymns, and Dr. Martin Haug allows 2,000 to 1,400 B.C. for those hymns, while, for the earliest of them he claims a still remoter date. It is unnecessary to cite the authority of other scholars; we think we agree with the general opinion on the subject when we fix 2,000 to 1,400 B.C. for the first period of Hindu history. And, for the sake of convenience, we will call this period the *Vedic Petiod.*

SECOND EPOCH

When once the Hindu Āryans had come as far as the Sutlej, they did not lose much time in crossing that river and pouring down in numbers in the valley of the Ganges. We have rare mention of the Ganges and the Jumna in the Ṛg Veda, shewing that they were not yet generally known to the Hindus in the *India : what can it teach us* ? (1883), p. 83. *Lectures on the Origin and Growth of Religion,* Lecture VII first or Vedic Period, although adventurous colonists must have issued out of the Punjab and settled in the shores of those distant rivers. Such settlements must have multiplied in the second period, until, in the course of some centuries, the entire valley of the Ganges, as far down as modern Tirhoot, was the seat of powerful kingdoms and nationalities, who cultivated science and literature in their schools of learning, and developed new forms of religion and of civilization widely different from those of the Vedic Period.

Among the nations who flourished in the Gangetic valley, the most renowned have left their names in the epic literature of India. The Kurus had their kingdom round about modern Delhi. The Pāñcālas settled further to the south-east, round about modern Kanouj.

The Kosalas occupied the spacious country between the Ganges and the Gunduck, which includes modern Oadh; the Videhas lived beyond the Gunduck, in what is now known as Tirhoot; and the Kāsīs settled down near and about modern Benares. These were the most renowned nations of the second period, though other less powerful nationalities also flourished and extended their kingdoms from time to time.

When the first Kurus and Pāñcālas settled in the Doab, they gave indications of a vigorous national life, and their internecine wars form the subject of the first national Epic of India, the Mahābhārata. And although this work, in its present shape, is the production of a later age—or rather of later ages—yet, even in its present form, it preserves indications that rude and sturdy vigour and warlike jealousies which must have characterised the early conquerers of the Gangetic valley. The Hindus did not, however, live many centuries in the soft climate of this valley before losing their vigour and manliness, as they gained in learning and civilization. As they drifted down the river they manifested less and less of the vigour of conquering races. The royal courts of the Videhas and the Kāsīs were learned and enlightened, but contemporary literature does not bear witness to their warlike qualities. The Kosalas, too, were a polished nation, but the traditions of that nation, preserved in the second national Epic of India, the Rāmāyaṇa, (in its present form, a production of later ages,) shew more devotion to social and domestic duties, obedience to priests, and regard for religious forms, than the sturdy valour and the fiery jealousies of the Mahābhārata. This gradual enervation of the

Hindus was the cause of the most important results in religious and social rules. Religion changed its spirit. The manly but simple hymns with which the sturdy conquerors of the Punjab had invoked nature-gods scarcely commended themselves to the more effete and more ceremonious Hindus of the Gangetic valley. The hymns were still repeated, but lost their meaning and sense, and vast ceremonials and observances took the place of simple forms, The priestly class increased in number and in influence, until they formed a hereditary caste of their own. The kings and warriors of the Gangetic valley lived in more splendid courts, and had more gorgeous surroundings than the simple agricultural warriors of the Punjab, and soon separated themselves from the people and formed a caste of their own. The mass of the people—the Vaiśyas or Visas of the Ṛg Veda—became more lifeless than their forefathers in the Punjab, and wore, without a protest, the chains which priests and warriors—the Brāhmaṇs and the Kṣatriyas—threw around them. And as subjection means demoralization, the people in Hindu kingdoms never afterwards became what the people in ancient and modern Europe have striven to be. And lastly, the aborigines who were subjugated and had adopted the Āryan civilization formed the low caste of Śūdras, and were declared unfit to perform the Āryan religious rites or to acquire religious knowledge.

Such was the origin of the Caste-system in India, in the second period of Hindu history. The system arose out of weakness and lifelessness among the people, and to a certain extent, it has perpetuated that weakness ever after.

It will be observed that this Second Period was a period of the submission of the people under the Brāhmans and the Kṣatriyas, and of the submission of the Kṣatriyas themselves under the Brāhmans. At the close of the period, however, there appears to have been a reaction, and the proud Kṣatriyas at last tried to shake off the galling yoke, and to prove their equality with the Brāhmans in learning and religious culture. Weaned with the unmeaning rituals and ceremonials prescribed by priests, 'the Kṣatriyas started new speculations and bold enquiries after the truth. The effort was unavailing. The priests remained supreme. But the vigorous speculations which the Kṣatriyas started form the only redeeming portion of the inane and lifeless literature of this period. And these speculations remained as a heritage of the nation, and formed the nucleus of the Hindu philosophical systems and religious revolutions of a later day.

It was in this period of Āryan expansion in the Gangetic valley that the Ṛg Veda and the three other Vedas—Sāman, Yajus and Atharvan—were finally arranged and compiled. Then followed another class of compositions known as the Brāhmaṇas, and devoted to sacrificial rites; and these inane and verbose compositions reflect the enervation of the people and the dogmatic pretensions of the priests of the age. The custom of retirement from the world into forest life, which was unknown in the earlier ages, sprang up, and the last portions of the Brāhmaṇas are Āraṇyakas devoted to forest rites. And lastly the bold speculations started by Kṣatriyas are known as the Upaniṣads, and form the last portions of the literature of this period, and close the so-called *Revealed Literature* of India.

Dr. H.H. Wilson, when reviewing Professor Max Müller's great work on Sanskrit literature thirty years ago, declared that a period of five centuries was not too long to account for the great political, social and religious changes which occurred in this period. And Dr. Wilson was right. Within this period the valley of the Ganges, as far as Tirhoot, was cleared, Colonized, and Hinduized, and formed the sites of powerful kingdoms. Religious observances were vastly elaborated; social rules were changed; the caste-system was formed; the supremacy of priests was established and confirmed, and ultimately questioned by the Kṣatriyas; and lastly, within this age, a varied and voluminous literature was recorded. The period may, therefore, be supposed to have extended approximately from 1,400 to 1,000 B.C.

One or two facts may be cited here which confirm these dates. The central historical fact of this period was a great war between the Kurus and the Pāñcālas which forms the subject of the Mahābhārata, and of which we shall have something to say further on. The central literary fact of this period was the compilation of the Vedas. Tradition and the Epic itself inform us that the compiler of the Vedas was a contemporary of the war; but we may accept or reject this as we like. We will examine these two facts separately.

Tradition, again, has it that when the Vedas were compiled, the position of the solstitial points was observed and recorded to mark the date. The Jyotiṣa in which this observation is now found is a late work, not earlier than the third century before Christ, but the observation was certainly made at an ancient date, and Bentley and Archdeacon Pratt—both able mathematicians—have gone over the calculation and found that it was made in 1,181 B C.

Much has been written of late in Europe, America, and India against the value of this discovery, but we have found nothing in these discussions which goes against the genuineness of the astronomical observation. We are inclined to believe that the observation marks approximately the true date of the final compilation of the Vedas; and as the work of compilation probably occupied numerous teachers for generations together, we may suppose that the Vedas were complied during the 14th and 13th centuries B.C. And this date falls within the period which we have assigned for the second epoch.

Now with regard to the Kuru-Pāñcāla War. The annals of different kingdoms, in India allude to this ancient war and some of these annals are not unreliable. The founder of Buddhism lived in the sixth century B.C., and we learn from the annals of Magadha that 35 kings reigned between the Kuru-Pāñcāla War and the time of Buddha. Allowing 20 years to each reign, this would place the war in the 13th century B.C.

Again we know from coins, that Kaniṣka ruled in Kashmir

in the first century A.D., and his successor Abhimanyu probably reigned towards the close of that century. The historian of Kashmir informs us that 52 kings reigned for 1,266 years from the time of the Kuru Pāñcāla War to the time of Abhhimanyu, and this would place the war in the 12th century B.C.

We do not ask the reader to accept any of the particular dates given above. It is almost impossible to fix any precise date in the History of India before Alexander the Great visited the land; and we may well hestitate, even when astronomical calculations point to a particular year or historical lists point to particular century. All that we ask, and all that we are entitled to ask, is that the reader will now find it possible to accept the fact that the Vedas were finally compiled and the Kuru Pāñcāla War was fought some time about the 13th century or the 12th century B.C.

And, if the Kuru Pāñcāla War was fought in the 13th century B.C. (*i.e.*, about a century before the Trojan War), it is impossible to fix a date later than 1,400 B.C. for the commencement of the second epoch of which we are speaking. For at the time of the Kuru Pāñcāla War, the tracts round modern Delhi and Kanouj were the seats of powerful nations who had developed a civilization and literature of their own. And two centuries must be allowed between the date when the Āryans issued out of the Punjab and the date when these results had been achieved in the Gangetic valley.

To accept 1,400 B.C. as the date when the Āryans issued out of the Punjab, is to confirm the dates we have given (2,000 to 1,400 B.C.) for the first epoch, the Vedic Period.

Again, many of the Brāhmaṇas contain internal evidence that they were composed at the time or after the time of the Kurus and the Pāñcālas. We may, therefore, suppose these to have been composed in the 13th and I2th centuries B.C. And the Upaniṣads, which mark the close of Brāhmaṇa literature, were composed about the 11th century B.C. Janaka, the King of the Videhas, give a start to the Upaniṣads; we may, therefore, suppose the Videhas and the Koshalas to have flourished about

1,200 to 1,000 B. C , as the Kurus and the Pāñcālas flourished about 1400 to 1,200 B.C.

For the sake of convenience we will call this second period the *Epic Period.* It was the period when the nations described in the national Epics of India lived and fought; when the Kurus and the Pāñcālas, the Kosalas, and the Videhas held sway along the valley of the Ganges.

THIRD EPOCH

The Third Epoch is, perhaps, the most brilliant period of Hindu history. It was in this period that the Āryans issued out of the Gangetic valley, spread themselves far and wide, subjugated and occupied the whole of India, and introduced Hindu civilization and founded Hindu kingdoms as far as the southernmost limits of India. Magadha which was already known to the Hindus in the Epic Period was completely Hinduized in the Third Epoch; and the young and powerful kingdom founded here soon eclipsed and then subjugated all the ancient kingdoms of the Gangetic valley. The descendants of the proud races who had fought the Epic wars in the Ganges valley, the descendants of the older and sturdier races who had first founded Āryan dominions in the Indus valley—all quailed before this new and rising power. Chandragupta, the contemporary of Alexander the Great, brought the whole of Northern India, from the Punjab to Behar, under the rule of Magadha; and his grandson Aśoka the Great, the promulgator of Buddhism, was the greatest Emperor that ever ruled in India within the thirty centuries of Hindu independence. With the time of Aśoka, the third Epoch ends, and the Fourth or Buddhist Epoch begins.

Āryan colonists penetrated to Bengal and introduced Hindu religion and civilization among the aborigines. But Bengal never made any mark in the history of Ancient India, The kingdoms founded in the south won greater distinction. The Andhras founded a powerful kingdom in the Deccan, founded great schools of learning, and were destined, at a later period, to extend their sway over Northern India also. Further south, the Āryans came in contact with the old and imperfect Dravidian civilization. The more perfect Hindu civilization prevailed, and the Dravidians were Hinduized and founded kingdoms which became distinguished for learning and power. The three sister-kingdoms of the Choḷas, the Cheras, and the Pāṇḍyas made their mark before the third century B .C. and Kānchī (Conjeveram), the capital of the Choḷas, distinguished itself as the seat of Hindu learning at a later day.

In the west the Saurāṣṭras (including Guzrat and the Maharatta.country) received Hindu civilization from the Andhras of the Deccan; while, beyond a strip of the sea, Ceylon was discovered, and formed a great resort of Hindu traders, until Aśoka the Great sent his son to that land and converted the people to Buddhism. In the east, Buddhist pilgrims came and settled in Orissa and excavated caves in rocks centuries before Aśoka.

The practical and enterprising spirit of the age shews itself in literature as well as in territorial conquests. The whole of the verbose teachings and rites of the Brāhmaṇas and Āraṇyakas were condensed into Sūtras or aphorisms so as to form handy manuals for the sacrifice. Other Sūtras were framed for laying down the rules of domestic rites and social conduct Sūtra schools sprang up all over India, in the north and in the south, and works multiplied. Besides these religious works, phonetics, metre, grammar, and lexicons, were studied, and Yāska wrote his Nirukta, and Pāṇini his grammar, early in this period. And the construction of sacrificial altars according to fixed rules gave rise to geometry which was first discovered in India.

And, lastly, the lessons of the Upaniṣads were not lost. The bold speculations started in these works were pursued, until Kapila arose in the eighth or seventh century B .C. and started the Sāṅkhya philosophy—the first closely-reasoned system of mental philosophy known in the world. Other systems of philosophy were started by other thinkers, but the Sāṅkhya philosophy was destined to have the greatest influence on the future of India; for Gautama Buddha was born in the sixth century B. C, and he added to the cold logic of the Sāṅkhya philosophy a world-embracing sympathy and love for mankind which has made his religion the religion of a third of the human race.

Buddhism spread slowly among the poor and the lowly, for it was a protest against caste-privileges, a religion of equality of men. It spread slowly—as Christianity spread in Europe in the early days—until Aśoka embraced Buddhism in the third century B.C., as Constantine the Great embraced the new faith in Europe. As in the case of Christianity, so in the case of Buddhism, it fast became a national religion under imperial favour, and from the third century B.C., the Fourth or Buddhist Epoch begins.

Our readers will perceive that we have no difficulty in fixing the dates of the Third Epoch. Aśoka the Great ascended the throne about 260 B. C., and held his great Buddhist Council to settle the Buddhist Scriptures about 242 B.C. Two such Councils had been held before, one in the year of Gautama's death in 477 B.C., and one a hundred years after in 377 B.C. But the Council held by Aśoka in 242 B.C. finally settled the Scriptures, and the great Emperor then promulgated them all over India, and beyond the limits of India. At this date, therefore, 242 B.C., the Third Epoch ends, and the Fourth or Buddhist Epoch begins. And we have seen before that the Second Epoch closes about 1,000 B.C. We may, therefore, date the Third Epoch from 1,000 B.C. to 242 B.C. For the sake of convenience, we will call it the *Rationalistic Period,*

The great political, literary, and religious incidents of the period require the wide space of seven centuries and a half that we have allotted to the Epoch; and all the facts that we know confirm these dates. Dr. H. H. Wilson considers that the first incursions of the Āryans to the south began about 1,000. B. C., and we have adopted this date as the commancement of the

Third Period. The dates which Dr. Bühler has given to the Sūtras of Gautama, Baudhāyana, and Āpastamba fall within the dates given above. Dr. Thibaut assigns the eighth century B.C. to the Sulva Sūtras or geometry. Writers on Sāṅkhya philosophy assign the eighth or seventh century B .C. to Kapila's philosophy, and Gautama Buddha lived, as we know, in the sixth century B.C. Chandragupta was a contemporary of Alexander the Great, and ascended the throne probably in 320 B.C., and his grandson, as we have seen before, became king sixty years later.

These dates, which have been ascertained with tolerable certainty, confirm the dates which we have accepted for the previous or the Epic Period. For, if the philosophy of Kapila, which was a distant and matured result of the Upaniṣads, was started in the eighth or seventh century, the Upaniṣads themselves must have been composed at least two centuries earlier. And we are presumably correct in assigning B.C. 1,000 for the Upaniṣads,—the works which closed the Epic Period.

FOURTH EPOCH

The epoch begins with the brilliant reign of Aśoka the Great, who was the Emperor of Northern India, and published his edicts of humanity on stone pillars and on rocks all over Northern India, from Gujrat to Orissa. He prohibited the slaughter of animals, provided medical aid to men and cattle all over his empire, proclaimed the duties of citizens and members of families, and directed Buddhist missionaries to proceed to the ends of the earth, to mix with the rich and the poor, and to proclaim the truth. His inscriptions shew that he made treaties with Antioch of Syria, Ptolemy of Egypt, Antigonas of Macedon, Magas of Cyrene, and Alexander of Epiros, and sent missionaries to these kingdoms to preach the Buddhist religion. "Both here and in foreign countries," says Aśoka, "everywhere the people follow the doctrine of the religion of the Beloved of the Gods, wheresoever it reacheth."

"Buddhist missionaries,. "says a Christian writer[1], "preached in Syria two centuries before the teaching of Christ (which has so many moral points in common) was heard in Northern Palestine. So true is it that every great historical change has had its forerunner."

The Maurya dynasty which had commenced with Aśoka's grandfather Chandragupta about 320 B.C. did not last very long after the time of Aśoka. It was followed by two short-lived dynasties, the Śuṅga and the Kāṇva 183 to 26 B.C.), and then the great Andhras who had founded a powerful empire in the South, conquered Magadha and were masters of Northern India for four centuries and a half, B.C. 26 to A.D. 430. They were generally Buddhists, but respected Brāhmans and orthodox Hindus; and throughout the Buddhist Epoch, the two religions flourished in India side by side, and persecution was almost unknown. The Andhras were succeeded by the great Gupta emperors who were supreme in India till about 500 A.D., and then their power was overthrown. The Guptas were generally orthodox Hindus, but favoured Buddhism also, and made grants to Buddhist churches and monasteries.

In the meantime India was the scene of continual foreign invasion. The Greeks of Bactria, expelled by Turanian invaders, entered India in the second and first centuries before Christ, founded kingdoms, introduced Greek civilization and knowledge, and had varied fortunes in different parts of India for centuries after. They are said to have penetrated as far as Orissa. The Turanians themselves of the Yu-Chi tribe next invaded India, and gave a powerful dynasty to Kashmir; and Kaniṣka the Yu-Chi king of Kashmir, had an extensive empire in the first century A.D., which stretched from Kabul, and Kashgar, and Yarkand to Gujrat and Agra. He was a Buddhist, and held a great council of the Northern Buddhists in. Kashmir." The Cambojians and other tribes of Kabul then poured into India, and were in their turn followed by the locust-hordes of

1. Mahaffy, Alexander's Empire, Chapter XIII.

the Huns, who spread over Western India in the fifth century A.D. India had no rest from foreign invasions for six or seven centuries after the time of Aśoka the Great; but the invaders, as they finally settled down in India, adopted the Buddhist religion, and formed a part of the people.

Buddhism gradually declined during the centuries after the Christian era, much in the same way as the Hinduism of the Ṛg Veda had gradually become corrupted in the Epic Period when the Hindus had settled down in the Gangetic Volley. Buddhist monks formed a vast and unmanageable body of idle priesthood, owning vast acres of land attached to each monastery, and feeding on the resources of the people; and Buddhist ceremonials and forms bordered more and more on Buddha-worship and idolatry. A change was at hand; and that change was witnessed when Hindu genius and learning and a new form of Hinduism asserted themselves in the sixth century after Christ, first in Ujjayinī, and then all over India. An effete form of Buddhism lingered on for some centuries in some parts of India after this; but the Buddhist period may be said to close with the fifth century A.D.

We find an uninterrupted series of Buddhist rock-cut caves, stūpas, chaityas or churches, and vihāras or monasteries all over India, dating from the time of Aśoka to the 5th century A.D., but there are scarcely any specimens of Buddhist architecture of a later date. Temple-building and Hindu architecture flourished from the sixth century A.D., to long after the Mahommedan conquest.

The most valuable portions of Buddhist literature left to us are the scriptures as finally settled in the Council of Aśoka, and sent by him all over India and beyond India. These scriptures, preserved in the Pāli language in Ceylon, form our best materials for the history of early Buddhism, while later forms of this literature have been found in Nepal, in Thibet, in China, in Japan, and in all Buddhist countries.

We have said that Hinduism flourished in India side by side with Buddhism throughout the Buddhist Epoch. But

Buddhism had a marked effect on Hinduism which cannot be mistaken. Buddhism had questioned the sacredness of the Vedas; and the Hinduism of the Buddhist and subsequent times—though nominally revering the Vedas—shews a complete estrangement and emancipation from those ancient works. Hindu astronomy, mathematics, laws, and philosophical speculations had begun from the Vedas and the Vedic sacrifices, and belonged to different Vedic schools. But Hindu science and learning of the post-Buddhist age have no reliance on the Vedas, and do not belong to any Vedic school. Even the revived form of Hinduism of the sixth century and later ages is not a religion of Vedic sacrifices, but of worship of images and gods, unknown to the Vedas.

The Code of Manu represents Hindu thought and manners of the Buddhist Epoch. It is based on the ancient Dharmasutras or social laws of the Rationalistic Period; but while the Dharmasūtras belong to different Vedic schools, Manu's Saṁhitā knows of no such divisions and professes to be the law for all Āryans. It is remarkable that even so late as Manu's time, the whole Āryan population (leaving aside priests and soldiers), still formed one compact caste, the Vaiśyas, and had not been disunited and divided into the numerous trade and profession castes of modern times. Manu's mixed castes are mostly Hinduized aboriginal tribes.

For reasons which will appear from the foregoing remarks, we date the fourth, or *Buddhist Period,* from 242 B .C. to 300 A.D.

FIFTH EPOCH

The fifth or last Epoch of Hindu history is the Epoch of Hindu revival, and cover seven centuries, from 500 A.D. to 1194 A.D., the date of the Mahommedan conquest of Northern India.

The period begins with great deeds in politics and literature. Foreign invaders had harassed India for centuries before, and at last a great avenger arose. Vikramāditya the Great, of Ujjayinī, was the master of Northern India; he beat back the invaders known as the Śakas in the great battle of Korur, and asserted Hindu independence. Hindu genius and literature revived under his auspices, and a new form of Hinduism assented itself.

The two centuries and a half commencing with the time of Vikramāditya the Great (500 to 750 A.D.) may be called the Augustan era of later Sanskrit literature, and nearly all the great works which are popular in India to this day belong to this period. Kālidāsa wrote his matchless dramas and poems in Vikrama's court. Amara Sinha, the lexicographer, was another of the "nine gems" of this court. And Bhāravi was Kālidāsa's contemporary, or lived shortly after Śīlāditya II, a successor of Vikramāditya, ruled from 610 to 650 AD., and is reputed to have been the author of Ratnāvalī, though the work was probably composed by an author of his court. Daṇḍin, the author of Dasakumāra Charita, was an old man when Śīlāditya II reigned, and Bāṇabhaṭṭa, the author of Kādamvarī, lived in his court. Subandhu, the author of Vāsavadattā, also lived at the same time; and there are reasons to believe that the Bhaṭṭikāvya was composed by Bhartṛhari, the author of the Satakas, in the same reign.

In the next century Yaśovarman ruled between 700 and 740 A.D., and the renowned Bhavabhūti composed his powerful dramas in this reign. Bhavabhūti, however, was the last of the galaxy of poets and literary men— and no literary genius arose in India after the middle of the 8th century.

It was in this Augustan era also that the great national epics of India, the production of many ages, received their last additions and touches and assumed their final shape; and the voluminous Purāṇas, which have given their name to this Period, began to be composed in their present shape.

In modern Hindu science, too, we have the brightest names in these two centuries and a half. Āryabhaṭṭa, the founder of modern Hindu astronomy, was born in 476 A.D., and produced his work early in the sixth century. Varāha Mihira, his successor, was one of the "nine gems" of Vikrama's Court. Brahmagupta was born in 598 A.D., and was, therefore, a contemporary of Bāṇabhaṭṭa, the novelist. These three astronomers for the Triumvirate of modern Hindu Astronomy.

This brilliant period of two centuries and a half (500 to 750 A.D,) was followed by two centuries of impenetrable darkness ! The history of India from 750 to 950 A.D. is a perfect blank. No great dynasties rose to power, no literary or scientific men rose to renown, no great work of architecture or art was constructed in Northern India. History is silent over these two dread centuries !

But we have indications of what was transpiring. The two dark centuries witnessed the fall of ancient dynasties, and the crumbling down of ancient kingdoms and nationalities. They resemble the dark period of Europe, which witnessed the fall of the Roman power, and which cleared up when Feudal power arose. In India, too, the power of ancient races and dynasties was silently swept away during the period of darkness; and when light breaks in again, we see a new race of Hindu Feudal barons as the masters of India—the modern Rajputs ! In the general dissolution of ancient power and the struggle for supremacy, the youngest and the most vigorous race came to the forefront, and about 950 A.D. we find Rajput dynasties ruling everywhere in Northern India. They inherited the throne of Vikramāditya and his successors in Ujjayinī and Kanouj; they usurped the power of the powerful Valabhi or Sena Kings of Gujrat and Western India; and they tried to oppose the progress of Sabaktagin and Mahmud in the Punjab.

If the two dark centuries thus witnessed the rise of a new power, they also witnessed another great revolution. Decaying Buddhism, which in the time of Vikramāditya and his successors was allowed to exist side by side with Hinduism, was crushed out of existence during the dark centuries. Vikramāditya, though he favoured Hinduism, never persecuted Buddhists, and some of his most renowned courtiers, like Amara Sinha, the, lexicographer, were Buddhists. His successors favoured Hinduism and Buddhism by turns, but there was complete toleration throughout the period. Śilāditya II. the reputed author of Ratnāvalī, was a staunch Buddhist, and was visited by Houen Tsang, the Chinese traveller, about 640 A.D. There was no thought of persecution throughout this intellectual period, Hinduism was reviving with the vigour of new life, Buddhism was dying a slow and natural death. But there are reasons to suppose that persecution, the burning of monasteries and books, and the banishment of monks, were witnessed between 750 A.D. and 950 A.D. Śaṅkarācārya, the most determined foe of Buddhism, was born in 788 A.D., and the spirit which marks his literary labours soon found vent in the action of kings.

There are reasons to suppose that the new Rajput race is responsible for this persecution which finally stamped out Buddhism in India. Different theories have been put forward as to the origin of the Rajputs. Dr. H. H. Wilson, Col, Tod, and other authorities maintain that they were descended from the Scythian invaders of India, who poured in through successive centuries, who were once beaten back by Vikramāditya the Great, but who, like other invaders, settled down in the deserts of Western India, and ruled and conquered when they could. Be that as it may, the Rajputs certainly appear to have been new converts to Hindu civilization, for there is no mention of them in older records. Like all new converts, they espoused Hinduism with exceptional zeal; they were proud to be styled Kṣatriyas (descended from the Solar and Lunar races); and wherever they conquered, Buddhist churches and monasteries went down and Hindu temples and idols arose. Priestly monopoly in its closest form and the unhealthiest restrictions of modern Hinduism date from the rise of the Rajputs, and were perpetuated during the six centuries of national lifelessness under the Musalman rule.

It is impossible not to be struck with the resemblance

between European History and Indian History at the period which marks the close of the Ancient Age. The efforts of Vikramāditya to beat back the Śakas have a close resemblance to the efforts of the last Roman Emperors and armies to keep back the hordes of barbarians who pressed eagerly forward for conquests. For centuries the Hindus and the Romans succeeded; but the waves of invasion and conquest at last overwhelmed the ancient empires in India and in Italy, and marked the fall of ancient thrones and institutions! For centuries after this event, Western Europe and Northern India have scarcely any history; or the history is one of violence and wars which closed the Ancient Age and ushered in the Modern Age ! When, at last, the darkness clears up, we find a new Feudal power in Europe, and a new Rajput power in India. And the new dynasties of Europe had embraced Christianity, and exerted as zealously and enthusiastically for the medieval priests, as the newly-converted Rajputs did for the Brāhmans and the modern Hinduism of India.

But the parallel does not end here. The new masters of India had to fight as hard against the waves of Mahommedan invasion, as the new masters of Europe did in France, Spain, and in Syria. Richard the Lion-hearted was fighting at the same period as Prithu Rai of Delhi, and against the same rising power. In Europe the Christian barons saved their independence, and ultimately expelled the Musalmans even from Spain; in India the Hindu barons struggled and fell. Shahabuddin Ghori overthrew the Rajput kingdoms of Delhi and Ajmere, Kanouj and Benares in 1193 and 1194 A.D., and the boldest of the Rajputs retreated to their desert fastnesses, where they enjoy a sort of independence to the present day, through the generous sufferance of the British Government.

We have dated the Fifth or *Paurāṇik Period* from 500 A.D. to 1194 A.D., and we have supposed Vikramāditya the Great to have ruled shortly after 500 A.D, The Saṁvat Era, beginning in 56 B.C., is connected with Vikramāditya's name, and for a long time it was believed that the great king and the poet Kālidāsa flourished in the first century B.C. The researches of modern scholars which have confirmed and added to Vikramādityā's historic claims to renown, have, however, taken away from his antiquity, and his real date is no longer an open question. It is impossible for us to go fully into the evidence which places the great king and the great poet in the 6th century A.D.; but we will mention one or two facts for the curious reader.

Varāha Mihira was admittedly one of the "nine gems" of Vikrama's court, and it has been ascertained from his astronomy that he lived in the 6th century after Christ. Amara Sinha was admittedly another of the "nine gems," and it is believed he was the builder of the temple at Buddha Gayā, which was constructed after the 5th century A.D. Houen Tsang the Chinese traveller states that Vikramāditya was succeeded by Śīlāditya I., and Śīlāditya I. reigned 60 years before Houen Tsang's time. This gives us the 6th century for Vikrama's reign. And lastly, Kalhaṇa the historian of Kashmir informs us, that Durlabha-vardhana began his reign in Kashmir in 598 A.D., and that six kings ruled between Mātrigupta (Vikrama's contemporary) and Durḷabhavardhana. Allowing 15 years for each reign, we come to the beginning of the 6th century as the date of Mātrigupta and Vikrama.

But to those who are familiar with later Sanskrit literature, Kālidāsa's writings are the best evidence of his date. We know the dates of other writers and poets, of Bhavabhūti, Bāṇabhaṭṭa, Bhartṛhari, etc., and it is as impossible to separate Kālidāsa from this galaxy of literary men, and throw him six centuries backwards, *i.e.,* to within two centuries of Aśoka and his Buddhist council, as it is impossible to separate Shakespeare from the Elizabethan poets, and to assign to him a date within two centuries of Alfred's time !

DATES

What then is the origin of the *Saṁvat* Era, beginning at 56 B.C.? And what is the origin of the *Śakābda* Era, commencing at 78 A.D.? Scholars have experienced the greatest difficulty in finding out what great events these Eras really commemorate; and the conclusions arrived at are not yet beyond the Pale of controversy.

The Śakābda (78 A.D.) is supposed to commemorate the date on which a great Hindu king, Sālivāhana, or Vikramāditya, defeated the Śakas. But there is no evidence of Śaka invasions of that date, except that of the great king Kaniṣka of Kashmir, the greatest Buddhist king of India after Aśoka the Great, who, as we have seen before, conquered Western India as far as Agra and Gujrat, and held a great Council of the Northern Buddhists. History does not speak of any Hindu king who checked his progress; but on the other hand, there are inscriptions to shew that Kaniṣka himself established an Era which was used from his time for two or three centuries. It has been conjectured that this Era of Kaniṣka has subsequently been known as the Śakābda or the Era of the Śaka king; for the Śakābda was originally a Buddhist Era. It was adopted in Buddhist India, and it was known and used in all Buddhist countries—in Thibet and Burma, in Ceylan and Java. It was after the Hindu revival of the 6th century that the date was adopted by Hindus, and the story was added, that the Era marked not the reign of a Buddhist Śaka king, but the defeat of the Śakas by a Hindu king. Dr. Bhao Daji was the first to point out that this idea of the Śaka Era, commemorating the defeat and destruction of the Śakas, does not crop up before the 8th century A.D.

Wherever the Era is cited by ancient writers, it is cited as the Era of a Śaka king[1]; and to the present day the Era is

1. The exceedingly careful and observant scholar, Colebrooke, pointed out seventy years ago, that the astronomer, Varāhamihira, who lived in the 6th century A.D., cited the Sākā Era as the *Śaka Bhupā Kāla* or *Śakendra Kāla, i.e.*, the Era of the Śaka king. His commentator explains this as the Era when the barbarians called Śakas "*were discomfited by Vikramāditya*" Again, the astronomer, Brahmagupta, who flourished in the 7th century A.D., cites the Era as *Sāka Nripānte, i.e.*, after the Śaka King. His commentator explains this as "*after the reign oj Vikramāditya, who slew a people of barbarians called. Śakas.*" —Colebrooke's Algebra, ete. from the Sanskrit, p. xliii. London 1817.

known in our almanacs as the Śakābda, or more fully as *Śaka Narapater Atīlābda,* which means the Era of the Śaka king, not the Era of the destruction of the Śakas by a Hindu king.

The Saṁvat Era is still more perplexing. Popularly it is known as the Era of a great victory of Vikramāditya, but history knows of no Vikramādityā of Ujjayinī in 56 B.C.

It is still more curious that the Saṁvat Era has come into use in comparatively recent times. Dr. Bhao Daji says he knows of no inscription before the 11th century A.D. adopting this Era. Dr. Kern in his introduction to the Bṛhat Saṁhitā of Varāhamihira, declares that the use of the Saṁat Era in early times cannot be demonstrated, while Hindu astronomers begin to use it after the year 1000 or so. Westerguard holds that the grant of Dantidurga, dated *Śaka* 675, Saṁvat 811 (A.C. 754) is the earliest certain instance of its occurrence. And Dr. Burnell holds a similar opinion. No trace of this Era is found in the inscriptions of the Buddhist Period in India, or, in other Buddhist countries, Thibet and Burma, Ceylon and Java.

There certainly seems to be some mystery about the Saṁvat Era, 56 B.C. It pretends to commemorate a victory of a king of whom history knows nothing; and it is an Era which does not seem to have been used in the numerous inscriptions in India for several centuries, after it pretends to have been established.

Dr. Fergusson offers a bold solution of this mystery. That the real Vikramādityā—the patron of Kālidāsa—lived in the 6th century A.D., is now established beyond a doubt; that he defeated foreign invaders in the battle of Korur in the 6th century A.D., is a historic fact; that this year of a great Hindu victory (probably 544 A.D.), and of the revival of Hindu leaning, science, and religion., was a suitable date for the commencement of an Era, is apparent. But chronicles were not satisfied with an Era which was so long posterior to the Buddhist Era of the Śakābda, and so they fixed an Era sixth centuries before the battle of Korur—to make it anterior to the Śakābda Era—and called it by the name of Vikramāditya, the hero of the battle. And they fixed mother Era a thousand years before the battle of Korur. and called that Era, by the name of Śrī Harṣa, Vikramāditya's father. No Vikramāditya lived in 56 B. C., and no Śrī Harṣa lived in 456 B.C.; but the Eras named after them mean six and ten centuries before the victory of Vikramāditya. Śrī Harṣa's Era has fallen into disuse; the Saṁvat is still in universal use.

This is Dr. Fergusson's theory of the origin of the Saṁvat Era. But, probably, the true origin of the Era has been discovered by Mr. Fleet in his volume on the inscriptions of the Gupta kings. It would seem that the Era was originally a national Era of the Mālavā tribe, and came subsequently to be connected with the name of Vikramāditya who, in the 6th century A.D., raised the Mālavas to the rank of the first nation in India.

We now proceed, for facility of reference, to give a table of dates for the different Epochs, premising, that the dates should be taken as only approximately correct, and that the earlier dates are only supposed to be correct within two or three centuries.

DATES

Epoch I. Vedic Period

Āryan settlement in the Indus Valley Composition of the Ṛg Veda Hymns	B.C. 2000 to 1400

Epoch II. Epic Period

Āryan settlements in the Ganges Valley ...	B.C. 1400 to 1000
Lunar Zodiac fixed. Astronomical Observations	B.C. 1400 to 1200
Compilation of the Vedas	B.C. 1400 to 1200
Flourishing Period of the Kurus and the Pāñchālas	B.C. 1400 to 1200
Kuru Pāñchāla War	B.C. 1250

Flourishing Period of the Kosalas, the Kāsīs, and the Videhas	B.C. 1200 to 1000
Composition of the Brāhmaṇas and Āraṇyakas ...	B.C. 1300 to 1100
Composition of the Upaniṣads	B.C. 1100 to 900

Epoch III. Rationalistic Period

Āryan Conquest of all India	B.C.1000 to 242
Yāska...	B. C. 9th century
Pāṇini ...	B.C. 8th century
Sūtra Schools	B.C. 800 to 300
Sulva Sūtras (Geometry)	B.C. 8th century
Kapila and Sāṅkhya Philosophy	B.C. 700
Other Schools of Philosophy	B.C. 600 to 100
Gautama Buddha	B.C. 557 to 477
Bimbisāra, King of Magadha	B.C. 537 to 485
Ajāta Śatru	B.C. 485 to 453
First Buddhist Council	B.C. 477
Second Buddhist Council	B.C. 377
Nine Nandas, Kings of Magadha	B.C. 370 to 320
Chandragupta, King of Magadha	B.C. 320 to 291
Bindusāra, King of Magadha	B.C. 291 to 263
Aśoka, Sub-king of Ujjayinī	B.C. 263 to 259
Aśoka Emperor	B.C. 259 to 222
Third Buddhist Council	B.C. 242
Mahendra sent to Ceylon	B.C. 241
Kātyāyana attacks Pāṇinī	B.C. 4th century
Patañjali defends Pāṇini	B.C. 2nd century
Andhra Kingdom founded	B.C. 600
Choḷa, Chera, and Pāṇḍya Kingdoms founded	B.C. 400
Āryans colonize Bengal and Orissa ...	B.C. 500 to 200

Epoch IV. Buddhist Period

Prevalence of Buddhism	B.C. 242 to A.D. 500
The Maurya Dynasty (from Chandra gupta) in Magadha	B.C. 320 to B.C. 183
The Śuṅga Dynasty in Magadha ...	B.C. 183 to B.C. 71
The Kāṇva Dynasty in Magadha ...	B.C. 71 to B.C. 26
The Andhra Dynasty in Magadha...	B.C. 26 to A.D. 430
Parāsara's Astronomy.....	B.C. 200
Garga's Astromomy ...	B.C. 100
Astronomical Siddhāntas	A.D. 200 to A.D. 300
The Gupta Emperors ...	A.D. 400 to A.D. 500
The Bactrians invaded India	B.C. 2nd and 1st century
The Yu-Chi invaded India	B.C. & A.D. 1st century
Kaniṣka the Yu Chi King of Kashmir, commenced his reign and founded the Śaka Era	A.D. 78
The Shah Kings ruled in Saurāṣṭra ...	A.D. 150 to 300
The Cambojians (from Kabul and Kandahar) invaded India	A.D. 200 to 400
The White Huns invaded India	A.D. 4th and 5th centuries

Epoch V. Paurāṇik Period

Hindu Revival	A.D. 500 to 1194
Vikramāditya of Ujjayinī and Northern India	A.D. 515 to 550
Vikramāditya beat back the foreign invaders in the battle of Korur, about	A.D. 544
Kālidāsa. Amarasinha, Vararuchi, etc. ...	A.D. 500 to 550
Bhāravi. about	A.D. 550 to 600
Āryabhaṭṭa, Founder of Modern Hindu Astronomy	A.D. 476 to 530

Varāha mihira	A.D. 500 to	550
Brahmagupta	A.D. 598 to	650
Śīlādityā II. Emperor of Northern India ...	A.D. 610 to	650
Daṇḍin	A.D. 570 to	620
Bāṇa Bhaṭṭa and Subandbu	A.D. 610 to	650
Bhartṛhari and Bhaṭṭikāvya	A.D. 610 to	650
Houen Tsang visited Śīlāditya's courts ...	A.D. 640	
Yasovarman, King of Northern India	A.D. 700 to	730
Bhavabhūti	A.D. 700 to	730
Valabhi Kings of Western India	A.D. 470 to	720
Destruction of ancient dynasties and rise of the Rajputs...	A.D. 750 to	950
Śaṅkarāchārya	A.D. 788 to	850
Persecution of Buddhists	A.D. 750 to	950
Rajputs, masters of Northern India. Modern Hinduism finally established	A.D. 950 to	1194
Chālukya Kings of the Deccan	A.D. 500 to	1200
Pāla Kings of Bengal	A.D. 850 to	1150
Sena Kings of Bengal	A.D. 1000 to	1204
Kesari line of Orissa	A.D. 476 to	1132
Gaṅgetic line of Orissa	A.D. 1132 to	1534
The Bellala Dynasty of the Carnatic ...	A.D. 11th century.	
The Kakati Dynasty of Warrangal	A.D. 1200to	1323
The Kingdom of Vijayanagara	A.D. 1344 to	1565
Bhāskarāchārya	A.D. 12th century	
Jayadeva, Śrī Harṣa, Māgha, etc. ...	A.D. 12th century	
Sāyaṇāchārya	A.D. 14th century	

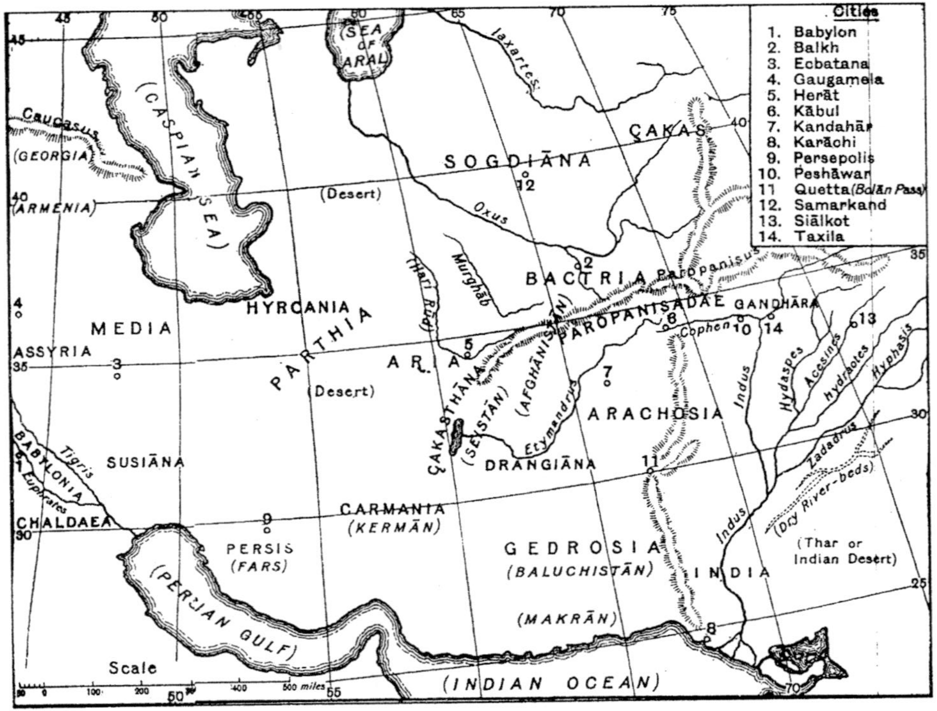

Map 1 : Map of N.W. India and Adjacent Countries in the time of Alexander the Great.

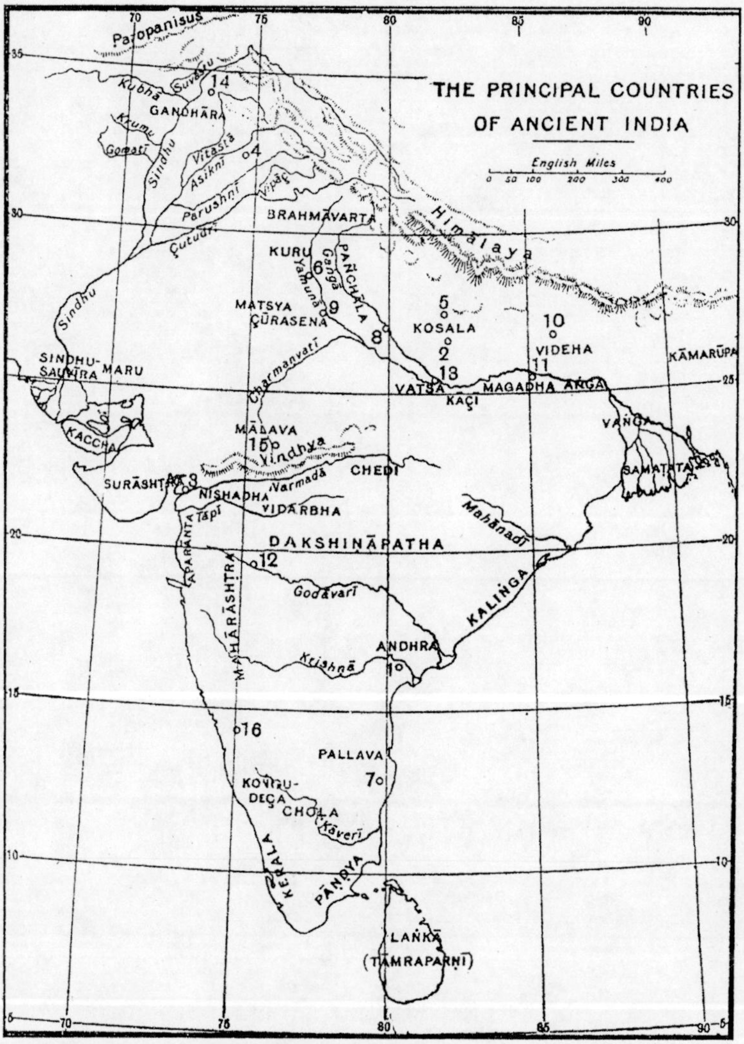

Map 2 : The Principal Countries of Ancient India.

1. Amarāvatī	5. Śrāvastī	9. Mathurā	13. Prayāga
2. Ayodhyā	6. Indraprastha	10. Mithilā	14. Takṣaśilā
3. Bhṛgu-kaccha	7. Kāñchī	11. Pāṭaliputra	15. Ujjayinī
4. Śākala	8. Kānyakubja	12. Pratiṣṭhāna	16. Vaijayantī

BOOK-I

VEDIC PERIOD

(B.C. 2000 to B.C. 1400)

CHAPTER – 1

IMMIGRATION OF THE INDO-ĀRYANS – THEIR LITERATURE

The site of the early home of the Āryans has been a subject of endless controversies among scholars. Enthusiastic and patriotic Hindu scholars will not admit that the first home of the Āryans was anywhere outside India; while equally patriotic European scholars would place the seat of the primitive Āryans on the shores of the Baltic Sea. We need hardly say that it is not our object to enter into this discussion; and we merely repeat here the belief of all moderate thinkers, that the early home of the Āryans was somewhere in Central Asia.

The main arguments on which this conclusion is based have been summed up by Professor Max Müller in a recent work, and we quote them for our readers :—

"Firstly, we have two streams of language, one tending south-east to India, and the other north-west to Europe. The point where these two streams naturally intersect, points to Asia."

"Secondly, the earliest centres of civilized life were in Asia." And we may add that the most primitive form of all Āryan languages—the nearest approach to that language which was spoken by the common ancestors of all Āryans races—is the Vedic Sanscrit of Ancient India.

"Thirdly, we see in later times large ethnic waves, rising

from Central Asia and overwhelming Europe. Such are the Huns in the fourth, and the Mongols in the thirteenth century.

"Fourthly, if the migration had taken place from Europe to Asia, particularly from Scandinavia, we should naturally look in the common Āryan language for a number of words connected with maritime life. But this is not the case. While we find common names for particular animals and birds, and even common names of animals (*paśu)* and birds (*vi*) in general, we find no names for special fishes, and no general name for fish, nor even is there a common name for the sea!"

Various pictures, more or less imaginary, of the civilization of the early Āryans before they separated, have been drawn by various scholars from the slender materials of the words which are found in common use among the different Āryan nations in the world. Pictet's work, in two large volumes, published in Paris in 1859-63, created a wider interest than any preceding attempt of a similar nature and this was followed by Dr. Fick's work in 1868, and Dr. Hehn's work in 1870. It is not our intention to draw such pictures here; we will only give a few facts about the life of the primitive Āryans, about which there is no dispute.

The domestic economy among the early Āryans was much the same as it is among the Āryan nations of the present day. The historian of man does not find in Āryan history any traces of Hatairism (or of promiscuous relationship between the sexes), of families being reckoned on the mother's side, or of inheritance by the female line. On the contrary, the father was the protector and the nourisher of the family, the mother looked after and fed the children, the daughter milked the cattle, and relationship by marriage was recognized. Probably the primitive Āryans had already reached a higher state of civilization than promiscuous living would imply. The family, and not the tribe, was the unit of society; and the father was the head of the family.

Many of the useful animals had been domesticated and brought under the service of man. The cow, the bull, the ox, the sheep, the goat, the swine, the dog, and the horse had all been domesticated. The wild bear, the wolf, the hare, and the dreaded serpent were known. Similarly among birds, the goose, the duck, the cuckoo, the raven, the quail, the crane, and the owl were well known to the early Āryans.

The various industries were still in their infancy; but a commencement in manufactures and arts had been made. The Āryans built houses, villages and towns, made roads, and constructed boats for communication by water or for a humble kind of trade. Weaving, spinning, and plaiting were known, and furs, skins, and woollen fabrics were made into garments. Carpentry must have made a considerable progress, and dyeing was known.

It need scarcely be stated that agriculture was practised by the primitive Āryans; and it was this occupation which probably gave them their name *(Arya* = cultivator). Many words familiar to cultivators like the plough, the waggon, the cart, the wheel, the axle, the yoke, in common use among the Āryan nations point to the same primitive roots from which they have been derived. Corn was ground, prepared and cooked in various ways; while the flocks of sheep and cows, by which every family was surrounded, afforded milk and meat. There can be little doubt, that, although agriculture was largely resorted to, many patriarchs of families used also to rove about from place to place with their attendants and flocks in search of new pastures, and a fairly large portion of the early Āryans led a nomad life. Of this we have some trace even in the Ṛg Veda, as we shall see farther on.

War was not infrequent in those primitive times, and weapons of bone and of wood, of stone and of metals, were known. The bow and the arrow, the sword and the spear seem to have been the weapons of war.

It argues some advance in civilization, that the use of gold and of silver was undoubtedly known to the early Āryans; and with the simplicity of early races, they called gold by the name "yellow," and silver by the name "white." A third metal *(ayas)* was also known, but it is doubtful if it was iron.

It is perhaps impossible to conjecture the sort of government which obtained in those olden days. Patriarchs of tribes and leaders of men undoubtedly obtained ascendancy, and the simple subjects looked up to them and called them the protectors or nourishers of men, or the shining chiefs *(Pati, Vispati, Raja)* in war as well as in peace. The natural feelings of civilized man distinguished between right and wrong, and custom, and a vague perception of what was good for the nation, had the force of law.

And lastly, the primitive religion of the Āryans was suggested by whatever was beautiful and striking in the phenomena of Nature. The sky, or the bright sky was an eternal object of wonder and of worship. The sun, the dawn, the fire, and the earth, the storms and the clouds and the thunder, all received worship. But religion was still simple and archaic. Myths and legends about the gods and their relationship had not yet multiplied; elaborate rites and ceremonials had not yet been fabricated. The bold forefathers of the Āryan nations looked up with a manly veneration to whatever was wondrous and beautiful in nature, imagined such manifestations as instinct with deity, and offered their praise and their prayers with a grateful and fervent heart.

Adventurous bands of Āryans left their home in Central Asia from time to time in quest of food or pasture, of kingdoms or plunder. The exact order in which the forefathers of the different nations left has not been ascertained, and will never be ascertained. Professor Max Müller holds that the first divizion of the Āryan race was into two branches, *viz.*, the North-Western or European, and the South-Eastern or Asiatic; and that, after they became once separated, the two branches never met again. The North-Western branch travelled towards Europe divisions took place, and five distinct races occupied five different portions of Europe at periods which cannot be ascertained. The Celts settled, or were more probably driven onwards by other races to settle, in the extreme west of Europe, in France, Ireland, Great Britain, and Belgium; the robust Tutons settled in central Europe, from which they issued after the downfall of Rome to conquer the whole of Europe; the Slavs settled in Eastern Europe, *i.e.*, in Russia and other places; and the Italic and Greek divizions settled in the south of Europe.

The Asiatic branch travelled southwards, and according to Max Müller, the still undivided Indo-Iranians came as far as the Indus, to the land of the seven rivers, or the Punjab. Here "within sight of the Indus and its tributaries, the undivided South-Eastern Āryans spoke a language more primitive than the Sanscrit or Zend." Religious schism then separated them; the worshippers of the Devas or the Hindus remained in the Punjab, the worshippers of the Asuras or the Iranians went away to Persia.[1]

It is the worshippers of the Devas—the Hindu Āryans—who have composed those hymns which are known as the Ṛg Veda and we will say a few words here about this ancient work. Probably there is not another work in the literature of mankind which is so deeply interesting, so unique in the lessons it imparts. The hoary antiquity of this ancient work, the picture it affords of the earliest form of civilization that the Āryans developed in any part of the world, and the flood of light it throws on the origin of the myths and religions of all Āryan nations—these alone would make the Ṛg Veda deeply interesting.

But the work has a yet higher import, a deeper significance. To the philosophical historian of man the Ṛg Veda discloses the origin of religious faith and religious feelings. It explains how the mind of man in its infancy worships what is bright and glorious in nature, what is powerful and striking.Among less happy nations, religion began with the dread of diseases and of evils, as these made the most lasting impression on the mind.But among the Āryans, the brighter and pleasanter aspects of nature–the bright sky' the blushing down, the rising sun, and the glowing fire, created the deepest impression, and called forth songs of gratitude and praise and worship. This is the Ṛg Veda Saṁhitā,– this is the earliest form of Āryan religion known.

But the Ṛg Veda is more than this.It shows us how the mind is led from Nature up to Nature's God. For the sages of the Ṛg Veda do not always remain satisfied with the worship of the manifestation of Nature; they sometimes soar higher, and dare to conceive that all these phenomena – the sun, the sky, the storms, and the thunder – are but the action of the Unknowable One. It is in the very latest hymns of the Veda that we find these daring guesses after oruth – this bold conception of one God.

And if such is the value of the Ṛg Veda to the historian of man, its value to the historian of Āryan nations is still greater. It is the oldest work in the Āryan world.It gives us a picture of the oldest civilization which the Āryans developed in any part of the world; and as we have said before, it enlightens and clears up much that is dark and obscure in the religions and myths of Āryan nations all over world. It would be entirely foreign to our present object to illustrate this by instances, but some instances are so well known as to merely require a mention to illustrate our views.

Zeus or Jupiter is the Vedic Dyu, or the sky; Daphne and Athena are the Vedic Dahanā and Ahanā the down; Uranus is Varuṇa, the sky; and probably, Prometheus and Hephaistos are the Vedic Pramantha and Yaviṣṭa, the fire!

To the Hindus the Ṛg Veda is a work of still higher importance. It explains the whole fabric of the later Hindu religion; it clears all the complications of later mythology; it throws light on the history of the Hindu mind from its earliest stage of infancy to the latest times. The Hindu learns from this ancient and priceless volume that Viṣṇu the supreme preserver, and his three steps covering the universe meant the sun at its rise, its zenith, and when setting; that the terrible god Rudra, the supreme destroyer originally meant the thunder or thunder-cloud; and that Brahmā the supreme creator, was originally prayer or the god of prayer. And lastly, he learns that Rāma and Kṛṣṇa, Durgā and Lakṣmī Gaṇiśa and Kārtikeya, are later creations of the Paurāṇik fancy, and were unknown to the first Āryans in India.

Historically, and socially too, the Hindu has much to learn from the Veda. For the Ṛg Veda gives us a picture of society when there were no caste distinctions, when widows were married, and women had their legi timate influence in the society in which they lived and moved.

The Veda consists of 1,028 hymns, comprising over ten

thousand verses. The hymns are addressed to Nature-gods, of whom a full account will be given later on.

The hymns are generally simple, and betray a child- like and somple faith in the gods, to whom sacrifices are offered, and libations of the Soma juice are poured, and who are asked for increase of progeny, cattle, and wealth, and implored to help the Āryans in their still doubtful struggle the black aborigines of the Punjab.

The hymns of the Ṛg Veda are divided into ten Maṇḍalas or Books, and with the exception of the first and the last books, every one of the remaining eight books contains hymns said to have been composed or rather proclaimed by one Ṛṣi, – by which we may understand one family or time of teachers. Thus the second book is by Gṛtsamada, who is said to be the same as Śaunaka; the third by Viśvāmitra; the fourth by Vāmadeva; the fifth by Atri; the sixth by Bhāradvāva; the seventh by Vasiṣṭha; the eighth by Kaṇva; and the ninth by Angiras. The first book contains 191 hymns, which with scattered exceptions, are composed by fifteen Ṛṣis; and the tenth book also contains 191 hymns, which are mostly ascribed to fictitious authors.

The attempt to separate the older hymns from the new, and to assign a separate period for each, has not succeeded, and is never likely to succeed. Nevertheless, the most careless student of the Veda cannot help noticing that the tenth or last Maṇḍala of the Ṛg Veda stands apart from the other nine, and look like a later appendage; and most of the hymns of this book are comparatively recent hymns. One can almost lay his finger on many of the hymns of this book which are undoubtedly recent, comparatively speaking. They disclose a higher development of ideas, a more matured state of speculations, and often a grosser superstition, and a more artificial state of society. Such are the hymns which describe the future world, or lay down the rituals for marriage or funeral; and such are the obscure speculations about the unity of God. Such again are the Mantras against diseases, etc, similar to the hymns of the Atharva Veda, which is admittedly a later work. Most of the hymns of the tenth Book of the Ṛg Veda again are ascribed to gods, as if the real authors were anxious to conceal the late origin of the hymns by this device!

The hymns of the Ṛg Veda were handed down from father to son, or from teacher to pupil, for centuries together, and it was in a later age, in the Epic Period, that they were arranged and compiled. The whole, or greater portion of the tenth Book, seems to have been the production of this later period, but was thrown in and preserved with the body of the older hymns.

The arrangement and compilation of the Ṛg Veda hymns in their present shape must have been completed within the Epic Period. In Aitareya Āraṇyaka II, 2, we have fanciful derivations given of the names of the Ṛṣis of the Ṛg Veda in the order in which the Maṇḍalas are arranged. And this is followed by an account of a Sūkta or hymn, of a Ṛk or verse, of a half Ṛk, of a Pada or word, and of an Akṣara or syllable. The Ṛg Veda Saṁhitā therefore had not only been arranged Maṇḍala by Maṇḍala, but had been carefullly divided, subdivided, and analysed within the Epic Period.

By the close of the Epic Period, every verse, every word, every sylllable of the Ṛg Veda had been counted. The number of verses, as computed, varies from 10,402 to 10,622, that of words is 153,826, that of sylllables 432,000.

REFERENCE

1. The opinion, however, which has hitherto been generally accepted, is at the separation between the Hindus and the Iranians took place before the race came to the Indus; and that the Indo-Āryans came to India in consequence of the religious schism and subsequent dissensions.

CHAPTER–2

AGRICULTURE, PASTURE AND COMMERCE

The main industry of the ancient Hindus, as of the modern Hindus, was agriculture; and, as might be expected, we have frequent allusions to it in the Ṛg Veda. The very name Ārya by which the Āryan conquerors of India have distinguished themselves from the aborigines or Dāsas, is said to come from a root which means to cultivate. Professor Max Müller has traced the progress of this word all over the Āryan world, from Iran or Persia, to Erin or Ireland, and argues with considerable force that the word was invented in the primeval home of the Āryans in Central Asia, to indicate their partiality to cultivation, as distinguished from the nomadic habits of the Turanians, whose name indicates their rapid journies or the fleetness of their horse. Certain it is that the word Ārya is the one word in the Ṛg Veda which distinguishes the conquerors as a class, or even as a caste, from the aborigines of the country. And there are remarkable passages also which show that the new settlers, in calling themselves Ārya, had not altogether forgotten the real signification of the word. One instance will suffice:—

"O ye two Aśvins! you have displayed your glory by teaching the *Ārya* to cultivate with the plough and to sow corn, and by giving him rains for (the production of) his food, and by destroying the *Dasyu* by your thunderbolt." (I, 117, 21.)

There are two other words in the Ṛg Veda which are synonymous, not so much with the Āryan tribe, but rather with man generally; and both of them come from roots which indicate cultivation. The words are *Charshana* (1, 3, 7, etc.) and *Kṛṣṭi* (1, 4, 6, etc), and both these words come from modifications of the same root *Kṛṣ* or *Chṛṣ* to cultivate.

Thus the very names which the Āryan conquerors of India gave themselves, are names which indicate, that useful occupation which distinguishes the civilized man from the barbarian, *viz.*, cultivation of the soil.

There are numerous direct allusion in the Ṛg Veda to agriculture, but the most remarkable among them is a hymn which is dedicated to a supposed god of agriculture, the Lord of the Field as he is called, and which we will translate in full :—

"1. We will win (cultivate) this field with the Lord of the Field; may he nourish our cattle and our horses; may he bless us thereby.

"2. O Lord of the Field! bestow on us sweet and pure and butter-like and delicious and copious rain, even as cows give us milk. May the Lords of the Water bless us.

"3. May the plants be sweet unto us; may the skies and the rains and the firmament be full of sweetness; may the Lord of the Field be gracious to us. We will follow him uninjured by enemies.

"4. Let the oxen work merrily; let the men work merrily, let the plough move on merrily. Fasten the traces merrily; ply the goad merrily.

"5. O Suna and Sīra! accept this hymn. Moisten this earth with the rain you have created in the sky.

"6. O fortunate Furrow! proceed onwards, we pray unto thee; do thou bestow on us wealth and an abundant crop.

"7. May Indra accept this Furrow; may Pūṣan lead her onwards. May she be filled with water, and yield us corn year after year.[1]

" 8. Let the ploughshares turn up the sod merrily; let the men follow the oxen merrily; may Parjanya moisten the earth with sweet rains. O Suna and Sīra! bestow on us happiness." (IV, 57).

We shall seek in vain in the entire range of later Sanscrit literature for a passage in which the humble hopes and wishes of simple agriculturists are so naturally described. This is the unique charm of the Ṛg Veda as a literary composition. Whether it is an account of a battle with aborigines, or a prayer to friendly Indra to come and have a cup of Soma, or a song of the simple cultivator—the Ṛg Veda hymn always takes us nearer to the simple workings of a simple but straightforward and manly heart, than anything in the literature of later times.

We will translate a portion of another hymn, also dedicated to agriculture :—

"3. Fasten the ploughs, spread out the yokes, and sow the seed on this field which has been prepared. Let the corn grow with our hymns; let the scythes fall on the neighbouring fields where the corn is ripe.

"4, The ploughs have been fastened; the labourers have spread the yokes; the wise men are uttering prayers to gods,

" 5. Prepare troughs for the drinking of the animals. Fasten the leather-strings and let us take out water from this deep and goodly well which never dries up.

" 6. The troughs have been prepared for the animals; the leather-string shines in the deep and goodly well which never dries up, and the water is easily got. Take out water from the well.

" 7. Refresh the horses; take up the corn stacked in the field; and make a cart which will convey it easily. This well full of water for the drinking of animals, is one *droṇa* in extent, and there is a stone wheel to it. And the reservoir for the drinking of men is one *skanda*. Fill it with water." (X, 101.)

Irrigation and cultivation in the Punjab are only possible by means of wells, and wells are reserved also for the drinking of men and beasts; and it is not surprising therefore that we should find references to wells in the Ṛg Veda. Another remarkable fact which appears from the passages translated above is that horses were used for cultivation in those days, a custom still common in Europe, but not in India in modern times.

In X, 25, 4, and in many other places we have allusions to wells. In X,, 93, 13 we are told how water was raised from wells for irrigation. The contrivance is the same as is still in vogue in Northern India; a number of pots are tied to a string, and as the pots go up and down by the movement of a wheel, they are filled in the well and pulled up and emptied and sent down again. The contrivance is called *ghaṭichakra,* or the circle of pots, and bears the same name to the present day.

In X, 99, 4, we have another allusion to irrigation of fields by means of canals which were replenished with water by means of a *droṇa*. And in X, 68, 1, we are told that cultivators who irrigated their fields kept away birds by uttering loud cries.

As stated above, the allusions to pasture are by no means so frequent as the allusions to agriculture. Pūṣan is the god of shepherds—he is the sun as viewed by shepherds—and is supposed to protect them and travellers generally in their wanderings over the country. And here and there in a hymn to Pūṣan, we find that the Āryans of India had brought with them recollections and songs about those migrations which they occasionally undertook in Central Asia, if not after their settlement in India. We translate one such hymn below :—

"1. O Pūṣan! help us to finish our journey, and remove all dangers. O Son of the Cloud, do thou march before us!

"2. O Pūṣan! do thou remove from our path him who would lead us astray, who strikes and plunders and does wrong.

"3. Do thou drive away that wily robber who intercepts journeys.

"4. Do thou trample under thy foot the vile carcass of him who plunders us in both ways (by stealth and by force) and who commits outrages.

"5. O wise Pūṣan, destroyer of enemies! we implore of thee the protection with which thou didst shield and encourage our forefathers.

"6. O Pūṣan, possessed of all wealth, possessed of golden

weapons, and chief among beings! bestow on us thy riches.

"7. Lead us so that enemies who intercept may not harm us; lead us by an easy and pleasant path. O Pūṣan! devise means (for our safety) on this journey.

"8, Lead us to pleasant tracts covered with green grass; let there be no extreme heat by the way. O Pūṣan! devise means (for our safety) on this journey.

"9 Be powerful (in thy protection); fill us (with riches; bestow on us (wealth); make us strong and give us food! O Pūṣan! devise means (for our safety) on this journey.

"10. We do not blame Pūṣan; but we extol him in our hymns. We solicit wealth from the handsome Pūṣan." I, 42

There is also another interesting hymn on the practice of taking out cattle to pasture fields, and then bringing them back. A few verses are worth translating :—

"4. We call the cowherd, let him take out these cows; let him pasture them in the fields; let him know and pick out the animals; let him bring them back to the house; let him pasture them on all sides.

"5. The cowherd seeks for the cows and brings them back to the house; he pastures them on all sides. May he come home safe.

"8. O cowherd! pasture the cows in all directions, and bring them back. Pasture them in various parts of the earth, and then bring them back." (X, 19.)

There are allusions in the preceding passages to robbers who infested outlying tracts of the country— probably to the cattle-lifters and thieves among the aboriginal races, who hung around the Āryan villages and clearances, and lived by intercepting peaceful industry. We shall speak of them further on.

Allusions to trade and commerce must be necessarily rare in a collection of hymns to gods; but, nevertheless, we are here and there surprised by passages which throw a curious light on the manners of the times. Loans and usury were well understood in those days, and Ṛṣis (who, we should always remember, were worldly men in those days, and not hermits or anchorites) occasionally lament their state of indebtedness with the simplicity of primitive times. In one remarkable verse again, we are reminded of the finality of a sale-transaction, when once the sale is completed :—

"One sells a large quantity for a small price, and then goes to the purchaser and denies the sale, and asks for a higher price. But he cannot exceed the price once fixed on the plea that he has given a large quantity. Whether the price was adequate or inadequate, the price fixed at the time of sale must hold good." IV, 24, 9.

A passage like the above would indicate the existence of current money for the purposes of buying and selling. We have numerous instances of Ṛṣis acknowledging the gift of a hundred piece of gold (V, 27, 2, etc.), and there can be no doubt, pieces of gold of a certain fixed weight were used as money and indicated in these passages. Professor Wilson in his note on the above verse (V, 27, 2), thinks "that pieces of money are intended; for if we may trust Arian, the Hindus had coined money before Alexander." We must admit, however, that there is no distinct allusion to *coined* money in the Ṛg Veda. The word *Niṣka* (1, 126, 2, etc.) is often used in the Ṛg Veda in a dubious sense. In some passages it means money, in others it means a golden ornament for the neck;—the two interpretations are not necessarily contradictory, for in India pieces of gold used as money have habitually been used as ornaments for the neck since time immemorial.

On the other hand, there are distinct references to voyages by sea, though of course, the words used may mean rivers only, and not the sea. The shipwreck of Bhujyu, and his deliverance by the gods Aśvins, is constantly alluded to (I, 116, 3, etc), and in 1, 25, 7, the god Varuṇa is said to know the paths of the birds through the sky, and the paths of the ships over the sea. In IV, 55, 6, the poet refers to the "people who desiring to acquire wealth, pray to the sea before undertaking a voyage ;" while in VII, 88, 3, Vasiṣṭha says :—

"When Varuṇa and I went on a boat and took her out to sea, I lived in the boat floating on the water and was happy in it, rocking gracefully (on the waves)."

While there are these and other distinct allusions to voyages, there is absolutely no prohibition against voyages in the Ṛg Veda.

REFERENCE

1. In these two remarkable verses, the furrow, Sītā is addressed as a female, and asked to yield copious harvests. In the Yajur Veda also, the furrow is similarly worshipped. And when the Āryans gradually conquered the whole of India, and primeval jungles and waste lands were marked with the furrow, the furrow or Sītā assumed a more definite human character, and became the heroine of the Epic which describes the Āryan conquest of Southern India,

CHAPTER – 3

FOOD, CLOTHING AND THE ARTS OF PEACE

Barley and wheat seem to have been the principal produce of the field, and the principal articles of food. The names of grain found in the Ṛg Veda are somewhat misleading, as they have come to bear a different signification in modern days from what they had in the ancient times. Thus the word *Yava,* which, in modern Sanscrit implies barley only, was used in the Veda for implying food-grains generally, including wheat and barley. And the word *Dhāna* which, in Bengal at least, means paddy or rice, implies in the Ṛg Veda fried barley, which was used as food and offered to the gods. There is no allusion to *vrīhi* (rice) in the Ṛg Veda.

We also find mention of various kind of cakes prepared from these grains and used as food and offered to the gods. *Pakti* (from *pach,* to cook, or to prepare) means prepared cakes, and various other terms like *Puroḍāsa* and *Apūpa* and *Karambha,* are also used. (III, 52, 1 & 2; IV, 24, 7, etc.)

It may be easily imagined that animal food was largely used by the early Hindus of the Punjab. We have frequent allusions to the sacrifice and to the cooking of cows, buffaloes, and bulls. (I, 61, 12; II, 7, 5; V, 29, 7 and 8; VI, 17, 11; VI, 16, 47; VI, 28, 4; X, 27, 2; X, 28, 3, etc.)

In X, 89, 14, there is mention of slaughter-houses where cows were killed, and in X, 91, 14, there is an allusion to the sacrifice of horses, bulls, and rams. The allusions to the sacrifice of horses are extremely rare, showing that, although the custom was introduced into India by the early Āryans from heir primitive home in Central Asia, the flesh of the horse as an article of food soon fell into disuse. In later times the sacrifice of the horse at the *Aśvamedha* was performed on rare occasions with great pomp and circumstance by powerful kings, after they had subdued their neighbours and assumed a title answering to the Imperial title in Europe. There can be no dealt this great imperial rite rose out of the simple sacrifice of the horse practised in primitive times when the horse was still an article of food. The pomp and ceremony, as well as certain revolting rites connected with horse-sacrifice in later days, were unknown in Vedic times.

A fairly complete account of the sacrifice of the horse, such as it prevailed in the Vedic times, is to be found in hymn 162 of the first Maṇḍala of the Ṛg Veda. It is too long for translation, but a few verses may interest our readers :—

"2. The men have brought the prepared offering before the horse which is covered with gold trappings. The piebald goat bleats and goes towards the horse; may it be an acceptable offering for Indra and Pūṣan.

"11. O horse! the gravy which comes out of your body when you are roasted, escaping from the roasting spit, should not fall to the ground nor get mixed with the grass. The gods are eager for the food; let it be offered to them !

"12. Those who stand around and watch the cooking of the horse, those who say—Its smell is delicious, take it down now—and those who beg a portion of the meat—let the aims of all of them be in furtherance of our aims.

"13. The stick, which is dipped into the boiling pot, the vessels in which the gravy is kept, the covers which keep it warm, the cane by which the body of the horse is first marked, and the knife by which the body is dissected (along the lines marked), all these implements help in the cooking of the horse.

"18. The knife goes as a friend of the gods to separate the thirty-four ribs of the horse. Cut them out, so that the separate parts may not be cut or mangled. With a loud voice, and with circumspection, cut away along the joints.

"20. Go to the gods, O horse! let not thy dear body pain thee; let not the knife rest long on thy limbs; let not a greedy and ignorant immolator cut thy body needlessly, disregarding the separate limbs,"

Who could have believed that this simple horse sacrifice of the Ṛg Veda, the carving and the roasting and the boiling of the horse for worship and for the purposes of food, would have developed into the imperial ceremony of *Aśvamedha* of later times? But many a practice which we see in its simple and natural aspect in the Veda has developed into mighty and often monstrous ceremonies in later days; and many a simple Vedic allegory relating to the striking phenomena of Nature has also developed into equally monstrous Paurāṇik legends. Herein constitutes the true value of the Veda; we trade in it Hindu rites and institutions and the Hindu religion itself to their simple natural beginnings.

The fermented juice of the plant called *Soma* appears to have been the only intoxicating drink used in the Vedic times. So much were the ancient Āryans addicted to this drink, that Soma was soon worshipped as a deity both in India and in Iran (under the name *Haoma* in the latter country), and we find one entire Maṇḍala or Book of the Ṛg Veda dedicated to this deity. The Indo-Āryans appear to have been more addicted to fermented and intoxicating Soma than their peaceful brethren of Iran; and many are the allusions in the Zendavesta to the hateful customs of their Indian brethren. Some antiquarians think that this was one great reason of those dissensions which broke out among the southern Āryans, and which led to the final separation of the Iranians from the Hindus.

The process by which the Soma-juice was prepared has been fully described in IX, 66, and in other hymns. We will translate a few verses from this hymn :-

"2. O Soma! your two leaves alternated, and you attained a wonderful glory thereby.

"3. O Soma! the leaves covered thee—a creeper— on all sides, and you flourished in all seasons.

"7. O Soma! you have been crushed; you flow as a stream to Indra, scattering joy on all sides; you bestow immortal food.

"8. Seven women stir thee with their fingers, blending their voices in a song to thee; you remind the sacrificer of his duties at the sacrifice.

"9. You mix with water with a pleasing sound; and the finders stir you over a woollen strainer, and filter you. Your particles are thrown up then, and a sound arises from the woollen strainer.

"11. The woollen strainer is placed on a vessel, and the finger repeatedly stir the Soma, which sends out a sweet stream into the vessel.

"13. O Soma! you are then mixed with milk. Water runs towards thee with a pleasing sound."

From this description it would appear that the juice of Soma used to be taken—much as *Siddhi* is taken in our times—mixed with milk. The poets of the Ṛg Veda go into ecstasy over the virtues and the exhilarating powers of the Soma; and some of their descriptions have developed into strange Paurāṇik legends in subsequent times. One or two verses will illustrate this :—

"O Soma! there is nothing so bright as thou. When poured out, thou welcomest all the gods, to bestow on them immortality." (IX, 108, 3.)

"The praiseworthy Soma has from ancient times been the drink of the gods; he was milked from the hidden recesses of the sky; he was created for Indra and was extolled." (IX, 110, 8.)

"In that realm where there is perennial light, and where the heaven is placed, O Soma, lead me to that deathless and immortal realm! Flow thou for Indra." (IX, 113,7)

Such passages as these are to be found throughout the Ninth Book of the Ṛg Veda. Who could have guessed that the strange Paurāṇik legends of the churning of the ocean and the discovery of the *Amṛta* or immortal drink could have arisen from these simple Vedic descriptions of Soma ? The sky in the Veda is considered watery, and is often confused with the sea, and the milking of Soma from the sky would, with the help of a strong Paurāṇik imagination, be translated into the churning of the ocean for the *Amṛta !*

It would appear from many passages in the Ṛg Veda that many arts were carried to a high state of excellence. Weaving was well-known, of course, and deft female fingers wove the warp and the woof in ancient times as in modern days. (II, 3, 6; II, 38, 4, etc.) In one curious passage (VI, 9, 2), the Ṛṣi laments his ignorance of the mysteries of religious rites by saying : "I know not the warp and I know not the woof of religious rites; and in another place (X. 26, 6.) the weaving and bleaching of sheep's wool is attributed to the god Pūṣhan, who, as we have already seen, is the god of sheperds.

Every Āryan village had probably its barber then as now; and the clearances of forests by fire are in one passage somewhat mysteriously described as the *shaving* of the earth. (I, 164, 44.) Carpentry was also well known, and we have frequent allusions to the construction of carts and chariots. (III, 53, 19; IV, 2, 14; IV, 16, 20, etc.) The use of iron, of gold, and of other metals was well known; in V, 9, 5, we have a reference to the work of an ironsmith, and in VI, 3, 4, we are told of goldsmiths melting metal.

But we get a better idea of working in metals in the Vedic times from the description of various gold ornaments and iron utensils and implements of war which is to be found throughout the Ṛg Veda. The allusions are numerous, and we can therefore only make a selection here which will convey a fair idea of the manufactures of those days. We are told of armours used in war in I, 140, 10, in II, 39, 4, in IV, 53, 2, and in various other places. In II, 34, 3, we have reference to golden helmets, and in IV, 34, 9, there is mention of armour for the shoulders or arms, probably a shield. The lightning has been compared to a javelin *(ṛṣṭi)* in V,

52, 6, and in V, 54, 11; and also to a sword or battle-axe *(bāṣi),* and to bows and arrows and quivers in V, 57, *2*. Three thousand mailed warriors are spoken of in VI, 27, 6; feathered, sharp-pointed, shining shafts are described in VI, 46, 11; and sharp-edged swords are spoken of in VI, 47, 10. And in verses 26 and 29 of the same hymn we are told of war-chariots and war-drums. And lastly, in the 75th hymn of the sixth Maṇḍala, we have a spirited account of the arms and accoutrements of war which we will translate for our readers further on.

In IV, 2, 8, we have a reference to horses with golden caparisons, and in IV, 37, 4, V, 19, 3, and many other places, we have allusions to the *Niṣka,*. a golden ornament worn in the neck. In V, 53,4, the lightning ornaments of the Maruts are compared with ornaments *(Añji)* with necklaces *(Srak),* with golden breast plates *(Rukma),* and with bracelets and anklets *(Khadi)*. In V, 54, 11, we are again told of anklets for the feet, and golden breastplates for the breast, and of golden crowns *(Siprāh hiraṇmayiḥ)* for the head.

Thus it will be seen that a very considerable advance was made in the manufacture of arms, weapons, and various kinds of ornaments. We have references also to skin vessels for curds (VI, 48, 18), and iron vessels (V, 30, 15), and in several places to iron towns, which must be taken in a figurative sense as signifying strong forts (VII, 3, 7; VII, 15, 14; VII, 95, 1, etc). We have also references to a hundred stone-built towns in IV, 30, 20, and other places.

There can be no doubt that in the various rocky and mountainous tracts where the early Hindus extended their colonies, they soon learnt to utilize stone as a durable and cheap material for architecture; and there can be no difficulty in believing that in numerous Hindu towns many structures and surrounding walls were of stone. That the art of building was carried to some degree of excellence appears from many allusions to mansions with thousand pillars (II, 41, 5; *V, 62, 6,* etc); but at the same time it must be admitted that there is no distinct allusion in the Ṛg Veda to the art of sculpture properly so-called. The researches of antiquarians have failed to discover in any part of India traces of sculptured stone of a time long previous to the Buddhist era; and in the numerous great museums of Europe— which are filled with the ancient stone monuments of Egypt and Babylon, of Greece, and of Rome—India is not represented by any such monuments dating much before the Buddhist Period.

Most of the animals domesticated at the present day were domesticated in India in the remote period of the Ṛg Veda. We have spirited accounts of the war-horse in several places. (VI, 46, 13, and 14, etc.)

Indeed, these war-horses were so highly prized by the early Āryans in their battles against the aborigines, that the horse under the name of *Dadhikrā* soon became an object of worship; and in IV, 38, we have a spirited account of the respect paid to this god-like being.

In IV, 4, 1, we have a reference to a king riding with his ministers on an elephant. Among other domesticated animals, we have frequent mention of cows, goats, sheep, buffaloes, and dogs, which last were used in carrying burdens.

CHAPTER – 4

WARS AND DISSENSIONS

As has been stated before, the early Hindus wrested the fertile tracts on the banks of the Indus and its tributaries from the primitive aborigines of the Punjab; but the aborigines did not give up their birthright without a struggle. Retreating before the more civilized organization and valour of the Hindus in the open field, they still hung round in fastnesses and forests near every Hindu settlement and village, harassed them in their communications, waylaid and robbed them at every opportunity, stole their cattle, and often attacked them in considerable force. Well might they exclaim with the Gaels of Scotland, who had been similarly dispossessed of their fertile soil by the conquering Saxons and had similarly retreated to barren fastnesses :

" These fertile plains, that softened vale,
Were once the birthright of the Gael;
The stranger came with iron hand,
And from our fathers left the land.
Where dwell we now ? See rudely swell
Crag over crag, and fell o'er fell.

Pent in this fortress of the North,
Think'st thou we will not sally forth
To spoil the spoiler as we may,
And from the robber rend his prey ?
Aye, by my soul! while on yon plain
The Saxon rears one shock of grain,
While, of ten thousand herds, there strays

But one along yon river's maze—
The Gael, of plain and river heir,
Shall, with strong hand, redeem his share !"

Unfortunately, however, they had no poet to hand down to us their view of the case, and the only account we have of this long war of centuries, is from the conquering Hindus. It is needless to say that the conquerors viewed the aborigines with the contempt and hatred which have marked the conduct of all conquering tribes, whether on the banks of the Indus seventeen hundred years before Christ, or on the banks of the Mississipi seventeen hundred years after Christ! History repeats itself; and the Punjab was cleared of its non-Āryan aborigines just as the United States of America have, in modern times, been cleared of the many powerful and brave Indian races who lived and hunted and ruled within its primeval forests.

Of these wars with the aborigines we have frequent allusions in the Ṛg Veda; and a translation of some of these passages will give a better idea of these interminable hostilities than any account that we can give of them. The allusions are so numerous that our only difficulty is in making a selection.

"Indra, who is invoked by many, and is accompanied by his fleet companions, has destroyed by his thunderbolt the *Dasyus* and *Simyus* who dwelt on earth, and then he distributed the fields to his white-complexioned friends (Āryans). The thunderer makes the sun shine and the rain to fall." (I, 100, 18.) "Indra with his weapon (the thunderbolt), and full of vigour, destroyed the towns of the *Dasyus,* and wandered at his will. O holder of the thunderbolt! be thou cognizant (of our hymns), and cast thy weapon against the *Dasyu,* and increase the vigour and the fame of the *Ārya?* (I 103, 3)

In the very next hymn we come across a curious allusion to aboriginal robbers who dwelt on the banks of four small streams called the Sifā, the Añjasī, the Kulisī, and the Vīrapatnī, whose courses cannot now be determined. These robbers issued from their fastnesses and harassed the civilized Āryan villages, much in the same way, we suppose, as a true descendant of those aborigines—the Bhil Tantia in our own time—is harassing the peaceful villages of Central India! We translate the two verses below :—

"Kuyava gets scent of the wealth of others and appropriates them. He lives in water and pollutes it. His two wives bathe in the stream; may they be drowned in the depths of the Sifā river !

" Ayu, lives in water in a secret fastness. He flourishes amidst the rise of waters. The rivers Añjasī, Kulsī and Vīrapatnī protect him with their waters. (I, 104, 3 & 4.)

We proceed with some more extracts :—

"Indra protects his *Ārya* worshipper in wars. He who protects him on countless occasions, protects him in all wars. He subdues the people who do not perform sacrifices for the benefit of men (Āryans). He flays the enemy of his black skin and kills him and reduces him to ashes. He burns down all who do injury, and all who are cruel. (I, 130, 8.)

"O destroyer of foes! collect together the heads of these marauding troops, and crush them with thy wide foot! Thy foot is wide !

"O Indra! destroy the power of these marauding troops! Throw them into the vile pit—the vast and vile pit!

"O Indra! thou hast destroyed three times fifty such troops! People extol this thy deed; but it is nothing compared to thy prowess !

"O Indra! destroy the Pīśāchis who are reddish in appearance and utter fearful yells. Destroy all these Rākṣhasas."[1] (I, 133, 2 to 5.)

"O Indra! the poet prays to thee for pleasant food. Thou hast made the earth the bed (burial ground) of the *Dāsas*. Indra has beautified the three regions with his gifts; he has slayed *Kuyavācha* for king *Daryoni*.

"O Indrā! Ṛṣis still extol that ancient deed of prowess! Thou hast destroyed many marauders to put an end to war;

thou hast stormed the towns of enemies who worship no gods; and thou hast bent the weapons of foes who worship no gods. (I, 174, 7 & 8).

"O Aśvins! destroy those who are yelling hideously like dogs, and are coming to destroy us! Slay those who wish to fight with us! You know the way to destroy (them. Let each word of those who extol you bring wealth in return. O you truthful ones! accept our prayers. (I, 182,4.)

"The far-famed and graceful Indra is gracious to men (Āryans)! The destroying and powerful Indra has cast down the head of the malignant *Dāsa !*

"Indra, who slayed Vṛtra and stormed towns has destroyed the troops of the black *Dāsas* and has made the earth and the water for Manu.[2] May he fulfil the wishes of the sacrificer." (II, 20, 6 & 7.)

We know how the Spaniards, the cenquerors of America, owed their successes, to a very great extent, to their horses—animals previously unknown to the American aborigines, and therefore regarded with a strange terror. It would seem that the war-horses of the early Indo-Āryans inspired the aborigines of India with a similar fear. The following passages, translated from a hymn to *Dadhikrā,* or the deified war-horse will, therefore be regarded with interest:—

"As people shout and raise a cry after a thief who has purloined a garment, even so the enemies yell and shout at the sight of Dadhikrā! As birds make a noise at the sight of the hungry hawk on its descent, even so the enemies yell and shout at the sight of Dadhikrā careering in quest of plunder of food and cattle !

"Enemies fear Dadhikrā who is radiant and destroying as a thunderbolt. When he beats back a thousand men around him, he becomes excited and uncontrollable in his strength." (IV, 38, 5 & 8.)

It would seem from numerous passages in the Ṛg Veda that Kutsa was a powerful warrior and a mighty destroyer of the black aborigines. We are told in hymn 16 of the fourth Maṇḍala, that Indra slew the š*Dasyu,* who is wily and impious," to bestow wealth on Kutsa (verse 9); that he helped Kutsa and came to his house with the common object of slaying the *Dasyu* (verse 10); and that he slew fifty thousand "black complexioned enemies" in the battle- (verse 13). In IV, 28, 4, we are told that Indra has made the *Dasyus* devoid of all virtues, and the object of hatred of all men; and in IV, 30, 15, we learn that Indra destroyed five hundred and a thousand *Dāsas*.

We have similar allusions to the subjugation and destruction of *Dasyus* or *Dāsas* in V, 70, 3; VI, 18, 3; and VI, 25, 2; while there is a curious reference to an unknown region inhabited by the *Dasyus* in VI, 47, 20, which deserves translation :—

"O ye gods! We have travelled and lost our way, and come to a region where cattle do not pasture. The extensive region gives shelter to *Dasyus* only. O Bṛhaspati! lead us in our search for cattle. O Indra! shew the way to your worshippers who have lost their way."

We have seen that the Āryan poets are sufficiently uncomplimentary in speaking of the shouts and yells of the aboriginal barbarians. The civilized conquerors could scarcely imagine that these yells could form a language, and have therefore in some places described the barbarians as without a language. (V, 29, 10, etc.)

We have spoken before of Kuyava and Ayu, two aboriginal robbers who dwelt in fastnesses surrounded by rivers, and harassed the Āryan villages. We have frequent allusions to another powerful aboriginal leader who is called Kṛṣṇā, probably because of his black complexion. One of the passages relating to him deserves translation :—

"The fleet Kṛṣṇā lived on the banks of the Ansumatī river

with ten thousand troops. Indra of his own wisdom became cognizant of this loud-yelling chief. He destroyed the marauding host for the benefit of men.

"Indra said : 'I have seen the fleet Kṛṣṇā. He is lurking in the hidden region near the Ansumatī, like the sun in a cloud, O Maruts! I desire you to engage in fight, and to destroy him.'

"The fleet Kṛṣṇā then appeared shining on the banks of the Ansumatī. Indra took Bṛhaspati as his ally, and destroyed the fleet and godless army." (VIII, 96, 13 to 15.)

Not only have the aborigines been described as fond of yells and devoid of a language, but they are in other places considered as scarcely human. We are told in one place :

"We are surrounded on all sides by *Dasyu* tribes. They do not perform sacrifices; they do not believe in anything; their rites are different; they are not men! O destroyer of foes! kill them. Destroy the *Dāsa* race !" (X, 22, 8.)

In X. 49, Indra proclaims that he has deprived the *Dasyu* race of the name of *Ārya* (verse 3); that he has destroyed Navavāstva and Bṛhadratha of the *Dāsa* race (verse 6); that he cuts the *Dāsas* in twain, "it is for this fate that they have been born! "(verse 7.)

Such were the aborigines with whom the early Hindus carried on an interminable war, and such was the fate to which they consigned their less civilized neighbours, the primeval owners of the Indian soil! It is abundantly evident that no love was lost between the conquerors and the conquered. It was by ceaseless fighting that the conquerors protected themselves in their newly-conquered country, gradually extended the limits of cultivation, built new villages, threw out new colonies in primeval jungles, and spread the light of civilization and the fame of their prowess around. They dreaded and hated the despised barbarians with a genuine hatred, killed numbers of them when they could, thinned their ranks with their cavalry, called them yelling hounds and men without a tongue and brutes below the rank of men, and almost believed they were born to be slain,—"it is for this fate that they have been born !" On the other hand, the stubborn barbarians had their revenge too. Retreating before the more civilized valour of the Hindus, they hung about in every fastness and every bend of a river, they waylaid and robbed travellers, harassed villages, killed or stole cattle, and sometimes fell on the Hindus in great numbers. With that dogged tenacity which is peculiar to barbarians they disputed every inch of ground as they retreated, they interrupted the religious rites of the conquerors, despised their gods, and plundered their wealth. But in spite of every resistance the colonies of the more civilized races extended on every-direction, the area of civilization widened, jungles and wastes were brought under cultivation and dotted with villages and royal towns, and the kingdoms of the early Hindus extended over the whole of the Punjab. The barbarians were either exterminated, or retreated before the ever-advancing line of Āryan civilization into those hills and fastnesses which their children still inhabit.

It may be imagined, however, that some among the weaker barbarians preferred abject subjection to extermination or exile. We find traces accordingly in the Ṛg Veda of *Dasyus* who at last owned the domination of the more powerful race, and who adopted their religion and their rites and even their language. They learnt cultivation and the arts of civilized life; settled down in Āryan villages at Dāsas or serfs; and ministered to the wants of their masters—the white men. There are frequent references to such *Dāsas* who had been subjugated by the Āryans. These, then, were the first *Hinduized aborigines* of India.

Our extracts on the subject of wars with the aborigines have been somewhat numerous, but we cannot refrain from quoting one or two passages more about the wars of the mighty conqueror Sudās :

"8. The wily foes planned destruction, and broke down the embankment of Ādīnā river (to cause an inundation.) But Sudās filled the earth with his prowess, and Kavi, the son of Chayamāna, fell like a victim.

"9. For the waters of the river flowed through their old channel and did not take a new course; and Sudās' horse marched over the country. Indra subdued the hostile and talkative men and their children under Sudās.

"11. Sudās earned glory by killing twenty-one men of both regions. As the young priest cuts the kusa grass in the house of sacrifice, even so Sudās cuts down his enemies. The hero Indra sent the Maruts for his succour.

"14. The sixty-six thousand six-hundred and sixty-six warriors of Anu and Druhya, who had desired for cattle, and were hostile to Sudās, were laid low. These deeds proclaim the glory of Indra !

"15. It was Indra who enabled the poor Sudās to achieve these deeds. Indra enabled the goat to kill the strong lion. Indra felled the sacrificial post with a needle. He bestowed all the wealth on Sudās." VII, 18.

The poet who sings these deeds of Sudās' glory is not unrewarded for his immortal verse. For in verses 22 and 23, he acknowledges with gratitude that the valiant conqueror and beneficent king had rewarded him with two hundred cows and two chariots and four horses with gold trappings !

In a subsequent hymn we are told how ten kings combined against Sudās, and Sudās was victorious over them all. A curious description of a battle in this hymn deserves translation :—

"2. Where men raise their banners and meet in bat' tle, where nothing seems to favour us, where the men look up to the sky and tremble, then, O Indra and Varuṇa! help us and speak to us (words of comfort.)

"3. O Indra and Varuṇa! the ends of the earth seem to be lost, and the noise ascends to the skies! The troops of the enemy are approaching. O Indra and Varuṇa! who ever listen to prayers, come near us with your protection.

"4. O Indra and Varuṇa! you pierced the yet unassailed

Bheda, and saved Sudās. You listened to the prayers of the Tritsus. Their priestly vocation bore fruit in the hour of battle.

"5. O Indra and Varuṇa! the weapons of the enemy assail me in all directions, the foes assail me among marauding men. You are the owners of both kinds of wealth! Save us in the day of battle.

"6. Both parties invoked Indra and Varuṇa for wealth at the time of war. But in this battle you protected Sudās with the Tritsus who were attacked by ten kings.

"7. O Indra and Varuṇa! the ten kings who did not perform sacrifices were unable, though combined, to beat Sudās." (VII, 83.)

In VI, 47, there is an address to the war-drum on the eve of battle; and the poet asks that martial instrument to fill the earth and skies with its sound, to rouse movable and immovable objects, to instil fear into the enemy and to drive them away. The address ends with these portentous words : "The drum *(Dundubhī)* sounds loud to proclaim to all men (the hour of battle). Our leaders have mounted their steeds and have collected together. O Indra! let our warriors who fight in chariots win victory."

In a still more remarkable hymn, VI, 75, the preparations and weapons of war have been described in some detail, and a few extracts from it will convey to our readers some idea of military weapons in use in those days :—

"I. When the battle is nigh, and the warrior marches in his armour,, he appears like the cloud! Warrior, let not thy person be pierced; be victorious; let thy armour protect you !

"2. We will win cattle with the bow, we will win with the bow; we will conquer the fierce and proud enemy with the bow! May the bow foil the desires of the enemy! We will spread our conquests on all sides with the bow !

"3. The string of the bow when pulled approaches the ear of the archer, making way in battle. It whispers words of consolation to him, and with sound it clasps the arrow, even as a loving wife clasps her husband.

"5. The quiver is like the parent of many arrows; the many arrows are like its children. It makes a sound, and hangs on the back of the warrior, and furnishes arrows in battle, and conquers the enemy.

"6. The expert charioteer stands on his chariot and drives his horses wheresoever he will. The reins restrain the horses from behind. Sing of their glory !

"7. The horses raise the dust with their hoofs, and career over the field with the chariots, with loud neighings. They do not retreat, but trample the marauding enemies under their feet.

"11. The arrow is feathered; the deer (horn) is its teeth. Well pulled and sent by the cow-leather-string, it falls on the enemy. Wherever men stand together or are separate, there the shafts reap advantage.

"14. The leather guard protects the arm from the abrasion of the bow-string, and coils round the arm like a snake in its convolutions. It knows its work, and is efficient, and protects the warrior in every way.

"15. We extol the arrow which is poisoned, whose face is of iron;[3] whose stem is of Parjanya. "(VI, 75.)

Before concluding our extracts, we will make one more from a hymn about the coronation of kings. It belongs, like all hymns relating to pompous ceremonies, not to the earlier, but to the latest period of the Vedic Age :—

"1. O king! I place you in the station of a king. Be the lord of this country! Be immovable and fixed! Let all the subjects cherish thee! Let not your kingdom be destroyed!

"2. Remain here fixed as the mountain; do not be dethroned! Remain fixed like Indra, and support the kingdom !

"3. Indra has received the sacrificial offerings, and supports the newly-coronated king! Soma blesses him.

"4. The sky is fixed, the earth is fixed, the mountains are

fixed, this universe is fixed. He also is fixed as king among his subjects !

"5. May King Varuṇa make you immovable! May the good Bṛhaspati make you immovable; may Indra and Agni support you and make you immovable.

"6. See, I mix these immortal offerings with the immortal Soma-juice. Indra has brought your subjects under your rule, and made them willing to pay you revenue !" (X, 173.)

These extracts are enough. We have elsewhere shewn that the warriors used not only armours but helmets, and also protecting armours for the shoulder, probably shields. They used javelins and battle-axes, and sharp-edged swords, beside bows and arrows, All the weapons of wars known elsewhere in ancient times were known in India nearly four thousand years ago. Drums assembled men in battle, banners led them on in compact masses, and the use of war-horses and chariots was well-known. Tame elephants were in use too, and we have allusions to kings riding on richly caparisoned elephants with their ministers (IV, 4, 1); but it does not appear that elephants were regularly used in wars in the Vedic period, as they were in the third and fourth centuries before Christ when the Greeks came to India. For the rest, it was a turbulent time when the Vedic warriors lived and fought. They had not only to wage an interminable war against the aborigines, but the Hindu States were divided among themselves, and a powerful leader was often bent on annexing his neighbour's state. Ṛṣis engaged in sacrifices asked for prowess to conquer the foe's, or prayed to the gods for a son who would win victory in battles. Every able-bodied man was a warrior, and was ever prepared to defend his home and his fields and his cattle with his strong right arm. Each Hindu colony or tribe, while attentive to the worship of the gods and to the cultivation of the various arts of peace, was at the same time alive to the fact, that its national existence depended on a constant preparedness for war. And the great conglomeration of Hindu tribes which spread from the banks of the Indus to the banks of the Sarasvatī consisted of hardy, brave, and warlike peoples, who maintained their footing in the land, and their independence and national existence by constant struggles, and a determination to win or die.

It is sad to contemplate this state of things. But where is the country in which, in ancient times, tribes and nations had not to maintain a ceaseless war for their aggrandizement, or even for their very existence ?And even in modern times, during the two thousand years which have elasped since Gautama Buddha and Jesus Christ preached their messages of peace, where shall we seek for the tribe or nation which could hope, to reap the results of its peaceful industry without a constant struggle against its neighbours ? If a generation has passed in Europe without a dreadful war, that period is marked in history as a period of exceptional bliss. And even in our own times, with the exception of a few countries advantageously situated, all the nations of Europe are armed to the teeth; all the individuals, by millions, of great kingdoms and empires, are eternally prepared for war, ready on a week's notice to leave their homes and occupations and march to the frontier! Civilization has done much for the cause of humanity; but civilization has not yet converted the sword into the scythe, or enabled man to reap the results of his peaceful Industry without a struggle to the death against his neighbour.

REFERENCES

1. Pishāchis and Rākṣasas may mean imaginary demons. I would rather think, however, that they here refer to the aborigines.
2. Here, as elsewhere, Manu is spoken of as the ancestor of the Āryan man. In many places is spoken of as the originator of cultivation and of the worship of fire which distinguished the Āryans.
3. "This passage shews that the arrow-heads were of iron. Parjanya is the god of rains. Stem of Parjanya probably means stem of reed growing in the rains, Verse II shews that arrow-heads were sometimes of deer-horn.

CHAPTER – 5

SOCIAL AND DOMESTIC LIFE : THE POSITION OF WOMEN

It was by such continuous wars against the aborigines of the soil that the Āryans at last conquered the whole of the Punjab from the Indus to the Sarasvatī, and from the mountains probably to the sea.

As might be expected, we have frequent allusions to the Indus and its five tributaries. Hymn 75 of the tenth Maṇḍala is a remarkable instance, and we will give our readers a translation of the entire hymn :—

"1. O ye streams! The bard celebrates your excellent prowess in the house of the worshipper. They flow in three systems, seven streams in each system. The prowess of the Indus is superior to that of all others.

"2. O Indus! when you ran towards lands rich in food, Varuṇa opened out the way for you. You flow over a spacious path on the land. You shine above all flowing rivers.

"3. The mighty sound of the Indus ascends above the earth to the sky! She flows with mighty force and radiant form. Her mighty sound is heard as if rains are decending from the clouds with great noise. The Indus comes roaring like a bull.

"4. As cows bring milk to their calves, even thus, O Indus, the other streams come sounding to you with their waters! As a king marches with his forces to battle, even thus you march in front with two systems of rivers flowing by your side ![1]

"5 O Gangā! O Yamunā and Sarasvatī and Sutadru (Sutlej) and Paruṣṇī (Ravi)! share this my praise among you! O river combined with Asiknī (Chinab)! O Vitastā (Jhilam)! O Ārjīkīyā (Beas), combined with Susomā (Indus)! hear my words.

"6. O Indus! first thou flowest united Triṣtāmā with Susartu and Rasā and the Śvetī. You unite Krumu (Kurum river) and Gomatī (Gomal river) with Kubhā (Cabul river) and Mehatnu. You proceed together with these rivers,

"7. The irresistible Indus proceeds straight, white and dazzling in splendour! She is great, and her waters fill all sides with mighty force. Of all the flowing rivers, none is flowing like her! She is wild like a mare, beautiful like a well developed woman!

"8. The Indus is ever young and beautiful. She is rich in horses, in chariots, and in garments; she is rich in gold and is beautiously clad! She is rich in corn and in wool and in straw, and has covered herself with sweet flowers.

"9. The Indus has fastened horses to her easy chariot, and has brought food therein to us. The greatness of the chariot is extolled as mighty; it is irresistible and great and rich in its fame!"

The hymn is remarkable for its power and its beauty, and remarkable also for the extensive vision of the poet who, as Professor Max Müller says, takes in at one swoop three great river-systems, those flowing from the north-west into the Indus, those joining it from the north-east, and in the distance the Ganges and the Jumnā with their tributaries. "It shows the widest geographical horizon of the Vedic poets, confined by the snowy mountains in the north, the Indus and the range of the Suleiman mountains in the west, the Indus or the sea in the south, and the valley of the Jumnā and Ganges in the east. Beyond that the world, though open, was unknown to the Vedic poets."

The rivers of the Punjab are sometimes spoken of together as the "seven rivers," and it is explained in one place (VII, 36, 6), that the seven rivers have the Indus for their mother and the Sarasvatī as the seventh. The Indus and its five branches still water the primeval home of the early Hindus, but the Sarasvatī which was the most sacred of ancient rivers and was worshiped even in that remote time as a goddess, has since ceased to flow. Antiquarians state that it has been lost in the deserts of Rajputana.

There is one somewhat curious passage in which the Ṛṣi Viśvāmitra, encumbered with the chariots and horses and other rewards bestowed on him by king Sudās. finds a difficulty in crossing the confluence of the Beas and the Sutlej, and pours out an entire hymn (III, 33) to appease the anger of the roaring flood! We have seen that this Sudās was a mighty conqueror and subjugated ten surrounding kings, and was the victor of numerous battles which form the theme of some spirited hymns. This mighty conqueror seems also to have been a patron of learning and religion, and liberally rewarded the sages of the houses of Viśvāmitra and of Vasiṣṭha alike. As a consequence, there was jealousy between these two priestly houses to which we will allude further on.

While references to the rivers of the Punjab are thus frequent, allusions to the Ganges and the Jumnā are rare. We have already translated a hymn in which both those rivers are named.

The only other passage in the Ṛg Veda where the Ganges is alluded to, is VI, 45, 31, where the high banks of the Ganges are the subject of a simile. The famed cattle in the pasture-fields along the banks of the Jumnā are alluded to in V, 52, 17.

Thus the land of the five rivers was the earliest home of the Āryan settlers in India; and it would seem that the settlers along the five rivers gradually formed themselves into five tribes or nations. The "five lands" *(Pañca-Kṣiti)* are alluded to in I, 7, 9 ; I, 176, 3; VI, 46, 7, and in other places. Similarly we read of the "five cultivating tribes" *(Pañca-Kṣṭi)* in II, 2, 10; IV, 38, 10, , and other places, and we read of "five peoples" *(Pañca-jana)* in VI, 11,4; VI, 51, II; VIII, 32, 22,; IX, 65, 23, and other places.

It was these "five tribes" of simple, bold, and enterprising Āryans, living by agriculture and by pasture the fertile banks of the Indus and its tributaries, who were the progenitors of the great Hindu nation, which has spread from the Himalayas to Cape Comorin.

We now turn to the interesting and pleasing subject of the social and domestic rules and the home-life of these five tribes of the Punjab. The first thing that strikes us here is the absence of those unhealthy rules and restrictions, those marked distinctions between man and man and between class and class, which form the most unpleasant feature of later Hindu society. We have already seen that the sturdy Hindus of the Vedic times recognized no restrictions against the use of beef, and that they refer with pride to their merchants going to the sea. We have seen, too, that the Ṛṣis did not form a separate and exclusive class, and did not pass their lives away from the world in penance and contemplation. On the contrary, the Ṛṣis were practical men of the world, who owned large herds of cattle, cultivated fields, fought against the aboriginal enemies, in times of war, and prayed to their gods for wealth and cattle, for victory in wars, and for blessings on their wives and children. Every father of a family was in fact a Ṛṣi on a small scale, and worshipped his gods in his own house in his own humble fashion, and the women of the family joined in the worship, and helped in the performance of the ceremonies. Some among the community were of course prominent in the composition of hymns and the performance of great sacrifices; and kings and rich men sent for them on great occasions, and rewarded them handsomely. But even these great composers—these great Ṛṣis of the Ṛg Veda—did not form an exclusive caste of their own. They were worldly men, mixed and married with the people, shared property with the people, fought the wars of the people, and were of the people.

One martial Ṛṣi for instance (in V, 23, 2) prays for a son who will conquer enemies in war. Another (in VI, 20, I) prays for wealth and corn-fields and a son who will destroy his foes. Another (in IX, 69, 8) prays for wealth and gold, for horses and cows, for profuse harvests, and excellent progeny. Another Ṛṣi, with naive simplicity, says that his cattle are his wealth and his Indra! (VI, 28, 5.; Throughout the Ṛg Veda the Ṛṣis are the people. There is not the shadow of any evidence that the Ṛṣis or priests were a "caste" of their own, different from the fighters and cultivators.[2]

This will be considered by impartial judges to be very good evidence that the caste-system did not exist. It proves a negative much more convincingly than many positive facts can be proved. In a vast collection of hymns, composed during six hundred years and more, and replete with references to the habits and manners and customs of the people—replete with allusions to agriculture and pasture and manufacture, to wars against aborigines, to marriage and domestic rules, and the duties and position of women, to religious observances and to elementary astronomy as then known— we have not one single passage to show that the community was cut up into hereditary "*Castes.*" Is it possible to suppose that that wonderful system existed, and yet there is no allusion to that fundamental principle of society in the ten thousand verses of the Ṛg Veda ? Is it possible to find a single religious work of later times, of one-tenth the dimensions of the Ṛg Veda, which is silent on that system ?

So far, then, we have proved a negative in the only way in which a negative can be proved. But curiously enough there is positive proof, and various passages in the Ṛg Veda shew that the caste-system did not exist. The very word "*varṇa*" which in later Sanskrit indicates caste, is used in the Ṛg Veda to distinguish the Āryans and non-Āryans, and nowhere indicates separate sections in the Āryan community (III, 34, 9, etc.) The very word *Kṣatriya,* which in later Sanskrit means the military caste, is used in the Veda simply as an adjective which means strong, and is applied to gods! (VII, 64, 2; VII, 89, etc.) The very word *Viprā,* which in later Sanskrit means the priestly caste, is used in the Ṛg Veda merely as an adjective which means wise, and which is applied to gods! (VIII, II, 6, etc.) And the every word *Brāhmaṇa,* which in later Sanskrit means also the priestly caste, is used in a hundred places in the Ṛg Veda to imply the composers of hymns, and nothing else. (VII, 103, 8, etc.)

We would gladly multiply evidences, but our limits forbid. But we cannot help producing one piece of evidence. With that charming simplicity which is the characteristic beauty of the Ṛg Veda, one Ṛṣi says pathetically of himself:—

"Behold, I am a composer of hymns, my father is a physician, my mother grinds corn on stone. We are all engaged in different occupations. As cows wander (in various directions) in the pasture-fields (for food), so we (in various occupations), worship thee, O Soma! for wealth. Flow thou for Indra !" (IX, 112, 3.) Those who suppose that the hereditary caste-system existed in the Vedic times will have a hard nut to crack in explaining passages like the above, where father, mother, and son are described as physician, corn-grinder, and composer of hymns !

Later asserters of the caste-system have sometimes tried to crack these nuts, and with the most wonderful results! Like most other Ṛṣis of the Ṛg Veda (who, we have seen before, constantly prayed for warlike sons), Viśvāmitra was a warrior and a composer of hymns. Later Hindus were shocked at this, and invented a beautiful Paurāṇik myth to explain how Viśvāmitra was first a Kṣhatriyā and then became a Brāhman. Needless endeavour, for Viśvāmitra was neither a Kṣatriya nor a Brahmān! He was a Vedic Ṛṣi, *i. e.*, a warrior and priest, long before the Brāhmans and the Kṣatriyas, as such, were known ![3]

As we have seen, then, every father of a family was his own priest, and his home was his temple. There is no mention of idols in the Ṛg Veda, none of temples or places of worship where the people were to congregate. The sacred fire was lighted in the house of every householder, and he chanted the beautiful and simple hymns which were the national property. We have a pleasing picture of women who assisted at these sacrifices, who ordered the necessary things, prepared them with pestle and mortar, extracted the Soma-juice, stirred it with their graceful fingers and strained it through a woollen strainer. In numerous places we find mention of wives joining their husbands, and performing the sacrifice together. They offer the oblations together, and hope thereby to go to heaven together (I, 131, 3; V, 42, 15, etc.) A few verses from a pious hymn on this subject will no doubt interest our readers.

"5 O ye gods! The married couple who prepare oblations together, who purify the Soma-juice and mix it with milk.

"6. May they obtain food for their eating, and come united to the sacrifice. May they never have to go in quest of food.

"7. They do not make vain promises oi offerings to the gods, nor withhold your praise. They worship you with the best offerings.

"8. Blest with youthful and adolescent offspring they acquire gold, and they both attain to a mature age.

"9. The gods themselves covet the worship of such a couple who are fond of sacrifices, and offer grateful food to the gods. They embrace each other to continue their race, and they worship their gods !" (VIII, 31.)

Still more grateful to us is the picture of cultured ladies who were themselves Ṛṣis, and composed hymns and performed sacrifices like men. For there were no unhealthy restrictions against women in those days, no attempt to keep them secluded or uneducated or debarred from their legitimate place in society. There is mention of veiled wives and brides, but no allusion to women being kept in seclusion. On the contrary, we meet them everywhere in their legitimate spheres of action, taking a share in sacrifices, and exercising their in fluence on society. We cherish the picture of the cultured lady Viśvavārā, which has been handed down to us through thousands of years—a pious lady who composed hymns, performed sacrifices, and with simple fervency invoked the god Agni to regulate and keep within virtuous bounds the mutual relations married couples. (V, 28. 3.) We meet with the names of other ladies also who were Ṛṣis of the Ṛg Veda.

In a society so simple as that of the Vedic times, the relations of life were determined by the needs and requirements of individuals rather than by cast-iron rules as in later days; and there was no religious obligation therefore that every girl must be married. On the contrary, we find allusions to unmarried women who remained in the homes of their fathers, and naturally claimed and obtained a share of the paternal property. (II, 17, 7.) On the other hand, we have frequent references to careful and industrious wives who superintended the arrangements of the house, and like the dawn roused and sent every one in the house to his work in the morning (I, 124, 4), and who possessed those domestic virtues for which Hindu wives have always been noted from the earliest to the present times. Occasionally we have allusions to women who went astray (II, 29, 1); of maidens who had no brothers to watch over their morals; and wives who were faithless to their husbands. (IV, 5, 5; X, 34, 4.) And we are told of the wife of a ruined gambler who becomes the object of other men's lust. (X, 34, 4.)

It would seem that girls had some voice in the selection of their husbands. Their selection was not always happy, for "many a woman is attracted by the wealth of him who seeks her. But the woman who is of gentle nature and of graceful form selects, among many, her own loved one as her husband." (X, 27, 12.) We can almost imagine we see the *Svayamavra* system of later times foreshadowed in the above verse. There can be no doubt, however, that fathers always exercised a wise control in the selection of husbands for their daughters, and as at the present day, fathers gave away their girls gracefully adorned and decked with golden ornaments. (IX, 46, 2; X, 39, 14.)

The ceremony of marriage was an appropriate one, and the promises which the bridegroom and bride made to each other were suitable to the occasion, We will translate some verses from a hymn in the later portion of the Ṛg Veda, in which we find a pleasing picture of the ceremony. The first two among the following verses will shew that the unnatural custom of early marriage was unknown, and that girls were married after they had attained their youth.

"21. O Visvavasu! (god of marriage), arise from this place, for the marriage of this girl is over. We extol Visvavasu with hymns and prostrations. Go to some other maiden who is still in her father's house and has attained the signs of the age of marriage. She will be your share, know of her.

"22. O Visvavasu! arise from this place. We worship thee, bending in adoration. Go to an unmarried maiden whose person is well developed; make her a wife and unite her to a husband.

"23. Let the paths by which our friends go in quest of a maiden for marriage be easy and free of thorns. May Aryaman and Bhaga lead us well. O gods! may the husband and wife be well united.

"24. O maiden! the graceful sun had fastened thee with ties (of maidenhood), we release thee now of those ties. We place thee with thy husband in a place which is the home of truth and the abode of righteous actions.

"25. We release this maiden from this place (her father's house), but not from the other place her (husband's house). We unite her well with the other place. O Indra! may she be fortunate and the mother of worthy sons.

"26. May Pūṣan lead you by the hand from this place. May the two Aśvins lead you in a chariot. Go to your (husband's) house and be the mistress of the house. Be the mistress of all, and exercise your authority over all in that house.

"27, Let children be born unto thee, and blessings attend thee here. Perform the duties of thy household with care. Unite thy person with the person of this thy husband; exercise thy authority in this thy house until old age.

"40. First Soma accepts thee; then Gandharva accepts thee; Agni is thy third lord; the son of man is the fourth to accept thee.[4]

"41. Soma bestowed this maiden to Gandharva, Gandharva gave her to Agni, Agni has given her to me with wealth and progeny.

"42. O bridegroom and bride! Do ye remain here together; do not be separated. Enjoy food of various kinds; remain in your own home, and enjoy happiness in company of your children and grandchildren.

"43. (The bride and bridegroom say), May Prajāpati bestow on us children; may Aryaman keep us united till old age. (Address to the bride), O bride! Enter with auspicious signs the home of thy husband. Do good to our male servants and our female servants, and to our cattle.

"44. Be thy eyes free from anger; minister to the happiness of thy husband; do good to our cattle. May thy mind be cheerful;

and may thy beauty be bright. Be the mother of heroic sons, and be devoted to the gods. Do good to our male servants and our female servants, and to our cattle.

"45. O Indra! make this woman fortunate and the mother of worthy sons. Let ten sons be born of her, so that there may be eleven men (in the family) with the husband.

"46. (Address to the bride), May thou have influence over thy father-in-law and over thy mother-in-law, and be as a queen over thy sister-in-law and brother-in-law.

"47. (The bridegroom and bride say), May all the gods unite our hearts; may Mātarisvan and Dhātri and the goddess of speech unite us together." (X, 85.)

Our extract has been somewhat lengthy, but our readers will not regret it. The extract shews at once the appropriate nature of the ceremony that was performed, and the position which the young bride occupied in the home and the affections of her lord.

Polygamy was allowed among kings and the rich people in Vedic times, as it was allowed in olden times in all countries and among all nations. Domestic dissensions were the natural result in such instances, and we have hymns in the latter part of the Ṛg Veda, in which wives curse their fellow-wives. (X, 145; X, 159.) The evil seems, however, to have grown in the latter part of the Vedic age, for there are scarcely any allusions to it in the earlier hymns.

We need scarcely allude to hymns suited to the occasions of conception and childbirth. (X, 183 ;X, 184; X, 162 ;V, 78, 7 to 9.) These hymns also belong to the last portion of the Vedic age when superstition and priestly influence were gaining on the people, and ceremonies multiplied. We must allude, however, to two curious verses which seem to lay down the law of inheritance, and is therefore of peculiar interest. We give a translation below :

"1. The father who has no son honours his son-in-law, capable of begetting sons, and goes *(i. e.,* leaves his property) to the son of his daughter. The (sonless) father trusts in the daughter's offspring, and lives content.

"2. A son does not give any of his father's property to a sister. He gives her away to be the wife of a husband. If a father and mother beget both son and daughter, then one (*i.e.*, son) engages himself in the acts and duties of his father, while the other (daughter) receives honour." (III, 31.)

This is the first germ of the Hindu law of inheritance, which makes the son, and not the daughter, the inheritor of his father's property and religious duties, and which allows the property to go to the daughter's son only in the absence of male issue. We think we discover the first germs of the Hindu law of adoption, too, in such passages as the following :—

"As a man who is not indebted gets much wealth, so we too shall get the treasure that endures (*i. e.*, a son,). O Agni! let us not have a son begotten of another. Do not follow the ways of the ignorant.

"A son begotten of another may yield us happiness, but can never be regarded or accepted as one's own. And verily he ultimately goes back to his own place. Therefore, may a son be newly born unto us who will bring us food and destroy our foes." (VII, 4, 7 & 8.)

As we have spoken in this chapter of marriage and inheritance, it is necessary to complete our account of social and domestic customs and speak of the funeral ceremony also. Yama in the Ṛg Veda is not the god of hell, but the god of the heaven of the righteous, the god who rewards the virtuous man after his death, in a happy land. His two dogs however are objects to be avoided or propitiated. The following verses are taken from a hymn composed, it is needless to say, not in the earlier but in the latest period of the Vedic age when ceremonies multiplied :

"7. O thou deceased! proceed to the same place where our forefathers have gone, by the same path which they followed. The two kings, Yama and Varuṇa, are pleased with the offerings; go and see them.

"8, Go to that happy heaven and mix with the early forefathers. Mix with Yama and with the fruits of thy virtuous deeds. Leave sin behind, enter thy home,

"9. O ye ghosts! leave this place, go away, move away. For the forefathers have prepared a place for the deceased. That place is beautified with day, with sparkling waters and with light; Yama assigns this place to the dead.

"10. O thou deceased! these two dogs have four eyes each, and a strange colour. Go past them quickly. Then proceed by the beautiful path to those wise forefathers, who spend their time in joy and happiness with Yama." (X, 14.)

The above passages give us an idea of the belief in future happiness as it was developed in the latest period of the Vedic era.

There are some passages which shew that burial, without cremation, was practised in those times.

"10. O thou deceased! go to the extended earth who is as a mother; she is extensive and beautiful. Her touch be soft as that of wool or of a female. You have performed sacrifices, let her save thee from unrighteousness.

"11. O earth! rise up above him, do not give him pain. Give him good things, give him consolation. As a mother covers her child with the hem of her cloth, so cover the deceased.

"12. Let the earth, raised on him as a mound, lie light. Let a thousand particles of dust rest on him. Let them be to him as a house filled with butter, let them form a shelter to him." (X 18.)

That cremation was also practised in the Vedic times will be shewn by the following extract:—

"O fire! do not reduce this deceased into ashes; do not give him pain. Do not mangle his skin or his person. O fire! send him to the home of our fathers as soon as his body is burnt in thy heat." (X, 16, 1.)

It remains only to allude to one more remarkable verse of the 18th hymn which distinctly sanctions the marriage of widows.

"Rise up, woman, thou art lying by one whose life is gone, come to the world of the living, away from thy husband, and become the wife of him who holds thy hand, and is willing to marry thee." (X, 18, 8.)

The translation is based on Sāyaṇa's rendering of the passage in the *Taittiriya Āraṇyaka,* and there can be no doubt as to its correctness, because the word Didhiṣu used in the passage has only one meaning in the Sanskrit language, *viz.,* the second husband of a woman. We quote here with pleasure the following remarks with which Dr. Rajendra Lala Mitra winds up a paper on Funeral Ceremony in Ancient India: "That the remarriage of widows in Vedic times was a national custom, can be established by a variety of proofs and arguments; the very fact of the Sanskrit language having, from ancient times, such words as Didhiṣu, 'a man that has married a widow Parapūrvā, 'a woman that has taken a second husband,' Paunarbhava, 'a son of a woman by her second husband,' are enough to establish it."

It is with pain and regret that we will in conclusion refer to another passage also belonging to this remarkable hymn. and which is perfectly harmless in the Ṛg Veda itself, but which was altered and mistranslated in later times to sanction the barbarous custom of *Suttee,* or the burning of the widow on the pyre of her husband. That most cruel of all human institutions finds no sanction in the Ṛg Veda. There is a perfectly harmless passage (X, 18,7,) which refers to a procession of women at a funeral ceremony. The passage may be thus translated :—

"May these women not suffer the pangs of widowhood. May they who have good and desirable husbands, enter their houses with collyrium and butter. Let these women, without shedding tears, and without any sorrow, first proceed to the house, wearing valuable ornaments."

There is not a word in the above relating to the burning of widows. But a word in it *Agre* was altered into *Agne,* and the text was then mistranslated and misapplied in Bengal to justify the detestable custom of widow burning. In the words of Professor Max Müller,This is perhaps the most fragrant instance of what can be done by an unscrupulous priesthood. Here have thousands of lives been sacrificed and a fanatical rebellion been threatened on the authority of a passage which was mangled, mistranslated and misapplied." The censure is strong, but is deserved; it does not matter whether the alteration in the text and the mistranslation were made in recent times or a few hundred years ago.

REFERENCES

1. *i.e.* the tributaries coming from Cabul in the west, and the tributaries flowing through the Punjab in the east, as named in the two following verses.
2. The solitary mention of the four castes, in X, 90, 12, will not be considered an exception, or weaken out argument. The hymn itself was composed centuries after the time when the Ṛg Veda hymns were generally composed, as is proved by its language and its ideas. It was composed after the Ṛik, and the Saman and the Yajur Vedas had been separately classified (verse 9), and after the idea of the Sacrifice of the Supreme Being (unknown elsewhere in the Ṛg Veda) find found a place in the Hindu religion. It was composed, as Colebrooke states, after the rude versification of the Ṛg Veda had given place to the more sonorous metre of a later age. Weber, Max Müller, Muir, and other scholars all agree as to this hymn being comparatively modern.
3. It gives us much pleasure to be able to cite here the authority of two scholars who have devoted their lifetime to the study of the Veda :—

   "If, then, with all the documents before us, we ask the question, does caste, as we find it in Manu, and at the present day. form part of the most ancient religious teaching of the Vedas? We can answer with a decided 'No.' "—Max Müller, *Chips from a German Workshop, Vol. II,* (1867), p. 307.

   There are no castes as yet, the people are still one united whole, and bear but one name, that of *Visas.* "—Weber, *Indian Literature* (translation), p. *38.*
4. "This, and the following verse would shew that the bride was offered to the three gods before she was united to the bridegroom.

CHAPTER – 6

VEDIC RELIGION

An account of the social life and the civilization of the early Hindus will not be complete without some account of their religion. The religion of the Ṛg Veda is well known. It is pre-eminently the worship of Nature in its most imposing and sublime aspects. The sky which bends over all, the beautiful and blushing dawn which like a busy housewife wakes men from slumber and sends them to their work, the gorgeous tropical sun which vivifies the earth, the air which pervades the world, the fire which cheers and enlightens us. and the violent storms which in India strike terror into the boldest, but usher into those copious rains which fill the land with plenty, —these were the gods whom the early Hindus loved to extol and to worship. And often when an ancient Ṛṣi sang the praises of any of the gods with devotion and fervour, he forgot that there was any other god besides, and his sublime hymn has the character and the sublimity of a prayer to the one God of the universe. This is what makes many scholars often pause and hesitate before they *give* the Vedic religion any other name than Monotheism. Indeed the Ṛṣis themselves often rose higher than the level of their primitive Nature-worship, and boldly declared that the different gods were but different manifestations or different names of the One Primal Cause. Towards the end of the Ṛg Veda, we often come across hymns sung to the One Being. The landmarks between Nature-worship and Monotheism have been passed, and the great Ṛṣis of the Ṛg Veda have passed from Nature up to Nature's God.

This is the characteristic beauty of the Ṛg Veda as compared with other religious works of other nations. We do not find in the

Veda any well defined system of religion or any one particular stage of thought or civilization. On the contrary we watch with interest how the human mind *travels,* travels from an almost childlike but sincere invocation of the rising sun or the beneficent sky to the sublimer idea that neither the sun nor the sky is the Deity—that the Deity is greater and higher than these, and has created these objects. We know of no other work in any language which possesses such interest for the philosophic enquirer into the progress of the human mind, or which shows, as the Ṛg Veda does show, how human intelligence travels step by step, higher and higher, until from the created objects it grasps the sublime idea of the Creator.

The sky was naturally the most prominent object of worship, and as the sky assumes various aspects, various names were given to it, and the conception of various deities was formed. The oldest propably is Dyu (literally the shining), the Zeus of the Greeks the first syllable of Jupiter among the Romans, the Tiu of the Saxons, and the Zio of the Germans. This common name among many Āryan rages indicates that the deity was worshipped by the ancestors of all these nations in their first primeval abode in Asia.

But while Zeus and Jupiter maintained their supremacy among the gods of Greece and Rome, in India he soon lost his place, and the sky *in one of its peculiar functions* soon usurped his place. For in India the annual rise of rivers, the fertility of land, and the luxuriance of crops depend, not on the sky which shines above us, but on the *sky that rains,* and *Indra,* which means the rain-giver, soon became the first among the Vedic gods.

Another ancient name of the sky was Varuṇa, the Uranus of the Greeks. The word signifies to cover; and Varuṇa was the sky which covered the earth, probably the sky without light, the nightly sky. For we find another name for the bright sky of day, *viz.,* Mitra, the Mithra of the Zendavesta. Sanskrit commentators naturally explain Varuṇa as night and Mitra as day, and the Iranians worshipped the sun under the name of Mithra, and gave the name of Varuṇa to a happy region, if not the sky.

These facts show that the idea and name of Varuṇa as a god of sky was known to the ancestors of Āryan nations before those nations separated and migrated to Greece, to Persia, and to India. Indeed the eminent German scholar Dr. Roth and many others are of opinion that before the Indo-Āryans and the Iranians separated, Varuṇa was the highest and holiest of the gods of their common ancestors, and represented the spiritual side of their religion. After the separation had taken place, this deity of righteousness was, it is alleged, translated in Iran into Ahura Mazd,the Supreme Deity. And although in India, Varuṇa yielded the foremost place among gods to the young and vigorous rain-giver Indra, still he never became divested of that sanctity and holiness which entered into his first conception, and the holiest hymns of the Ṛg Veda are his, not Indra's. Whatever be the value of these opinions, the fact of Varuṇa's pre-eminent sanctity in the Ṛg Veda, cannot be denied, and we will give a few short translations from the hymns to Varuṇa to illustrate this :

"6. O Varuṇa! the birds that fly have not attained thy power, or thy vigour; the water which flows ceaselessly and the moving wind do not surpass thy speed.

"7. King Varuṇa of unsullied power remains in the firmament, and holds on high the rays of light. Those rays descend downwards, but proceed from above. May they sustain our existence.

"8. King Varuṇa has spread out the path for the course of the sun. He has made the path for the sun to traverse in pathless space. May he rebuke our enemies who pierce our hearts.

"9. O King Varuṇa! a hundred and a thousand medicinal drugs are thine; may thy beneficience be vast and deep. Keep unrighteousness away from us, deliver us from the sins we have committed.

"10. Yonder stars [1] which are placed on high, and are seen by night,--where do they go by day ? The acts of Varuṇa are irresistible; the moon shinews brightly by his mandate." (I, 24.)

"3. O Varuṇa! with an anxious heart I ask thee about my sins, I have gone to learned men to make inquiry; the sages have all said to me :—'Varuṇa is displeased with thee.'

"4. O Varuṇa! what have I done that thou wishest to destroy thy friend, thy worshipper ? O thou of irresistible power, declare it to me, so that I may quickly bend in adoration and come unto thee.

"5. O Varuṇa! deliver us from the sins of our fathers. Deliver us from the sins committed in our persons. O royal Varuṇa! deliver Vasiṣṭha, like a calf from its tether, like a thief who has feasted on a stolen animal.

"6. O Varuṇa! all this sin is not wilfully committed by us, Error or wine, anger or dice, or even thoughtlessness has begotten sin. Even an elder brother leads his younger astray, sin is begotten even in our dreams.

"7. Freed from sin, I will faithfully serve as a slave, the Varuṇa who fulfils our wishes and supports us. We are ignorant, may the Ārya god bestow on us knowledge. May the wise deity accept our prayer and bestow on us wealth." (VII, *86.)*

"1. O King Varuṇa! may I never go to the earthen home. O thou of great power! have mercy, have mercy.

"2. O Varuṇa with thy weapons! I come trembling even like a cloud driven by the wind. O thou of great power! have mercy, have mercy.

"3. O rich and pure Varuṇa! I have been driven against righteous acts through weakness. O thou of great power! have mercy, have mercy.

"4. Your worshippers hath thirsted even when living in water. O thou of great power! have mercy, have mercy.

"5. O Varuṇa! we are mortals. In whatever way we have sinned against gods, in whatever manner we have through ignorance neglected thy work—O! do not destroy us for these sins." (VII, 89.)

These and many other hymns show that Varuṇa was never divested in India of that idea of holiness which is said to have entered into his original conception. But nevertheless, Varuṇa like Dyu was supplanted in power by the younger Indra, a god who is peculiarly Indian, and is unknown to other Āryan nations.

One of the most famous legends about Indra, the most famous legend probably in the Āryan world, is about the production of rain. The dark heavy clouds to which man looks up with wistful eyes, but which often disappoint him in seasons of drought, are called by the ancient name of Vṛtra.

Vṛtra is supposed to confine the waters, and will not let them descend until the sky-god or rain-god Indra strikes the monster with his thunderbolt. The captive waters then descend in copious showers, rivers rise almost instantaneously, and gods and men rejoice over the changed face of nature. Many are the spirited hymns in the Ṛg Veda in which this combat is narrated with much glee and rejoicing. The storm-gods, Maruts, help Indra in the combat, the sky, and earth tremble at the noise, Vṛtra long wages an unequal combat, and then falls and dies—the drought is over, and rains begin.

We have said that Indra is a peculiarly Indian name, and is unknown to other Āryan nations. But the legend given above and the name of Vṛtra, appear in various shapes among various Āryan nations. Vṛtraghna, or the slayer of Vṛtra, is worshipped in the Zendavesta as Verethraghna, and we also find in the same work an account of the destruction of Ahi, which in the Veda is another name for Vṛtra. Threyetana is the slayer of Ahi, and the genius of the great French scholar Burnouf has recognized this identical Threyetana in the Ferudin of Ferdusi's Shah Nama—translated from mythology to history after thousands of years! It will probably surprise modern readers more to know that scholars have traced this Ahi of the Veda and the Zendavasta in the dragon Echis and Echidna of Greek mythology; that in the dog Orthros, the offspring of Echidna, they have recognized our old friend Vṛtra or the rain-cloud, and Hercules therefore, the slayer of Orthros, is the counterpart of Threyetana of Zendavesta, and of Indra of the Ṛg Veda!

It would be easy to multiply such legends, but our limits forbid such a course. We will therefore only make a passing mention of one more legend, *viz.*, that about the recovery of light by Indra after the darkness of night. The rays of light are compared to cattle which have been stolen away by the powers of darkness, and Indra (the sky) seeks for them, in vain. He sends *Saramā, i.e.*, the dawn, after them, and Saramā finds out the *Bilu,* or fortress, where the *Panis*. or powers of darkness, have concẹaled the cattle. The Panis try to tempt Saramā, but in vain. Saramā comes back to Indra, and Indra marches with his forces, destroys the fort and recovers the cattle; darkness in gone, and it is day! This is a well-known Vedic legend, and there are constant allusions to it in the hymns to Indra.

Professor Max Müller maintains that the story of the siege of Troy is a development of this simple Vedic myth, and is "but a repetition of the daily siege of the East by the Solar powers that every evening are robbed of their brightest treasures in the west." Ilium according to the Professor is *Bilu,* the cave or the fortress of the Ṛg Veda. Paris is the *Panis* of the Veda who tempt, and Helena is the Vedic *Saramā* who resists the temptation in the Veda, but succumbs to it in Greek mythology.

Historical evidence of an actual siege of Troy need not necessarily disprove this theory, for nothing is more common in ancient history than the blending of mythical names and incidents with historical events. Arjuna the hero of a historical Kuru Pāñcāla war is a myth, and is a name of the rain-god Indra; and it is not impossible that the poet who sang of a historical seige of Troy blended with it a solar myth with its names and incidents. We will now make short extracts from the Ṛg Veda illustrating these two legends :—

"1. We sing the heroic deeds which were performed by Indra the thunderer. He destroyed Ahi (cloud) and caused rains to descend, and opened out the paths for the mountain streams to roll.

"2. Indra slayed Ahi resting on the mountains, Tvaṣṭṛi had made the far-reaching thunderbolt for him. Water in torrents flowed towards the sea, as cows run eagerly towards their calves.

"3. Impetuous as a bull, Indra quaffed the Soma-juice; he drank the Soma libations offered in the three sacrifices. He then took the thunderbolt, and thereby slayed the eldest of the Ahis.

"4. When you killed the eldest of the Ahis, you destroyed the contrivances of the artful contrivers. You cleared the sun and the morning and the sky, and left no enemies behind.

"5. Indra with his all destructive thunderbolt slayed the darkling Vṛtra (cloud), and lopped his limbs. Ahi now lies touching the earth like the trunk of a tree felled by the axe.

"6. The proud Vṛtra thought that he had no equal, and defied the destroyer and conqueror Indra to combat. But he did not escape destruction, and Indra's foe fell, crushing the rivers in his fall.

"8. Glad waters are bounding over the prostrate body as rivers flow over fallen banks. Vṛtra when alive had withheld the water by his power, Ahi now lies prostrate under that water.

"10. The prostrate body lies concealed and nameless under ceaseless and restless waters, and the waters flow above. Indra's foe sleeps the long sleep." (I, 32)

The above is one of the hymns relating to the legend of Vṛtra. We now turn to a hymn relating to the legend of Saramā.

1. The *Panis* say :— "O Saramā! why hast thou come here? It is a long distance. He who looks back cannot come this way. What have we with us for which thou hast come ? How long hast thou travelled ? How didst thou cross the Rasā ?

2. *Saramā* replies :—" I come as the messenger of Indra. O Panis! it is my object to recover the abundant cattle which you have hidden. The water has helped me, the water felt a fear at my crossing, and thus I crossed the Rasā.

3. *Panis,*—"What is that Indra like, whose messenger thou art, and hast come from a long distance ? How does he look ? (To

one another:) Let her come, we will own her as a friend. Let her take and own our cows.

4. *Saramā,*—"I do not see any one who can conquer the Indra whose messenger I am, and have come from a long distance. It is he who conquers everybody. The deep rivers cannot restrain his course. O Panis! you will surely be slain by Indra and will lie down.

5. *Panis.*—"O beautiful Saramā! thou hast come from the farthest ends of the sky, we will give thee without any dispute these cows as thou desirest. Who else would have given the cattle without a dispute. We have many sharp weapons with us.

9. *Panis.*—"O Saramā! thou hast come here because the god threatened thee and sent thee here. We will accept thee as a sister, do not return. O beautiful Saramā! we will give thee a share of this cattle.

10. *Saramā.*—"I do not comprehend your words about brothers and sisters. Indra and the powerful sons of Aṅgiras know all. They sent me here to guard the cattle until recovery. I have come here under their shelter, O Panis! run away far, far from here." (X, 108.)

It will be seen from the few extracts we have made, that the hymns to Indra are characterized by force and vigour as those to Varuṇa are marked with a feeling of righteousness. Indra is, in fact, the most vigorous of Vedic gods, fond of Soma wine, delighting in war, leading his comrades, the Maruts, to fight against drought, leading hosts of Āryans against the black aborigines, and helping them to carve out for themselves, with their strong right arm, the most fertile spots along the five rivers of the Punjab. The sky and earth gave him birth as a cudgel for the enemies. (III, 49, 1.) The young and vigorous infant went to his mother Aditi for food, and saw Soma wine on her breast; he drank Soma before he drank from his mother's breast. (III, 48, 2 & 3.) And the great drinker and fighter often hesitates between the temptation of Soma libations at sacrifices, and the temptation of his home where a beautiful wife awaits him. (III, 53, 4 to 6.)

We have so long spoken of Dyu and Varuṇa and Mitra and Indra as the principal sky-gods of the Ṛg Veda. All these gods may however also be considered as gods of light, as the idea of the bright light of sky enters into the conception of all the deities, even of Varuṇa in some passages. We will now, however, speak of some deities who have more distinctly a solar character, and some of whom are grouped together under the common name of Ādityas or sons of Aditi, and this brings us to the most remarkable name that occurs in the Ṛg Veda mythology. Unlike Indra, which comes from *Ind* to rain, and Dyu which comes from *Dyu* to shine, the word Aditi involves a more complicated idea. Aditi means the undivided, the unlimited, the eternal. It is in reality, as has been stated, the earliest name invented by man to express the Infinite—the vizible infinite, the endless expanse, beyond the earth, beyond the clouds, beyond the sky. The fact that such an idea should enter into the conception of a deity argues a remarkable advance in the culture and thought of the early Hindus. The word has no counterpart among the names of the deities of other ancient Āryan nations, and must have been coined in India after the Indo-Āryan section had settled in this country. It means, according to the eminent German scholar Dr. Roth, the eternal and inviolable principle, the celestial light.

There is much confusion in the Ṛg Veda as to who are the Ādityas—the sons of this celestial light. In II, *27,* Aryaman and Bhaga and Dakṣa and Ansa are named besides Varuṇa and Mitra of whom we have spoken before. In IX, 114, and in X, 72, the Ādityas are said to be seven in number, but are not named. We have seen before that Indra is called a son of Aditi. Savitri, the sun, is often described as an Āditya, and so are Pūṣan and Viṣṇu, who are also different names of the sun. We will therefore leave alone the word Āditya and make a few remarks on the different names by which the sun, in its different aspects, was worshipped.

Sūrya and Savitri are the most common names of the sun in the Ṛg Veda, the former word answering to the Greek Helios, the Latin Sol, the Tuton Tyr and the Iranian Khorshed. Commentators draw a distinction between Savitri the rising or the unrisen sun, and Sūrya the bright sun of day. The golden rays of the sun were naturally compared with arms, until a story found its place in the Hindu mythology, that Savitri lost his arm at a sacrifice, and it was replaced by a golden arm. The same story reappears in a different form in German mythology, in which the sun-god Tyr placed his hand in the mouth of a tiger and lost it!

The only extract we will make from the hymns to the sun will be that most celebrated of all the verses in the Ṛg Veda, the Gāyatrī, or the morning hymn of the later Brāhmans. But the Ṛg Veda recognized no Brāhmans, the caste system was not formed then, and the sublime hymn was the *national* property of the early Hindus who dwelt on the banks of the Indus. We give the original verse and Dr. Wilson's translation :

> *"Tat savitur vareṇyam bhargo devasya dhīmahi*
> *"Dhiyo yo nahprachodayāt."*

"We mediate on the desirable light of the divine Savitri who influences our pious rites." (III, 62. 10.)

Pūṣan is the sun as viewed by shepherds in their wanderings in quest of fresh pasture lands. He travels in a chariot yoked with goats, guides men and cattle in their travels and migrations, and knows and protects. — the flocks. The hymns to Pūṣhan therefore Soften breathe a simplicity which is truly pastoral. A few extracts from such hymns have been given before.

Viṣṇu has obtained such a prominent place as the Supreme Deity in later Hinduism, that there is a natural reluctance among orthodox modern Hindus to accept him in his Vedic character as a mere sun-god. Yet such he is in the Ṛg Veda, and he is quite an inferior deity in the Vedic pantheon, far below Indra or Varuṇa, Savitri or Agni. It was not till the days of the Śatapatha Brāhmaṇa that Viṣṇu obtained some prominence among gods; and it was not till the Paurāṇik times, long after the Christian Era, that Viṣṇu was considered as a Supreme Deity. in the Veda Viṣṇu is said to traverse space in three steps, *viz.*, the sun at rising, at zenith and at setting. In the Purāṇas this simple metaphor has led to a long story.

Fire was an object of worship among all ancient nations, and in India sacrificial fire received the highest regard. As no sacrifice could be performed without fire, Agni or fire was called the invoker of the gods. He was called Yavishṭha, or the "youngest" among the gods, because he was, kindled anew at each time of sacrifice by the friction of *araṇi,* or the sacrificial wood. For this reason, he also received the name of Pramantha, *i.e.*, produced by friction.[2]

So high was the esteem in which fire was held among the gods of the Ṛg Veda, that when the ancient commentator Yāska, tried to reduce the number of the Vedic gods into three, he named Agni or fire as the god of the earth, Indra or Vāyu as the god of the firmament, and the Sun as the god of the sky.

But Agni is not only terrestrial fire in the Ṛg Veda; he is also the fire of the lightning and the sun, and his abode was the invizible heaven. The Bhṛgus discovered him there, Mātarisvan brought him down, and Atharvan and Aṅgiras, the first sacrifices, first installed him in this world as the protector of men.

Vāyu, or the air, has received less consideration from the Vedic bards, and there are but few hymns assigned to him. But the Maruts or the storm-gods are oftener invoked, as we have seen before, probably because they inspire more terror, and they are considered as the companions of Indra in obtaining rain from the reluctant clouds! The earth trembles as they move in their deer-yoked chariots, and men see the flashing of their arms or the sparkle of their ornaments, the lightning. But they are benevolent all the same, and they milk from the udder of their mother Pṛṣni (cloud) copious showers for the benefit of man. Rudra, a fierce deity, is the father of the Maruts, loud-sounding as his name signifies, and a form of fire as the commentators Yāska and Sāyaṇa explain. There can be no doubt, therefore, as to the correctness of Dr. Roth's conclusion, that the original meaning of this loud-sounding fire, this father of storms, is thunder. Nevertheless Rudra, though awful, is not a malevolent deity, he is beneficent and helpful and knows many remedies.

Like Viṣṇu, Rudra is a second rate deity in the Ṛg Veda, and only a few hymns are assigned to him. But like Viṣṇu,

Rudra has attained prominence in later times, and is one of the Hindu Trinity of the Paurāṇik religion, a portion of the Supreme Deity. In some of the Upaniṣads we find the names Kālī, Karālī, etc, used as the names of different kinds of flame, and in the White Yajus Saṁhitā, we find Ambikā spoken of as the sister of Rudra. But when Rudra assumed a more distinct individuality in the Purāṇas, all these names were construed as, the different names of his wife! We have only to add that none of these goddesses, nor Lakṣmī, the wife of Paurāṇik Viṣṇu, is so much as mentioned even by name in the Ṛg Veda.

Another god who has also changed his character in the Purāṇas (and very much for the worse!) is Yama, the king of the dead. In the Purāṇas he is called the child of the Sun, and there are some reasons (which Professor Max Müller explains with his usual eloquence), for supposing that the original conception of Yama in the Ṛg Veda is the conception of the departing sun. The sun sets and disappears, just as a man's life ends : and the imagination of a simple race would easily conjure up an after world, where that departed deity would preside over departed spirits.

According to the Ṛg Veda, Vivasvat the sky is the father, and Saraṇyu the dawn is the mother of Yama and his sister Yamī.

Who can be the offspring of the sky and the dawn but the sun or the day ? It is difficult to resist the conclusion that the twins Yama and Yamī are, as Professor Max Müller explains, day and night in their original conception. There is a curious passage in the Ṛg Veda in which the amorous sister Yamī desires to embrace, her brother as her husband, but the brother declines such union as unholy (X, 10). It is not difficult to fathom the import of this conversation :—Day and Night, though eternally pursuing each other, can never be united.

But whatever the original conception of Yama may be, there is no doubt that even in the Ṛg Veda itself, that deity has attained a distinct individuality, and he is the king of the departed. So far his Vedic character agrees with his Paurāṇic character, but here the parallel ends. In the Veda, he is the beneficient king of the happy world where the virtuous live and enjoy themselves in after-life, Clothed in a glorious body, they sit by the side of Yama in the realms of light and sparkling waters, they enjoy endless felicity there, and are adored here below under the name of Pitṛs or fathers. How different is the character which Yama bears in the Purāṇas as the cruel and dread Punisher of the guilty!

The following extract embodies the Vedic idea of future happiness. We will only remark here, that allusions to the future world are brief and rare in the earlier portions of the Veda, and that there is no description of future life, like the one we quote below, except in the very latest hymns.

"1. Worship Yama the son of Vivasvat with offerings. All men go to him. He takes men of virtuous deeds to the realm of happiness. He clears the way for many.

"2. Yama first discovered the path for us. That path will not be destroyed again. All living beings will, according to their acts, follow by the path by which our forefathers have gone." (X, 14.)

We may also quote here another passage from a hymn to Soma, which contains a fuller allusion to the future world. Soma it is well known was the juice of a plant made into wine, and used as libation in sacrifices. Soma soon attained the rank of a deity, and all the hymns of the ninth Maṇḍala are dedicated to him.

"7. O flowing Soma! take me to that immortal and imperishable abode where light dwells eternal, and which is in heaven. Flow, Soma! for Indra.

"8. Take me where Yama is king, where there are the gates of heaven, and where mighty rivers flow. Take me there and make me immortal. Flow, Soma! for Indra.

"9. Take me where there is the third heaven, where there is the third realm of light above the sky, and where one can wander at his will. Take me there and make me immortal. Flow, Soma! for Indra.

10. Take me where every desire is satiated, where Pradhma

has his abode, where there is food and contentment. Take me there and make me immortal. Flow, Soma! for Indra.

"11. Take me where there are pleasures and joys and delights, where every desire of the anxious heart is satiated. Take me there, and make me immortal. Flow, Soma! for Indra." (IX, 113.)

We have spoken above of Yama and Yamī as twin children of Vivasvat the sky, by Saraṇyu the dawn. It is remarkable that the same parents begot another twin offspring, the two Aśvins. There can be little doubt that they, too, like Yama and Yamī, were in their original conception the day and the night, or the dawn and the evening.

But whatever the original conception of the Aśvins may be, they appear in the Ṛg Veda as great physicians, healers of the sick and the wounded, and tending many persons with kindness. Long lists of the kind acts of the two Aśvins are given in several hymns, and the same cures are spoken of over and over. On their three-wheeled chariot, they make the circuit of the world day by day, and succour men in their distress.

Bṛhaspati or Brāhmaṇaspati is the lord of hymns, Brahmān in the Ṛg Veda meaning hymn. The conception of this deity arose in much the same way as the conception of the deities Agni and Soma. As there is power in the flame and the libation of the sacrifice, so there is power in the prayer uttered; and this power of prayer is personified in the Vedic god Brāhmaṇaspati.

He is quite a second rate god in the Ṛg Veda, but has a great future. For in course of centuries, the thinkers of the Upaniṣads conceived of a Supreme Universal Being, and gave him the Vedic name Brahmā. Then, when Buddhism flourished in the land, the Buddhists themselves tolerated Brahmā as a gentle and beneficent spirit in their pantheon. And when at last Paurāṇik Hinduism supplanted Buddhism in India, the Paurāṇik thinkers gave the name of Brahmā to the Supreme Creator of the Universe. Thus by looking into our national records of the farthest antiquity, we trace the simple beginnings of that gorgeous Paurāṇik mythology which has for over a thousand years swayed the opinions and conduct of hundreds of millions of our countrymen and countrywomen. It is like tracing one of our great indian rivers which spreads for miles together at its mouth, to its very source, where a narrow but pure and crystal streamlet issues from the eternal mountains! Ideas develope in the course of time, just as rivers expand and receive fresh supplies of water in their course, until they lose all their primitive character, although still bearing the same names. And we can no more recognize the simple Vedic character of Brahmā the prayer, of Viṣṇu the sun, and of Rudra the thunder, in the Supreme Creator, the Preserver and the Destroyer of the Purāṇas, than we can recognize the crystal streamlet at Hard war in the sea-like expanse of the Ganges where it mingles with the Bay of Bengal.

These are the important gods of the Ṛg Veda. Of the goddesses there are only two who have any marked individually, *viz.*, Uṣas, the dawn, and Sarasvatī, the goddess of the river of that name, and afterwards the goddess of speech.

There is no lovelier conception in the Ṛg Veda than that of the dawn. There are no hymns in the Veda more truly poetical than those dedicated to her, and nothing more charming is to be found in the lyrical poetry of any ancient nation. We can make room here for only a few extracts :

"20. What mortal knoweth thee, O immortal Uṣas fond of our praise! Whom, O mighty one, dost thou favour ?

"21. Far-extending, many-tinted, brilliant Uṣas! we know not thy abode, whether it be nigh or remote.

"22. Daughter of the sky! accept these offerings, and perpetuate our welfare." (I, 30,)

"7. Auspicious Uṣas has harnessed her chariots from afar, before the rising of the sun! She comes in radiance and glory on us in her hundred chariots." (I, 48.)

"7. She, the young, the white-robed daughter of the sky, the mistress of all earthly treasure, dawns upon us, dissipating darkness! Auspicious Uṣas! shine upon us to-day in this spot.

"8. Following the path of mornings that have passed, to

be followed by endless mornings to come, bright Uṣas dispels darkness, and awakens to life all beings unconscious like the dead in sleep.

"10. How long have the Dawns risen ? How long will the Dawns arise? The present morning pursues those that are gone, future mornings will pursue this resplendent Uṣas.

"11. Mortals who beheld the pristine Uṣas have passed away; we behold her now; and men will come after us who will behold Uṣas in the future." (I, 113.)

"4. Ahanā gently proceeds to every house; she comes ever diffusing light, and blesses us and accepts our offerings.

"11. Radiant as a bride decorated by her mother, thou displayest thy person to the view. Auspicious Uṣas! remove the investing darkness; no other dawns but thee will disperse it." (I, 123.)

The Dawn was known by various names, and most of these names and the legends connected with them were brought by the Hindus from their original abode, since we find phonetical equivalents of these names, and a repetition of some of the legends, too, in Greek mythology. Uṣas is the Eos of the Greeks and the Aurora of the Latins. Arjunī (the white one) is the Greek Argynoris, Brisayā is Briseis, Dahanā is Daphne, Saramā is phonetically equivalent to the Greek Helena, and Saraṇyu, the mother of Yama and of the Aśvins, is the Greek Erinys, and Ahanā is the renowned goddess Athena.

We have already alluded to the legend of Saraṇyu running away from her husband Vivasvat, and then giving birth to the twin Aśvins. We find the same legend among the Greeks who believed in Erinys Demeter running away in the same manner, and giving birth to Areion and Despoina. The idea in both cases is the same, it is the dawn disappearing as the day advances. The same idea has given rise to another beautiful Greek legend whose origin, too, we trace in the Ṛg Veda. In many passages (I, 115, 2, for instance,) we find allusions of the sun pursuing the dawn as a man pursues a woman. The Greek Apollo in the same way pursues the Greek Daphne, until she is metamorphosed, *i. e.,* the dawn disappears !

Sarasvatī, as her name signifies, is the goddess of the river of that name, which was considered holy because of the religious rites performed on its banks and the sacred hymns uttered there. By a natural development of ideas, she was considered the goddess of those hymns, or, in other words, the goddess of speech, in which character she is worshipped now. She is the only Vedic goddess whose worship continues in India to the modern day; all her modern companions, Durgā, Kālī, Lakṣmī and others, are creations of a later day.

Such is the nature-worship of the Ṛg Veda; such were the gods and goddesses whom our forefathers worshipped near four thousand years ago on the banks of the Indus. The conception of the nature-gods, and the simple and manly fervency with which they were adored, argue the simplicity and vigour of a manly conquering race, as well as the culture and thoughtfulness of a people who had already made considerable progress in civilization. Again, the very conception of the Vedic gods argues an elevated sentiment, a high tone of morality in the men who conceived such deities. As M. Barth justly observes, the Vedic gods are masters close at hand, and require a due performance of duty by man. "He must be sincere towards them, for they cannot be deceived. Nay he knows that they in turn do not deceive, and that they have a right to require his affection and confidence as a friend, a brother, a father. .... How could it be permitted to men to be bad when the gods are good, to be unjust while they are just, to be deceitful when they never deceive. It is certainly a remarkable feature of the hymns that they acknowledge no wicked divinities, and no mean and harmful practices.....We must acknowledge then that the hymns give evidence of an exalted and comprehensive morality, and that in striving to be 'without reproach before Aditi and the Ādityas' the Vedic minstrels feel the weight of other duties besides those of multiplying offerings to the gods.[3]

There are no indications in the Ṛg Veda of any "temples reared by mortal hands" and consecrated as places of worship.

On the contrary, every householder, every patriarch of his family lighted the sacrificial fire in his own home, and poured libations of the Soma-juice, and prayed to the gods in the hymns which were then the common property of the nation, for happiness to his family, for abundant crops and wealth of cattle, for immunity from sickness and victory over the black aborigines. There was no separate priestly caste, and men did not retire into forests, and subject themselves to penances in order to meditate on religion, and chant these hymns. On the contrary, the old Ṛṣis, the real Ṛṣis as we find them in the Ṛg Veda, stories not the fabled ones of whom we have legendary stories in the Purāṇas, were worldly men, men with considerable property in crops and in cattle and surrounded by large families, men who in times of danger exchanged the plough for the spear and the sword, and defended against the black barbarians those blessings of civilization which they solicited from their gods, and secured with so much care.

But though each householder was himself the priest, the warrior and the cultivator, yet we find evidence of kings and rich men performing rites on a large scale by men specially proficient in the chanting of hymns and other religious rites, and engaged and paid for the purpose. And as we go towards the later hymns of the Ṛg Veda, we find this class of professional priests gaining in reputation and in wealth, honoured by chiefs and kings, and rewarded by gifts of cattle and cars, We find mention of particular families specially proficient in the performance of religious rites, and in the composition of hymns; and many of the existing hymns of the Ṛg Veda were composed by members of these families, and were traditionally learnt by rote and preserved in those families.

The hymns of the Ṛg Veda are divided into ten *maṇḍals,* so arranged according to the Ṛṣis by whom they were composed. The first and the last maṇḍalas contain hymns composed by numerous Ṛṣis, but the remaining eight maṇḍalas belong, each of them, to a particuiar Ṛṣi, or rather to a particular house or school of Ṛṣis. Thus the second maṇḍala is a collection of hymns composed by Gritsamada of the house of Bhṛgu and his descendants, the third maṇḍala belongs to

Viśvāmitra, the fourth maṇḍala belongs to Vāmadeva, the fifth to Atri, the sixth to Bhāradvāja, the seventh to Vasiṣṭha, the eighth to Kaṇva, and the ninth to Aṅgiras, All these names are familiar to modern Hindus through the numberless legends which have surrounded them in Paurāṇik times, and modern Hindus still love to trace their descent from these ancient and revered houses. We shall have something to say about these Ṛṣis and their legends in our next chapter.

It is to these and other venerable houses that the Āryan world owes the preservation of the most ancient compositions of the Āryan race. From century to century the hymns were handed down without break or intermission, and the youths of the priestly houses spent the prime of their life in learning by rote the sacred songs from the lips of their grey-headed sires. It was thus that the inestimable treasure, the Ṛg Veda, was preserved for hundreds of years by memory alone.

With the progress of civilization, and as religious rites were more and more monopolized by professional priests, the simple religion of the earlier times underwent a change. Priests boldly grappled with the deeper mysteries of nature, they speculated about creation and about the future world, and while continuing the worship of the nature-gods, they attained to the conception of the Supreme Deity. We find evidence of all this in the last portions of the Veda. We have already quoted some verses about the future world, we will add here some about creation and about the great Creator:—

"1. That all wise Father saw clearly, and after due reflection, created the sky and the earth in their watery form, and touching each other. When their boundaries were stretched afar, then the sky and the earth became separated.

"2. He who is the all-creator (Viśvakarman) is great; he creates and supports all; he is above all and sees all. He is beyond the seat of the seven Ṛṣis. So the wise men say, and the wise men obtain fulfilment of all their desires.

"3. He who has given us life, he who is the creator, he who knows all the places in this universe—*he is one although he bears the names of many gods*. Other beings wish to know of him.

"7. You cannot comprehend him who has created all this; he is incomprehensible to your mind. People make guesses, being shrouded in a mist; they take their food for the support of their life, and utter hymns and [wander about." (X. 82.)

The incomprehensible nature of the Deity has never been more clearly put than in the preceding hymn composed over three thousand years ago.

1. At that time what is, was not, and what is not, was not. The earth was not, and the far-stretching sky was not. What was, there that covered ? Which place was assigned to what object ? Did the inviolate and deep water exist ?

2. At that time death was not nor immortality; the distinction between day and night was not. There was only ONE who lived and breathed without the help of air, supported by himself. Nothing was, except HE.

"3. At first darkness was covered in darkness.. All was without demarcation; all was of watery form. The world that was a void was covered by what did not exist and was produced by meditation.

"4. Desire arose on the mind, the cause of creation was thus produced. Wise men reflect, and in their wisdom ascertain the birth of what is from what is not.

"5. Males with generating seed were produced, and powers were also produced. Their rays extended on both sides and below and above, a self-supporting principle beneath, an energy aloft.

"6. Who knows truly ? Who will describe ? When was all born ? Whence were all these created ? *The gods have been made after the creation.* Who knows whence they were made ?

"7. Whence all these were created, from whom they came, whether any one created them or did not create— is known only to Him who lives as Lord in the highest place. If he knows not (no one else does.)" (X. 129.)

Such is the first recorded attempt among the Āryan nations of the earth to pierce into the mysteries of creation; such are the bold and sublime if somewhat vague ideas which dawned in the minds of our forefathers over three thousand years ago, regarding the commencement of this great universe. One more hymn we will quote here, a remarkable hymn, shewing how the later Ṛṣis soared beyond the conception of the nature-gods to the sublime idea of One Deity.

"1. In the beginning he of the golden womb (Hiraṇya-garbha) existed. He was the Lord of all from his birth. He placed this earth and sky in their respective places. Whom shall we worship with offerings ?

"2. Him who has given life and strength; whose will is obeyed by all the gods; whose shadow is immortality, and whose slave is death. Whom shall we worship with offerings ?

"3. Him who by his power is the sole king of all the living beings that see and move; him who is the Lord of all bipeds and quadrupeds. Whom shall we worship with offerings ?

"4. Him by whose power these snowy mountains have been made, and whose creations are this earth and its oceans. Him whose arms are these quarters of space. Whom shall we worship with offerings ?

"5. Him who has fixed in their places this sky and this earth; him who has established the heavens and the highest heaven; him who has measured the firmament. Whom shall we worship with offerings ?

"6. Him by whom the sounding sky and earth have been fixed and expanded; him whom the resplendent sky and earth own as Almighty; him by whose support the sun rises and gains its lustre. Whom shall we worship with offerings ?" (X, 121.)

We now see the force of the remark that the religion of the Ṛg Veda is a progressive religion, that it travels from nature up to nature's God. We see the entire journey of the human mind in this wonderful book, from the simple childlike admiration of the ruddy dawn, to the deep and sublime attempt to grasp the mysteries of creation and its great Creator.

But unfortunately this prossess was not unattended with evils. As the priestly grass rose in power and in knowledge, in worldly influence and in true wisdom, the worship of the ancestral gods fell almost entirely into their hands, and the people lost their manly self-reliance and sank under priestly influence. In the concluding portions of the Ṛg Veda, therefore, we find evidences on the one hand of the high thought and bold speculations of the priests, and, on the other hand, of the-growing superstition of the people. The numerous mantras prescribed for snake-bite, for diseases and evil omens, all belong to the last period of the Vedic Age, and betoken a growing superstition and a greater dependence on the priestly class. At the close of the Ṛg Veda, therefore, we discern the first germs of all that was the glory, and all that was the shame of Hindu civilization. The first speculations of philosophy and science have commenced,—and the subjection of the nation to a priestly class has also commenced !

REFERENCES

1. The word used in the text is Ṛkṣa, which may either mean stars generally, or the stars of the constellation Great Bear. The root *rich* means to shine, whence in course of time the word Ṛkṣa came to have two meanings—the shining stars of a particular constellation, and an animal with bright eyes and shining glossy hair. By a natural confusion of ideas, therefore, the constellation itself ultimately came to be called the Bear. The question is discussed with remarkable eloquence and learning by Max Müller in his Science of Language, and he explains that "the surprise with which many a thoughtful observer has looked at these seven bright stars, wondering why they were ever called the Bear, is removed by reference to the early annals of human speech."
2. According to Mr. Cox, many of the Greek and Latin deities owe their name to the Sanscrit names of Fire. "In this name, Yaviṣṭha, which is never given to any other Vedic god, we may recognize the Hellenic Hephaistos.

   Note.—Thus, with the exception of Agni, all the names of the Fire and the Fire-gods were carried away by the Western Āryans; and we have Prometheus answering to Pramantha, Phuronus to Bharanyu, and the Latin Vulcanus to the Sanscrit Ulka."—*Cox's Mythology of Āryan Nations*.

   "Agni is the god of fire; the Ignis of the Latins, the Ogni of the Sclavonias."—*Muir's Sanscrit Texts*.
3. *The Religions of India*. (Translation), p. 32, *et seq*.

CHAPTER – 7

VEDIC ṚṢIS

We have stated in the last chapter that certain pious and learned families obtained pre-eminence in the Vedic Period by their knowledge of performing religious sacrifices and their gift of composing hymns; that kings and wealthy lords delighted to honor and reward these families; and that it is to them that the Āryan world is indebted for handing down the Vedic hymns from generation to generation. Modern Hindus take a pride in tracing their descent from these ancient families, and their names are a household word in modern Hindu society. Some account of these ancient Ṛṣis—the revered pioneers of the Hindu religion— will therefore not be unwelcome to Hindu readers.

Pre-eminent among the Vedic Ṛṣis, or rather Ṛṣi families, stand the Viśvāmitras and the Vasiṣṭhas, The learned and industrious scholar Dr. Muir has, in the first volume of his Sanscrit Texts, collected many legends about these Ṛṣis from later Sanscrit literature; but there is no Hindu who has not read in books or heard from his boyhood, innumerable legends of this kind, connected with those revered names.

The Vasiṣṭhas and the Viśvāmitras were both honored by the powerful conqueror, Sudās. The hymns of the third maṇḍala are ascribed to the Viśvāmitras, and in the 53rd hymn we find the following passage : "The great god born, god commissioned Ṛṣi, the beholder of men, has stayed the watery current. When Viśvāmitra sacrificed for Sudās, then Indra was propitiated through the Kauśikas." Again, the hymns of the seventh maṇḍala are ascribed to the Vasiṣṭhas, and in the 33rd hymn we find the following passage : The Vasiṣṭhas in white robes, with their hair knots the right, devoted to sacred rites, have gladdened me. Rising up, I call the people round the sacrificial grass. Let not the Vasiṣṭhas depart from my door." And in the celebrated 83rd hymn, we find the well known passage : "Ye, O Indra and Varuṇa, have succoured Sudās, when hemmed in on every side in the combat of the ten kings, where the white robed Tritsus with braided hair adored you reverently with prayers."

There was naturally some jealousy between these two priestly houses, and hard words were exchanged. The following verses in III, 53, are said to contain an imprecation against the Vasiṣṭhas :

"21. Indra, approach us to-day with many excellent succour: be propitious to us. May he who hates us fall low; and let the breath of life forsake him whom we hate.

"22. As the tree suffers from the axe; as the Simbala flower is broken; as the cauldron boiling over casts forth foam; so may the enemy, O Indra.

"23. The might of the destroyer is not perceived. Men lead away the Ṛṣi as if he were a beast. The wise do not condescend to ridicule the fool. They do not lead the ass before the horse.

"24. These sons of Bharata have learnt to turn away from, not to associate with (the Vasiṣṭhas). They urge the horse against them as against a foe. They bear about the bow in battle."

Two other verses in the same hymn are also supposed to refer to the same hostility between the two families, though no imprecation, is apparent in them.

"15. The daughter of the sun, given by Jamadagni, everywhere diffusing herself and removing darkness, has produced a great sound, and has conveyed imperishable food for the gods.

"16. May she, everywhere diffusing herself, speedily supply abundant food to these men of the five tribes-- she, the daughter of the sun, possessing new life, and given by Jamadagni to me."

Vasiṣṭha is supposed to have hurled back the imprecations in the following verses of VII, 104:

"13.Soma does not bless the wicked nor the ruler who abuses his power. His slays the demon; he slays the untruthful man; both are bound by the fetters of Indra.

"14.If I had worshipped false gods, or if I had called upon the gods in vain,—but why art thou angry with me O Jātavedas ? May vain talkers fall into thy destruction.

"15.May I die at once if I be a Yātudhana, or if I hurt the life of any man. But may I be cut off from his ten friends who falsely called me a Yātudhāna.

"16,He who called me a Yātudhāna, when I am not so, or who said I am a bright devil—may Indra strike him down with his great weapon, may he fall the lowest of all beings."

So far the jealousy of the two angry priests is intelligible and even natural, however unbecoming of their great learning and sanctity. But when we proceed from the Ṛg Veda to later Sanscrit literature, incidents which are human and natural become lost in a cloud of miraculous and monstrous legends.

It is assumed from the commencement in these later legends, that Vasiṣṭha was a Brāhman and Viśvāmitra was a Kṣatriya, although the Ṛg Veda justifies no such assumption and knows no Brāhmans and Kṣatriyas as castes. On the contrary, Viśvāmitra is the composer of some of the finest hymns cherished by later Brāhmans, including the sacred Gāyatri, or the sacred morning prayer of modern Brāhmans.

Having assumed that Viśvāmitra was born a Kṣatriya, the Mahābhārata, the Harivaṁśa, the Viṣṇu Purāṇa, and other later works repeat an amusing story to account for the sage's attaining Brāhmanhood. Satyavati, a Kṣatriya girl, had been married to Ṛchika, a Brāhman. Ṛchika prepared a dish for his wife, which would make her conceive a son with the qualities of a Brāhman, and another dish for his mother-in-law (a Kṣatriya's wife) which would make her conceive a son with the qualities of a Kṣatriya. The two ladies however exchange dishes; and so the Kṣatriyani conceived and bore Viśvāmitra with the qualities of a Brāhman, and the Brāhman's wife Satyavati bore Jamadagni, whose son, the fiery Parasurāma, though a Brāhman, became a renowned and destructive warrior! Such were the childish stories which the later writers had to invent to remove the difficulty they had created for themselves by assuming that Vedic Ṛṣis belonged to particular castes!

But the Vedic account of the jealousy between Vasiṣṭha and Viśvāmitra has led to wilder legends. A legend is told in the Rāmāyaṇa and the Mahābhārata that Viśvāmitra, a king's son, went out hunting and came to the heimitage of Vasiṣṭha. He was received with honor and entertained with delicious food and drink, and presented with precious jewels and dresses, all obtained by the sage from his wonder-working cow! The prince coveted this wonderful cow, and failing to persuade the Brāhman to relinquish it, wished to take it by force. But the might of the Kṣatriya was unavailing against the power of the Brāhman; and the humbled Viśvāmitra then began his austerities which continued for thousands of years (!) until he became a Brāhman.

In the celebrated legend of Hariśchandra, Viśvāmitra appears as a rapacious Brāhman. He not only made the king give up his whole empire, but compelled him to sell his queen, his boy and himself as slaves to pay the inexorable Brāhman's fee! If such stories are invented to teach respect and duty due to Brāhmans, they fail in their object and inspire other sentiments. The bereaved Hariśchandra was, however, rewarded in the end, and Viśvāmitra anointed his son as king, and Hariśchandra went to heaven. Vasiṣṭha became angry and cursed Viśvāmitra to be a Vaka or crane, and Viśvāmitra, too, transformed Vasiṣṭha into an Ali bird! The two birds began a furious contest which shook the whole world, until Brahmā had to interpose, and restored the saints to their own forms, and reconciled them !

In the legend of Trisanku, we are told that that prince wished to go bodily to heaven. Vasiṣṭha declared the thing impossible, and in return for the king's angry words changed him to a Chaṇḍāla. The fiery Viśvāmitra now appeared on the scene. He declared the thing quite possible, and began a great sacrifice and proceeded with it in spite of Vasiṣṭha's absence. Trisanku ascended to heaven, but Indra refused to receive him, and threw the intruder, head downwards, towards the earth. The irrepressible Viśvāmitra however threatened to create another heaven with Indra and gods and stars! The gods had to give in, and Trisanku ascended to heaven, and shone like a star beyond the sun's course, but in a somewhat uncomfortable position, with his head still downwards!

The legend of Sunahśepha has arisen out of some hymns in the first maṇḍala which are ascribed to him. The later legend says that he was the son of Ṛchīka (and therefore nephew of Viśvāmitra), and was sold by his father to be the victim of a sacrifice. He was bound to the stake and was about to be sacrificed when he repeated the hymns alluded to above, which his maternal uncle Viśvāmitra had taught him, and was released. We shall have to allude to Sunahśepha's story in a later chapter, and examine some theories about the prevalence of human sacrifice which have been built on it.

In the legend of Kalmāṣapāda, we are told that Viśvāmitra caused that king to kill a hundred sons of Vasiṣṭha. In various other legends which have almost become household stories for Hindu boys and girls, these two sages continually appear, in defiance of chronology and date, and are always at enmity with each other. The rival priests appear in courts of kings, twenty, thirty, or fifty generations removed from each other, and there is hardly a classical composition of note about a royal house, or a semi-divine hero, in which we do not find mention of Vasiṣṭha and Viśvāmitra, eternally the rivals of each other. Thus the Viṣṇu Purāṇa makes Vasiṣṭha the priest of Ikṣvāku's son Nimi, as well as the priest of Sāgara who was 37th in descent from Ikṣvāku; and the Rāmāyānā makes Vasiṣṭha the priest of Rāma who was 61st in descent from Ikṣvāku! Such is the use which later romancers have made of the simple materials furnished by the Ṛg Veda, and such is the manner in which they have piled story upon story, and myth upon myth, in connection with incidents which, in the ancient Veda, are simple, natural and human. Not only the Ṛṣis of the Veda but every deity, and we may almost say every simile or allegory in the Ṛg Veda about a natural phenomenon, has received such treatment in the hands of later imaginative Hindus.

But while a hundred wild stories were invented in later days to account for Viśvāmitra's attaining Brāhmanhood, there was no thought of denying that accepted fact. Every legend, every learned disquisition, every sacred tale, every great work, from the Mahābhārata to Manu and the Purāṇas—admit that Viśvāmitra was a Kṣatriya and a Brāhman, Yudhiṣṭhira in the Anusāsana Parva (section 3) of the Mahābhārata enquires of Bhīṣma how Viśvāmitra had not only become a Brāhman but had established "the great and wise family of the Kusikas *which included Brāhmans and hundreds of Brāhman Ṛṣis.*" The question would be a difficult one to answer in the Paurāṇik Age in which the Mahābhārata received its last touches. The question would not be difficult of solution in the Epic Age when the caste-system was still a pliable institution. And the question would not arise at all in the *Age* of Viśvāmitra himself, *i. e.,* in the Vedic Age, when caste as such did not exist.

Again in the same Anuśāsana Parva (section 52), Yudhiṣṭhira enquires how Parasurāma, the son of the Brāhman Jamadagni, was possessed of the qualities of a Kṣatriya Later legends have made Jamadagni's son the converse of Viśvāmitra. Parasurāma is represented to have been a fiery Brāhman who killed his mother, and then destroyed the Kṣatriya race twenty-seven times, just as Viśvāmitra is represented as a pious Kṣatriya who rose to Brāhmanhood by his holiness and austerities. We have seen one attempt to solve the difficulty by the story that Viśvāmitra's mother and Parasurāma's grandmother exchanged dishes! But it is scarcely necessary to descend to such childish tales if we only remember the fact that both Viśvāmitra and Jamadagni were Vediç Ṛṣis; and they bore arms and composed hymns when Kṣatriyas and Brāhmans, as such, were unknown.

Jamadagni's name occurs in the Ṛg Veda, but not that of his renowned son Parasurāma. That character therefore is a later invention, and the story of his wars with Kṣatriyas is probably based on actual hostilities which may have taken place early in the Epic Age between stalwart priests and proud kings, just when the caste-system was forming itself. An institution like this is not formed in a day, and some centuries must have elapsed, even after the commencement of the Epic Period, before professions became absolutely hereditary. Even in the Mahābhārata which, however altered in later ages, is based on the traditions of the Epic Age, we find the most holy and religious character is Yudhiṣṭhira, a Kṣatriya, and the most renowned strategist and warrior is Droṇa, a Brāhman.

From the legends of the Viśvāmitra's and the Vasiṣṭhas let us now turn to the scarcely less renowned houses of the Bhṛgus, the Kaṇvas, the Bhāradvājas and the Aṅgirases. All these are families of Vedic Ṛṣis, composers of Vedic hymns; and later writers therefore feel somewhat uncertain about their caste. They are sometimes called Brāhmans with the character of Kṣatriyas, sometimes Kṣatriyas with the character of Brāhmans; and occasionally the bold truth is conjectured, that these Ṛṣis lived before the institution of caste was formed.

The Aṅgirases are the reputed authors of the ninth maṇḍala of the Ṛg Veda. About the Aṅgirases, the Viṣṇu Purāṇa (IV, 2, 2) has the following : "The son of Nabhāga was Nābhāga; his son was Ambarīṣa; his son was Virūpa; from him sprang Prishadasva, and from him Rathinara. On this subject there is this verse : These persons *descended from a Kṣatriya stock and afterwards known as Aṅgirases were* the chief of the Rathīnaras, *Brāhmans possessing also the character of Kṣatriyas!*"

The Viṣṇu Purāṇa in another place (IV, 3, 5) traces the descent of the Aṅgiras Hāritas *from the Kṣatriya king Ikṣvāku.* The Vāyu Purāṇa says of the Hāritas that "they were sons of Aṅgiras *and Brāhmans with the properties of Kṣatriyas!'* The Liṅga Purāṇa also maintains that they were the followers of Angiras, "*and Brāhmans with the properties of Kṣatriyas.*" He will be a wise reader who will unravel from these statements the caste of the Aṅgirases !

Vāmadeva and Bhāradvāja are reputed to be the authors of the fourth and the sixth maṇḍalas of the Ṛg Veda. The Matsya Purāṇa includes them (section 132) among the Aṅgirases of whom we have spoken before.

To the Gritsamadas are attributed the hymns of the second maṇḍala of the Ṛg Veda. The commentator Sāyaṇa says of him, that he was formerly the son of Sunahotra of the Aṅgiras race, but he afterwards became Gritsamada, son of Sunaka, of the Bhṛgu race. This somewhat mystic legend is elaborated in the Mahābhārata Anuśāsana Parva (section 30), in which we are told that Vitahavya, a Kṣatriya king, had taken shelter with Bhṛgu, and Bhṛgu, in order to save the fugitive from his pursuer, stated "there is no Kṣatriya here, all these are Brāhmans." The word of Bhṛgu could not prove untrue, and the fugitive Kṣatriya Vitahavya forthwith bloomed into Brāhmanhood and became Gritsamada! It must be allowed that this was an easier process than the penance of thousands of years which Viśvāmitra had to go through—not to mention that his mother had exchanged dishes with a Brāhman's wife !

But the story of Gritsamada's change of caste is not universally accepted. The Viṣṇu Purāṇa and the Vāyu Purāṇa conjecture the bold truth that Gritsamada lived before the caste institution was formed. "From Gritsamada was decended Śaunaka *who originated the four castes.*" *(Vish. Pur., IV, 8,)* "The son of Gritsamada was Sunaka from whom sprang Śaunaka. *In this race were born Brahmāns, Kṣatriyas, Vaiśyas, and Śūdras.*" (*Vāyu Purāṇa.*) The Harivaṁśa (section 29) repeats this statement.

But the Viṣṇu and the Vāyu Purāṇas and the Harivaṁśa are scarcely consistent, for we find elsewhere in these works that the four castes originated with Bhārgabhūmi who was the *twentieth in descent* from the brother of Gritsamada. Both these accounts, however, point to the ancient tradition that Gritsamada lived before the caste-system was instituted.

If we turn from the Gritsamadas to the Kaṇvas, authors of the eighth maṇḍala of the Ṛg Veda, we find the same uncertainty about their caste. The Viṣṇu Purāṇa (IV, 19), and the Bhāgavata Purāṇa (IX, 20, 6, 7), maintain that Kaṇva was the son of Apratiratha or of Ajāmīdha, both being descendants of Puru a Kṣatriya. Nevertheless the Kaṇvas were regarded as Brāhmans. "From Ajāmīḍha sprang Kaṇva, and from him Medhātithi, *from whom were descended the Kaṇvanaya Brāhmans" (Vish. Pur.*, IV, 19.)

Of the same race we read in the Viṣṇu Purāṇa (IV, 21), that "*the race which gave origin to Brāhmans and Kṣatriyas,* and was purified by regal sages shall terminate with Kṣemaka in the Kali age." Again in (IV, 19), we read of Garga of the same race, that "from Garga sprang Śivi; from him were descended the Gārgyas and Śaivyās, *who, having the character of Kṣatriyas, became Brāhmans."* Regarding Garga's brother Mahāvīrya, we read (IV, 19) that he had three grandsons, Trayaruna, Puṣkari, and Kapi, who *attained to Brāhmanhood*" And of Bali, one of the descendants of Anu, brother of Puru, we read in the Matsya Purāṇa and in the Vāyu Purāṇa, that *he established the four castes;* and the Harivaṁśa (section 31) repeats this story.

And lastly, if we turn from the Kaṇvas to Atri, the reputed author of the fifth maṇḍala of the Ṛg Veda, we find the name connected by later legends with the creation of the human race itself. Thus the Viṣṇu Purāṇa (IV, 6), calls him the son of Brahmā, and the grandfather of Pururavas *who belonged to the Kṣatriya race.*

These extracts are enough. The extracts are made from works composed or revised two or three thousand years after the time of the Vedic Ṛṣis, but those "extracts enable us to comprehend the status and position of the Vedic religious leaders and warriors, and are therefore not out of place in an account of the Vedic Period. Writing at such a long distance of time from the Vedic Age, the modern authors often misapprehended ancient facts and traditions. But nevertheless, the unswerving loyalty to the past which has ever characterised Hindu writers, prevented them from tampering with such traditions. Those traditions pointed to a state of society which had long past away, and which had become almost unintelligible. Paurāṇic writers could scarcely comprehend that priests and warriors could spring from the same race, that a Ṛṣi could be a warrior, or that a warrior could be a priest. They tried to explain such traditions by a hundred different theories and legends, but nevertheless they have faithfully and piously handed down the traditions unchanged and unaltered. Thus to make only one more extract, the Matsya Purāṇa enumerates 91 Vedic Ṛṣis, and concludes with the following suggestive passage, (section 132) : "Thus 91 persons have been declared, by whom the hymns have been given forth. *They were Brāhmans, Kṣatriyas and Vaiśyas,* all sons of Ṛṣis. They were the offspring of the Ṛṣikas, sons of Ṛṣis, Vedic Ṛṣis." .

Thus the Purāṇa faithfully preserves the ancient tradition, that the Vedic hymns were the common property of the entire Āryan population. And when the writer tell us that the composers of those hymns were Brāhmans, Kṣatriyas, and Vaiśyas, we have little difficulty in discovering in that statement, a dim recollection of the truth that the hymns were composed by the *undivided ancestors of those castes.*

For the rest, these invaluable traditions—that priests and warriors were descended from the same races, and that the same Ṛṣis were often both priests and warriors—enable us to comprehend the true position of Vedic Ṛṣis. For, divested of their miraculous and legendary character, what do these traditions indicate ? They indicate that the venerable families of the olden times—like those of the Vasiṣṭhas, the Viśvāmitras, the Aṅgirases and the Kaṇvas—furnished renowned warriors and eminent priests at the same time. A Percy or a Douglas might be an ambitious priest or a fiery warrior, and so might a Kaṇva or an Aṅgiras. To be sure, the Hindu houses were pre-eminently priestly as the European houses were military, but *caste* was as unknown to the one as to the other. Many a baron of medieval Europe whose name is still preserved in the history of the crusades, had his father or uncle, son or nephew, immured in the solitude of holy monasteries; and many a Vasiṣṭha or Viśvāmitra, whose religious hymns we still cherish and revere, had his son or nephew, engaged in the wars of the Vedic Period; in the unending contests against the aborigines of the soil. These, facts are proved by the texts of the Ṛg Veda itself which we have quoted in a previous chapter; and they are confirmed by the legends and traditions which we have quoted in this chapter from later Sanscrit literature. The Vedic Ṛṣis composed their hymns, fought their wars, and ploughed, their fields; but were neither Brāhmans, nor Kṣatriyas, nor Vaiśyas. The great Ṛṣi houses of the Vedic Age furnished priests and soldiers, but were no more Brāhmans or Kṣatriyas than the Percies or Douglases of medieval Europe were Brāhmans or Kṣatriyas.

BOOK II

EPIC PERIOD

(B.C. 1400 to 1000)

CHAPTER – 1

LITERATURE OF THE PERIOD

We have closed our account of the Vedic Age, when the Hindu Āryans crossed the Indus and gradually conquered and occupied the whole tract of country watered by the Indus and its five tributaries. We have seen that the sole work of this period which remains to us is the collection of hymns known as the Ṛg Veda Saṁhitā, and we have also seen how these hymns illustrate the civilization of the Vedic Period. We now proceed to describe the civilization of the Epic Period, when the Hindus crossed the Sutlej, moved down the basin of the Ganges and the Jumnā, and founded powerful kingdoms along the entire valley as far down as modern Benares and North Behar. And as in the case of the Vedic Age, so in the case of the Epic Age, we will base our account on contemporaneous literature.

What is the contemporaneous literature of the Epic Age ? And what is the contemporaneous literature of the Philosophical or Rationalistic Age that followed ? The Brāhmaṇas, the Āraṇyakas, and the Upaniṣads which constantly refer to the actions of the Kurus, the Pāñcālas, the Kosalas, and the Videhas *living in the valley of the Ganges,* form the literature of the Epic Age. The Sūtras which presuppose the rise of rationalism in India, and which were composed when the Āryans *had expanded all over Southern India,* form the literature of the Rationalistic Age.

About thirty years ago Professor Max Müller published his great work on Sanskrit literature and gave reasons, which have since generally been accepted for considering the mass of Sūtra literature as subsequent to the Brāhmaṇa literature. He shewed that the Sūtra literature presupposed and quoted the Brāhmaṇa literature, and the converse was never the case. He shewed that the Brāhmaṇa literature reflected an age of priestly supremacy and unquestioning obedience on the part of the people, which was anterior to the practical and philosophical and sceptical age of the Sūtras. He shewed that the Brāhmaṇa literature down to the Upaniṣads was considered *revealed* in India, while all Sūtra works were ascribed to human authors. And he enforced these and similar arguments by a wealth of illustrations and a degree of erudition which left nothing to be desired.[1]

It is needless to say that we cannot enter into the details of these learned discussions. True to the plan of the present work, we will make only a few remarks not on the *literary,* but on the *historical* bearings of the facts stated above. What is the *historical* import of this sequence in the different glasses of Ancient Sanskrit literature ? What is the *historical* reason of this sequence ? Why did the Ancient Hindus compose their works in one particular form, the Vedic hymns, for a number of centuries ? Why did they gradually abandon that style of composition, and write the prolix and dogmatic prose Brāhmaṇas, for some succeeding centuries ? And why again did they gradually change this for the concise aphorisms of the Sūtras during the next few centuries ? What is there in the nature of things that would induce the Ancient Hindus to take up different styles of composition at different periods of their history—as if to afford the future historian a clue to the dates of their writings ?

The question is more easily asked than answered. It may be answered, however, by a counter question. What is there in the nature of things which prevented the Chronicles and Romances of Medieval Europe being composed after the 14th and 15th centuries? Why did not Humes and Gibbon compose Chronicles? Why did not Fielding and Scott compose Medieval Romances ? The subjects were still the same—why was the composition so different that it would be possible to demarcate the feudal ages from the modern period on the testimony of European literature, even if every vestige of European history was destroyed ?

An Englishman would answer : it was impossible that Chronicles and feudal Romances should be continued after Elizabeth had reigned and Shakespeare and Bacon had written. A new light had dawned on Europe. The human mind had expanded. Religion was purified. A new world had been discovered. Modern philosophy had taken its rise. Commerce and maritime enterprise had received a wonderful development. Feudalism had died a natural death. The face of the European world had been changed.

Were it possible to bring before the reader the history of Hindu civilization as vividly as he has before him the history of European civilization, he would give similar replies with regard to the epochs of Indian History. It was impossible, in the nature of things, that hymns like those of the Ṛg Veda should be composed after the Hindus had achieved the elaborate civilization and adopted the pompous religious rites of the Epic Period. The simple fervency with which the Punjab Āryans looked up to the Sky, the Dawn, or the Sun had passed, once and for ever. Simple natural phenomena did not excite the wonder and religious admiration of the cultured and somewhat artificial Gangetic Āryans engaged in solemn rites and pompous sacrifices. The fervent prayer to the rain god Indra, or the loving address to the blushing goddess Uṣas (Dawn) was almost impossible. The very import and object of the old simple hymns were forgotten, and sacrifices of various descriptions, from the simple morning and evening libations, to the elaborate royal sacrifices lasting for many years, formed the essence of the later religion. The rules of the sacrifices, the import and object of every minute rite, the regulations for each insignificant observance—these occupied the religious minds of the people, these formed the subject of discussions between learned kings and royal priests, these formed the bulk of the Brāhmaṇa literature. It was as impossible for the cultured writers and thinkers of the day to go back to the buried past and disinter the simple faith of the Vedic Hymns, as it was impossible for the erudite schoolmen of Medieval Europe to produce the wild and simple Norwegian Sagas of a bygone age.

Again, the elaborate and dogmatic trifling of the scholastic philosophy of Europe was impossible after Descartes had lived and Bacon had written. In the same way, and for the same reason, the elaborate trifling and priestly pedantry of the Brāhmaṇas was impossible in the Hindu world after Kapila had taught and Gautama Buddha had preached. The human mind in India had received a new impetus. A new world had been discovered beyond the Vindhya range, though the name of the Indian Columbus, who first planted the Hindu flag in a southern kingdom, is forgotten. The earnest and fervent Upaniṣads had been written and marked a strong reaction against priestly pedantry. Kapila—the Descartes of India—had startled the Hindu world by his Sāṅkhya philosophy; and Gautama—the Luther of India—had proclaimed a reformed faith for the poor and the lowly, and protested against the privileges of priests. New sciences had started into existence. A new light had dawned in the Hindu world.

The Brāhmaṇa literature died a natural death. The elaborate and unmeaning dogmas were left in the shade; the rules for the performance of the ancient sacrifices were condensed for practical purposes. It was a practical age when everything was condensed and codified. The rules of life were codified. Philosophy was condensed into aphorisms, science and learning in every department were condensed. Treatises were composed in every branch of human knowledge in a concise style, in which teachers could teach and learners could learn by rote. And thus it is that we have the entire literature of Rationalistic Age in the shape of aphorisms— or Sūtras.

This is the historical import of the three different classes of Ancient Sanskrit literature, which represent three distinct epochs of Hindu history. The hymns reflect the manly simplicity of the Vedic Age. The Brāhmaṇas reflect the pompous ceremonials of the Epic Age. The Sūtras reflect the science and learning, and even the scepticism of the Rationalistic Age.

We have said before that the tide of Hindu colonization rolled eastward and southward in each successive period, and the different classes of Sanskrit literature spoken of above attest to this onward movement. In Europe feudal literature and modern literature were developed on the same arena, in Italy and Germany, in France and England. In India, the case was different. For the Āryans of India went on conquering through successive periods, and the literature of each period speaks of the portion of India under the Āryan influence and domination in that particular period. This in itself is an invaluable index to the dates of the different classes of literature. The hymns of the Ṛg Veda speak of the Punjab and Cabul alone,—India beyond the Punjab is unknown to the Ṛg Veda. The banks of the distant Ganges and the Jumnā are rarely alluded to; the scene of all the wars and social ceremonies and religious sacrifices of the Ṛg Veda are the banks of the Indus and its tributaries and the Sarasvatī. This was the Hindu world when the hymns were composed.

But the Hindus soon threw out colonies all over Northern India. In course of centuries these colonies rose into importance and formed powerful kingdoms, and by their progress and learning threw the mother-country, the Punjab, into shade. In the Brāhmaṇas we bear of the mighty Kurus in the tract of the country round modern Delhi; we hear of the powerful Pāñcālas in the country round modern Kanouj; we read of the Videhas in the country now known as North Behar, we read of the Kosalas in Oude, and we read of the Kāsis in the country round modern Benares. These colonists developed pompous sacrificial rites, had illustrious and learned courts like those of Janaka and Ajātaśatru and Janamejaya Parīkṣita, they founded schools or pariṣads in villages and towns, and they developed a new social system based on caste distinctions. It is of these colonists and their civilization that we mostly read in the Brāhmaṇas—the Punjabis almost forgotten, and Southern India is still unknown, or is referred to as the home of wild beasts and wild men.

On the other hand, the Sūtra literature makes us familiar with great Hindu kingdoms in Southern India, and some of the existing Sūtras were composed in Southern India, and lay down rules for the conduct of Southern Hindus.

We have spoken of the Vedic period and the Ṛg Veda

Hymns in the First Book of this work. We will speak of the Epic period and the Brāhmaṇa literature in this Second Book. And we will speak of the Rationalistic Period and the Sūtra literature in the Third Book.

We have seen before that the Ṛg Veda Hymns were *composed* in the Vedic Age and were finally *compiled* in the Epic Age. The other three Vedas known as the Sāma Veda, the Yajur Veda (White and Black), and the Atharva Veda, were also compiled in this Epic Age.

The reasons which led to the compilation of the Sāma Veda and the Yajur Veda have been ascertained with a fair degree of certainty. We find mention in the hymhs of the Ṛg Veda of different classes of priests who performed different duties at sacrifices. The Adhvaryus were entrusted with the material performance of sacrifice. They measured the ground, built the altar, prepared the sacrificial vessels, fetched wood and water, and immolated animals. The Udgātṛs on the other hand were entrusted with the duty of singing, as according to ancient custom, some parts of the sacrifice had to be accompanied by songs. The Hotris had to recite hymns. And lastly, the Brāhmans presided at sacrifices over all the rest.

Of these four classes of priests, neither the Brāhman nor the Hotri required any special manual. For the Brahmān was required to know the entire ceremonial, to be able to superintend the performance of the sacrifice, to advise the other priests on doubtful points, and to correct their mistakes. The Hotri, too, had simply to recite, and if he knew the hymns of the Ṛg Veda, he did not require any separate compilation. But the duties of the Adhvaryu and the Udgātṛ required special training. Special sacrificial formulas must have existed for the former, and a stock of the Ṛg Veda Hymns, set to music, must have also existed for the latter in the Vedic Period, for we find the names Yajus and Sāman in the Ṛg Veda Hymns. These formulas and chants were however separately collected and compiled at a later age in the Epic Period; and these separate compilations, in the shape which they last took, are the Yajur Veda and the Sāma Veda as we have them now.

No name has been handed down to us as the compiler of the Sāma Veda, Professor Benfey has pointed out, what Dr. Stevenson previously suspected, that all the verses of the Sāma Veda, with the exception of a few, are to be found in the Ṛg Veda; and it is supposed that these few verses, too, must have been contained in some other recension of the Ṛg Veda now lost to us. It is quite clear, therefore, that the Sāma Veda is only a selection from the Ṛg Veda set to music for a special purpose.

Of the compilers of Yajur Veda, we have some information. The more ancient or Black Yajur Veda is called the Taittiriyā Saṁhitā from Tittiri, who probably compiled or promulgated it in its present shape. In the Anukramaṇī of the Aitreya recension of this Veda, however, we are told that the Veda was handed down by Vaiśampāyana to Yāska Paingi, by Yāska to Tittiri, by Tittiri to Ukha, and by Ukha to Ātreya. This would shew that the existing oldest recension of the Yajur Veda was not the first recension.

We have fuller information with regard to the more recent White Yajur Veda, It is called the Vājasaneyi Saṁhitā, from Yājñavalkya Vajasaneya, the compiler or promulgator of that Veda. Yājñavalkya held the influential position of chief priest in the court of Janaka, king of the Videhas, and the promulgation of this new Veda proceeded probably from the court of that learned king.

There is a striking difference in arrangement between the White Yajur Veda and the Black Yajur Veda. In the latter, the sacrificial formulas are followed by dogmatic explanation, and by accounts of ceremonials belonging to them, In the former, the formulas only find place in the Saṁhitā, the explanation and the ritual being assigned to the Brāhmaṇa. It it not improbable, as has been supposed, that it was to improve the old arrangement, and to separate the exegetic matter from the formulas, that Yājñavalkya, of the court of Janaka, founded the new school known as the Vājasaneyins, and that their labors resulted in a new (Vāyasaneyi) Saṁhitā and an entirely separate (Śatapatha) Brāhmaṇa. But although the promulgation of the White Yajur Veda is ascribed to Yājñavalkya, a glance at its contents will show that it is not the compilation of any one man or even of one age. Of its 40 chapters only the first 18 are cited in full and explained in due order in the first nine books of the Śatapatha Brāhmaṇa; and it is the formulas of these 18 chapters only which are found in the older Black Yajur Veda. These 18 chapters, then, are the oldest portion of the White Yajur Veda, and may have been compiled or promulgated by Yājñavalkya Vājasaneya. The next 7 chapters are very likely a later addition. The retraining 15 chapters are undoubtedly a still later addition, and are expressly called Pariśiṣṭā or Khila, *i.e.,* supplement.

Of the Atharva Veda, we need only state that it was not generally recognised as a Veda till long after the period of which we are speaking, though a class of literature known as the Atharvāṅgiras was growing up during the Epic Period, and is alluded to in the later portions of some of the Brāhmaṇas. Throughout the first three Periods of Hindu history, and even in Manu and other metrical codes, three Vedas are generally recognised. And although the claims of the Atharvan were sometimes put forward, still the work was not generally recognised as a fourth Veda till long after the Christian era. Hundreds of passages recognising three Vedas only could be cited from the literature of the period of which we are now speaking; but we are unable to make room for such passages. We will only refer our readers to a few passages, *viz.,* Aitareya Brāhmaṇa V, 32; Śatapatha Brāhmaṇa IV, 6, 7,; Aitareya Āraṇyaka III, 2, 3; Brihadāraṇyaka Upaniṣad I, 5; and Chhāndogya Upaniṣad III and VII; and in this last work, after the three Vedas are named, Atharvāṅgiras is classed with Itihāsa. It is only in the Brāhmaṇa and Upaniṣads of the Atharvā Veda itself that we find a uniform recognition of this work as a Veda. For instance, it is the principal object of the Gopatha Brāhmaṇa to show the necessity of four Vedas. A carriage, we are told, does not proceed with less than four wheels, an animal cannot walk with less than four feet, nor can sacrifice be perfect with less than four Vedas! Such special pleading only proves that the fourth Veda was not yet recognised generally, even in the comparatively recent times when the Gopatha Brāhmaṇa was composed.

Atharvan and Aṅgiras are, as Professor Whitney remarks, half mythical names of ancient and venerated Indian families, and it was sought to bring the recent composition into connection with these ancient names! The Veda is divided into twenty books, and contains nearly six thousand verses, and a 6th of this is in prose. Of the remaining, one-sixth is found among the hymns of the Ṛg Veda, mostly in the tenth book. The 19th book is a kind of supplement to the previous 18, while the 20th book is made up of extracts from the Ṛg Veda.

The entire Veda principally consists of formulas intended to protect men against the baneful influences of divine powers, against diseases, noxious animals, and curses of enemies. It knows a host of "imps and hobgoblins." and offers homage to them to prevent them from doing harm. The Mantra brings from the unwilling hands of gods the favours that are wanted. The book is full of incantations calculated to procure long life or wealth or recovery from illness. It also contains invocations for good luck in journeys, in gaming, etc. These hymns resemble similar hymns in the last book of the Ṛg Veda; only as Professor Weber has pointed out, in the Ṛg Veda they are apparently additions made at the time of the compilation, while in the Atharva Veda they are the natural utterance of the present.

We must now hasten to an account of those compositions called the Brāhmaṇas, after which the literature of this Age has been named the Brāhmaṇa literature. We have seen that in the Black Yajur Veda the texts are, as a rule, followed by their dogmatic explanations. These explanations were supposed to elucidate the texts and to explain their hidden meanings, and they contained the speculations of generations of priests. A single discourse of this kind was called a Brāhmaṇa; and in later times collections or digests of such discourses were called Brāhmaṇas.

The Ṛg Veda has two Brāhmaṇas, viz., the Aitareya and the Kauṣītaki. The composition of the former is attributed to Mahidāsa Aitareya, son of Itarā, one of the many wives of a Ṛṣi. The story is given by Sāyaṇa in his introduction to the Aitareya

Brāhmaṇa. In the Kauṣītaki Brāhmaṇa, on the other hand, special regard is paid to the sage Kanṣītaka, whose authority is considered to be final. For the rest, these two Brāhmaṇas seem to be only two recensions of the same work, used by the Aitaryins and the Kauṣītakins respectively, and they agree with each other in many respects, except that the last ten chapters of the Aitareya are not found in the Kauṣītaki, and belong probably to a later age.

The Sāma Veda has the Tāṇḍya or Pañcaviṁśa Brāhmaṇa, the Ṣaḍviṁśa Brāhmaṇa, the Mantra Brāhmaṇa and the Upaniṣad. Pandit Sāmasramin has pointed out that these works, comprising 40 chapters, form the real Brāhmaṇas of the Sāma Veda.

The Black Yajur Veda or Taittirīya Saṁhitā has its Taittirīya Brāhmaṇa, and the White Yajur Veda or Vājasaneyi Saṁhitā has its voluminous Śatapatha Brāhmaṇa. We have already stated that the Śatapatha Brāhmanā is attributed to Yājñavalkya, though it is more likely the handiwork of the school he founded, as he is often quoted in the work. Nor does the work belong entirely to one school or to one age. On the contrary, as in the case of the White Yajur Veda Saṁhitā, so in the case of its Brāhmaṇa, there are reasons to think that the work belongs to different periods. The first 18 chapters of the Saṁhitā are the oldest part of the work, and the first nine books of the Brāhmaṇa, which comment on these 18 chapters, are the oldest part of the Brāhmaṇa. These nine books contain 60 chapters, and were called. Shashtipatha in the time of Patañjali, as Professor Weber has pointed out. The remaining five books with their 40 chapters are of later date than the first nine books.

Even in the first nine books Yājñavalkya is not always quoted as the final authority, His opinions are authoritative in the first five books, while the remaining four quote Śāṇḍilya. The two lines of teachers meet in their common successor Sañjiviputra (named after his mother according to the custom of the times), and it is supposed that Sañjiviputra reconciled the two schools, and finally adjusted the first nine books. Thus this famous Brāhmaṇa seems to have been first started by the school of Yājñavalkya, and the work of that school appears to have been combined with the work of the school of Śāṇḍilya; and to the nine books thus formed, five more books were added at a later age.

The Atharva Veda has its Gopatha Brāhmaṇa—a comparatively recent production—the contents of which are a medley, derived to a large extent from other sources.

Next after the Brāhmaṇas come the Āraṇyakas, which may, indeed, be considered as the last portions of the Brāhmaṇas. They are so-called, as Sāyaṇa informs us, because they had to be read in the forest, while the Brāhmaṇas were for use in sacrifices performed by householders in their homes. We scarcely meet with any allusions to retirement in forests in the Hymns of the Ṛg Veda, and forest life and retirement are undoubtedly a far later institution than sacrifices in the householder's own fireside.

The Ṛg Veda has its Kauṣītaki Āraṇyaka and its Aitareya Āraṇyaka, the latter ascribed to Mahidāsa Aitareya. The Black Yajur Veda has its Taittiriya Āraṇyaka, and the last book of the Śatapatha Brāhmaṇa is called its Āraṇyaka. The Sāma Veda and the Atharva Veda have no Āraṇyakas.

What gives these Āraṇyakas a special importance, however, is, that they are the proper depositories of those celebrated religious speculations known as the Upaniṣads. The Upaniṣads which are the best known, and which are undoubtedly ancient, are the Aitareya and the Kauṣītaki, found in the Āraṇyakas of those names, and belonging to the Ṛg Veda; the Chāndogya and the Talavakāra (or Kena) belonging to the Sāma Veda; the Vājasaneyi (or Isa) and the Bṛhadāraṇyaka belonging to the White Yajur Veda, and the Taittiriya belonging to the Black Yajur Veda. The Kaṭha, too, is said to belong to the Black Yajur Veda, but more probably belongs to the Atharva Veda, together with the Muṇḍaka and the Praśna. These ten are the ancient Upaniṣads to which Śaṅkarā chārya principally appeals in his great commentary on the Vedānta Sūtras. But once after the Upaniṣads had come to be considered sacred and authoritative works, new compositions of the class began to be added until the total number reaches 200 or more. The later Upaniṣads, which are generally known as the Atharva Upaniṣads, come down as far as the Paurāṇik times, and as Professor Weber points out, enter the lists in behalf of sectarian views, instead of being devoted to an inquiry into the nature of Brāhman or the Supreme Spirit, like the old Upaniṣads. Indeed, the later Upaniṣads come down to a period long subsequent to the Mahommedan Conquest of India, and, the idea of a universal religion which was cherished by the great Emperor Akbar finds expression in an Upaniṣad called the Allah Upaniṣad! We need hardly say that we well refer in this work only to the ten ancient Upaniṣads, and not to the later Upaniṣads.

With the Upaniṣads the Epic Period ends, and the so-called revealed literature of India ends also. Other classes of works, besides those named herein, undoubtedly existed in the Egic period, but have now been lost to us, or more frequently replaced by newer works. A fragment only of the vast literature of the Epic Period has come down to us, and the principal works which remain have been detailed above.

Of the Epics themselves, the Mahābhārata and the Rāmāyaṇa, we will speak in the next two chapters.

REFERENCES

1. Later researches have confirmed the view that not only are the Sūtras of a particular school subsequent to the Brāhmaṇas of the same school, but that the body of the Sūtra literature as a whole is subsequent to the body of the Brāhmaṇa literature. Thus to quote one instance only, Dr. Bulher, who does not altogether agree with Max Müller on this point, nevertheless points out in his introductions of the Dharma Sūtras, that those Sūtras repeatedly quote from Brāhmaṇas of different schools. He shews that the oldest Dharma Sūtra extant presupposes an Āraṇyaka of the black Yajur Veda, a Brāhmaṇa of the Sāma Veda, and even an Upaniṣad of the Atharva

Veda! He points out that Vasiṣṭha's Dharma Sūtra quotes from a Brāhmaṇa of the Ṛg Veda, an Āraṇyaka of the Black Yajur Veda and a Brāhmaṇa of the White Yajur Veda, and also mentions an Upaniṣad of the Atharva Veda. So also Baudhāyana's Dharma Sūtra quotes from the Brāhmaṇas both of the Black and the White Yajur Veda. On the other hand, no Brāhmaṇa ever quotes from any Sūtra work.

No scholar maintains that the last Brāhmaṇa work was composed before the first Sūtra work was written. But there can be little doubt on the evidence now before us, that there was a period when the *prevailing style* of writing was the prose style of the Brāhmaṇas, and that this period was followed by a period when the *prevailing style* was aphorisms or Sūtras.

CHAPTER – 2

KURUS AND PĀÑCĀLAS, B.C. 1400 To 1200.

The tide of Āryan conquests rolled onward. If the reader will refer to a map of India, he will find that from the banks of the Sutlej to the banks of the Jumnā there is not a very wide strip of country to cross. The Āryans who had colonized the whole of the Punjab were not likely to remain inactive on the banks of the Sutlej or of the Sarasvatī. Already in the Vedic Period bands of enterprising colonists had crossed those rivers and explored the distant shores of the Jumnā and the Ganges, and those noble streams, though alluded to in the hymns as on the very horizon of the Hindu world, were not unknown. In course of time the emigrants to the fertile banks of the two rivers must have swelled in number, until. the colonists founded a powerful kingdom of their own in the country near modern Delhi,—the kingdom of the Kurus.

From what part of the Punjab the Kuru colonists came, is a question still involved in obscurity. In the Aitareya Brāhmaṇa (VIII. 14,) it is stated that the Uttara Kurus and the Uttara, Mādras lived beyond the Himālaya. In later works, the Mahābhārata (I, 47, 19, etc.) and the Rāmāyaṇa (IV, 44, 88, etc.), the land of the Uttara Kurus, has already become a mythical country. Uttara Kuru is identified with Ottorakorra of Ptolemy, and Lassen places the country somewhere east of modern Kashgar; but we would place the Uttara Kuru alluded to in the Aitareya Brāhmaṇa somewhere north of the Sub-Himalayan range, *i.e.*, in Kashmir, the Ṛg Veda itself, we find mention of the Kuru-Kriviz; and Professor Zimmer supposes that they lived in the valleys of Kashmir. There are reasons, therefore, for supposing that the Kurus originally lived among the hills in the extreme north of the Punjab; and that large numbers of this tribe moved southwards until they formed a powerful colony or kingdom between the Jumnā and the Ganges. We assume that this kingdom rose to prowess and fame about 1400 B..C,

When the Hindus had once beġun to colonize the fertile banks of the Jumnā and the Ganges, swarms of the colonists would naturally march down the course of those streams and soon occupy the whole of the Doab, *i.e.,* the tract of country between those rivers. And this was what they did. While we find the Kurus settling down in the country near modern Delhi, we find another adventurous tribe, the Pāñcālas occupying the tract of country near modern Kanouj. The original seat of the Pāñcālas is still less known than that of the Kurus. Professor Zimmer thinks that they also came from the northern hills like the Kurus. Indeed, it has been supposed that the allied tribes known in the Ṛg Veda as the Kuru-Kriviz were the ancestors of the allied tribes of the Doab, known as the Kuru Pāñcālas. The Pāñcāla kingdom probably rose to distinction about the same timers the kingdom of the Kurus, and the Brāhmaṇa literature frequently refers to these allied tribes as forming the very centre of the Hindu world, and renowned by their valour, their learning, and their civilization. Many of the Brāhmaṇas allude to the culture of their schools (Pariṣads), the sanctity of their priests, the ostentatious religious sacrifices of their kings, and the exemplary lives of the people.

For centuries had elapsed, since the Āryans had first settled on the banks of the Indus, and the centuries had done their work in progress and civilization. The Kurus and the Pāñcālas were no longer like the warrior-cultivators who battled against the black aborigines and won the banks of the Indus and its tributaries. Manners had changed, society had be come more refined and polished, learning and arts had made considerable progress. Kings invited wise men in their polished courts, held learned controversies with their priests, performed elaborate sacrifices according to the dictates of religion, led respectable and trained armies to the field, appointed duly qualified men to collect taxes and to administer justice, and performed all the duties of civilized administrators. The relations and friends of the king and all the warriors of the nation learnt archery and riding and driving the war chariot from their early youth, and also learned the Vedas and all the holy learning that was handed down from generation to generation. The priests multiplied religious rites and observances, preserved the traditional learning of the land, and instructed and helped the people in their religious duties. And the people lived in their towns and villages, cherished the sacred sacrificial fire in their houses, cultivated the arts of peace, trained their boys from early youth in the Vedas and in their social and religious duties, and gradually developed those social customs which in India have the force of laws. Women had their legitimate influence in society, and moved without restriction or restraint. Society in India, fourteen hundred years before Christ, was more polished and refined than that of the preceding Vedic Age, and had more of healthy life and vigour than Hindu society has had in succeeding ages.

Civilization, however, does not necessarily put a stop to wars and dissensions; and of the political history of the Kurus and the Pāñcālas, the only reminiscences we possess are those of a sanguinary war in which many neighbouring tribes took part, and which form the subject of one of the two great epics of India. There is a passage in the 13th book of the Śatapatha Brāhmaṇa, in which Bharata the son of Duḥṣḥanta and Śakuntalā, Dhṛtarāṣṭra the king of the Kāsis, and Janamejaya Pārikṣita and his three brothers Bhīmasena, Ugrasena and Śrautasena are named, *and these last are absolved by a horse-sacrifice from all guilt, all Brahmāhatyā.* Again, in the 14th Book we find an account of a discussion between Yājñavalkya and his rivals in Janaka's court, and one of the questions put to Yājñavalkya by one of his rivals is, "*Whither have the Pārikṣitas gone ? "and Yājñavalkya answers, "Thither where all Aśvamedha Sacrificers go?*

Professor Weber's remarks on these passages are worthy of reflection. He says : "The Pārikṣitas must at that time have been altogether extinct. Yet their life and end must have been still fresh in the memory of the people, and a subject of general curiosity. It almost seems as though their guilt, their *Brahmāhatyā* had been too great for the people to believe that it could have been atoned for by sacrifices, were they ever so holy."[1]

On the whole, Professor Weber adopts Lassen's view that there was a destructive conflict between the Kurus and the Pāñcālas, and that this feud is the leading and central fact round which the stories of the great epic Mahābhārata have since grown. Professor Weber further maintains that this war must have taken place after the Śatapatha Brāhmaṇa had been commenced, and before the final books of that work were written. For in the earlier books of the Brāhmaṇa, "we find the Kurus and the Pāñcālas still in full prosperity, and also united in the closest bonds of friendship as one people. Consequently, this internecine strife cannot have taken place. On the other hand, in the latest portions of the Brāhmaṇa, we find the prosperity, the sin, the expiation, and the fall of Janamejaya Pārikṣita and his brothers Bhīmasena, Ugrasena and Śrautasena, and of the whole family of the Pārikṣitas, apparently still fresh in the memory of the people and discussed as a subject of controversy."[2]

Without assenting to the inference that the Śatapatha Brāhmaṇa was commenced before the war, we think there can be little doubt as to the war itself in which the Kurus, the Pāñcālas, and other races were engaged. There can be as little doubt that this war was the subject of the Mahābhārata in its original shape, and that this original Mahābhārata began to be composed within a few centuries after the war, probably within the Epic Period. The name of Mahābhārata occurs in Āśvalāyana's Gṛhya Sūtra, and scholars like Max Müller, Goldstucker, and Weber agree in maintaining that the original Mahābhārata existed in Āśvalāyana's time, *i.e.,* in the Rationalistic Age which immediately followed the Epic Period.

What a historical treasure, what an invaluable record of the manners and customs and annals of the Epic Period we have lost in that original Epic of India. Where is the Indian historian who would not willingly sacrifice one-half of the voluminous later literature of the Paurāṇik Period to get this single work back again in its integrity ? But this may not be. Every later poet and editor has contributed his mite towards enlarging, altering and distorting the ancient epic; every new sect has been careful to incorporate its new-fangled tenets in this national work; and Kṛṣṇa-worship, which is of later origin, has been bodily transplanted into the ancient narrative of the Kuru-Pāñcāla war !

As a historical narrative of the principal incidents of the war, the present epic is utterly valueless. For the events and incidents have been changed, and the names of the heroes are later interpolations. The very geography of the ancient work has been changed. Sahadeva in the existing epic travels as far south as Mysore and Ceylon, which countries it is needless to state were unknown to the Hindus at the time when the war was waged.

The heroes of the existing epic are the five sons of Pāṇḍu, called the Pāṇḍavas, and these heroes are myths and later interpolations. The literature of the time which makes frequent mention of Janamejaya Pārikṣita and numerous other kings of the time, has not a word to say about the Pāṇḍavas who are entirely unknown to Ancient Sanskrit literature! In the Buddhist work, Lalita Vistāra, the Pāṇḍavas are described as a wild mountain tribe; but if so, how do they come to be enrolled as heroes in a war among Āryan nations ? We will not try to conjecture an answer.

The five heroes of the existing epic are myths pure and simple. Yudhiṣṭhira, the eldest, represents virtue. Bhīma, the second, represents untrained valour; Arjuna, the third, represents skill in war; and the other two brothers similarly represent distinct qualities. It is remarkable that in the Epic Period, when the war took place, Arjuna was still a name of Indra, and Indra's Vedic combats with the rain cloud have thus been mixed up with the facts of a historical war! To take one more instance, Janamejaya Pārikṣita was, according to contemporaneous testimony, himself stained with the guilt of the war. In the modern epic, Janamejaya is the great grandson of Arjuna who was engaged in the war.

And if the heroes of the modern epic are mythical, the heroine is still more so. Draupadī the daughter of the king of the Pāñcālas, marries the Pāṇḍavas in the modern epic—yes, marries all five of them! And yet polyandry was not only unknown to the Hindus at the time of the Kurus and the Pāñcālas, but that barbarous custom was not known to the Indo-Āryans in any age or period within the four thousand years of their history. We know enough of the manners of the polished court of the Pāñcālas to be able boldly to assert that the king of that race would not have given his daughter to *five husbands,* to save his empire or even his head! Draupadi is only a myth, or perhaps an allegory representing the alliance of the Pāñcāla king with the Pāṇḍava tribe or party.

Thus the existing epic is utterly valueless as a record of the incidents and characters of the real war. Nevertheless this work, so changed and altered, has a unique value as a record of the manners and civilization of the ancient time. The generations of authors who have tampered with this ancient epic, who have been assiduous in altering characters and incidents, in preaching new cults and amassing ancient and modern legends, have not had the time or the motive to wipe out many a lifelike picture of the manners of the Kurus and the Pāñcālas which has been preserved to us. We still see in this venerable volume how the Hindus lived and fought, acted and felt, three thousand years ago. We find how young princes were early trained to arms, and how Kuru mothers and sisters and wives came out in public and witnessed with pride the tournaments in which their sons and brothers and husbands distinguished themselves! We find how girls married at an advanced age, and princesses famed for their beauty often selected their husbands among the princes who came to seek their hands. We find how jealousies among kings broke out into sanguinary wars, and how the bitterness of such feuds was restrained by the laws of chivalry. Victors in such wars performed the great horse-sacrifice, and all the princes of the Hindu world were invited to those grand imperial festivities.

It is because the story of the existing epic throws such valuable side lights on the state of the society of the ancient Hindus that we think it necessary to briefly narrate it here. Let the reader attach no value to the names which are mostly myths, or to the incidents which are mostly imaginary; let him only endeavour to draw from it a picture of Hindu life in the Epic Period, *i.e.,* the period of Āryan expansion in the Gangetic Valley.

The capital of the Kurus at the time of which we are speaking was the city of Hastināpura, the supposed ruins of which have been discovered on the upper course of the Ganges about 65 miles to the north-east of Delhi. Śāntanu, the old king of Hastināpura, died, leaving two sons, Bhīṣma who had taken a vow of celebacy, and a younger prince who became king. This young prince died in his turn, leaving two sons, Dhṛtarāṣṭra the blind, and Pāṇḍu who ascended the throne.

Pāṇḍu died, leaving five sons who are the heroes of the epic. Dhṛtarāṣṭra remained virtually the king during the minority of the five Pāṇḍavas and of his own children, while Dhṛtarāṣṭra's uncle Bhīṣma, a renowned warrior, remained the chief councillor and friend of the state.

The account of the training of the young Pāṇḍavas and the sons of Dhṛtarāṣṭra to arms throws much light on the manners of royal houses. Droṇa was a Brāhman, and a renowned warrior, for caste had not yet completely formed itself, Kṣatriyas had not yet obtained the monopoly of the use of arms, nor Brāhmans of religious learning. He had been insulted by his former friend the king of the Pāñcālas, and had retired in disgust to the court of the Kurus and undertook to train the princes in arms.

Yudhiṣṭhira, the eldest of the Pāṇḍavas, never became much of a warrior, but became versed in the religious learning of the age, and is the most righteous character in the epic. Bhīma the second, learnt to use the club, and was renowned for his gigantic size and giant strength, and is indeed the Hercules of the poem. The third Pāṇḍava, Arjuna, excelled all other princes in the skill of arms, and aroused the jealousy and hatred of the sons of Dhṛtarāṣṭra, even in their boyhood. Nakula, the fourth, learned to tame horses, and Sahadeva became proficient in astronomy. Duryodhana, the eldest son of Dhṛtarāṣṭra, was proficient in the use of the club, and was a rival to Bhīma.

At last the day came for a public exhibition of the proficiency which the princes had acquired in the use of arms. A spacious area was enclosed. Seats were arranged all round for the accommodation of ancient warriors and chieftains, of ladies and courtiers. The whole population of Kuruland flocked to see the skill of their young princes. The blind king Dhṛtarāṣṭra was led to his seat; and foremost among the ladies were Gāndhāri, the queea of Dhṛtarāṣṭra, and Kuntī, the mother of the first three Pāṇḍavas. The last two were Pāṇḍu's sons by another wife.

There was shooting of arrows at a butt, and there were fights with swords and bucklers and clubs. Duryodhana and Bhīma soon began to fight in right earnest, and rushed towards each other like mad elephants. Shouts ascended to the sky, and soon the fight threatened to have a tragic end. At last the infuriated young men were parted, and peace was restored.

Then the young Arjuna entered the lists in golden mail, with his wondrous bow. His splendid archery surprised his most passionate admirers and thrilled the heart of his mother with joy, while shouts of admiration rose from the multitude like the roar of the ocean. He played with his sword which flashed like lightning, and also with his sharp-edged quoit or chakra and never missed his mark. Lastly, he brought down horses and deer to the ground by his noose, and concluded by doing obeisance to his worthy preceptor Droṇa, amidst the ringing cheers of the assembled multitude.

The dark cloud of jealousy lowered on the brow of Dhritarāṣṭra's sons, and soon they brought to the field an unknown warrior Karṇa, who was a match for Arjuna in archery. Kings' sons could only fight with their peers like the knights of old, and Duryodhana therefore knighted the unknown warrior, or rather made him a king, on the spot, so that Arjuna might have no excuse for declining the fight. To awkward questions which were put to him, the haughty Karṇa replied that rivers and Warriors knew not of their origin and birth—their prowess was their geneology. But the Pāṇḍavas declined the fight, and the haughty Karṇa retired in silence and in rage.

Droṇa now demanded the reward of his tuition. Like doughty warriors of old he held revenge to be the dearest joy of a warrior, and for his reward he asked the help of the Kurus to be revenged on Drupada, king of the Pāñcālas, who had insulted him. The demand could not be refused. Droṇa marched against Drupada, conquered him and wrested half his kingdom. Drupada swore to be avenged.

Dark clouds now arose on the horizon of Kuru land. The time had come for Dhṛtarāṣṭra to name a Yuvarāja,—or a prince who would reign during his old age. The claim of Yudhiṣṭhira to the throne of his father could not be gainsaid, and he was appointed Yuvarāja. But the proud Duryodhana rebelled against the arrangement, and the old monarch had to yield, and sent the five Pāṇḍavas in exile to Vāraṇāvata, said to be the modern Allahabad, and then the very frontier of Hindu settlements, The vengeance of Duryodhana pursued them there, and the house where the Pāṇḍavas lived was burnt to ashes. The Pāṇḍavas and their mother escaped by an underground passage, and for a long time roamed about disguised as Brāhmans.

Heralds now went from country to country, and proclaimed in all lands that the daughter of Drupada, king of the Pāñcālas, was to choose for herself a husband among the most skilful warriors of the time. As usual on such occasions of *Svayamvara,* or self-choice of a husband by a princess, all the great kings and princes and warriors of the land flocked to the court of Drupada—each hoping to win the lovely bride who had already attained her youth and was renowned for her beauty. She was to give her hand to the most skilful archer, and the trial ordained was a pretty severe one. A heavy bow of great size was to be wielded, and an arrow was to be shot through a whirling chakra or quoit into the eye of a golden fish set high on the top of a pole !

Not only princes and warriors, but multitudes of spectators flocked from all parts of the country to Kāmpilya the capital of the Pāñcālas. The princes thronged the seats, and Brāhmans filled the place with Vedic Hymns. Then appeared Draupadī with the garland in her hand which she was to offer to the victor of the day. By her appeared her brother, Dhṛṣṭadyumna, who proclaimed the feat which was to be performed.

Kings rose and tried to wield the bow, one after another, but in vain. The skilful and proud Kaṇa stepped forth to do the feat, but was prevented from doing it.

A Brāhman suddenly rose and drew the bow and shot the arrow through the whirling chakra into the eye of the golden fish. A shout of acclamation arose! And Draupadī, the Kṣatriya princess, threw the garland round the neck of the brave Brāhman who led her away as bride. But murmurs of discontent arose like the sound of troubled waters from the Kṣatriya ranks at this victory of a Brāhman, and the humiliation of the warriors; and they gathered round the bride's father and threatened violence. The Pāṇḍavas now threw off their disguise, and the victor of the day proclaimed himself to be Arjuna, a true born Kṣatriya !

Then follows the strange myth that the Pāṇḍavas went back to their mother and said, a great prize had been won. Their mother, not knowing what the prize was, told her sons to share it among them. And as a mother's mandate cannot be disregarded, the five brothers wedded Draupadī as their wife. It is needless to say that the story of Draupadī herself and of the five Pāṇḍavas is an allegory. The Pāṇḍavas now formed an alliance with the powerful king of the Pāñcālas, and forced the blind king Dhṛtarāṣṭra to divide Kuru land between his sons and the Pāṇḍavas. The division, however, was unequal; the fertile tract between the Ganges and the Jumnā was retained by the sons of Dhṛtarāṣṭra, while the uncleared jungle in the west was given to the Pāṇḍavas. The jungle Khāṇḍava Prastha was soon cleared by fire, and a new capital called Indraprastha was built—the supposed ruins of which are shewn to every modern vizitor to Delhi.

Military expeditions were now undertaken by the Pāṇḍavas on all sides, but these need not detain us, specially as the accounts of these distant expeditions are very modern interpolations. The scene of action of the Kurus and the Pāñcālas was the Doab, and the country beyond the basin of the Ganges and the Jumnā was yet almost unknown to Hindus.

We do not even hear that the Kosalas and the Videhas took any active part in the Kuru-Pāñcāla war, and this shews that Oude and North Behar, if already colonized by Āryans, had not risen to power and fame. When, therefore, we find in the Mahābhārata accounts of expeditions to Ceylon, to Bengal, to Dvarika in Guzerat, we may unhesitatingly put them down as later interpolations.

And now Yudhiṣṭhira was to celebrate the Rājasūya or coronation ceremony, and all the princes of the land, including his kinsmen of Hastināpura, were invited. The place of honor was given to Kṛṣṇa, king of Dvārikā in Guzerat; but Śiśupāla of Chedi violently protested, and Kṛṣṇa killed him on the spot, The whole story of Kṛṣṇa,—a deity and a king—appears to us to be a very modern interpolation.

The tumult having subsided, the consecrated water was sprinkled on the newly-created monarch, and Brāhmans went away loaded with presents.

But the newly-created king was not long to enjoy his kingdom. With all his righteousness, Yudhiṣṭhira had a weakness for gambling, like the other chiefs of the time, and the unforgiving and jealous Duryodhana challenged him to a game. Kingdom, wealth, himself, and his brothers, and even his wife were staked and lost—and behold now, the five brothers and Draupadī the slaves of Duryodhana! The proud Draupadī refused to submit to her position, but Duhśāsana dragged her to the assembly-room by her hair, and Duryodhana forced her down on his knee in the sight of the stupified assembly. The blood of the Pāṇḍavas and the other chieftains was rising, when the old Dhṛtarāṣṭra was led to the assembly-room and stopped a tumult. It was decided that the Pāṇḍavas had lost their kingdom, but should not be slaves. They agreed to go in exile for twelve years, after which they should remain concealed for a year. If the sons of Dhṛtarāṣṭra failed to discover them during the year, they would get back their kingdom.

Thus the Pāṇḍavas again went in exile; and, after twelve years of wanderings in various places, disguised themselves in the thirteenth year and took service under the king of Virāṭa. Yudhiṣṭhira was to teach the king gambling; Bhīma was the head cook; Arjuna was to teach dancing and music to the king's daughter, Nakula and Sahadeva were to be master of horse and master of cattle respectively, and Draupadī was to be the queen's hand-maid. A difficulty arose. The queen's brother was enamoured of the new attendant of superb beauty, and insulted her and was resolved to possess her. Bhīma interfered and killed the lover in secret.

Cattle-lifting was not uncommon among the princes of those days, and the princes of Hastināpura carried away some cattle from Virāṭa. Arjuna, the dancing master, could stand this no longer, he put on his armour, drove out in a chariot, and recovered the cattle, but was discovered! The question whether the year of secret exile had quite expired was never settled.

And now the Pāṇḍavas sent an envoy to Hastināpura to claim back their kingdom. The claim was refused, and both parties prepared for a war, the like of which had never been seen in India. All the princes of note joined one side or the other, and the battle, which was fought in the plains of Kurukṣetra, north of Delhi, lasted for 18 days, and ended in fearful slaughter and carnage.

The long story of the battle with its endless episodes need not detain us, Arjuna killed the ancient Bhīṣma unfairly, after that chief was forced to desist from fighting. Droṇa, with his impenetrable "squares" or phalanxes, killed his old rival Drupada, but Drupada's son revenged his father's death and killed Droṇa unfairly, Bhīma met Duhsāsana who had insulted Draupadī in the gambling room, cut off his head, and in fierce vindictiveness drank his blood! Lastly, there was the crowning contest between Karṇa and Arjuna who had hated each other through life; and Arjuna killed Karṇa unfairly, when his chariot wheels sank into the earth, and he could not move or fight. On the last or eighteenth day, Duryodhana fled from Bhīma, but was compelled by taunts and rebukes to turn round and fight, and Bhīma by a foul blow (because struck below the waist) smashed the knee on which Duryodhana had once dragged Draupadī, And the wounded warrior was left there to die. The bloodshed was not yet over, for Droṇa's son made a midnight raid into the enemy's camp and killed Drupada's son, and thus an ancient feud was quenched in blood,

The remainder of the story is soon told. The Pāṇḍavas went to Hastināpura, and Yudhiṣṭhira became king. He is said to have subdued every king in Āryan India and at last celebrated the Aśvamedha ceremony or the Imperial horse-sacrifice. A horse was let loose and wandered at its will for a year, and no king dared to stop it, This was a sign of submission of all the surrounding kings, and they were then invited to the great horse-sacrifice. We have seen that in the Vedic times the horse was sacrificed simply for eating; in the Epic Period the horse-sacrifice became a means of expiation of sin, and of the assumption of the Imperial title.

Such is the story of the great Epic divested of its numerous legends and episodes, its supernatural incidents and digressions. Kṛṣṇa, the island-born compiler of the Vedas (not Kṛṣṇa, the king of Dvārikā), is said to have been the son of the unmarried girl who afterwards married Sāntanu. He was therefore half brother of Bhīṣma. He often appears on the scene abruptly and in a supernatural manner, and imparts instruction and advice. The story has a historical interest, and shews that the three ancient Vedas were compiled before the time of the Kuru-Pāñcāla war.

For the rest, it will appear from the above brief account that the first Hindu colonists of the Gangetic Valley had not yet lost the sturdy valour and the stubborn warlike determination of the preceding Vedic Age. Kings now ruled over larger countries and peoples, manners were more polished, the rules of social life and of chivalry were more highly developed, and the science of war itself was better organized. But nevertheless the stern and relentless determination of the Vedic warriors to quell the foe breaks through the polished manners of the Kurus and the Pāñcālas, and those nations, if they had gained in civilization, had scarcely yet lost much in the vigour of national life. How imperfectly the caste-system flourished among these sturdy races is shewn by many facts which still loom out in bold outline amidst the interpolations and additions of later writers. Sāntanu, the ancient king of Hastināpura, had a brother Devapi, who was a priest. The most learned character in the epic, Yudhiṣṭhira, is a Kṣatriya, and the most skilful warrior, Droṇa, is a Brāhman. And the venerable compiler of the Vedas, Kṛṣṇa Dvaipāyana himself—was he a Brāhman or a Kṣatriya ?

REFERENCES

1. *Indian Literature* (translation), p. 126.
2. *Ibid*, p. 135.

CHAPTER – 3

VIDEHAS, KOSALAS AND KĀSĪS B.C. 1200 To B. C. 1000

The tide of Āryan conquests rolled onward. Soon after the country between the Jumnā and the Ganges had been completely conquered, peopled and Hinduized, new bands of adventurous settlers crossed the Ganges and marched further eastwards to found new colonies and new Hindu kingdoms. Stream after stream was crossed, forest after forest was explored and cleared, region after region was slowly conquered, peopled and Hinduized in this onward march towards the unknown east. The history of the long struggles and the gradual development of the Hindu power in these regions has been lost to us; and we only see, in the literature which has been preserved, the establishment of powerful and civilized Hindu kingdoms east of the Ganges—the kingdom of the Kosalas in the country known as modern Oude, of the Videhas in North Behar, and of the Kāsīts in the country round modern Benares.

Some recollections of this eastern march has been preserved in stray passages, and attention was directed many years ago by Professor Weber to one such passage in the Śatapatha Brāhmaṇa.

"10. Mādhava the Videgha carried Agni Vaiśvānara in his mouth. The Ṛṣi Goṭama Rāhūgana was his family priest. When addressed (by the latter) he made no answer fearing lest Agni might fall from his mouth.

"13. Still he did not answer. (The priest continued) : 'Thee O butter sprinkled one, we invoke !' (Ṛg Veda V, 26, 2.) So much he uttered when, at the very mentioning of butter, Agni

Vaiśvānara flashed forth from the king's mouth; he was unable to hold him back; he issued from his mouth and fell down on this earth.

"14. Mādhava the Videgha was at that time on the (river) Sarasvatī. He (Agni) thence went burning along this earth towards the east; and Gotama Rāhūgana and the Videgha Mādhava followed after him as he was burning along. He burnt over (dried up) all these rivers. Now that (river) which is called Sadānīra (Gunduck river) flows from the northern (Himālaya) mountain : that one he did not burn over. That one the Brāhmans did not cross in former times, thinking it has not been burnt over by Agni Vaiśvānara.

"15. Now-a-days, however, there are many Brāhmans to the east of it. At that time it (the land east of the Sadānīra) was very uncultivated, very marshy, because it had not been tasted by Agni Vaiśvānara.

"16. Now-a-days, however, it is very cultivated, for the Brāhmans have caused (Agni) to taste it through sacrifices. Even in late summer that (river), as it were rages along; so cold it is, not having been burnt over by Agni Vaiśvānara.

"17. Mādhava the Videgha then said (to Agni), Where I am to abide ?' To the east of this (river) be thy abode!' said he. Even now this river forms the boundary of the Kosalas and Videhas; for these are the Mādhavas (or descendants of Mādhava)." (Śatapatha Brāhmaṇa, I, 4, 1.)

Here then we have an account, in a legendary form, of the gradual march of the colonists from the banks of the Sarasvatī eastwards until they came to the Gunduck. That river formed the boundary between the two kingdoms; the Kosalas lived to the west of it, and the Videhas to the east of it.

In course of years, probably of centuries, the kingdom of the Videhas rose in power and in civilization, until it became the most prominent kingdom in Northern India.

Janaka, king of the Videhas, is probably the most prominent figure in the history of the Epic Period in India! That monarch had not only established his power in the farthest confines of the Hindu dominions in India, but he gathered round him the most learned men of his time; he entered into discussion with them, and instructed them in holy truths about the Universal Being. It is this that has surrounded the name of Janaka with undying glory. King Ajātaśatru of the Kāsīs, himself a learned man and a most renowned patron of learning, exclaimed in despair, "Verily, all people run away, saying, Janaka is our patron!" (Bṛhadāraṇyaka Upaniṣad, II, 1, 1.)

The great fame of Janaka is partly owing to the culture and learning of the chief priest of his court Yājñavalkya Vājasaneyin. Under the royal auspices of Janaka this priest probably conceived the bold conception of revising the Yajur Veda as it then existed, of separating the formulas from the exegetic matter, of condensing the former in the shape of a new Yajur Veda (the White Yajur Veda known as the Vajasaneyi Veda). and of amplifying the latter into a vast body of Brāhmaṇa known as the Śatapatha Brāhmaṇa, Generations of priests laboured at this stupendous work, but the glory of starting the work belongs to the founder of the school, Yājñavalkya Vājasaneyin and his learned patron, King Janaka of the Videhas.

But Janaka has a still higher claim to our respect and admiration. While the priestly caste was still multiplying rituals and supplying dogmatic and ridiculous explanations for each rite, the royal caste seems to have felt some impatience at priestly supremacy and pedantry, and also at the ridiculous dogmas which were so authoritatively preached. Thinking, and earnest Kṣatriyas must have asked themselves if these rites and dogmas were all that religion could teach. Learned Kṣatriyas, while still conforming to the rites laid down by priests, gave a start to healthier speculations, and inquired about the destination of the human soul and the nature of the Supreme Being. So bold, so healthy and vigorous were these new and earnest speculations, that the priestly classes, who were wise in their own esteem, at last felt their inferiority, and came to Kṣatriyas to learn something of the wisdom of the new school. The Upaniṣads contain the healthy and earnest speculations which were started at the close of the Epic Period; and King Janaka of Videha is honored and Inspected—more than any other king of the time—as an originator of the earnest speculations of the Upaniṣads.

The teaching of the Upaniṣads will be dwelt on more fully in a subsequent chapter of this book, but an account of Janaka and of the other kings of the period and their place in Hindu literature, will not be complete unless we cite a few passages here, illustrating their relations with their priests, and their labours in the cause of earnest philosophical speculations in India.

"Janaka of Videha once met some Brāhmans who had just arrived. They were Śvetaketu Āruṇeya, Somasuṣma Satyayajñi and Yājñavalkya. He said to them : 'How do you perform the Agnihotra ?' "

The three Brāhmans replied as best they could; but not correctly. Yājñavalka came very near the mark, but was not quite correct. Janaka told them so, and mounted his car and went away !

The priests said : "This fellow of a Rājanya has insulted us." Yājñavalkya mounted his car, followed the king, and had the difficulty explained. (Śatapatha Brāhmaṇa, XI, 4, 5.)

We find in Chāndogya Upaniṣad, V, 3, that one of the three Brāhmans named above, Śvetaketu Āruṇeya came to an assembly of the Pāñcālas, and Pravāhana Jaivali, a Kṣatriya, asked him some questions which puzzled him. He came back sorrowful to his father and said : "That fellow of a Rājanya asked me five questions, and I could not answer one of them." father, Gautama, was himself puzzled and went to the Kṣatriya to have his difficulty removed. Pravāhana Jaivali replied : "Gautama, this knowledge did not go to any Brāhman before you, and therefore this teaching belonged in all the worlds to the Kṣatra class alone." And then he imparted the knowledge to Gautama,

In another place in this Upaniṣad (I, 8,) this Pravāhana silenced two boastful Brāhmans and then imparted true knowledge of the Highest Brāhman to them.

A story is told in the Śatapatha Brāhmaṇa (X, 6, I, I), and is repeated in the Chandogya Upaniṣad (V, II) that five Brāhman householders and theologians became anxious to know, What is our Self and what is Brahmān ? ' They came to Uddālaka Āruṇi to obtain the knowledge, but Āruṇi had his misgivings, and therefore took them to the Kṣatriya king, Aśvapati Kaikeya, who courteously invited them to stay at a sacrifice he was going to perform. He said : "In my kingdom there is no thief, no miser, no drunkard, no man without an altar in his house, no ignorant person, no adulterer, much less an adulteress. I am going to perform a sacrifice, Sirs, and as much wealth as I give to each Ṛtvik priest, I shall give to you, Sirs. Please to stay here."

They stayed and told him what they had come for, and "on the next morning they approached him, carrying fuel in their hands (like students), and he, without any preparatory rites," imparted to them the knowledge they had come for.

It is curious how we meet the same names over and over in the different Upaniṣads, and often the same story too in different forms, showing that the old recognised Upaniṣads were composed at much the same time. We find Uddālaka Āruṇi, also called Gautama and his son Śvetaketu, again in the Kauṣītaki Upaniṣad; and the father and the son went to Chitrā Gāngyāyani, fuel in hand, to learn the truth. Chitra, Kṣatriya king, said : You are worthy of Brāhman, Gautama, because you were not led away by pride. Come hither, I shall make you know clearly." (I, 1.)

A celebrated story is told in the Kauṣītaki Upaniṣad (IV), of a conversation between Gārgya Bālāki, a celebrated man of learning, and Ajātaśatru, the learned king of the Kāsīs. The boastful Brāhman challenged the king; but in course of the learned dispute which followed, he collapsed and became silent. Ajātaśatru said to him :' Thus far do you know O Bālāki ? ' 'Thus far only,' replied Bālāki. Then Ajātaśatru said to him : 'Vainly did you challenge me, saying, shall I tell you Brāhman ? ' 'O Bālāki, He who is the maker of those persons (whom you mentioned), He of whom all this is the work, He alone is to be known.

"Then Bālāki came, carrying fuel in his hand, saying : 'May I come to you as a pupil ? ' Ajātaśatru said to him : "I deem it improper that a Kṣatriya should initiate a Brāhman. Come, I will make you know clearly."

This story as well as the story of Śvetaketu Āruṇeya and the Kṣatriya King Pravāhana Jaivali are repeated in the Bṛhadāraṇyka Upaniṣad.

There are numerous such passages in the Upaniṣads in which the Kṣatriyas are represented as the wisest teachers and the boldest speculators. But it is needless to multiply instances here. What we have said is enough to indicate the place which belongs to the royal caste at the close of the Epic Period in the history of Hindu religion and philosophy. The Upaniṣads mark a new era in the history of human knowledge, and this knowledge which dates about 1000 B. C. "did not belong to any Brahmān before," "it belonged in all the worlds to the Kṣatra class alone."

These are real claims of Janaka, king of the Videhas, to the admiration and gratitude of posterity. Curiously enough, posterity remembers him and the Videhas and the Kosalas also, through a myth which has clung round their revered names. That myth relates to the Āryan conquest of Southern India; and with a fervid and blind gratitude poets of subsequent ages have connected that great historical event with the names of ancient kings who had nothing to do with the conquest! Historical knowledge in Europe, even in the dark ages, was never so dim as to allow a poet to conjecture the conquest of Jerusalem by Charlemagne or Alfred the Great! But the second great epic of India conceives and describes the conquest of Ceylon by a king of the Kosalas who had married the daughter of Janaka king of the Videhas.

It is not possible with our present knowledge to state when the Rāmāyaṇa was composed in its original shape. literature, but we find no such reference to the Rāmāyaṇa. The discovery and conquest of Ceylon by Vijaya from Bengal took place in the fifth century B. C. and at first sight one would be inclined to refer the first conception of the epic, which has its scene of action in that island, to that date. On the other hand, there is nothing to shew that the existence of the island was utterly unknown before its conquest by Vijaya. It seems on the contrary very probable that the island was darkly known, and believed to be inhabited by monsters and giants for centuries before it was conquered by the Hindus. And the composition of the Rāmāyaṇa which makes no allusion to Vijaya's conquest, may with greater probability be referred to an age anterior to Vijaya, when the darkness of ignorance and myths still obscured the island from the Hindus.

That this view is more probable appears from the fact that the whole of India, south of the Vindhya chain, is described in the Rāmāyaṇa as one interminable forest, inhabited by barbarous aborigines, who are described as monkeys and bears of different kinds. Now we know that the banks of the Godāvarī and even of the Kṛṣṇā river were colonized by the Āryans early in the Rationalistic Period, and great empires like that of the Andhras rose to power and started new schools of science and learning several centuries before Christ. The first conception of the Rāmāyaṇa must be referred to a period anterior to these movements in the South, for the Rāmāyaṇa speaks of no Āryan civilization south of the Vindhyas.

The Rāmāyaṇa in its original shape must therefore be referred to a period anterior to the Āryan subjugation of Southern India, and must therefore belong to the close of the period of which we are now speaking, *i. e.* the Epic Period. What was the original shape of the Rāmāyaṇa and what incidents have been bodily added at a latter period are questions which we are unable to discuss here.

The Rāmāyaṇa then, like the Mahābhārata, is utterly Valueless as a narrative of historical events and incidents. As in the Mahābhārata, so in the Rāmāyaṇa, the heroes are myths, pure and simple.

Sītā, the field furrow, had received divine honors from the time of the Ṛg Veda, and had been worshipped as a goddess.

When cultivation gradually spread towards Southern India, it was not difficult to invent a poetical myth that Sītā was carried to the South. And when this goddess and woman—the noblest creation of human imagination—had acquired a distinct and lovely individuality, she was naturally described as the daughter of the holiest and most learned king on record, Janaka of the Videhas !

But who is Rāma, described in the epic as Sītā's husband and the king of the Kosalas ? The later Purāṇas tell us that he was an incarnation of Viṣṇu—but Viṣṇu himself had not risen to prominence at the time of which we are speaking! Indra was still the chief of the gods of the Epic Period. And in the Sūtra literature (*e.g.*, Pāraskara Gṛhya Sūtra II, 17, 9.) we learn that Sītā, the furrow goddess, is the wife of Indra. Is it then an untenable conjecture that Rāma, the hero of the Rāmāyaṇa, is in his original conception like Arjuna, the hero of the Mahābhārata, only a new edition of India of the Ṛg Veda battling with the demons of drought? The myth of Indra has thus been mixed up with the epic which describes a historic war in Northern India, and the epic which describes the historic conquest of Southern India!

But though the Rāmāyaṇa is utterly valueless as a narrative of events, still like the Mahābhārata it throws side-lights of the state of ancient society in India, and the story of the epic therefore needs be briefly told. Only we must premise that even as a picture of life, the Rāmāyaṇa is long posterior to the Mahābhārata, and belongs (in its first conception) to the very close of the Epic Period. We miss in the Rāmāyaṇa the fiery valour and the proud self-assertion of the Kṣatriyas of the Mahābhārata; and the subordination of the people to the priestly caste is proud asserter of Kṣatriya learning and dignity that he was, but as a humble servant of the priests. And Rāma himself, the hero of the epic, though he encounters and defeats a Brāhman warrior, Parasu Rāma, does so with many apologies and due submission! The story of Parasurāma probably conceals a great historic truth. He is said to have fought against the Kṣatriyas and exterminated the caste twenty-seven times, and then he was conquered by the Kṣatriya Rāma, the hero of the epic. It would seem that this story indicates the real rivalry and hostilities between the priestly and warrior castes—indications of which we have found in a literary form in the Upaniṣads.

For the rest, one feels on reading the Rāmāyaṇa that the real heroic age of India had passed, and that centuries of residence in the Gangetic Valley had produced an enervating effect on the Āryans. We miss the heroic, if somewhat rude and sturdy manners and incidents which mark the Mahābhārata. We miss characters distinguished by fiery valour, and battles fought with real obstinacy and determination. We miss men of flesh and blood, and pride and valour and stern determination like Karṇa and Duryodhana and Bhīma; and the best developed characters in the Rāmāyaṇa are women like the proud and scheming Kaikeyī or the gentle and ever suffering Sītā. The heroes of the Rāmāyaṇa are somewhat tame and commonplace personages, very respectful to priests, very anxious to conform to the rules of decorum and etiquette, doing a vast amount of fighting work mechanically, but without the determination, the persistence of real fighters! A change had come over the spirit of the nation; and, if princes and men had become more polished and law-abiding, they had become less sturdy and heroic. For a picture of Hindu life of the fourteenth and thirteenth centuries, when the hardy and conquering Kurus and the Pāñcālas ruled in the Doab, we would refer our readers to the Mahābhārata. For a picture of Hindu-life of the tenth century, when the Kosalas and the Videhas had, by a long residence in the Gangetic Valley, become law-abiding and priest-ridden, learned and polished, enervated and dutiful, we would refer our readers to the Rāmāyaṇa. The two epics represent the change which Hindu life and society underwent from the commencement to the close of the Epic Age.

We proceed now with the story of the Rāmāyaṇa. The people who lived in the wide tract of country between the Ganges and the Gunduck were known by the general name of the Kosalas as we have seen before. Daśaratha, a distinguished king of this nation, had his capital in Ayodhyā (or Oude), the ruins of which ancient town are still shown to travellers in some shapeless mounds.

Daśaratha had three queens honored above the rest, of whom Kausalyā bore him his eldest born Rāma, Kaikeyī was the mother of Bharata, and Sumitrā of Lakṣmaṇa and Śatrughna. Daśaratha in his old age decided on making Rāma the Yuvarāja or reigning prince, but the proud and beauteous Kaikeyī insisted that her son should be Yuvarāja, and the feeble old king yielded to the determined will of his wife.

Before this Rāma had won Sītā, the daughter of Janaka, king of the Videhas, at a Svayamvara. Kings and princes had assembled there, but Rāma alone could lift the heavy bow, and bent it till it broke in twain. But now, when Ayodhyā was still ringing with acclamation at the prospect of Rāma's being installed as Yuva rāja, it was decided in queen Kaikeyī's chambers, that Bharata must be the Yuvarāja, and further that Rāma must go in exile for fourteen years.

Rāma was too obedient and dutiful to resist or even resent this decision. His faithful half brother Lakṣmaṇa accompanied him, and the gentle Sītā would not hear of parting with her lord. Amidst the tears and lamentation of the people of Ayodhyā, Rāma and Sītā and Lakṣmaṇa walked out of the city.

The exiles first went to the hermitage of Bhāradvāja in Prayāga (Allahabad), and then to that of Vālmīki in Chitrakūṭa, somewhere in modern Bandelkund. Vālmīki is reputed to be the author of the epic Rāmāyaṇa just as Kṛṣṇa Dvaipāyana Vyāsa, the compiler of the Vedas is said to be the author of the Mahābhārata. There is as little truth in the one tradition as in the other. Dasaratha died of a broken heart on the departure of Rāma.

Bharata followed Rāma to Chitrakūṭa and informed him of their fathers death and implored his return. But Rāma felt himself bound by the promise he had made, and it was agreed that Rāma would return after fourteen years and ascend the throne. Bharata returned to Ayodhyā.

Leaving Chitrakūṭa, Rāma wandered in the Daṇḍaka forest and towards the sources of the Godāvarī among jungles and non-

Āryan tribes—for Southern India had not yet been colonized by Āryans. Thirteen years thus passed away.

Rāvaṇa, the monster king of Laṅkā or Ceylon and of Southern India, heard of the beauty of Sītā now dwelling in jungles, and in the absence of Rāma took her away from their hut, and carried her off to Ceylon. Rāma, after a long search; obtained clue of her; he made alliances with the non-Āryan tribes of Southern India who are described as monkeys and bears, and made preparations for crossing over to Ceylon to recover his wife.

Bāli was a great king among the non-Āryans, but his brother Sugrīva thirsted after his kingdom and his wife, and Rāma fought and killed Bāli; helped Sugrīva to win the kingdom and Bāli's widow; and Sugrīva then marched with his army to Laṅkā.

Hanumat, the commander-in-chief of the non-Āryan or monkey army, led the way. He leaped over the Strait of sixty miles which separates India from Ceylon, found Sītā, and gave her the ring sent by Rāma, caused a conflagration in the capital of Rāvaṇa, and then returned to Rāma.

A causeway was then built across the Strait by boulders and stones. The reader is aware that a natural causeway runs nearly across the Strait, and there is no doubt that the physical geography of this locality suggested to the poet the idea that the causeway was built by the superhuman labours of Rāma's monkey army. The whole army then crossed over and laid siege to the capital of Rāvaṇa.

The account of the war which follows, though full of poetical incidents and stirring description, is unnatural and tedious. Chief after chief was sent out by Rāvaṇa to beat back the invaders, but they all fell in the war. Rāma using his supernatural weapons and mystic mantras. Indrajit, the proud son of Rāvaṇa, battled from the clouds, but Lakṣmana killed him. Rāvaṇa came out in a rage and killed Lakṣmana, but the dead hero revived under the influence of some medicine brought by the faithful Hanumat. One of Rāvaṇa's brothers, Bibhīṣaṇa, had turned a traitor, and had joined Rāma, and told him the secret by which each warrior would be killed, and thus chief after chief of Rāvaṇa's proud host fell. At last Rāvaṇa himself came out, and was killed by Rāma. Sīta was recovered, but she had to prove her untainted virtue by throwing herself into a lighted pyre, and then coming out of it uninjured.

The fourteenth year of exile being now accomplished, Rāma and Sītā returned to Ayodhyā and ascended the throne. But the suspicions of the people fell on Sītā who had been in Rāvaṇa's house, and could not, they thought, have returned untainted. And Rāma, as weak as his father had been, sent poor, suffering Sītā —then gone with child—to exile.

Vālmīki received her at Chitrakūṭa, and then her two sons, Lava and Kusa, were born. Vālmīki composed the poem of the Rāmāyaṇa and taught the boys to repeat the piece, and thus years were passed.

Then Rāma decided to celebrate the Aśvamedha sacrifice, and sent out the horse. The animal came as far as Vālmīki's hermitage, and the boys in a playful humour caught it and detained it. Rāma's troops tried in vain to recover the animal. At last Rāma himself saw the princely boys, but did not know who they were; he heard the poem Rāmāyaṇa chanted by them, and it was in a passion of grief and regret that he at last knew them and embraced them as his own dear boys.

But there was no joy in store for Sītā. The people's suspicions could not be allayed, and Rāma was too weak to act against his people. The earth which had given poor Sītā birth yawned and received its long-suffering child. To this day Hindus hesitate to call their female children by the name of Sītā; for if her gentleness, her virtue, her patient uncomplaining faithfulness and her unconquerable love for her lord were more than human, her sufferings and woes too were more than what usually fall to the lot of woman. There is not a Hindu woman in the length and breadth of India to whom the story of suffering Sītā is not known, and to whom her character is not a model to strive after and to imitate. And Rāma, too, though scarcely equal to Sītā in the worth of character, has been a model to men for his faithfulness, his obedience and his piety. And thus the epic has been for the millions of India a means of moral education, the value of which can hardly be over estimated.

CHAPTER – 4

BELT OF NON-ĀRYAN TRIBES

The great river system of Northern India determined the course of Āryan conquests; when we survey the course of these rivers, we comprehend the history of Āryan conquests during ten centuries. And when we have traced the course of the Indus and its tributaries and of the Ganges and the Jumnā as far as Benares and North-Behar, we have seen the whole extent of the Indo-Āryan world as it existed at the close of the Epic Period, or about 1000 B. C. Beyond this wide tract of Hindu kingdoms lay the whole extent of India yet unexplored or rather unconquered by the Āryans and peopled by various aboriginal tribes, A Vide belt of this Non-Āryan tract, surrounding the Hindu world to the east, south and west was becoming known to the Hindus about the very close of the Epic Period. East and South Behar, Malwa and a portion of the Deccan, and the regions near Guzerat and the Rajputana desert, formed a wide semi-circular belt of country, as yet not Hinduized, but becoming gradually known to the Hindus, and therefore finding occasional mention in the latest works of the Brāhmaṇa literature, as regions peopled by *Satvas, i.e.,* living creatures, hardly human beings. We can imagine hardy colonists penetrating into this encircling belt of unknown and uncivilized regions, obtaining a mastery over the aborigines wherever they went, establishing some isolated settlements on the banks of fertile rivers, and presenting to the astonished barbarians some of the results of civilized administration and civilized life. We can imagine also saintly anchorites retiring into these wild jungles, and fringing the tops of hills or fertile valleys with their holy hermitages, which were the seats of learning and of sanctity. And lastly adventurous royal huntsmen not unoften penetrated into these jungles, and unhappy princes exiled by their more powerful rivals often chose to retire from the world and took up their abodes in these solitudes. In such manner was the belt of Non-Āryan country described above, gradually known to the Hindus, and we will cite a passage or two which will shew how far this knowledge extended, and how the civilized Hindus named the different aboriginal tribes dwelling in this tract, probably in the tenth century B. C.

There is a passage in the last book of the Aitareya Brāhmaṇa which, along with an account of the principal Hindu kingdoms of the time, makes some mention of the aboriginal races in the south and south-west; and the passage deserves to be quoted.

"The Vāsavas then inaugurated him (Indra) in the eastern direction during thirty-one days by these three Ṛk verses, the Yajus verse, and the great words (all just mentioned), for the sake of obtaining universal sovereignty. Hence all kings of eastern nations are inaugurated to universal sovereignty and called *Samrāj, i e.,* universal sovereign, after this precedent made by the gods.

"Then the Rudras inaugurated Indra in the southern region during thirty-one days, with the three Ṛk verses, the Yajus, and the great words (just mentioned), for obtaining enjoyment of pleasures. Hence all kings of living creatures[1] in the southern region, are inaugurated for the enjoyment (of pleasures) and called *Bhoja, i.e.,* the enjoyer.

"Then the divine Ādityas inaugurated him in the western region during thirty-one days, with those three Ṛk verses, that Yajus verse, and those great words for obtaining independent rule. Hence all kings of the *Nīcyas* and *Apācyas* in the western country[2] are inaugurated to independent rule, and called 'independent rulers.'[3]

"Then the Visvedevāḥ inaugurated him during thirty-one days in the northern region by those three Ṛk verses, etc, for distinguished rule. Hence all people living in northern countries beyond the Himālaya, such as the *Uttāra Kurus, Uttara Mādras,* are inaugurated for living without a king (*Vairājyam),* and called *Virāj, i.e.,* without king.

"Then the divine Sādhyas and Aptyas inaugurated Indra during thirty-one days in the middle region, which is a firmly established footing (the immovable centre) to the kingship *(Rājya)*. Hence the kings of the *Kuru Pāñcālas* with the *Vasas* and *Usīnaras* are inaugurated to kingship and called kings (Rāja)."

This passage shows us at one glance the whole of the Hindu world as it existed in the close of the Epic Period. To the farthest east lived the Videhas and the Kāsīs and the Kosalas as we have seen before, and those newest and youngest of the Hindu colonists excelled in learning and reputation their elder brethern in the west. Their kings, Janaka and Ajātaśatru and others, took the proud title of *Samrāj,* and worthily maintained their dignity by their learning and their prowess.

In the south some bands of the Āryan settlers must have worked their way up the valley of the Chumbal, and become acquainted with the aboriginal tribes inhabiting the country now known as Malwa. These tribes were called *Satvas, i.e.,* living creatures, scarcely human beings! We note, however, that the kingdoms in this direction already went by the name of *Bhoja* (however fanciful the derivation which the author gives to the word), and *Bhoja* was in later times the name of the same region, immediately to the north of the Vindhya chain, and along the valley of the Chumbal.

Westwards from this place surged the waves of Āryan settlers or adventurers, until the invaders came to the shores of the Arabian sea, and could proceed no further. The aboriginal races in these distant tracts were looked upon with some degree of contempt by the civilized colonists or invaders and were significantly called *Nīcyas* and *Apācyas,* and their rulers had the significant name of *Svarāt* or independent rulers.

These races dimly known at the very close of the Epic Period were the ancestors of the proudest and most warlike Hindu tribes of later times, the Maharattas. Surat and Guzerat were named after the same race-name.

To the north the Uttara Kurus and the Uttara Mādras and other tribes lived—beyond the Himālaya we are told—but which probably means beyond the lower ranges and among the valleys of the Himālaya.

To the present day these men live in communes, and have very little concern with chief or king; and it is no I wonder that in ancient times they should be known as peoples without kings.

And then, in the very centre of the Hindu world, along the valley of the Ganges, lived the powerful tribes of the Kurus and the Pāñcālas, and the less known tribes, the Vasas and the Usīnaras.

In the west, the deserts of Rajputana were wholly unexplored by the Āryans. The Bhil aborigines of those deserts and mountains were left undisturbed until new and hardy tribes of invaders entered India after the Christian era and settled down in these parts.

In the far east, south Behar was not yet Hinduized. In a passage in the Atharva Veda pointed out by Professor Weber, special and hostile notice is taken of the Aṅgas and the Magadhas. The passage shews that the people of east and south Behar did not yet belong to the Hindu confederation of nations; but were nevertheless becoming known to the Āryans. Bengal Proper was as yet simply unknown.

And the whole of southern India, *i.e.,* India south of the Vindhya range, was yet unoccupied by the Hindus. The Aitareya Brāhmaṇa gives (VII, 18,) the names of certain degraded barbarous tribes, and among others that of the Andhras. We will see that in the Rationalistic Period the Andhras rose to be a great civilised Hindu power in Southern India.

We have now spoken of all the principal Āryan races and kingdoms which flourished in the Epic Period, and of the Non-Āryan kingdoms which formed a semicircular belt in the south of the Hindu world. It will be our pleasanter task in the following chapters to give some account of the social customs and the domestic life of the people. But before we take leave of kings, we must make some mention of the great coronation ceremony, as it has been described in many works of the Epic Period. This ceremony and the imperial horse-sacrifice were the most imposing and ostentatious royal ceremonials of Ancient India, and we have already said something of the horse-sacrifice in connection with the two Epics of the Hindus. An extract or two about the coronation ceremony are all that is needed here.

"He spreads the tiger skin on the throne in such a manner that the hairs come outside, and that part which covered the neck is turned eastward. For the tiger is the Kṣatra (royal power) of the beasts in the forests. The Kṣatra is the royal prince; by means of this Kṣatra, the king makes his Kṣatra (royal power) prosper. The king, when taking his seat on the throne, approaches it from behind, turning his face eastwards, kneels down with crossed legs, so that his right knee touches the earth, and holding the throne with his hands, prays over it the following mantra :—

"May Agni ascend thee, O throne, with the Gāyatrī Metre, etc.

"They now put the branch of the udambara tree on the head of the Kṣatriya, and pour the liquids (which are in the large ladle) on it. (When doing so) the priest repeats the following mantras :—

'With these waters which are happy, which cure every thing, increase the royal power, the immortal Prajāpati sprinkled Indra, Soma the king, Varuṇa, Yama, Manu, with the same sprinkle I thee! Be thou ruler over kings in this world. The illustrious mother bore thee as the great universal ruler over men; the blessed mother has borne thee, etc.'

"Now, he gives into his hand a goblet of spirituous liquor, under the recital of the verse Svadiṣṭhayā . Madiṣṭhayā, etc. (9, 1, 1), *i.e.*, Purify O Soma! with thy sweetest, most exhilarating drops (the sacrifice?), thou who art squeezed for Indra to be drunk by him. After having put the spirituous liquor into his hand, the priest repeats a propitiatory mantra, etc.

"He now descends (from the throne seat) facing the branch of the udamdara tree,"—Aitareya Brāhmaṇa. VIII, 6 to 9.

We are then told that with this ceremony priests invested a number of kings whose names are already known to us. Tura, the son of Kavaṣa, thus inaugurated Janamejaya, the son of Parikṣit "Thence Janamejaya went everywhere, conquering the earth up to its ends, and sacrificed the sacrificial horse." Parvata and Nārada thus invested Yudhamsranshti, the son of Ugrasena. Vasiṣṭha invested Sudās, the great conqueror of the Ṛg Veda hymns; and Dīrghatamas invested Bharata, the son of Duḥṣanta, with this ceremony.

We have also an excellent account of the coronation rite in the Vājasaneyi-Saṁhitā, from which we quote a remarkable passage in which the priest blesses the newly crowned king :—"May God who rules the world bestow on you the power to rule your subjects. May fire, worshipped by householders, bestow on you supremacy over the householders. May Soma, the lord of trees, bestow on you supremacy over forests. May Bṛhaspati, the god of speech, bestow on you supremacy in speech. May Indra, the highest among gods, bestow on you the highest supremacy. May Rudra, the cherisher of animals, bestow on you supremacy over animals. May Mitra, who is truth, make you supreme in truth. May Varuṇa, who cherishes holy works, make you supreme in holy acts."—IX, 39.

In the address to the people which follows, the priest tells them : "This is your king, O ye such and such tribes." The Kāṇva text reads thus : "This is your king, O ye Kurus, O ye Pāñcālas."

We will conclude this chapter with an excellent piece of advice which is given to kings further on, which modern rulers will do well to remember : "*If thou shalt be a ruler, then from this day judge the strong and the weak with equal justice, resolve on doing good incessantly to the public, and protect the country from all calamities"—X,* 27.

REFERENCES

1. *Sātvānām* is the word in the original.
2. *Prātīcyām* is the word in the original.
3. *Svarāṭ* is the word in the original, whence *Sāurāṣṭrā* and Surat.

CHAPTER – 5

CASTE

As we drift down the history of Hindu civilization, we notice, along with a remarkable progress in sciences and learning and the arts of peace, an unhappy sign of social institutions being more and more crystalised into hard-and-fast rules, which gradually contracted the liberties and the free energies of the people. Four or five centuries of peaceful residence in a genial climate in the fertile basin of the Ganges and the Jumnā enabled the Hindus to found civilized kingdoms to cultivate philosophy, science and arts, and to develop their religious and social institutions; but it was under the same gentle but enervating influences that they also unconsciously surrendered all social freedom, and were gradually bound down by unhealthy priest-imposed laws and restrictions which made further progress on the part of the *people* impossible. This is the dark side of Hindu civilization. Priestly supremacy threw its coils round and round the nation from its early youth, and the *nation* never attained that political and social freedom and strength which marked the ancient nations of Europe.

But the worst results of priestly supremacy were not brought about in a day. We see the dark cloud slowly forming itself at the close of the Vedic Period. We see it increasing in strength and volume in the Epic Period. We shall see it casting a still gloomier shadow on the society of the Rationalistic Period. But it is only in the Paurāṇik Period, which followed the Buddhist Era, that it threw an utter impenetrable gloom over a gifted but ill-fated nation. In the earlier periods, so long as the nation had the life and the strength of youth, it made repeated attempts to throw off priestly supremacy and to assert its free-born rights. The Kṣatriyas made an attempt to assert themselves in the very period of which we are now speaking, as we have already seen. And the Kṣatriyas made a still mightier attempt later on to throw Brāhmanism overboard, and adopted the Buddhist religion all over the land. With the extinction of Buddhism such attempts seemed to end, and priestly supremacy became ten times worse than before. The energies of the nation were cramped, the natural boldness of martial races was subdued by superstitious beliefs, the feeling of political unity was almost annihilated, and the descendants of those who had fought the Kuru-Pāñcāla war, and had opposed the march of Alexander, fell before petty adventurers. The great nation was conquered by an adventurer from Ghor, who had scarcely a kingdom of his own, and whose successors soon lost all connection with their mother country, and ruled in India through the weakness of the Hindus. And in the five or six centuries that followed the conquest, there was not life enough in the millions of martial men who inhabited Northern India, from the Punjab to Behar to enable them to make one serious effort to send out the handful of aliens who held them in chains. Ancient Greece fell through dissensions among her petty states; Rome fell on account of her luxury and vice; India fell on account of her superstition and consequent life lessness.

We have seen that about the close of the Vedic Period, the priests had already formed themselves into a separate profession, and sons stepped forward to take up the duties of their fathers. When religious rites became vastly more elaborate and pompous in the Epic Period, when, with the founding of new kingdoms along the fertile Doab, polished and great kings prided themselves on the performance of vast sacrifices with endless rites and observances, it is easy to understand that the priests, who alone could undertake such complicated rites, rose in the estimation of the people, until they were naturally regarded as aloof from the ordinary people, as a distinct and superior race—as a caste. They devoted their lifetime to learn these rites, and they alone were able to perform them in all their details; and the natural inference in the popular mind was that they alone were worthy of the holy task. And when hereditary priests were thus completely separated from the people by their fancied sanctity and real knowledge of elaborate rites, it was scarcely considered "good form" on their part to form "misalliances" with the people outside their holy rank. They might still condescend to honor particular families by choosing brides from among them, but young ladies of priestly houses must never give their hands to men outside their ranks. What is a feeling and a custom among modern nations, soon became an inviolable and religious rule among a passive and custom-abiding people like the Gangetic Hindus.

The very same causes led to the rise of a royal caste. Royalty had not assumed a high dignity among the Punjab Hindus. Warlike chiefs led clans from conquests to conquests; and the greatest of them like Sudās, the patron of the Vasiṣṭhas and the Viśvāmitras, were looked upon more as leaders of men and protectors of clans than as mighty kings. Far different was the state of things with the Gangetic Hindus; Probably in the early days of the martial Kurus and Pāñcālas, caste distinctions had not yet been fully matured. But later in the day, the kings of the peaceful Kosalas and Videhas, surrounded with all the paraphernalia of august and learned and pompous courts, were looked upon by the humble and lowly and extremely law-abiding and loyal people as more than human. As kings became more rich and more august and more addicted to the forms which indicate royalty, as the people became more enervated and submissive and loyal, it was scarcely possible that maidens of the royal or warlike classes should condescend to marry men from the ranks. The stigma which attaches to such misalliances all over the world gave rise to an inviolable rule in India. And when priests and warriors were thus separated by such absolute and inviolable rules from the people, the humblest girls of the former classes were debarred from marriage with the greatest and richest among the Vaiśyas.[1]

It is difficult to find in the history of European institutions any parallel to the caste-system of India. Yet there was a time in Europe when institutions, somewhat similar to the caste-system of India, sprang from the same causes which operated in India, *viz.*, the feebleness and enervation of the people, and the pride and power of warriors and priests. When the Roman Empire fell to pieces, and barbarian chiefs and barons carved out among themselves the fairest portions of Europe, the mass of the people were devoid of political life and political freedom. Never in Europe was there such a wide distinction between a powerful clergy and powerful soldiery on the one hand, and a lifeless and powerless people on the other, as in the days of feudalism in Europe. Vast monasteries arose all over Europe; great feudal towers frowned on every navigable river and every humble village; and the dwellers of villages and the humble artizans in little towns were scarcely regarded as better than slaves. The clergy, the knighthood and the people of Europe in the Middle Ages answered in some respects to the Brāhmans, the Kṣatriyas and the Vaiśyas of India.

But the resemblance is in appearance only. The clergy of Feudal Europe did not marry, and its ranks were recruited from the ablest, the cleverest, the most learned among the people. The knights, too, were glad to welcome into their ranks doughty squires and brave warriors among the people. The people, too, in the darkest days of feudal oppression, had more of tough life and rude vigour than the passive and submissive citizens of the Gangetic plain. The people in Europe soon formed leagues to protect their commerce, fortified their towns to meet the marauding barons, formed municipal corporations, and trained themselves to arms to defend their interests in those insecure times. Ambitious scions of baronial houses often mixed with the people, and fought their battles in the field and in the council board; and this healthy admixture, which the caste-system prevented in India, revived and strengthened the people in Europe. Feudalism and the absolute power of the clergy decayed as trade and commerce and political life rose among the people; and the danger of the people being divided into three "castes," if it ever existed in Europe, passed away once and for ever.

From what has been stated before, it will appear that the caste-system arose in India from the permanent separation of the priestly and warrior classes from the people, in an age when the people had become enervated and feeble, and those two classes usurped all power and dignity. Superficial and impulsive writers often hold the Brāhmans of India to blame for monopolizing religious knowledge and observances, and creating a harmful and permanent disunion in the nation. The charge, however, is unphilosophical and unjust. Priestly supremacy and royal despotism are inevitable when the people become enervated and feeble, and are incapable of taking care of their consciences or their political rights. Priests and kings are no more responsible for these results than the people themselves; indeed, the former are less responsible for assuming undue authority than the latter for submitting to such authority. Such chains are received ungrudgingly by a feeble and lifeless people; when the people awake to life and vigour, the chains fall asunder.

The simple origin of the caste institution as narrated above is obscured in later Hindu literature in a cloud of strange myths and legends. But in spite of such wonderful legends, later Hindu writers never completely lost sight of the fact, that caste was originally only a distinction based on professions. And this simple and natural account of the origin of caste often occurs in the same Paurāṇik works which elsewhere delight in strange and monstrous myths about the origin of the institution. We have room only for one or two extracts.

In the Vāyu Purāṇa we are told that in the first or Kṛta Age, *there were no castes,* and that subsequently, Brahmā established divisions among men *according to their works,* "Those of them who were suited for command and prone to deeds of violence, he appointed to be Kṣatriyas, from their protecting others. Those disinterested men who attended upon them, spoke the truth and declared the Veda aright, were Brāhmans, Those of them who formerly were feeble, engaged in the work of husbandmen, tillers of the earth, and industrious, were Vaiśyas, cultivators and providers of subsistence. Those who were cleansers and ran about on service, and had little vigour or strength, were called Śūdras." Accounts, more or less similar to this, occur in the other Purāṇas also.

The Rāmāyaṇa in its present shape is, as we have seen before, the work of later ages. In the Uttara Kāṇḍa, Chapter 74, we are told that in the Kṛta Age Brāhmans alone practised austerities : that in the Tretā Age, Kṣatriyas were born, *and then, was established the modern system of four castes.* Reduced from mythical to historical language, the above account may be read united body and practised Hindu rites. In the Epic Age, however, priests and kings separated themselves as distinct castes, and the people also formed themselves into the lower orders, the Vaiśyas and Śūdras.

The Mahābhārata also, as we have seen before, is in its present shape a work of later ages, but here also we occasionally meet with a sensible and honest attempt to account for caste. In the Śānti Parva, section 188, we are told that red-limbed twice-born men who were fond of sensual pleasure, fiery, irascible, daring and forgetful of their sacrificial duties, fell into the caste of Kṣatriyas. Yellow twice-born men, who derived their livelihood from cows and agriculture, and did not practise religious performances, fell into the caste of Vaiśyas. Black twice-born men, who were impure and addicted to violence and lying, and were covetous and subsisted by all kinds of works, fell into the caste of Śūdras. *Being thus separated by these their works, the twice-born men became of other castes!"*

The composers of these and similar passages no doubt knew of the legend of the four castes springing from four members of Brahmā's body; but they ignored it, and treated it as an allegory which it is. They maintain that in the earliest age there were no castes, and they make a very fair and sensible conjecture, that castes were developed in a later age from distinctions in work and professions. We must now, however, return from this degression, and examine the caste-system as it prevailed in the Epic Period.

As we have stated before, the caste system first formed itself among the peaceful citizens of the ancient Gangetic India; it never should be forgotten, however, that the worst results of that system did not appear, and could not appear until the Hindus had ceased to be a free nation. In the Epic Period the body of the people (except the priests and soldiers) still formed one united Vaiśya caste, and had not been disunited into such miserably divided communities as in the modern day. The body of the people were still entitled to religious knowledge and learning, and to perform religious rites for themselves— just like Brāhmans and Kṣatriyas. And even inter- marriage between Brāhmans, Kṣatriyas and Vaiśyas was flowed under certain restrictions. However much, therefore, we may deplore the commencement of the caste-system, we should never forget that the worst results of that system—*the priestly monopoly of learning, the disunion in the body of the people*, and *the absolute social separation among castes*—were unknown in India until the Paurāṇik times.

In the sixteenth chapter of the White Yajur Veda, we meet with the names of various professions which throw some light on the state of the society at the time the chapter was compiled. It is apparent, however, the list is one of different professions, not of different castes. Thus, various kinds of thieves are enumerated in Kandikās, 20 and 21, and horsemen, charioteers and infantry are spoken of in 26. Similarly the carpenter, the chariot-maker, the potter and the blacksmith, mentioned in 27, also formed different professions and not castes. The Niṣāda and others, also mentioned in the same Kandikā, were obviously aboriginal tribes, who, then as now, formed the lowest strata of the Hindu society.

The list is very much enlarged in the 30th chapter of the same work which, as we have seen before, is of a considerably later date, and indeed belongs to the *Khila* or the supplement. But here, too, we meet with many names which indicate professions only, and many others which undoubtedly refer to the aborigines; and we find no evidence that the mass of the Āryan population (leaving aside the priests and warriors) had been divided into castes. We find names of different kinds of thieves, of dancers, speakers, and frequenters in assemblies; of lewd men, and sons of unmarried women; of chariot-makers, carpenters, potters, jewellers, cultivators, arrow-makers, and bow-makers; of dwarfs and crookedly formed men, and blind and deaf persons; of physicians and astronomers; of keepers of elephants, horses and cattle; of servants, cooks, gate-keepers, and wood-cut-and barbers; of learned men and proud men; of women of various descriptions; of tanners, fishermen, and hunters and fowlers; of goldsmiths and merchants; of men with various diseases; of wig-makers and imaginative men (poets); of musicians of various kinds, and men of other descriptions. It is plain that this is not a list of castes. On the other hand, the Māgadha and Sūta and Bhīmala and Mṛgayu and Svanin, and Niṣāda and Durmada, and others mentioned in the list, are clearly aborigines, living under the shadow of the Āryan society. We have only to add that the same list, with slight modifications, is given in the Taittirīya Brāhmaṇa.

The above lists throw some light on the state of the society and the professions which were recognized in the period of which we speak; but they have nothing to do with caste. Throughout the Epic Period and throughout the Rationalistic and Buddhist Ages which followed, the great body of the Āryan people were the undivided Vaiśyas, although they followed numerous professions. Along with the Brāhmans and the Kṣatriyas, they formed the Āryan nation; and were entitled to all the rights and privileges, and the literary and religious heritages of the nation. The conquered aborigines, who formed the Śūdra caste, were alone debarred from the heritage of the Āryans.

This is the cardinal distinction between the ancient caste system, and the caste system of the modern age. Caste reserved some privileges for priests, and some privileges for warriors, in ancient times; but *never divided and, disunited the Āryan people.* Priests and warriors and citizens, though following their hereditary professions from generation to generation, felt that they were, one nation and one race, received the same religious instructions, possessed the same literature and traditions, ate and drank together, intermarried and held social communion in all respects, and were proud to call themselves the Āryan race as against the conquered aborigines. Caste in modern times has cut up the Āryan people into scores of communities, has opened the wide gulf of race distinctions among the different communities, has interdicted marriage and social communion among them, has starved the sons of the ancient Vaiśyas—the entire body of the people—of religious knowledge and literature, and has degraded them to the rank of Śūdras.

There are numerous passages in the Brāhmaṇa literature which shew that the distinctions between the castes were by no means so rigid in the early times as at a later period. We learn from Aitareya Brāhmaṇa (I, 16, and II, 17, that one who was not recognised as a Brāhman (Abrāhmaṇokta) could be the performing priest and bring a sacrifice. A still more remarkable passage, however, occurs in the same Brāhmaṇa (VII, 29 which would seem to show that caste rules were by no means rigid, and persons born in one community might enter into another. When a Kṣatriya eats at a sacrifice the portion assigned for the Brāhmans, his progeny has the characteristics of a Brāhman "ready to take gifts, thirsty after drinking Soma, and hungry of eating food, and ready to roam about everywhere according to pleasure." And "*in the second or third generation he is then capable of entering completely the Brāhmanship*" When he eats the share of Vaiśyas his "offspring will be born with the characteristic of the Vaiśyas, paying taxes to another king ;" "and in the second or third degree they are capable of entering the caste of the Vaiśyas ." When he takes the share of the Śūdras, his progeny "will have the characteristics of the Śūdras; they are to serve another (the three higher castes), to be expelled and beaten according to the pleasure (of their masters)." And "in the second or third degree, he is capable of entering the condition of the Śūdras."

In a previous chapter we have seen that Janaka, king of the Videhas, imparted to Yājñavalkya learning unknown to the priest before. On this "Yājñavalkya offered the king the choice of a boon. He replied 'let me enquire of thee whatever I desire, O Yājñavalkya !' Henceforth Janaka became a Brāhman." (Śatapatha Brāhmaṇa, XL 6, 2, 1.)

We have other evidences to show, that men not born Brāhmans became Brāhmans by their reputation and their learning. In Aitareya Brāhmaṇa (II, 19), we are told of Kavaṣa, the son of

Ilușā, whom the other Ṛṣis expelled from a sacrificial session, saying," how should the son of a slave girl, a gamester, who is no Brāhman, remain among us and become initiated?" But Kavasha knew the gods and all the gods knew him, and he was admitted as a Ṛṣi. Similarly, in the beautiful legend of Satyakāma Jabāla in the Chāndogya Upaniṣad (IV, 4), is exemplified the fact that truth and learning opened out in those days a path to the highest honor and to the highest caste. The legend is so beautiful in its simplicity and its poetry, that we feel no hesitation in quoting a portion of it :—

"1. Satyakāma, the son of Jabālā, addressed his mother and said : 'I wish to become a Brahmāchārin (religious student), mother. Of what family am I?'

"2. She said to him : 'I do not know, my child, of what family thou art. In my youth when I had to move about much as a servant, I conceived thee. I do not know of what family thou art. I am Jabālā by name, thou art Satyakāma, say that thou art Satyakāma Jabāla.'

"3. He going to Gautama Haridrumata, said to him : 'I wish to become a Brahmāchārin with you, Sir. May I come to you, Sir ?'

"4. He said to him : 'Of what family are you, my friend ?' He replied : 'I do not know, Sir, of what family I am. I asked my mother, and she answered '— "In my youth when I had to move about much as a servant, I conceived thee. I do not know of what family thou art. I am Jabālā by name, thou art Satyakāma." 'I am therefore Satyakāma Jabāla, Sir.'

"5. He said to him : 'No one but a true Brāhman would thus speak out. Go and fetch fuel, friend, I shall initiate you. You have not swerved from the truth.'"

And this truth-loving young man was initiated, and according to the custom of the times, went out to tend his teacher's cattle. In time he learnt the great truths which nature, and even the brute creation, teach those whose minds are open to instruction. Yes, he learned truths from the bull of the herd that he was tending, from the fire that he had lighted, and from a flamingo and a diverbird which flew near him, when in the evening he had penned his cows and laid wood on the evening fire, and sat behind it. The young student then came back to his teacher, and his teacher at once said : "Friend, you shine like one who knows Brahmān: who then has taught you ?" "Not men," was the young student's reply. And the truth which the young student had learnt (though clothed in the fanciful and somewhat grotesque style of the period) was that the four quarters, and the earth, the sky, the heaven and the ocean, and the sun, the moon, the lightning, and the fire, and the organs and mind of living beings, yea, the whole universe was Brahmān or God.

Such is the teaching of the Upaniṣads, and such are the poetical legends in which the teaching is clothed as we shall see further on. A legend like that of Satyakāma Jabāla in the Upaniṣads, which is full of human feeling and pathos and the highest moral lessons, cheers and refreshes the student after he has waded through pages of the dry and meaningless dogmas and rituals of the Brāhmaṇas. But our purpose in quoting the legend here is to show that the rules of caste had not become yet rigid when such legends were composed. We find in the legend that the son of a servant girl, who did not know his own father, became a religious student simply through his love of truth, learnt the lessons which nature and the learned men of the time could teach him, and subsequently became classed among the wisest religious teachers of the time. Surely the caste-system of that ancient time must have been freedom itself compared to the enslaving system of later times, when the entire nation, except the priests, was cruelly debarred from knowledge, —that knowledge which is the food of a nation's mind, and the life of a nation's life.

There is another legend in the same Upaniṣad (IV, 2), in which we find a Brāhman imparting knowledge to a Śūdra, accepting presents from him, and taking his daughter for his wife. The legend is in the usual simple language of the Upaniṣad, and we will therefore quote it:—

"1. Then Jānaśruti Putrāyana took six hundred cows, a necklace, and a carriage with mules, went to Raikva and said—

"2. 'Raikva, here are six hundred cows, a necklace, and a carriage with mules; teach me the deity which you worship?'

3. The other replied : 'Fie, necklace and carriage be thine O Śūdra, together with the cows.' Then Jānasruti Putrāyana took again a thousand cows, a necklace, a carnage with mules, and his own daughter and went to him.

"4. He said to him : 'Raikva, there are a thousand cows, a necklace, a carriage with mules, this wife, and this village in which thou dwellest, Sir, teach me?'

"5. He opening her mouth, said : 'You have brought these (cows and other presents), O Śūdra, but only by that mouth did you make me speak."

The Śūdra, however, though in exceptional cases admitted to knowledge, does not appear to have been ever admitted to the sacrifice. On the other hand, the Brāhmans, Kṣatriyas and Vaiśyas were all able to sacrifice (Śatapatha Brāhmaṇa, III, 1, 9), and therefore the distinctions between these castes was small, and the suppremacy of the Brahmān was almost nominal yet. In one passage, indeed, we have it boldly stated that a Brāhman may be of uncertain birth, but that he only is a true Brāhman who is born ot the *Brahmān* of the sacrifice; wherefore *even a Rājanya or a Vaiśyas should be addressed as Brāhman,* "since who is born of the sacrifice is born of the *Brahmān* and hence a Brāhman." (Śatapatha Brāhmaṇa, III, 2, 1, 40).

It was in the Epic Period that the sacrificial cord Yajñopavīta came to use. We are told in the Śatapatha Brāhmaṇa, II, 4, 2, that when all beings came to Prajāpati, the gods and the fathers came, wearing the sacrificial cord. And we are told in Kauṣītaki Upaniṣad, II, 7, that the all-conquering Kauṣītaki adores the sun when rising, having put on the sacrificial cord.

The Yajñopavīta was worn in this ancient period by Brāhmaṇs, Kṣatriyas and Vaiśyas alike, but only at the time of performing Yajña or Vedic worship and sacrifices.

Things have changed since those ancient times. The

Yajñopavīta is now habitually and ostentatiously worn at all times—by the members of one caste only—the Brāhmans, and that caste has forgotten to perform the Vedic Yajña!

REFERENCE

1. We have in a previous chapter (see p. 70, *note)* quoted the authority of Weber and Max Müller to shew that *caste* did not exist in the Vedic Age. We have much pleasure in adducing here the testimony of another eminent scholar, who with Weber and Max Müller may be said to form the Triumvirate of Vedic scholarship in Europe.

   Dr. Roth maintains that in the first or Vedic Age, Brāhmans were the domestic priests of the kings, and that gradually the dignity became hereditary in certain families. How these isolated priestly families were impelled by similarity of interests to form a common *caste* in the Epic Age, may be described best in Dr. Roth's own words.

   "When, at a period more recent than the majority of the hymns of the Ṛg Veda, the Vedic people, driven by some political shock, advanced from their abodes in the Punjab further and further to the south, drove the aborigines into the hills, and took possession of the broad tract of country lying between the Ganges, the Jumnā and the Vindhya range, the time had arrived when the distribution of power, the relation of king and priest, could become transformed in the most rapid and comprehensive manner.....This era is perhaps pourtrayed to us in the principal subject of the Mahābhārata, the contest between the descendants of Pāṇḍu and Kuru.....It is not difficult to comprehend how, in such a period of transition, powerful communities should arise among the domestic priests of petty kings, and their families should attain to the highest importance in every department of life, *and shoud grow into a caste."— Quoted in Muir's Sanscrit Texts, Vol. I (1872), p.291.*

CHAPTER – 6

SOCIAL AND DOMESTIC LIFE : THE POSITION OF WOMEN

The great distinction then between the society of the Vedic times and the society of the Epic Period is, that the caste-system was unknown in the former, and was developed in the latter. But this was not the only distinctive feature of the times. Centuries of culture and progress had their influence on society, and the cultured Hindus of the Epic Period were as widely different in their social manners from the warrior-cultivators of the Vedic Period as the Greeks of the time of Pericles were different from the Greeks of the time of Agamemnon and Ulysses.

The Hindus of the period of which we are speaking, had attained a high degree, of refinement and civilization and had developed minute rules to regulate their domestic and social duties. Royal courts were the seats of learning, and the learned and wise of all nations were invited, honored and rewarded. Justice was administered by learned officers, and laws regulated every duty of life. Towns with their strong walls and beautiful edifices multiplied among all nations, and had their judges, their executive officers, and their police. Agriculture was fostered, and the king's officers settled all disputes and looked to the collection of taxes and the comforts of cultivators.

We have said that the courts of enlightened and learned kings, like those of the Videhas, the Kāsīs, and the Kuru-Pāñcālas, were the principal seats of learning in those times. Learned priests were retained in such courts for the performance of sacrifices, and also for the purpose of the cultivation of learning; and many of the Brāhmaṇas and Upaniṣads which have been handed down to us, were probably composed in the schools which these priests founded. On great occasions men of learning came from distant towns and villages, and discussions were held not only on ritualistic matters, but on such subjects as the human mind, the destination of the soul after death, the future world, the nature of the gods, the fathers, and the different orders of being, and lastly, on the nature of that Universal Being who has manifested himself in all the works we see.

But learning was not confined to royal courts. There were Pariṣads or Brāhmanic settlements for the cultivation of learning, answering to the Universities of Europe; and young men went to these Pariṣads to acquire learning. Thus in Bṛhadāraṇyaka Upaniṣad VI, 2, we learn that Śvetaketu went to the Pariṣads of the Pāñcālas for his education. Max Müller in his History of Sanscrit Literature, quotes passages which show that, according to modern writers, a Pariṣad ought to consist of twenty-one Brāhmans well versed in philosophy, theology, and law; but these rules, as he points out, are laid down in later law books, and do not describe the character of the Pariṣads of the Epic Period. Parāsara says that four, or even three able men from amongst the Brāhmans in a village, who know the Veda and keep the sacrificial fire, form a Pariṣad.

Besides these Pariṣads, individual teachers established what would he called private schools in Europe, and often collected round themselves students from various parts of the country. These students lived with their teachers, served them in a menial capacity during the time of their studentship, and then after twelve years or longer, made suitable presents and returned to their homes and their longing relatives. Learned Brāhmans who had retired to forests in their old age often collected such students round them, and much of the boldest speculations in the Epic Period has proceeded from these sylvan and retired seats of sanctity and learning. Such is the way in which learning has been cultivated and preserved during thousands of years among Hindus, a nation who valued learning and knowledge perhaps more than any other nation in ancient or modern times. Good works and religious rites lead, according to the Hindu creed, to happier states of life and to their due reward; but true knowledge alone leads to final union with God.

When students had thus acquired the traditional learning either in Pariṣads or underprivate teachers, they returned to their homes, married, and settled down as householders. With marriage began their duties as householders, and the first duty of a householder was to light the sacrificial fire under an auspicious constellation, to offer morning and evening libations of milk to the fire, to perform other religious and domestic rites, and above all, to offer hospitality to strangers and to receive and honor guests. The essence of a Hindu's duties are inculcated in passages like the following :—

"Say what is true! Do thy duty! Do not neglect the study of the Veda! After having brought to thy teacher the proper reward, do not cut off the lives of children! Do not swerve from the truth! Do not swerve from duty! Do not neglect what is useful! Do not neglect greatness! Do not neglect the learning and teaching of the Veda !

Do not neglect the (sacrifice) works due to the gods and fathers! Let thy mother be to thee like unto a god! Let thy father be to thee like unto a god! Let thy teacher be to thee like unto a god! Whatever actions are blameless, those should be regarded, not others. Whatever good works have been performed by us, those should be observed by thee."—(Taittirīya Upaniṣad, I, 2.)

Pleasing pictures of a happy state of society are presented in many passages which we meet with in the literature of the period : "May the Brāhmans in our kingdom," says the priest at a horse-sacrifice, "live in piety; many our warriors be skilled in arms and mighty; may our cows yield us profuse milk, our bullocks carry their weights, and our horses be swift; may our women defend their homes, and warriors be victorious; may our youths be refined in their manners.........May Parjanya shower rain in every home and in every region; may our crops yield grains and ripen, and we attain our wishes and live in bliss."—(White Yajur Veda, XXII, 22.)

The wealth of rich men consisted in gold and silver and jewels; in cars, horses, cows, mules and slaves; in houses and fertile fields, and even in elephants. (Chāndogya Upaniṣad, V, 13, 17, and 19; VII, 24; Śatapatha Brāhmaṇa, III, 2, 48; Taittirīya Upaniṣad, I, 5, 12, etc, etc.) Gold is considered a proper gift at sacrifice, the gift of silver (Rajatam Hiraṇyam) being strictly prohibited. The reason is sufficiently grotesque, as the reasons given in the Brāhmaṇas generally are. When the gods claimed back the goods deposited with Agni, he wept, and the tears he shed became silver; and hence if silver is given as *dakṣiṇā,* there will be weeping in the house! The reason scarcely veils the cupidity of priests which was the real cause of gifts in gold.

Not only was the use of gold and silver known, but several other metals are mentioned in White Yajur Veda, XVII, 13. The following passage from the Chāndogya Upaniṣad specifies some metals then in use :

"As one binds gold by means of *lavaṇa* (borax), and silver by means of gold, and tin by means of silver, and lead by means of tin, and iron *(loha)* by means of lead, and wood by means of iron, and also by means of leather," (IV, 17, 7.)

In Aitareya Brāhmaṇa, VIII, 22, we are told, evidently in the language of exaggeration, that the son of Atri presented ten thousand elephants and ten thousand slave girls, "well endowed with ornaments on their necks, who had been gathered from all quarters."

As in the Vedic Period, the food of the people consisted of various kinds of grain as well as the meat of animals. In the Bṛhadāraṇyaka Upaniṣad, VI, III, 13, ten kinds of seeds are mentioned, *viz.,* rice and barley (brīhiyavās), sesamum and kidney bean (tila-māṣās), millet and panic seed (anupriyāngavās), wheat godhūmās), lentils (masūrās), pulse (khalvās) and vetes (khalakulās)

In the White Yajur Veda, XVIII, 12, we have a list of these grains, beside mudga, nīvāra, and syāmākarā. Grains were ground and sprinkled with curds, honey and clarified butter, and so made into different kinds of cake. Milk and its various preparations have ever been a favorite food in India.

Animal food was in use in the Epic Period, and the cow and the bull were often laid under requisition. In Aitareya Brāhmaṇa, 1, 15, we learn that an ox or a cow which miscarries is killed when a king or an honored guest is received.

In the Brāhmaṇa of the Black Yajur Veda, the kind and character of the cattle which should be slaughtered in minor sacrifices, for the gratification of particular divinities, are laid down in detail. Thus a dwarf one is to be sacrified to Viṣṇu, a drooping horned bull to Indra, a thick-legged cow to Vāyu, a barren cow to Viṣṇu and Varuṇa, a black cow to Pūṣan, a cow having two colors to Mitra and Varuṇa, a red cow to Indra, etc., etc. In a larger and more important ceremonial, like the Aśvamedha, no less than 180 domestic animals, including horses, bulls, cows, goats, deer, etc, were sacrificed. The same Brāhmaṇa lays down instructions for carving, and the Gopatha Brāhmaṇa tells us who received the different portions. The priests got the tongue, the neck, the shoulder, the rump, the legs, etc while the master of the house (wisely) appropriated to himself the sirloin, and his wife had to content herself with the pelviz! Plentiful libations of the Soma beer were allowed to wash down the meat!

In the Śatapatha Brāhmaṇa, IV, 5, we have a detailed account of the slaughter of a barren cow and its cooking. In III, 1, 2, 21 of the same Brāhmaṇa, there is an amusing discussion as to the propriety of eating the meat of an ox or a cow. The conclusion is not very definite : "Let him (the priest) not eat the flesh of the cow and the ox." Nevertheless Yājñavalkya said (taking apparently a very practical view of the matter "I for one eat it, provided that it is tender !"

The practical Yājñavalkya could scarcely, however have

contemplated the wonderful effects of vegetable and animal diets, respectively, as laid down in the following passage from the Bṛhadāraṇyaka Upaniṣad, (VI, 4, 17 and 18) :—

"And if a man wishes that a learned daughter should be born to him, and that she should live to her full age, then, after having prepared boiled rice with sesamum and butter, they (the husband and wife) should both eat, being fit to have offspring.

"And if a man wishes that a learned son should be born to him, famous, a public man, a popular speaker, that he should know all the Vedas, and that he should live to his full age, then, after having prepared boiled rice with meat and butter, they (the husband and wife) should both eat, being fit to have offspring. The meat should be of a young or of an old bull."

We scarcely thought that the venerable composers of the Vedic Brāhmaṇas ever suspected any sort of connexion between beef eating and public speaking, such as has manifested itself in later days !

And now let our readers by an effort of their imagination construct for themselves the social life which the Hindus of the Epic Period, which the citizens of Hastināpura and Kāmpilya and Ayodhyā lived three thousand years ago. The towns were surrounded by walls, beautified by edifices, and laid out in spacious streets—which would not bear comparison with the structures and roads of modern days—but were probably the finest of their kind in ancient times. The king's palace was always the centre of the town, and was frequented by boisterous barons and a rude soldiery as well as by holy saints and learned priests. The people flocked to the palace on every great occasion, loved, respected and worshipped the king, and had no higher faith than loyalty to the king. Householders and citizens had their possessions and wealth in gold, silver and jewels, in cars, horses, mules, and slaves, and in the fields surrounding the town. They kept the sacred fire in every respectable household, honored guests, lived according to the law of the land, offered sacrifices with the help of Brāhmaṇs, and honored knowledge. Every Āryan boy was sent to his school at an early age. Brāhmans and Kṣatriyas and Vaiśyas were educated together, learnt the same lessons and the same religion, and returned home, married and settled down as householders. Priests and soldiers were a portion of the people, intermarried with the people, and ate and drank with the people. Various classes of manufacturers supplied the various wants of a civilized society, and followed their ancestral professions from generation to generation, but were not cut up into separate castes. Agriculturists lived with their herds and their ploughs round each town : while holy saints and men of learning sometimes lived away in forests to add day by day to that knowledge which was the most cherished heritage of the Āryans. The picture of ancient life can be indefinitely enlarged; but each reader will probably do this for himself. We will turn from this general account of ancient society to examine the position which women held in that society.

We have seen that the absolute seclusion of women was unknown in ancient India. Hindu women held an honored place from the dawn of Hindu civilization tour thousand years ago; they inherited and possessed property; they took a share in sacrifices and religious duties; they attended great assemblies on state occasions; they openly frequented public thoroughfares, according to their needs, every day of their life; they often distinguished themselves in the learning of their times; and they even had their legitimate influence on politics and administration. And although they never mixed so freely in the society of "men as women do in modern Europe, yet absolute seclusion and restraint are not Hindu customs; they were unknown in India till the Mahomedan times; and are to this day unknown in parts of India like the Mahārāṣṭra, where the rule of the Moslems was brief. No ancient nation held their women in higher honor than the Hindus, but the Hindus have been misjudged and wronged by writers unacquainted with their literature, and who received their notions of the women of the East from Turkish and Arab customs.

Innumerable passages could be quoted from the Brāhmaṇa

literature, showing the high esteem in which women were held, but we will content ourselves with one or two. The first is the celebrated conversation between Yājñavalkya and his learned wife Maitreyī on the eve of his retirement into forests :—

"1. Now when Yājñavalkya was going to enter upon another state, he said : 'Maitreyī, verily I am going away from this my house. Forsooth let me make a settlement between thee and Kātyāyanī.'

"2. Maitreyī said : 'My Lord, if this whole earth full of wealth belonged to me, tell me, should I be immortal by it ?' 'No,' replied Yājñavalkya; 'like the life of rich people will be thy life. But there is no hope of immortality by wealth ?'

"3. And Maitreyī said : 'What should I do with that by which I do not become immortal ? What my Lord knoweth of immortality, tell that to me?'

"4. Yājñavalkya replied : 'Thou who art truly dear to me, thou speakest dear words. Come, sit down, I will explain it to thee, and mark well what I say.'

And then he explained the principle which is so often and so impressively taught in the Upaniṣads, that the Universal Self dwells in the husband, in the wife, in the sons, and in wealth, in the Brāhmans and Kṣatriyas, and in all the worlds, in the Devas, in all living creatures, yea, in all the universe.—Bṛhadāraṇyaka Upaniṣad.

Our next quotation, which is also from the same Upaniṣad, relates to a great assembly of learned men in the court of Janaka, king of the Videhas :—

"Janaka Videha sacrificed with a sacrifice at which many presents were offered to the priests of (the Aśvamedha). Brāhmans of the Kurus and the Pāñcālas had come thither and Janaka wished to know which of those Brāhmans was the best read. So he enclosed a thousand cows, and ten padas (of gold) were fastened to each pair of horns.

"2. And Janaka spoke to them : 'Ye venerable Brāhmans, he who among you is the wisest, let him drive away these cows.'

Then those Brāhmans durst not, but Yājñavalkya said to his pupil 'Drive them away, my dear.' He replied, 'O glory of the Sāman !' and drove them away."

On this the Brāhmans became angry, and plied the haughty priest Yājñavalkya with questions, but Yājñavalkya was a match for them all. Aśvala the hotri priest, Jāratkarava Ārtabhāga, Bhujyu Lāhyāyani, Uṣasta Chākrāyana, Kahola Kauṣītakeya, Uddālaka Āruṇi, and others plied Yājñavalkya with questions, but Yājñavalkya was not found wanting; the learned men, one by one, held their peace.

There was one in the great assembly—and this is a remarkable fact which throws light on the manners of the time—who was not deficient in the learning and the priestly lore of those times, because she was a lady. She rose in the open assembly, and said : "O Yājñavalkya, as the son of a warrior from the Kāsīs or Videhas might string his loosened bow, take two pointed foe-piercing arrows in his hand and rise to battle, I have risen to fight thee with two questions. Answer me these questions." The questions were put and were answered, and Gārgī Vāchaknavī was silent.

Do not these passages and such passages as these indicate that women were honored in ancient India, more perhaps than among any other ancient nation in the face of the globe ? Considered as the intellectual companions of their husbands, as their friends and affectionate helpers in the journey of life, as the partners of their religious duties and the source of their pure domestic bliss, Hindu wives were honored and respected in ancient times. It was not often that they attained the abstruse learning of a Maitreyī or a Gārgī; but nevertheless they were well informed in general matters and well trained in their own domestic duties. Free from all undue restraint on their movements and actions, women moved freely in the society in which they lived, frequented public festivities and sights, performed religious sacrifices, vizited friends, and received vizits. More than this : they had their rights to property and to inheritance which indicate the honor and regard in which they were held. It would scarcely be fair to compare ancient customs with the institutions of modern civilization; but the historian of India, who has studied the literature of the ancient Hindus, will have no hesitation in asserting that never, in the most polished days of Greece or Rome, were women held in higher regard in those countries than they were in India three thousand years ago.

As we have said before, early marriage and child marriage were still unknown in the Epic Period, and we have numerous allusions to the marriage of girls at a proper age. Widow marriage was not only not prohibited, but there is distinct sanction for it; and the rites which the widow had to perform before she entered into the married state again, are distinctly laid down. As caste was still a pliable institution, men belonging to one caste not unoften married widows of another, and Brāhmans married widows of other castes without any scruple. "And when a woman has had ten former husbands, not Brāhmans, if a Brahmān then marries her, it is he alone who is her husband." *Atharvā Veda,* V, 17, 8.

Polygamy was allowed among the Hindus as among many other ancient nations, but was confined in India to kings and wealthy lords as a rule. Modern readers, who would judge harshly of ancient Hindu civilization from the prevalence of this custom, should remember that polygamy was nearly universal among the wealthy people of all nations in ancient times, and that, to take some instances, Alexander the Great and his successors Lysimachus, Seleucus, Ptolemy, Demetrius, Pyrrhus and others were all polygamists! Polyandry, we need hardly say, was unknown in Āryan India: "For one man has many wives, but one wife has not many husbands at the same time." Aitareya Brāhmaṇa, III, 23.

There is in the Śatapatha Brāhmaṇa (I, 8, 3, 6) a curious passage prohibiting marriages among blood relations to the third or fourth generation : "Hence from one and the same man spring both the enjoyer (the husband) and the one to be enjoyed (the wife)"; "for now kingsfolk live sporting and rejoicing together saying, in the fourth or third man (generation) we unite." The rule of prohibition became more strict in later times.

CHAPTER–7

LAW, ASTRONOMY AND THE PROGRESS OF LEARNING

The punishment of criminals and a proper administration of the law are the foundations on which all civilized societies are built, and we find a warm appreciation of law in some passages in the Brāhmaṇa literature : "Law is the Kṣatra (power) of the Kṣatra, therefore there is nothing higher than the law. Thenceforth even a weak man rules a stronger with the help of the law as with the help of a king. Thus the law is what is called the true. And if a man declares what is true, they say he declares the law; and if he declares the law, they say he declares what is true. Thus both are the same," (Bṛhadāraṇyaka I, 4, 14.) No nobler definition of law has been discovered by all the jurists in the world.

The judicial procedure was still, however, crude, and as among other ancient nations, criminals were often tried by the ordeal of fire.

"They bring a man hither whom they have taken by the hand, and they say : 'He has taken something, he has committed theft.' (When he denies, they say): ' Heat the hatchet for him.' If he committed the theft, then he . . grasps the heated hatchet, he is burnt, and he is killed. But if he did not commit the theft, then he . . grasps the heated hatchet, he is not burnt, and he is delivered.", (Chāndogya, VI, 16.) Murder, theft, drunkenness and adultery are generally the offences alluded to.

The first elementary knowledge of the astronomical science is discernable in the Ṛg Veda itself. The year was divided into twelve lunar months, and a thirteenth or intercalary month was added to adjust the lunar with the solar year (I, 25, 8.) The six

Women in India have ever been remarkable for their faithfulness and their duteous affection towards their husbands, and female unfaithfulness is comparatively rare. It would appear that Hindu priests, like Roman Catholic priests, found a way to discover the most hidden secrets of frail women, and the following reads like a rule of Roman Catholic confessional :

"Thereupon. the Pratiprasthātri returns (to the place where the sacrificed wife is seated). When he is about to lead the wife away, he asks her, 'With whom holdest thou intercourse ?' Now when a woman who belongs to one (man) carries on intercourse with another, she undoubtedly commits (a sin) against Varuṇa. He therefore asks her, lest she should sacrifice with a secret pang in her mind; for when confessed, the sin becomes less, since it becomes truth : this is why he thus asks her. And whatever (connexion) she confesses not, that indeed will turn out injurious to the relatives." (Śatapatha Brāhmaṇa, II, 5, 2, 20).

seasons of the year were named Madhu, Mādhava, Sukra, Suchi, Nabha and Nabhasya, and were connected with different gods (II, 36.) The different phases of the moon were observed and were personified as deities. Rākā is the full moon, Sinīvāli is the last day before the new moon, and Gungu is the new moon (II, 32). The position of the moon with regard to the Nakṣatras or the lunar mansions is also alluded to (VIII, 3, 20), and some of the constellations of the lunar mansions are also named in X, 85, 13; but these hymns were probably composed at the time of the compilation of the Ṛg Veda which falls within the Epic Period, when the lunar zodiac was finally settled.

As might be expected, there was a considerable progress made in the Epic Period. Astronomy had now come to be regarded as a distinct science, and astronomers by profession were called Nakṣatra Darsa and Ganaka. (Taittirīya Brāhmaṇa, IV, 5, and White Yajur Veda, XXX, 10, 20.) The twenty-eight lunar mansions are also enumerated singly in the Black Yajur Veda, and a second and later enumeration occurs in the Atharva Saṁhitā and in the Taittirīya Brāhmaṇa. An interesting passage in Śatapatha Brāhmaṇa (II, I, 2) shows how sacrificial rites were regulated by the position of the moon in reference to these lunar asterisms. It is too long to be quoted, and we will therefore give extracts :—

"1. He may set up two fires under the *Kṛttikās* (the pleiades), for they, the vrittikās, are doubtless Agni's asterism.

"6. He may also set up his fires under (the asterism of) *Rohiṇī*. For, under Rohiṇī it was that Prajāpati, when desirous of progeny set up his fires.

"8. He may also set up his fires under (the asterism of) *Mṛgaśīrṣa*. For Mṛgaśīrṣa, indeed, is the head of Prajapāti. He may also set up his fires under the *Phalgunīs*. They, the Phalgunīs, are Indra's asterism, and even correspond to him in name; for indeed Indra is also called Arjuna, this being his mystic name; and they (Phalgunīs) are also called Arjunīs 12, Let him set up his fire under the asterism *Hastā,* whosoever should wish that (presents) should be offered him : then indeed (that will take place) forthwith; for whatever is offered with the hand (hasta), that indeed is given to him.

"13. He may also set up his fires under *Chitrā?* etc, etc.

But not only was the setting up of the sacrificial fires regulated by the constellations, but sacrifices lasting for a year were regulated by the sun's annual course. Dr. Martin Haug, the editor and translator of the Aitareya Brāhmaṇa has made some excellent remarks on this subject which deserve to be quoted :—

"A regulation of the calendar by such (astronomical) observations was an absolute necessity for the Brāhmans; for the proper time of commencing and ending their sacrifices, principally the so-called *Sattras* or sacrificial sessions, could not be known without an accurate knowledge of the time of the sun's northern and southern progress. The knowledge of the calendar forms such an essential part of the ritual, that many important conditions of the latter cannot be carried out without the former. The sacrifices are allowed to commence only at certain lucky constellations and in certain months; so, for instance, as a rule, no great sacrifice can commerce during the sun's southern progress (*dakṣiṇāyāna*); for this is regarded, up to the present day, as an unlucky period for the Brāhmans, in which even to die is believed to be a misfortune, The great sacrifices take place generally in spring, in the months *Chaitra* and *Vaiśākha* (April and May.) The *Sattras,* which lasted for a year, were, as one may learn from a careful perusal of the 4th Book of the Aitareya Brāhmaṇa, nothing but an imitation of the sun's yearly course. They were divided into two distinct parts, each consisting of six months of thirty days each; in the midst of both was the Viṣuvan, *i.e.* equator or central day, cutting the whole *Sattra* into two halves. The ceremonies were in both the halves exactly the same; but they were in the latter half performed in an inverted order. This represents the increase of the days in the northern and their decrease in the southern progress; for both increase and decrease take place exactly in the same proportions."—Introduction, pp. 46 and 47.

We have said that the lunar zodiac was finally arranged in

India towards the close of the Vedic Period, or the commencement of the Epic Period, say, B. C, 1400. The illustrious Colebrooke first stated his opinion that the Hindus arranged the lunar mansions from their own observations; and later researches into the intimate connection between the Vedic rites and the position of the moon with regard to the stars, leave no doubt whatever as to the indigenous origin of Hindu astronomy. But, nevertheless, some European scholars have indulged in conjectures as to the origin of Hindu astronomy, and a controversy which may really be called a battle of books has raged in Europe and America !

The eminent French savant Biot writing in 1860, described the Chinese system of *Sieu* as an indigenous Chinese institution, and the inference was, that the Hindu *Nakṣatras* and Arab *Manazil* were borrowed from the Chinese. The German scholar Lassen was led to adopt this opinion. The profound scholar Weber, however, took up the subject, and in two elaborate essays published in 1860 and 1861, proved that the Chinese *Sieu* as well as the Arab *Manazil* "in respect of order, number, indentity of limiting stars, and inequality of distance correspond to one of the most modern phases of the Hindu *Nakṣatras,* prior to which these have their own peculiar history of development," Weber thus finally disposes of the theory of the Chinese origin of the *Nakṣatras,* and further proves that the Arab lunar mansions were imported by the Arabs from India. And this is exactly the conclusion to which Colebrooke had arrived as for back as 1807, when he wrote that the Hindus had an ecliptic, "seemingly their own : it was certainly borrowed by the Arabians."

Having thus finally disposed of the Chinese and Arabian theories, Professor Weber must needs start a theory of his own, which we may call the Chaldean theory! He conjectures that the Hindu system may have been derived from some foreign source, probably Babylon. This is nothing but a conjecture, a mere suspicion, for Assyrian scholars have not yet obtained any trace of a lunar zodiac among the archives of old Babylonian learning; but Professor Whitney of America supports this "suspicion," as he calls it, because he thinks the Hindus "were not a people of such habits of mind" as to make observations in the heavens and settle the lunar zodiac. The argument is so amusing, that the learned professor almost withdraws it himself, stating that the argument "is not of a character to compel belief."

When scholars condescend to such wild reasoning, it is idle to pursue the controversy. We will, therefore, conclude this subject with a passage in which Max Müller puts forward the common sense view of the subject. "The 27 Nakṣatras, or the 27 constellations which were chosen in India as a kind of lunar zodiac, were supposed to have come from Babylon. Now the Babylonian zodiac was solar, and in spite of repeated researches, no trace of a lunar zodiac has been found, where so many things have been found in the cuneiform inscriptions. But supposing even that a lunar zodiac had been discovered in Babylon, no one acquainted with Vedic literature, and with the ancient Vedic ceremonial, would easily allow himself to be persuaded that the Hindus had borrowed that simple division of the sky from the Babylonians."[1]

Besides fixing the lunar zodiac, the Hindus of this period observed the solstitial points to fix the dates of momentous events, and divided the year into months, naming each month after the lunar constellation at which the moon was at its full in the particular month. If we can rely on Bentley, this naming of the months must have taken place in 1181 B. C, and 1426 B. C. is given for the formation of the lunar mansions.[2] A knowledge of the solar zodiac was borrowed from the Greeks, after the Christian era, as we will see in a subsequent Book.

Besides astronomy, other branches of learning were also cultivated in the Epic Period. Thus in Chāndogya Upaniṣad (VII, 1, 2), we find Nārada saying to Sanatkumāra, "I know the Ṛg Veda, Sir, the Yajur Veda, the Sāma Veda, as the fourth the Atharvana, as the fifth the Itihāsa Purāṇa, the Veda of the Vedas (grammar); the Pitrya (rules for sacrifices for the ancestors); the Rāsi (the science of numbers); the Daiva (the science of portents); the Nidhi (the science of time); the Vākovākya (logic); the EkĒyana (ethics); the Deva Vidyā (etymology;) the Brahmā

Vidyā (pronunciation prosody, etc.); the Bhūta Vidyā (the science of demons); tbe Kṣatra Vidyā (the science of weapons); the Nakṣatra Vidyā (astronomy); the Sarpa Devañjana Vidyā (the science of serpents and of genii.) All this I know, Sir."

In Bṛhadāraṇyaka (II, 4, 10) we are told that "Ṛg-Veda, Yajur Veda, Sāma Veda, Atharvāṅgirasas, Itihāsa (legends), Purāṇa (cosmogonies) Vidyā (knowledge), the Upaniṣads, Ślokas (verses), Sūtras (prose rules) Anuvyākhyānas (glosses), Vyākhyānas (commentaries), have all been breathed forth from the Supreme Being.

Again, in the eleventh book of the Śatapatha Brāhmaṇa, we have mention of the three Vedas, the Atharvāṅgirasas, the Aunśāsanas, the Vidyās, the Vākovākya, the Itihāsa Purāṇa, the Narasansīs and the Gāthās. Professor Weber is of opinion that these names do not necessarily imply distinct species of work which existed in the Epic Period, and which have been since lost to us. He points out that many of the names merely imply the different subjects which we still find existing in the Brāhmaṇas. It was at a later age, in the Rationalistic Period, that these different subjects which we find interwoven in the Brāhmaṇas and Upaniṣads, branched out as separate subjects of study, and were taught in the separate Sūtra works and compositions which have come down to us.

There is considerable force in this supposition, but at the same time it seems very likely that, on many of the subjects enumerated above, separate works existed in the Epic Period, which have been lost to us because they have been replaced by more elaborate and scientific works of a later age on the same subjects.

REFERENCES

1. India: What can it teach us. (1883) p. 126.
2. Hindu Astronomy. London (1825), pp. 3 and 10.

CHAPTER – 8

THE SACRIFICIAL RITES AND LEGENDS OF THE BRĀHMANAS

The main feature which distinguishes the religion of the Epic Period from that of the preceding age, is the great importance which came to be attached to *sacrifice.* In the earlier portion of the Vedic Period, men composed hymns in praise of the most imposing manifestations of nature, they deified these various natural phenomena, and they worshipped these deities under the name of Indra or Varuṇa of Agni or the Maruts. The worship took the shape of sacrifice, *i. e.,* the offering of milk or grain food, of animals or libations of the Soma juice to the gods, Such offerings were but an accompaniment to the worship of the gods which proceeded from pious hearts and pious lips.

A gradual change, however, is perceptible towards the close of the Ṛg Veda, and in the period of the Brāhmaṇas sacrifice as such, the mere forms and ceremonials and offerings, had acquired such an abnormal importance, that everything else was lost in it. The priests appear to have believed that the ancient hymns had been composed simply and solely for the purpose of being uttered at sacrifices, and were only a means to the great end. They entirely forgot that the hymns were themselves the earliest expression of those feelings of gratitude and fervency in the human heart which found a later and a less pure form of expression in elaborate sacrifices.

It would be entirely foreign to our purpose to describe the various kinds of sacrifices of which we find accounts in the Brāhmaṇas, from the simple morning or evening sacrifice (Agnihotra), and the new and full moon sacrifices (Darsa

Pūrṇamāsa Iṣṭi), to the *sattras* or sacrificial sessions, which lasted for a whole year or even ten or twelve years !

Sacrifices were generally accompanied by gifts of cattle, gold, garments and food, and by the offering of animals as victims. There is a curious passage in Śatapatha Brāhmaṇa, 1, 2, 3, 7 & 8, about animal sacrifice which deserves to be quoted :

"At first, namely, the gods offered up a man as a victim. When he was offered up, the sacrificial essence went out of him. It entered into the horse. They offered up the horse. When it was offered, the sacrificial essence went out of it. It entered into the ox, when it was offered up, the sacrificial essence went out of it. It entered into the sheep. They offered up the sheep. When it was offered up, the sacrificial essence went out of it. It entered into the goat. They offered up the goat. When it was offered up, the sacrificial essence went out of it. It entered into this earth. They searched for it by digging. They found it in the shape of those two substances, the rice and barley : therefore, even now they obtain those two by digging; and as much efficacy as all those sacrificed animal victims would have for him, so much efficacy has this oblation (of rice, etc), for him who knows this."

Professor Max Müller infers from this passage that human sacrifices prevailed among the ancient Hindus, not in the Brāhmaṇa Period, not even in the Vedic Period, but at a still remoter age. Dr. Rajendra Lala Mitra, we regret to observe, follows the lead of Professor Max Müller, and infers from certain other passages which he quotes from the literature of this period, that the inhuman custom prevailed in the remote past. We demur to the conclusions of these two eminent scholars.

If human sacrifice had prevailed in India before the Ṛg Veda hymns which are now extant were composed, we should certainly have found allusions to it in the hymns themselves—allusions far more frequent than we find in the later Brāhmaṇa literature. We find no such allusions. The story of Sunaḥśepha, as told in the Ṛg Veda, is no evidence of human sacrifice. And there is absolutely nothing else in the Ṛg Veda which can be construed as evidence of this fact. It is impossible to suppose that such a striking and fearful custom should have existed and gradually fallen into disuse without leaving the slightest trace in the Vedic hymns, some of which have come down from a very ancient date.

And where do we find allusions to this custom in the literature of the Epic Period ? The Sāma Veda is compiled from the Vedic hymns, and of course there is no mention of human sacrifice in this Veda. There is no mention of the horrible custom in the Black Yajur Veda, and there is no mention of it in the White Yajur Veda, properly so called. It is in the very latest compositions of the Epic Period—in the *khila* or supplementary portion of the White Yajur Veda, in the Brāhmaṇa of the Black Yajur Veda, in the Aitareya Brāhmaṇa of the Ṛg Veda, and the last but one book of the Śatapatha Brāhmaṇa that we have accounts of human sacrifice. Is it possible to postulate the existence of a horrible custom in India in the remote past of which we find no mention in the Ṛg Veda, in the Sāma Veda, in the Black or White Yajur Veda, but the memory of which suddenly revived after a thousand years in the supplements and Brāhmaṇas of the Vedas ? Or is it not far more natural to suppose that all the allusions to human sacrifice in the later compositions are the speculations of priests? The practice never generally prevailed among Hindus, and if it was ever adopted in rare and exceptional cases, it was borrowed from the non-Āryans of India at a comparatively recent period of Hindu history. The institution was foreign to the Vedic *religion* and to the Vedic Hindus.

But though human sacrifices never prevailed among the ancient Āryan Hindus animal sacrifices, no doubt, prevailed in ancient times, but gradually fell into disuse after the Epic Period. It was the growing repugnance to the killing of animals which was one of the causes which led to the rise of Buddhism in the Rationalistic Period, and that faith was essentially a religion of humanity and protection to all living beings.

The different varieties of sacrifices certainly exceed 1,000, but Gautama classifies them as seven kinds of Pāka-sacrifice, seven kinds of Havih-sacrifice and seven kinds of Soma-sacrifice.

The Havih-sacrifices are :—

(1) Agnyādheya (Setting up the sacred fire).
(2) Agnihotra (Daily oblation).
(3) Darsapūrṇamāsa (Full and new moon sacrifice).
(4) Āgrayana (Harvest sacrifice).
(5) Chāturmāsya (Four monthly sacrifice).
(6) Nirūdhapaśubandha (Animal sacrifice).
(7) Sautrāmanī (An expiation for over-indulgence in Soma).

The Soma-sacrifices ar

(1) Agniṣṭoma.
(2) Atyagniṣṭoma.
(3) Ukthya.
(4) Ṣoḍaṣin.
(5) Vājapeyā.
(6) Atirātra.
(7) Aptoryāma.

] Different types of norms of ceremonials.

The 7 Pāka-sacrifices will be enumerated in the next Book.

An account of these 21 sacrifices would be beyond the scope of the present work. The first of the above rites, however, the setting up of the fire, had a most important bearing on the life of the ancient Hindus, and an account of it will illustrate sacrificial rites generally.

Aśvapti, as has been observed before, boasted that in his kingdom there was no thief, no miser, no drunkard, no ignorant person, no adulterer or adulteress, and "no man without an altar in his house." In those days, to keep the sacred fire in the altar was a duty incumbent on every householder, and the breach of this rule was regarded as positive impiety and irreligiousness, The student who had returned home from his teacher or his Pariṣad, married in due time, and then set up the sacrificial fires. This was generally done on the first day of the waxing moon, but sometimes also at full moon, probably to enable the newly married couple to enter on the sacred duties as early as possible. The performance of the Agniādhāna, or the establishment of the sacred fires, generally required two days. The sacrificer chose his four priests, the Brahmān, the Hotri, the Adhvaryu, and the

Agnīdhra, and erected two sheds or fire-houses, for the Gārhapatya and the Āhavanīya fires, respectively. A circle was marked for the Gārhapatya fire, and a square for the Āhvanīya fire, and if a southern or Dakṣiṇāgni was required, a semi-circular area was marked south of the space between the other two.

The Adhvaryu then procured a temporary fire, either producing it by friction, or obtaining it from certain specified sources in the village, and after the usual fivefold lustration of the Gārhapatya fire-place, he laid down the fire thereon. Towards sunset the sacrificer invoked the gods and manes. He and his wife then entered the Gārhapatya house, and the Adhvaryu handed him two pieces of wood, the *arani* for the production of the Āhavanīya fire on the next morning, and the sacrificer and his wife laid them on their laps, and propitiatory ceremonies were performed. The sacrificer and his wife remained awake the whole night and kept up the fire. In the morning the Adhvaryu extinguished the fire, or it there was to be a Dakṣiṇāgni, he kept it till that fire was made up. Such, in brief, is the ceremony of the Agni-ādhāna, or the setting up of sacrificial fires, which formed an important duty in the life of every Hindu householder in ancient days, when the gods were worshipped by each man in his fire-place, and temples and idols were unknown.

We will now briefly allude to some other ancient customs. The illustrious German scholar Dr. Roth first pointed out in 1854, from a passage in the Ṛg Veda, (X, 18, 11) that in ancient ages burial was practised by the Hindus. This custom was followed by the burning of the dead and the burial of the ashes. That this latter custom was also in vogue in the Ṛg Veda Period appears from other passages, such as X, 15, 14, and X, 16,1. In the Epic Period, of which we are now speaking, the Custom of burying had ceased altogether, and the dead were burnt, and the ashes were buried. We find an account of this in the 35th chapter of the White Yajur Veda. The bones of the deceased were collected in a vessel and buried in the ground near a stream, and a mound was raised as high as the knee and covered with grass. The relatives then bathed and changed their clothes and left the funeral ground. The same ceremony is more fully described in the Āraṇyaka of the Black Yajur Veda. It is scarcely necessary to add that the custom which now prevails among the Hindus is simple cremation, without the burial of the ashes. This recent custom began, according to Dr. Rajendra Lala, shortly after the commencement of the Christian era.

The interesting ceremony of the gift of cakes to the departed ancestor is described in the second chapter of the White Yajur Veda. The cakes are offered to the Fire and to Soma, and the Fathers are invoked to receive their shares. Then follows an address to the Fathers with reference to the six seasons of the year. The worshipper then looks at his wife and says: "Fathers! you have made us domestic men—we have brought these gifts to you according to our power." Then, offering a thread or wool or hair, he says : "Fathers! this is your apparel, wear it." Then the wife eats a cake with a desire to have children and says : "Fathers! let a male be born in me in this season. Do you protect the son in this womb from all sickness." Departed spirits, according to the Hindu religion, receive offerings from their living descendants, and get none when the family is extinct. Hence the extreme fear of Hindus to die without male issue, and the birth of a son is a part of the religion.

Turning now to legends we note with interest how simple metaphors and similes in the Ṛg Veda take shape as legends in the Brāhmaṇas, and then expand into the gorgeous myths of the Purāṇas.

We have seen that in Vedic hymns, Soma is said to be obtained from the sky, aud brought down by a falcon. The falcon in the Brāhmaṇa is the Gāyatrī Metre which flew up to the sky for Soma. But when Gāyatrī was carrying Soma, the Gandharvas stole it. As the Gandharvas are fond of women, Vāk or speech went in the shape of a woman without clothes to delude the Gandharvas. The Gandharvas were deluded, and recited the Vedas to her; but the gods sang to her and amused her, and so she turned to the gods; "wherefore even to this day women are given to vain things, and hence it is, to him who dances and sings that they most readily take a fancy !" (Sat. Br. III 2, 4, 6.) Thus both Soma and vāk came to the gods.

A most remarkable legend is told of Manu, who in the Vedic hymns is alluded to as the ancient progenitor of man, who introduced cultivation and worship by fire. The legend in the Śatapatha Brāhmaṇa (I, 8, 1), is not unlike the account of the Deluge in the Old Testament. As Manu was washing his hands a fish came unto him and said : "Rear me, I will save thee." Manu reared it and in time it told him "in such and such a year that flood will come. Thou shalt then attend to me (*i. e.* to my advice) by preparing a ship." The flood came, and Manu entered into the ship which he had built in time, and the fish swam up to him and carried the ship beyond the northern mountain. The ship was fastened to a tree, there, and as the flood subsided, Manu gradually descended. "The flood then swept away all these creatures, and Manu alone remained here."

We have elsewhere quoted a celebrated Vedic hymn in which the poet, with fervent piety, enquires, "To which god shall we give our offering." It is difficult to misunderstand the import of this simple and sublime hymn; but "the authors of the Brāhmaṇas had so completely broken with the past that, forgetful of the poetical character of the hymn and the yearning of the poets after the unknown god, they exalted the interrogative pronoun itself into a deity, and acknowledged a god Ka or Who."

There is a beautiful Vedic simile in which the Sun, pursuing the Dawn, is compared to a lover pursuing a maiden. Who could have imagined that this simile would give rise to the legend which is found in the Brāhmaṇas (Śatapatha, I, 7, 4; Aitereya, III, 33, etc.) that Prajāpati, the supreme god, felt a passion for his daughter, and this was the origin of creation! This legend in the Brāhmaṇas further developed itself in the Purāṇas, where Brahmā, is represented as amorous of his daughter. The whole of these monstrous legends arose from a simple metaphor in the Ṛg Veda about the Sun following the Dawn. That such is the origin of the Paurāṇik fables was known to Hindu thinkers and commentators, as will appear from the following well-known argument of Kumārila, the great opponent of Buddhism, and the predecessor of Saṅkarācārya,

"It is fabled that Prajāpati, the Lord of Creation, did violence to his daughter. But what does it mean ? Prajāpati, the Lord of Creation, is a name of the sun; and he is called so because he protects all creatures. His daughter Uṣas is the Dawn. And when it is said that he was in love with her, this only means that at sunrise the sun runs after the dawn; the dawn being at the same time called the daughter of the sun because she rises when he approaches. In the same manner it is said that Indra was the seducer of Ahalyā. This does not imply that the god Indra committed such a crime; but Indra means the sun, and Ahalyā the night; and as the night is seduced and ruined by the sun of the morning, therefore is Indra called the paramour of Ahalyā."

There is a myth in the Taittirīya Brāhmaṇa (I, 1, 3, 5) that nothing was seen in the beginning except water, and a lotus leaf standing out of it. Prajāpati dived in the shape of a boar and brought up some earth and spread it out and fastened it down, by pebbles. This was the earth.

A similar story is told in the Śatapatha Brāhmaṇa (II, 1, 1, 8), that the gods and Asuras both sprung from Prajāpati, and the earth trembled like a lotus leaf when the gods and Asuras contended for mastery. We know that in the Ṛg Veda, the word Asura is an adjective which means strong or powerful, and is invariably applied to gods except in the very last hymns of the last Maṇḍala. In the Brāhmaṇas the word changed its meaning altogether, and was applied to the enemies of gods about whom many new legends were invented.

The story of Prajāpati conceiving a passion for his daughter, and this being the origin of creation, has already been alluded to before. Another account is given in the Śatapatha Brāhmaṇa (II, 5, 1) : "Verily in the beginning Prajāpati alone existed here." He created living beings and birds and reptiles and snakes, but they all passed away for want of food. He then made the breasts in the forepart of their body (*i. e.,* of the mammals) teem with milk, and so the living creatures survived.

While thus legends and speculations were springing up in the Epic Period, religion and religious faith was still the same as in the Vedic Period. The gods of the Ṛg Veda were still worshipped, and the hymns of the Ṛk, Sāman or Yajus were still uttered as texts. Only the veneration with which the gods were looked up to in the Vedic Period was merged now in the veneration for the sacrificial ceremonies. And superstition had increased vastly since the Vedic Period. Every sacrifice, every act, every movement has been laid down and described in the Brāhmaṇas, and no departure is allowed. Superstitious reasons are alleged for every act enjoined on the worshipper, and penances ordained for all kinds of mishaps. There are penances, for instance, if the cow sits down when being milked, or if she cries, or moves and spills the milk, or if the milk is spoilt, or the spoon is broken, or if the Agnihotri sheds tears, or if his wife or cow gives birth to twins! (Aitareya Brāhmaṇa, V and VII.) Such are the inevitable results when priests are made the custodians of the conscience of a nation!

New gods however were slowly rinding a place in the Hindu pantheon—names which have acquired importance in latter times. We have already seen that Arjuna was another name of Indra, even in the Śatapatha Brāhmaṇa. In Chapter XVI of the White Yajur Veda, we find Rudra already assuming his more modern Paurāṇik names, and assuming a more distinct individuality. In the Ṛg Veda, as we have already seen, Rudra is the father of the storms, he is the thunder. In the White Yajur Veda he is also described as the thunder-cloud, but is specially represented as a fearful god, and often the god of thieves and criminals, and altogether a destructive power. He is called Girisha (because clouds rest on mountains); he is called *Tāmrā* or *Aruṇā* or *Babhru* (from the colour of the clouds); he is named Nīla-kaṇṭha or blue-necked (also from the same reason); Kapardin or the long-haired; Paśupati or the nourisher of animals; Śaṅkara or the benefactor; Śiva or the beneficent; and Rudra or the terrible. Thus, in the Epic Period, we find

Rudra in a transition stage, and we already see the origin of some of the Paurāṇik legends about Śiva. But nowhere in the Brāhmaṇa literature do we find those legends fully developed, or Rudra represented as the Paurāṇik Śiva, the consort of Durgā or Kālī. In the Kauṣītaki Brāhmaṇa, we find great importance attached in one passage to Iśāna or Mahādeva. In Śatapatha Brāhmaṇa we find the following remarkable passage :—"This is thy share, O Rudra Graciously accept it together with thy sister Ambikā! (II, 6, 2, 9.) And in a celebrated passage in the Muṇ-ḍaka Upaniṣad (which, it must be remembered, is an Upaniṣad of the Atharva Veda), we find Kālī, Karālī, Manojavā, Sulohitā, Sudhūmarvarṇā Sphuliṅginī, and Bisvarupī as the names of the seven tongues of fire. In Śatapatha Brāhmaṇa (II, 4, *4,* 6), we are told of a sacrifice being performed by Dakṣa Pārvatī; and in the Kena Upaniṣad we find mention of a female called Umā Haimavatī,, who appeared before Indra and explained to Indra the nature of Brahmān. These are a few specimens of the scattered materials in the Brāhmaṇa literature, out of which the gorgeous Paurāṇik legend of Śiva and his consort was reared.

In the Aitareya Brāhmaṇa (VI, 15), and in Śatapatha Brāhmaṇa (I, 2, 5), we are told the story of the gods obtaining from the Asuras the part of the world which Viṣṇu could stride over or cover, and thus they managed to get the whole world. It is in the last book of the Śatapatha Brāhmaṇa (XIV, 1, 1), that Viṣṇu obtains a sort of supremacy among gods, and his head is then struck off by Indra, Kṛṣṇa, the son of Devakī, is not yet a deity; he is a pupil of Ghora Angirasa in the Chāndogya Upaniṣad (III, 17, 6).

While in these scattered allusions we detect materials for the construction of the gorgeous Paurāṇik mythology of a later day, we also find in the Epic Period traces of that scepticism in Brāhmaṇical rites and creed which broke out also at a later day in the Buddhist revolution. The Tāṇḍya Brāhmaṇa of the Sāma Veda contains the Vrātyā—stomas by which the Vrātyas or *Āryans not living according to the Brāhmanical rites* could get admission into that community. Some of them are thus described :—"They drive in open chariots of war, carry bows and lances, wear turbans, robes bordered with red and having fluttering ends, shoes and sheep skins folded double; their leaders are distinguished by brown robes and silver neck ornaments; they pursue neither agriculture nor commerce; their laws are in a state of confusion; they speak the same language as those who have received Brāhmanical consecration, but nevertheless call what is easily spoken hard to pronounce." Is it possible that this description refers to some hordes—probably Turanians—who pressed into Behar through the Himalayas, and gradually adopted Hindu language and civilization ? For the rest, a Vrātya was not yet looked upon with contempt, and the Supreme Being is addressed in Praśna Upaniṣad as a Vrātya.

REFERENCE

1. Max Müller, Ancient Sanscrit Literature, p. 433.

CHAPTER – 9

THE RELIGIOUS AND PHILOSOPHICAL SPECULATIONS OF THE UPANIṢADS

It is a relief to pass on from the rituals and ceremonies of the Brāhmaṇas to the healthier and more vigorous speculations of the Upaniṣads. The Upaniṣads were generally composed about the close of the Epic Period, leaving out, of course, the later Upaniṣads which come down even to the Paurāṇik Period. Some impatience appears to have been felt with the elaborate and unmeaning rites, the dogmatic but childish explanations, and the mystic but grotesque reasoning which fill the voluminous Brāhmaṇas; and thinking men must have asked themselves if this was all that religion could teach. Earnest men, while still conforming to the rites laid down in the Brāhmaṇas, began to speculate on the destination of the human soul and on the nature of the Supreme Being. Learned Kṣatriyas, who became disgusted with the pretensions of really ignorant priests, must have given a start to these healthier speculations, or at least carried them on with vigour and success, until Brāhmans who were wise in their own esteem, felt their inferiority and came to them to learn something of the wisdom of the new school. And although there is much in the speculations of the new school which, after the lapse of nearly three thousand years, appears to us to be grotesque or fanciful, still it is impossible not to be struck with the vigour, the earnestness, and the originality which characterise the Upaniṣads.

The idea of a Supreme Being, a Universal Spirit, an all-pervading Breath or Soul is the keystone of the philosophy and thought of the Upaniṣads. This idea is somewhat different from Monotheism as it has been generally understood in later days. For monotheism generally recognises a God and Creator as distinct from the created beings; but the monotheism of the Upaniṣads, which has been the monotheism of the Hindu religion ever since, recognises God as the Universal Being ; all things else have emanated from him, are a part of him, and will mingle in him, and have no separate existence. This is the lesson which Satyakāma Jabāla learnt from Nature, and this is the lesson which Yājñāvalkya imparted to his beloved and esteemed wife Maitreyī. This, too, is the great idea which is taught in the Upaniṣads in a hundred similes and stories and beautiful legends, which impart to the Upaniṣads their unique value in the literature of the world.

"All this is Brahmān (the Universal Spirit). Let a man meditate on that vizible world as beginning, ending, and breathing in the Brahmān. * *

"The Intelligent, whose body is spirit, whose form is light, whose thoughts are true, whose nature is like either (omnipresent and invisible), from whom all works, all desires, all sweet odours and tastes proceed; he who embraces all this, who never speaks and is never surprised.

"He is my self within the heart, smaller than a corn of rice, smaller than a corn of barley, smaller than a mustard seed, smaller than a canary seed or the kernel of a canary seed. He also is my self within the heart, greater than the earth, greater than the sky, greater than heaven, greater than all these worlds.

"He from whom all works, all desires, all sweet odours and tastes proceed who embraces all this, who never speaks and is never surprised, he—my self within the heart—is that Brahmān. When I shall have departed from hence, I shall obtain him." *Chāndogyā, III,* 14.

Śvetaketu, as we have seen before, stayed with his teacher

from his twelfth year to his twenty-fourth, and then returned home, "having then studied all the Vedas, conceited, considering himself well read, and stern, "But he had yet things to learn which were not ordinarily taught in the schools of the age, and his father Uddālaka Āruṇeya taught him the true nature of the Universal Spirit in beautiful similes:

"As the bees, my son, make honey by collecting the juices of distance trees, and reduce the juice into one form.

"And as these juices have no discrimination, so that they might say, I am the juice of this tree or that, in the same manner, my son, all these creatures, when they have become merged in the True, know not that they are merged in the True. * *

"These rivers, my son, run, the eastern (like the Ganges), towards the east, the western (like the Indus) towards the west. They go from sea to sea (*i.e.*, the clouds lift up the water from the sea to the sky and send it back as rain to the sea). They become, indeed, sea. And as those rivers, when they are in the sea, do not know, I am this or that river." * *

"'Place this salt in water and then wait on me in the morning.'

"The son did as he was commanded. The father said to him; 'Bring me the salt which you placed in the water last night.' The son having looked for it found it not, for, of course, it was melted.

"The father said : 'Taste it from the surface of the water. How is it?' The son replied : 'It is salt.' 'Taste it from the middle. How is it ?' The son replied. 'It is salt.' 'Taste it from the bottom. How is it?' The son replied : 'It is salt.' The father said : 'Throw it away and then wait on me.' *

"Then the father said, in this body, forsooth, you do not perceive the True, my son; but there indeed it is."—*Chhāndogya, VI*

"At whose wish does the mind, sent forth, proceed on its errand," asks the pupil. "At whose command does the first breath go forth ? At whose wish do we utter this speech? What god directs the eye or the ear?"* *

The teacher replies: "It is the ear of the ear, the mind of the mind, the speech of the speech, the breath of the breath, and the eye of the eye.

"That which is not expressed by speech, and by which speech is expressed. That which does not think by mind, and by which mind is thought. that which does not see by the eye, and by which one sees.* * That which does not hear by the ear, and by which the ear is heard. * * That which does not breathe by breath, and by which breath is drawn—that alone know as Brāhman—*not that which people here adore"—Kena Upaniṣad, I.*

The italics are, of course, ours. But who does not see in the above passage an effort of the human mind to shake itself from the trammels of meaningless ceremonials, which priests taught and the "people here "practised, to soar into a higher region of thought and to comprehend the incomprehensible—the breath of the breath and the soul of the soul ? Who is not struck by this manly and fervent effort made by the Hindu nation, three thousand years ago, to know the unknown Maker, to comprehend the incomprehensible God ?

And the joy of him who has comprehended, however feebly, the incomprehensible God, has been well described :

"He who beholds all beings in the Self, and Self in all beings, he never turns away from it.

"When to a man who understands, the Self has become all things, what sorrow, what trouble can there be to him who office beheld that unity.

"He, the Self, encircled all bright, incorporeal, scatheless, without muscles, pure, untouched by evil, a seer, wise, omnipresent, self-existent, he disposed all things rightly for eternal years."—*Isa Upaniṣad.*

In the Bṛhadāraṇyaka Upaniṣad, we are told that all gods are the manifestation of Self or Puruṣa, "for he is all gods." (I, 4, 6). And likewise, that he exists in all men, in the Brāhman, the Kṣatriya, Vaiśya, and the Śūdra.—(1,4, 15.)

The idea of Monoism was carried to its farthest limits in the Upaniṣads, Dualism was never recognised. In the Sāṅkhya philosophy, which sprung up at a subsequent period, Nature is independent of Puruṣa; in the Upaniṣads it is not. The idea of one Universal Being was carried to its extreme limit. Everything else is a manifestation of this Being.

Our extracts on this subject have been somewhat lengthy, but the reader will not regret it. For the idea of one Universal Being is the very keystone of the Hindu religion, and it is necessary to examine how this idea was first developed in India in the Upaniṣads .We will now pass on to other matters which have also affected and shaped the Hindu religion of subsequent ages.

The creation of the world was still a mystery to those early thinkers, and the attempts to solve it were necessarily fanciful, and sometimes grotesque. A few passages should be quoted :

"In the beginning this was non-existent. It became existent as it grew. It turned into an *egg*. The *egg* lay for the time of a year. The *egg* broke open. The two halves were, one of silver the other of gold.

"The silver one became this earth, the golden one the sky, the thick membrance (of the white) the mountains, the thin membrance (of the yolk) the mist with the clouds, the small veins the rivers, the fluid the sea.

"And what was born from it was Āditya, the Sun. When he was born shouts of hurrah arose, and all beings arose and all things which they desired." *Chhāndogya, III,* 19.

A different account is given in VI, 2 of the same Upaniṣad, where we are told that—" In the beginning there was that only, which is,—One only without a second." And that sent forth fire, and fire sent forth water, and water sent forth the earth.

The Aitareya Āraṇyaka describes how Prāṇa, the breath, and his companions created the world, and then discusses the question of the material cause out of which the world was created. As in the Ṛg Veda (X, 129), and as in the Jewish account of creation, water is said to be the first material cause.

"Was it water really ? Was it water ? Yes, all this was water indeed. The water was the root, the world was the shoot. He (the person) is the father, they (earth, fire, etc), are the sons." Mahidāsa Aitareya knew this.—(II, 1, 8, 1.)

Another speculation is started in the same Upaniṣad :—

"Verily in the beginning all this was Self—one only. There was nothing else blinking whatsoever." And that Self sent forth the water (above the heaven), the lights which are the sky, the mortal which is the earth, and the waters under the earth. He then formed the Puruṣa. Fire was produced from this Puruṣa's speech, air from his nose, the sun from his eyes, the different quarters from his ear, shrubs and trees from the hairs of his skin, the moon from his mind, etc. The deities (fire, etc), then asked for a place of rest and food. A cow was led to them, and then a horse, and then a man, and they were satisfied with the man. Then *Mūrti,* Matter, was produced from water, and thus food was produced.

A story is told in the Bṛhadāraṇyaka that in the beginning there was Self alone, and he made himself into two parts, male and female, and the pair took different shapes successively, and men, cows, horses, asses, goats, sheep and all other creatures were born.

Such were the futile attempts made in India in ancient ages, to solve the great mystery of creation, which it has not been given man, either in the ancient or in modern times, to solve. One great generalisation was conceived by the early philosophers of India—they discovered a harmony or unity in the creation and the universe, and that unity was variously styled by them Brahmān or Ātman, Puruṣa or Prāṇa.

Similar guesses were made, imperfect and often fanciful, but nevertheless in a fervent spirit of piety, as to the destination of the soul after death. The central idea is that which has been adopted as the cardinal principle of the Hindu religion, that good acts lead to their rewards in future existences, but it is true knowledge only which leads to union with the Universal Spirit. "As here on earthy whatever has been acquired by exertion, perishes, so perishes whatever is acquired for the next world by sacrifices and other good actions performed on earth. Those who depart from hence without having discovered the Self and those true desires, for them there is no freedom in all the worlds."—*Chāndogya, VIII,* I, 6.

The doctrine of transmigration of souls of which we have found no trace in the Ṛg Veda, is fully developed in the Upaniṣads. Chitra Gāṅgāyani, the Kṣatriya king, explained to Uddālaka Aruṇi and his son Śvetaketu, of whom we have had repeated mention before, and who came to the Kṣatriya for instruction, that departed spirits go to the moon, and the moon sends them back to be born again. And according to his deeds and according to his knowledge he is born again here as a worm, or as an insect, or as a fish, or as a bird, or as a lion, or as a boar, or as a serpent, or as a tiger, or as a man, or as something else in different places." An account then follows of the passage of the dead to the world of Agni, to the world of Vāyu, to the world of Varuṇa, to the world of Prajāpati, and to the world of Brāhman. "In that world there is the lake Āra, the mountains called Yeṣṭ iha, the river Vijarā, (ageless), the tree Ilya, the city Salajya, the palace Aparājita (unconquerable), the door-keepers Indra and Prajāpati, the hall of Brāhman called Vibhu, the throne Vicakṣaṇa (perception), the couch Amitaujas (endless splendour), and the beloved Mānasi (mind), and her image Cakṣuṣi (eye), who, as if taking flowers, are weaving the worlds." And there he meets Brāhman.— *Kāuṣītaki, I.*

The above passage is a remarkable instance of the process by which simple metaphors and similes of poets lent themselves into the formation of those gorgeous legends of which the later Purāṇas are full. We cannot fail to see that the passage simply describes how the soul passes into Brāhman, and the throne of preception and the couch of splendour and the mind are simple metaphors. In the Purāṇas the metaphors have been crystalized into legends, and can no longer be distinguished as metaphors.

A somewhat similar doctrine of transmigration is also taught by the Kṣatriya king, Pravāhana Jaibali to the same Śvetaketu, son of Uddālaka Aruṇi. The passage of the soul through various stages to the moon is described :

"Having dwelt there, till their (good) works are consumed, they return again the way as they came, finally in the form of rain.

"Then he is born as rice and corn, herbs and trees, sesamum and beans. From thence the escape is beset with difficulties. For whoever the persons may be that eat the food, and beget offspring, he thenceforth becomes like unto them. Those whose conduct has been good will quickly attain some good birth, the birth of a Brāhman or a Kṣatriya or a Vaiśya. But those whose conduct has been evil will quickly attain an evil birth, the birth of a dog or a hog or a Caṇḍāla."—*Chāndogya, V,* 10.

The doctrine of transmigration of souls is again fully and beautifully explained in the Bṛhadāraṇyaka. (IV, 4), and we will make an extract from that Upaniṣad :—

"As a caterpillar, after having reached the end of a blade of grass, and after having made another approach to another blade; draws itself together towards it, thus does the Self, after having thrown off this body, and dispelled all ignorance, and after making another approach to another body, draw itself together towards it. "And as a goldsmith, taking a piece of gold, turns it into another newer and more beautiful shape, so does the Self, after having thrown off this body, and dispelled all ignorance, made unto himself another newer and more beautiful shape, whether it be like the Fathers, or like the Gandharvas, or like the Devas, or like Prajāpati, or like Brāhman, or like other beings.* *

"So much for the man who desires. But as to the man who does not desire; who, not desiring, free from desires, is satisfied in his desires, or desires the Self only, his vital spirits do not depart elsewhere; being Brāhman, he goes to Brāhman.

" And as the slough of a snake lies on an anthill, dead and cast away, thus lies the body; but that disembodied immortal spirit is Brāhman only, is only light."

Beautiful, indeed, are the passages which describe the final emancipation of the soul and its union with Brāhman. A little further on, after the passage quoted above, occurs the following passage; and the reader will see that the Buddhist idea of Nirvāṇa arose out of the Hindu idea of union with Brāhman:

"He, therefore, that knows it, after having become quiet, subdued, satisfied, patient, and collected, sees self in Self, sees all in Self. Evil does not overcome him, he overcomes all evil. Evil does not burn him, he burns all evil. Free from evil, free from spots, free from doubt, he becomes a true Brāhman; enters the Brahmā world."

Still finer is the hymn of triumph with which the soul comes to Brahmān :

"I come to the hall of Prajāpati, to the house : I am glorious among Brāhmans, glorious among princes, glorious among men. I am glorious among the glorious."—*Chāndogya, VIII,* 14, 1.

This beatitude, this union with Brāhman or Self, was what Death taught Nachiketas in that beautiful idyll of an Upaniṣad called Kaṭha. We will close the present chapter with an extract from that beautiful creation of fancy and of piety. We should remind our readers, however, that Kaṭha is very likely an Upanishad of the Atharva Veda, and apparently belongs to a later age than the other Upaniṣads from which we have quoted before.

Nachiketas was given by his father unto Death, and entered the abode of Yama Vaivasvata, and asked him for three boons, the last of which was this :

"There is that doubt, when a man is dead; some saying, he is; others, he is not. This I should like to know taught by thee, this is the third of my boons.

But Death was unwilling to reveal his secrets, and told Nachiketas to ask for other boons.

"Choose sons and grandsons who shall live a hundred years, herds of cattle, elephants, gold, horses. Choose the wide abode of the earth, and live thyself as many harvests as thou desirest.

"If you can think of any boon equal to that, choose wealth and long life. Be king, Nachiketas, on the whole earth. I make thee the enjoyer of all desires.

"Whatever desires are difficult to attain among mortals, ask for them, any thing to thy wish—these fair maidens with their chariots and musical instruments—such are, indeed, not to be obtained by men; be waited on by them whom I give thee, but do not ask me about dying."

Nachiketas said :"These things last till to-morrow, O Death, for they wear out this vigour of all the senses, Even the whole of life is short. Keep thou thy horses, keep dance and song for thyself."

Pressed by the pious enquirer, Death at last revealed the great secret, with is the principle of all the Upaniṣads and the principle of the Hindu religion :

"The wise who, by means of meditation on his Self, recognizes the Ancient, who is difficult to be seen, who has entered into the dark, who is hidden in the cave, 'who dwells in the abyss, as God—he, indeed, leaves joy and sorrow far behind.

"A mortal who has heard this and embraced it, who has separated from it all qualities, and has thus reached the subtle Being, rejoices because he has obtained what is a cause for rejoicing. The house of Brāhman is open, I believe, O Nachiketas!"

Who can, even in the present day, peruse these pious enquiries and fervent thoughts of a long buried past, without feeling a new emotion in his heart, without seeing a new light before his eyes! The mysteries of creation and of the unknown future will never be solved by human intellect or by human science; but the first recorded attempts to solve them in a pious, fervent, philosophical spirit will ever have an abiding, interest for every patriotic Hindu and for every thoughtful man.

In the words of the eminent German writer and philosopher Schopenhauer : "From every sentence deep, original and sublime thoughts arise, and the whole is pervaded by a high and holy and earnest spirit, Indian air surrounds us, and original thoughts of kindered spirits. In the whole world there is no study except that of the originals, so beneficial and so elevating as that of the Oupnekhat. (Latin translation of the Upaniṣads). It has been the solace of my life; it will be the solace of my death."

BOOK III

RATIONALISTIC PERIOD

(B.C. 1000 to 242)

CHAPTER – 1

LITERATURE OF THE PERIOD

A change came over the spirit of the Hindu world in the third Period and the change is reflected in the Sūtra literature of India. The Vindhya range was the extreme southern limit of the Hindu world in the Epic Period; but now the Hindus crossed that chain of mountains and penetrated beyond the wastes and jungles of Central India and founded powerful Hindu kingdoms on the banks of the Godāvarī and the Kṛṣṇā, extending to the blue waters of the ocean. In the east the kingdom of Magadha rose to power and greatness, and threw out colonies into Bengal and Orissa, and in the west the kingdom of Saurāṣṭra extended its limits to the Arabian Sea This expansion of the Hindu world had its effect on the Hindu mind; Hindus became more practical and more venturesome, and their ideas became more expanded. Whatever literature was handed down from ancient times was put in a condensed, practical shape, and new discoveries in every department of science were made with the boldness of new explorers and conquerors.

The practical spirit of the age shewed itself in the form which literature assumed. All learning, all sciences all religious teaching were reduced to concise practical manuals. Brevity is the characteristic of the Sūtra literature as verbosity is of the Brāhmaṇa literature Indeed, the writers went from one extreme to another; verbose prose was replaced by aphorisms, and the proverbial saying which applies to the Sūtra literature is often quoted, that "An author rejoiceth in the economising of half a short vowel as much as in the birth of a son!"

One main reason which led to this extreme conciseness was, that young Hindu students were expected in their early years to learn these Sūtras by rote. Āryan boys were expected to place themselves under some teacher at the early age of eight or ten or twelve, and for twelve years or more they remained in their teacher's house, doing menial services under him, begging alms for him, and learning day by day the ancestral religion by rote. The diffuse details of the Brāhmaṇas were therefore compressed into short treatises in order that they might be imparted and learnt with ease, and a separate body of Sūtras was thus composed for each Sūtra charaṇa or school. The names of the authors of many of these compositions have been handed down to us, and while the Vedas and the Brāhmaṇas are declared to be *revealed* no such claim is put forward for the Sūtras, which are admitted to be human compositions. The so-called *revealed* literature of India closes there fore with the Upaniṣads, which form the last portions of the Brāhmaṇas.

When once the Sūtras began to be composed, the system spread rapidly all over India, and Sūtra schools multiplied. The Chāranyavyūhā names five charaṇas of the Ṛg Veda, twenty-seven of the Black Yajur Veda, fifteen of the White Yajur Veda, twelve of the Sāma Veda, and nine of the Atharva Veda. Each Sūtra charaṇa must have had a separate body of Sūtras for itself, and the adherents of any particular charaṇa— in whatever part of India they might live—learnt and imparted to students the Sūtras of that particular school. A vast mass of Sūtra literature thus gradually sprung up in India, but of the numerous bodies of Sūtras which must have been composed and taught in these numerous Sūtra charaṇas, a lamentably small number has been left to us! As with the Brāhmaṇas, so with the Sūtras, a limited number of works have only been saved from the shipwreck of ancient Sanskrit literature.

We will now rapidly survey the different branches of learning which gradually assumed the Sūtra form, and we will begin with religion. Details of ceremonials relating to Vedic sacrifices were compressed into concise manuals, and these manuals are called *Śrauta Sūtras*. Two collections of these Śrauta Sūtras belonging to the Ṛg Veda called Āśvalāyana and

Śānkhayana; three belonging the Sāma Veda and called Māsaka, Lāṭyāyana and Drāhyayana; four belonging to the older or Black Yajur Veda and called Baudhāyana, Bhāradvāja, Āpastamba and Hiraṇyakeśin, and one belonging to the new or White Yajur Veda and called Kātyāyana, have been left entire. An account of these Śrauta Sūtras will not be interesting to our readers, but nevertheless, some facts about them deserve mention.

The Āśvalāyana Sūtra is divided into twelve chapters. Āśvalayana is said to have been the pupil of the celebrated Śaunaka, and the teacher and pupil are said to have been the joint authors of the last two books of the Aitareya Āraṇyaka. Hermann Oldenberg points out, however, that the fourth book of this Āraṇyaka is extremely short, and consist of verses which probably belong to an ancient age, while the fifth or last book is in genuine Sūtra style, and was the work of Śaunaka and Āśvalāyana. Whichever view is accepted, the facts clearly point to the interesting conclusion that the earliest works of the Sūtra literature connect themselves with the last works of the Brāhmaṇa or Epic Period.

Śaunaka is indeed an interesting figure towards the close of the Epic Period. In an anterior state of existence he is said to have been the "seer" of the second book of the Ṛg Veda, and by this legend we may probably understand that he belonged to the line of teachers or families by whom the book of the Ṛg Veda was handed down from century to century. Śaunaka was again the priest of Janamejaya Pārikṣita in the famous horse-sacrifice which he celebrated. We may infer therefore that a line of Śaunakas were celebrated priests and men of learning in the Epic Period. No wonder that the earliest compilers of Sūtras connect themselves with this honored name as pupils.

The Sāṅkhāyāna Śrauta Sūtra consists of 18 chapters. Professor Weber conjectures that this Sūtra beongs to the Western part of Hindustan as the Āśvalāyana belongs to the Eastern.

Of the Sāma Veda the Māsaka Śrauta Sūtra is only a tabular enumeration of prayers belonging to different ceremonies, the

Sātyāyana embodies the opinions of various teachers, and both these Sūtras connect themselves with the great Tāṇḍya or Pañcaviṁśa Brāhmaṇa of the Sāma Veda. The Drahyāyana differs but little from the Sātyāyana.

The Sūtras of the Black Yajur Veda have been chronologically arranged as those of Baudhāyana, Bhāradvāja, Āpastamba, and Hiraṇyakeśin; and Dr. Bühler, who has recovered the lost Bhāradvāja Sūtra, justly remarks that the distance in years between Baudhāyana and Āpastamba must be measured not by decades but by centuries. In a most valuable introduction to his translation of the Dharma Sūtra of Āpastamba, Dr. Bühler states that a powerful Hindu kingdom, *t.e.,* of the Andhras, had been founded in Southern India before the Christian era, that the capital of the empire was probably situated near modern Amarāvati on the river Kṛṣṇā, that Āpastamba was probably born or naturalized in this country and founded his Sūtra school there, and that the date of his work cannot be put down later than the third century before Christ. And as Āpastamba speaks not only of the six Vedaṅgas, but also of the Pūrva Mimāṁsā and the Vedānta schools of philosophy, we can conclude that the philosophical schools of India had begun their work previous to that date. He conjectures that Baudhāyana also was born and worked in Southern India.

The Śrauta Sūtra of the White Yajur Veda is in 26 chapters and is by Kātyāyana, who also claims to be a pupil of the renowned Śaunaka. Kātyāyana was a critic of Pāṇini the grammarian, and lived, according to Max Müller, in the fourth century before Christ. An interesting "battle of books" has been waged by scholars about the date of Pāṇini, but we must avoid entering into the arena reserved for doughty scholars, and only express our assent to the prevailing opinion that the grammarian must have lived some centuries before his critic. The Kātyāyana Sūtra strictly follows the Śatapatha Brāhmaṇa, and the first 18 chapters of the Sūtra correspond with the first nine books of the Brāhmaṇa. As in Lāṭyāyana so in Kātyāyana we find allusion to Magadhadesiya Brahmābandhu, who are supposed to be the first Buddhists.

We turn with pleasure from the Śrauta Sūtras to the *Dharma Sūtras,* which present to us the customs and manners and laws of the times, and are, therefore, far more valuable for our historical purposes. In the Śrauta Sūtras we see the Hindus as worshippers and sacrificers; in the Dharma Sūtras we see them as citizens.

But the Dharma Sūtras of this ancient period have a still further claim to our attention, because they are the originals which have been modified and copied and put into verse at a later age and transformed into those law-books with which modern Hindus are familiar, such as Manu, Yājñavalkya, Parāsara, etc. This was pointed out by Professor Max Müller thirty years ago, and the researches which have been made since have fully confirmed the fact. A world of conjectures and fancies about the Code of Manu being the work of legislators and rulers, has been exploded by this discovery, and we now know what the so-called codes are, and how and why they were framed. In their original Sūtra form (often in prose, sometimes in prose and verse—but never in continuous verse like the later codes), they were composed, just as the Śrauta Sūtras were composed, by the founders of the Sūtra charaṇas, and were learnt by rote by young Hindus, so that they might, in later life, never forget their duties as citizens and as members of society. No nation has taken ageater precaution than the Hindus to implant in the mind of every member of society his religious, social and legal duties.

Among the Dharma Sūtras which are lost, and have not yet been recovered, was the Mānava Sūtra or Sūtra of Manu, from which the later metrical Code of Manu has been compiled. It seems that the Dharma Sūtra of Manu was held in high honor in the Sūtra Period, as the metrical Code of Manu is held in honor in the present day. The references to Manu are frequent in the Sūtra literature, and Dr. Bühler has pointed out two quotations from Manu in Vasiṣṭha and Gautama's Dharma Sūtras, to which we will allude further on.

Among the Dharma Sūtras still extant, Vasiṣṭha belonging to the Ṛg Veda, Gautama belonging to the Sāma Veda, and Baudhāyana and Āpastamba belonging to the Black Yajur Veda, have been translated by Dr. Bühler.

In point of time Gautama is the oldest, and we find

Baudhāyana transferring a whole chapter of Gautama's into his Sūtra, and Vasiṣṭha again has borrowed the same chapter from Baudhāyana, And we have seen before that Āpastamba also comes after Baudhāyana.

We have spoken of the Śrauta Sūtras which treat of the duties of a worshipper, and of the Dharma Sūtras which treat of the duties of a citizen. But man has other duties and responsibilities beyond those of a worshipper and a citizen. As a son, a brother, a husband, and a father, he has duties to perform towards the members of his family. He has little rites to perform in connexion with domestic occurrences, which are quite different from the more elaborate ceremonials taught in the Śrauta Sūtras. A distinct class of rules was necessary to fix the details of these Gṛhya or domestic rites, and these rules are given in the *Gṛhya Sūtras*.

A great deal of interest attaches to these simple domestic rites performed at the domestic fireside, and not at the hearths which had to be specially lighted at great sacrifices. The domestic fire was lighted by each householder on his marriage, and the simple rites, the Pākayajñas, were easily performed. "A log of wood," says Professor Max Müller, "placed on the fire of the hearth, an oblation poured out to the gods, or alms given to Brāhmaṇas, this is what constitutes a Pākayajña." Gautama enumerates seven Pāka sacrifices, *viz.:*—(1) Astakā performed in the four winter months; (2) Pārvaṇa at full and new moon; (3) Śrāddha or monthly funeral oblations; (4 to 7) Srāvanī, Agrāhayani, Chiatri and Āśvajujī. performed on the days of full moon in the months from which the rites have been named: The account of these rites contained in the Gṛhya Sūtras is deeply interesting to Hindus, because after a lapse of over two thousand years we are still practising, as will be seen further on, the same interesting rites, sometimes under the same name, and often under a different name and in a somewhat different way. To the seven Pākajajñas enumerated above, may be added the five daily oblations, called emphatically the Mahājajñas, and which consisted in oblations to gods, to departed fathers, and to creatures in general, in the performance of duty towards Ṛṣis and hospitality towards men. The Gṛhya Sūtras also contain accounts of social ceremonies performed at marriage, at the birth of a child, at his first feeding, at his assuming the life of a student, etc. And thus we get a complete idea of domestic life among ancient Hindus from these invaluable Gṛhya Sūtras.

The Sāṅkhyāyana and Āśvalāyana Gṛhya Sūtras belonging to the Ṛg Veda and the Pāraskara Gṛhya Sūtra belonging to the White Yajur Veda, together with the Khādira, which is an abridgement of Gobhila Gṛhya Sūtra of the Sāma Veda, have been translated by Herman Oldenberg, A second volume which promises to contain a translation of Gobhila, etc, has been announced, but has not yet been published, but an excellent edition of Gobhila with notes has been published by Pundit Satyavrata Sāmasramin.

The Śrauta Sūtra, the Dharma Sūtra, and the Gṛhya Sūtra go collectively under the name of Kalpa Sūtra. Indeed, each Sūtra charaṇa is supposed to have had a complete body of Kalpa Sūtra, including the division mentioned above, but much of what existed has been lost, and we have only fragments of the Sūtra literature left. The entire Kalpa Sūtra of Āpastamba still exists, and is divided into thirty praśnas or sections. The first twenty-four of these treat of Śrauta sacrifices; the 25th contains the rules of interpretation; the 26th and 27th treat of the Gṛhya rites; the 28th and 29th contain the Dharma Sūtra, and the 30th section, the *Śulva Sūtra,* teaches the geometrical principles according to which the altars for the Śrauta sacrifices were to be constructed. These interesting Śulva Sūtras have been made known to the western world by Dr. Thibaut. The publication of his work only confirms the conclusions of Von Schrader, that Pythagoras learnt not only his theory of transmigration, but his mathematics also from India in the sixth century before Christ.

We have so long spoken of the Kalpa Sūtra, as the Kalpa Sūtra forms the most important and, historically, the most valuable portion of the literature of the period. Our ancient writers enumerate five other Vedāṅgas or departments of Vedic study, and we will briefly allude to them here.

Śikṣā or Phonetics is the science of pronunciation, and there is reason to believe that rules on the subject were formerly embodied in the Āraṇyakas and even in the Brāhmaṇas of the Epic Period, but that they have disappeared in consequence of the appearance of more scientific works on the same subject in the Rationalistic Period. These works are called Prātisākhyas, which were collections of phonetic rules applicable to each Śākhā, or recension of each Veda.

Many of the Prātisākhyas, however, have been lost, and only one Prātisākhya for each Veda (except the Sāma Veda) has been preserved to us. The Prātisākhya of the Sākala recension of the Ṛg Veda is ascribed to the renowned Śaunaka. But Dr. Goldstucker gives good grounds for doubting his authorship of this work. Similarly, a Prātisākhya of the Mādhyandina recension of the White Yajur Veda is also extant and is ascribed to Kātyāyana. A Prātisākhya of the Black Yajur Veda and one of the Atharva Veda are also extant, but the names of the authors are forgotten. It will interest our readers to learn that among the teachers named in the Prātisākhya of the Black Yajur Veda, we have the name of a Vālmiki!

Chandas or Metre is spoken of in the Vedas, and whole chapters in the Āraṇyakas and Upaniṣads are devoted to it. But as in the case of Śikṣā, so in the case of Chandas, we have a clear scientific treatment of the subject for the first time in the Sūtra literature. There are some chapters on the metre of the Ṛg Veda at the end of the Prātisākhya spoken of above. For the Sāma Veda we have the well-known Nidāna Sūtra in ten prapāṭhakas. Piṅgalanāga's work on Chandas does not belong to the Sūtra Period, but to a much later time.

The deservedly great fame of Pāṇini in the department of *Vyākaraṇa* or Grammar has eclipsed that of all other grammarians of the period. Pāṇini belonged to the extreme north-west corner of India where the Brāhmaṇas and Āraṇyakas and Upaniṣads, composed mostly on the banks of the Ganges and the Jumnā, were little known or respected; and Pāṇini therefore knew little of them. Dr. Goldstucker is right in holding Pāṇini to be anterior to Buddha, that is to the 6th century B. C.

Similarly, the great fame of Yāska (anterior to Pāṇini, according to Dr. Goldstücker and other scholars) in the department of *Nirukta* has eclipsed the fame of his predecessors, of whom we know little except from the mention made of them in Yāska's work. Professor Max Müller has pointed out a common mistake made in calling Yāska's work as the Nirukta. Nirukta is a work, as Sāyaṇa says, where only a number of words is given. Yāska takes up such an old-existing Nirukta, and on this text (which is usually known as the Nighaṇṭu) he writes a commentary, which is his work.

Colebrooke speaks of different treatises on *Jyotiṣa* or Astronomy of each Veda, and he calls one which has a commentary, the Jyotiṣa of the Ṛg Veda. Professor Max Müller, however, has found the works to be different manuscripts of the same work, and he believes the work to have been composed after the Sūtra Period, although the doctrines and rules propounded in it belong to the earliest stage of Hindu astronomy. Its practical object is to convey a knowledge of the heavenly bodies necessary for fixing the time for sacrifices, and to establish a sacred calendar. However recent the date of the existing work may be, it contains observations made in India during the Epic Period, *i.e.,* when the Vedas were collected and arranged, and it furnishes evidence therefore of the date of that period, which should not be lightly rejected or ignored.

Besides the six Vedāṅgas detailed above, there is another class of works called the Anukramaṇī or Index to the Vedas which also belongs to Sūtra literature. The Anukramaṇī of the Ṛg Veda is ascribed to Kātyāyana, and gives the first words of each hymn, the number of verses, the name of the poet, the metre and the deity. There were some older Anukramaṇīs of the Ṛg Veda, which are ascribed to Śaunaka, and one of which is still extant, but which have all been replaced by Kātyāyana's fuller work. The Bṛhaddevatā, which is a voluminous Anukramaṇī, is also ascribed to Śaunaka. Writers of the Rationalistic Period were very fond of citing that honored name in connection with many works.

The Yajur Veda has three Anukramaṇīs, *viz.,* one for the Ātreya recension of the Black Yajur Veda, one for the recension of the Charakas, and the third for the Māddhyandina recension of the White Yajur Veda.

Of the Sāma Veda we have an ancient index in the Ārṣeya Brāhmaṇa, and some more among the Pari-śiṣṭas, or supplementary works. An Anukramaṇī of the Atharva Veda was discovered by Professor Whitney in the British Museum.

We have still to refer to the most important product of the Hindu mind in the Rationalistic Period. The speculations and earnest enquiries started at the close of the Epic Period in the Upaniṣads led to those deeper investigations and subtle and profound researches which are known as the six schools of Hindu Philosophy. We have seen that Āpastamba mentions two of them in his Dharma Sūtra, and there is evidence that the commencement of all the six schools dates from the Rationalistic Period, though their further developments took place at a later date. Professor Weber justly remarks that it was in Philosophy as well as in grammar that the speculative Hindu mind attained the highest pitch of its marvellous fertility. The abstrusest questions of matter and spirit and creation were dealt with, not as in the Upaniṣads in guesses and vague speculations, but with marvellous acumen and relentless logic. The natural result followed, and the fabric of faith tottered to its foundations. Learned men still paid a sort of nominal regard to the Vedas and the sacrifices they inculcated, but the support given was only nominal and half-hearted. Large portions of thinking men saw the weakness of the existing rites in the light of the new philosophy, and boldly threw away the mask and embraced Buddhism, which was a legitimate product of Sāṅkhya philosophy. And the masses of ignorant Śūdras too, for whom a cruel fate had been reserved in the Hindu Dharma Sūtras, openly welcomed a religion which recognised no Brāhmans.

It is said of the French Revolution that it was mainly

brought about by two causes the oppression of kings and the intellectual reaction set in by the philosophers of the eighteenth century. The Buddhist revolution in India is still more distinctly the result of similar causes. The oppression of Brāhmaṇism made the people sigh for a revolution, and the work of philosophers opened the path to such a revolution.

Buddhism was at last accepted as the State religion in the reign of Aśoka, about 242 B. C. At this date the Rationalistic Period ends and the Buddhist Period, *i.e.,* the period when Buddhism was the prevailing religion in India, may be said to commence.

CHAPTER – 2

EXPANSION OF THE HINDUS AND THE RISE OF MAGADHA

The history of India receives a new light in the Rationalistic Period, as it was in this period that the Greeks visited India and also compiled accounts of it from report. Greek civilization and national life had not commenced during the long centuries of the Vedic Age in India, Again, the rude heroes of the Trojan War knew little of their civilized but distant contemporaries, the Hindus of the Epic Age. The first two epochs of Hindu history receive no light therefore from Greek literature. The first Greek who is supposed to have borrowed his learning from the Hindus is the philosopher Pythagoras. He lived in the sixth century before Christ, *i.e,* in the Rationalistic Period of Hindu history, and his theories and ideas throw some light on the prevailing ideas of the Hindus of that age. He learnt the doctrine of transmigration of souls and of final beatitude from the Upaniṣads and the current faith of the Hindus, and his ascetic observances and prohibition to eat flesh and beans were also borrowed from India. He learnt his elementary mathematics and geometry from the Śulva sūtras; his notion of the virtues of numbers is borrowed from the Sāṅkhya Philosophy; and lastly, his idea of the five elements is essentially an Indian idea.

Herodotus, the father of Greek history, lived in the fifth century before Christ; and although he never visited India, he gives accounts of the Hindus from report which are valuable, although he mixes them up with legends and stories, and often confounds the customs of the Hindus with those of the uncivilized aborigines who still inhabited large tracts in India. Herodotus tells us that the Indians were the greatest nation of the age, that they were divided into various tribes and spoke different tongues, that they procured great quantities of gold in their country, that India abounded in quadrupeds and birds larger than any other country, and produced wild trees which bore wool (cotton) from which the Indians made their clothing III, 94 to 106). Elsewhere, he says, speaking of the Thracians, that they were the greatest of nations among men, excepting only the Indians (V, 3.) Herodotus also mentions the fact, which is probably historically true, that Darius; king of Persia, subjugated a part of India, and his ships sailed down the Indus to the sea (IV, 44.)

And lastly Magasthenes came to India in the fourth century before Christ, and lived in the court of Chandra Gupta in Pāṭaliputra or ancient Patna. And although his original account is lost, still extracts from his writings are found scattered in many subsequent works. These have been carefully collected by Dr. Schwanbeck of Bonn and translated into English by Mr. MacCrindle, and are invaluable for the purposes of Indian History, and we shall frequently have occasion to quote them. Pythagoras, Herodotus and Megasthenes are unimpeachable witnesses to the high civilization of India during three successive centuries which fall within the Rationalistic Period, *viz,*, the sixth, fifth, and fourth centuries before Christ.

We have seen that by the end of the Epic Period the whole of the valley of the Ganges and Jumnā from Delhi to North-Behar had been conquered, peopled and Hinduized. We have seen that towards the very close of that period, *i.e.*, about 1000 B.C., Hindu settlers and adventurers, colonists, and "pilgrim fathers" had left the valley of the Ganges and had penetrated into remote unknown lands, into Southern and East Behar,. Malwa, Southern India and Gujrat. And we have seen that these Non-Āryan provinces were becoming gradually known to the Hindus, and were slowly coming under Hindu influence and power when the Epic Period closed and the Rationalistic Period began. The waves of Hindu conquests rolled further and further, and the aborigines submitted themselves to a higher civilization and a nobler religion. Rivers were crossed, forests were cleared, lands were reclaimed, wide wastes were peopled, and new countries hitherto aboriginal became the scenes of Hindu power and of Hindu religion. Where a few scanty settlers had penetrated at first, powerful colonies arose; where religious teachers had retired in seclusion, quiet villages and towns arose. Where a handful of merchants had made their way by some unknown river, boats navigated up and down with valuable cargoes for a civilized population. Where hardy warriors or scions of royal houses had dwelt in exile or by the chase, powerful monarchs reigned over a conquered civilized, Hinduized, aboriginal population. And where foresters had felled trees and cleared small tracts of land, smiling fields, covered with waving corn, spread for miles and miles around, betokening the spread of civilization and of the civilized arts of life.

Such was the history of Āryan conquests from generation to generation and from century to century in the Rationalistic Period; and each succeeding Sūtra work that we take up shews that the circle of civilization has spread wider, and that the zone of unreclaimed barbarism has receded furthur and further. And long before we come to the close of the Rationalistic Period, *i.e.,* the third century B. C. we find that the entire peninsula has been reclaimed, civilized, and Hinduized, and that primitive barbarians dwelt only in rocks, forests and deserts which the Āryans disdained to conquer. It is not possible within our limits to narrate fully this interesting story of Hindu conquests; nor are materials available which would enable such a succinct account to be written. We will, however, quote a passage or two which will indicate to our readers the march of events,

Baudhāyana lived probably in the sixth century before Christ, and was, as we have seen before, one of the earliest of the Sūtrakāras. In his time the zone of Hindu kingdoms and civilization extended as far south as Kalinga or the eastern seaboard, stretching from modern Orissa southward to the mouth of the Kṛṣṇā. The passage we refer to is interesting, because it shews that the ancient Hindu region along the Ganges and the Jumnā was still regarded as the suitable home of Āryans, while tracts of country Hinduized more recently were looked upon with some degree of contempt.

"9. The country of the Āryas (Āryāvarta, lies to the east of the region where the River (Sarasvatī) disappears, to the west of the Black-forest (Kālakavana), to the north of the Pāripātra (Vindhya mountains), and to the south of the Himālaya. The rule of conduct which prevails there is authoritative.

"10. Some declare the country between the Yamunā and Ganga (to be Āryāvarta).

"11. Now the Bhāllavins quote also the following verse:—

"12. In the west the boundary river, in the east the region where the sun rises, as far as the black antelopes wander, so far spiritual preeminence is found,

"13. The inhabitants of Avanti (Malwa), of Aṅga (East Behar), of Magadha (South Behar), of Saurāṣṭra (Guzerat), of the Deccan, of Upāvrit, of Sindh, and the Sauviras (of south Punjab) are of mixed origin.

"14. He who has visited the Ārattas (in the Punjab), Kāraskars (in South India), Pundras (in North Bengal) Sauviras. Vangas (in Eastern Bengal), Kalingas (eastern seaboard) or Prānūnas, shall offer a Punastoma or a Sarvaprishtha sacrifice." *Baudhāyana, I, 1, 2.*

The passage is interesting, because it shews us the extent of the Hindu world in the early part of the Rationalistic Period, and also because it divides the Hindu world into three circles at it were, which were regarded with different degrees of esteem. Āryāvarta stretching from the Sarasvatī to the confines of Behar,. and from the Himālaya to the Vindhya, forms the first circle; and it is remarkable that the Punjab, which was the earliest home of the Āryans in the Vedic Age, is not included in this sacred circle. That realm had since then been backward in the later developments of Hindu religion and culture, and was rarely alluded to even in the literature of the Epic Period. The second circle, the people of which are said to be of mixed origin, includes Southern Punjab, Siudh, Gujrat, Malwa, Deccan, and South and East Behar. If the reader refers to the fourth chapter of the last book, he will find that these were the very regions which were becoming dimly known to the Hindus at the very close of the Epic Period. Early in the Rationalistic Age they had already become recognized as Hindu kingdoms, and Hindu influence and civilization had travelled *beyond* these kingdoms to other regions which are included in the third circle. That third or last circle embraces the country of the Arattas in the Punjab, some parts of Southern India, Eastern and Northern Bengal, and the eastern sea-board, from Orissa to the Kṛṣṇā river. A person travelling in these places had to expiate the sin by a sacrifice. This was the extreme limit of the Hindu world—say in the sixth century before Christ.

That portions of Southern India had not only been colonized by this date, but had become the seats of Hindu kingdoms and of distinct schools of laws and learning, is proved by the writings of Baudhāyana. As we have said before, Baudhāyana himself was probably a southerner, and although he expresses high regard for Āryāvarta, or the valley of the Ganges, still he takes care to mention the peculiar laws and customs of Southern India. We will cite one passage :

"1. There is a dispute regarding five practices in the south and in the north.

"2. We will explain those peculiar to the south.

"3. They are to eat in the company of an uninitiated; person, to eat in the company of one's wife, to eat stale food, *to marry the daughter of a maternal uncle or of a paternal aunt.*[1]

"4. Now the customs peculiar to the north are, to deal in wool, to drink rum, to sell animals that have teeth in the upper and in the lower jaws, to follow the trade of arms, *and to go to sea.*[2]

"5. He who follows these practices, in any other country than where they prevail commits sin.

"6. For each of these customs the rule of the country should be the authority.

"7. Gautama declares that that is false." *Baudhāyana,* I, 1, 2.

Let us now take leave of Baudhāyana and come to the next Sūtrakāra of Southern India. If Baudhāyana be supposed to have flourished in the sixth century before Christ, Āpastamba probably flourished in the fifth.[3] There can be little doubt that Āpastamba lived and taught in the Andhra country, and the limits of that great monarchy embraced all the districts between the Godāvarī and the Kṛṣṇā. Dr. Bühler sup. poses that the capital of this southern empire was situated near modern Amarāvatī on the lower Kṛṣṇā. It was the Andhra text of the Taittiroya Āraṇyaka which Āpastamba recognized and followed, and his teachings are to this day held in regard by the Brāhmans of Nasik, Puna, Ahmadabad, Satara, Sholapur and Kolhapur, and other places in the Deccan who are Āpastambīyas.

Thus we find that the conquest of Southern India, which was commenced at the close of the Epic Period, went on through succeeding centuries : that by the sixth century, Bengal, the Deccan, and the whole of the sea-board to the mouth of the Kṛṣṇā had been conquered and Āryanized; and that by the fifth century the Deccan, as far south as the Kṛṣṇā river, was the seat of a powerful Hindu Empire, and the portion of India south of the Kṛṣṇā was also probably Hinduized, By the fourth century B. C. the whole of Southern India had been Hinduized, and three great Hindu kingdoms, those of the Choḷas, and Cheras and the Pāṇḍyas had been founded, stretching as far south as Cape Comorin; and Ceylon too had been discovered. And when we come to this (fourth) century, we issue now from the obscurity of isolated passages in the Sūtra works to the sunlight of Greek accounts of India! For it was in this century that Megasthenes, the ambassador of Seleucus, came to India and resided in the royal court of Chandragupta in Pāṭaliputra (or ancient Patna) between 317 and 312 B. C. The conquest of the whole of Southern India by the Hindus had been completed before this date.

The account of the races and kingdoms in India given by Megasthenes is full and intelligible, though scholars have found some difficulty in identifying the names of the places he mentions. He gives the distance from the Sutlej to the Jumnā to be 168 miles, from the Jumnā to the Ganges 112 miles, and thence 286 miles (119 + 167,) to Kalinipaxa which Lassen identifies with Konouj, but St. Martin places on the banks of the Kalinadi river. 625 miles is given as the distance to the confluence of the Jumnā, and this distance is supposed to be reckoned from the point of the Jumnā above referred to, and so measures the entire length of the Doab. The distance to Pāṭaliputra is stated as 425 miles, which is incorrect, the real distance being 248 miles; and from Pāṭaliputra to the mouth of the Ganges the distance is given as 738 miles.

The Prāchyas, by which name we are now to understand the Magadhas, had become the most powerful and foremost nation in India in the fourth century B. C, as the Kurus, the Pāñcālas, the Videhas and the Kosalas had been in the Epic Period. They had their capital at Pāṭaliputra, a flourishing town described at 80 stadia or 9 miles long (a stadium = 202.25 yards) and 15 stadia or nearly 2 miles wide. It was of the shape of a parallelogram, girded with a wooden wall[4] pierced with loopholes for the discharge of arrows, and defended by a ditch in front.

It would seem that the whole of the Doab or the an cient land of the Pāñcālas and the Kurus was now included in the powerful and extensive kingdom of Magadha, for the Jumnā flowing through Mathura and Caresbora, (identified with *Kalikāvāsta* or Brindaban by Cunningham, and with *Kṛṣṇapura* or Agra by Lassen), was said to run through the kingdom of Pāṭaliputra. The nation surpassed in power and glory every other people in India, and their king Chandragupta had a standing army of 600,000 foot soldiers, 30,000 cavalry, and 9,000 elephants, "whence may be formed some conjecture as to the vastness of his resources."

Speaking apparently of South Bengal, Megasthenes mentions the Calingoe living nearest the sea, the Mandu and the Malli living higher up, the Gangerides, near the mouths of the Ganges, and the Modo-Galingce in an island in the Ganges. It is impossible not to discover in the first and last of these names the ancient name of Kalinga, and the obvious inference is, that in the fourth century before Christ, not only Orissa, but the part of Bengal nearest to the sea was also called Kalinga. Indeed the whole of the sea-board from the mouths of the Ganges to those of the Kṛṣṇā went by that name.

Megasthenes describes Parthalis as the capital of the Calingoe, and Parthalis is supposed to be the modern Vardhamāna or Burdwan. The powerful king of this place had 60,000 foot soldiers, 1,000 horse and 700 elephants.

A large island in the Ganges is said to have been, inhabited by the Modogalingoe (Madhya-Kalinga,) and beyond them several powerful tribes lived under a king who had 50,000 foot soldiers, 4,000 cavarly, and 400 elephants. Beyond them again lived the Andaroe in whom it is impossible not to recognize the Andhras of Southern India, The Andhras were a great and powerful nation who had settled originally between the Godāvarī and the Kṛṣṇā, but who before the time of Megasthenes had extended their kingdom as far north as the Nurbudda. Megasthenes writes that they were a powerful race, possessed numerous villages and thirty walled towns, and supplied their king with 100,000 infantry, 2,000 cavalry, and 1,000 elephants.

In the extreme North-West, Megasthenes speaks of the Isari, the Cosyri, and other tribes located probably in Kashmir or its neighbourhood. The Indus is said to skirt the frontiers of the Prācyas, by which we are to understand that the powerful and extensive kingdom of Magadha extended as far as the frontiers of the Punjab, and embraced all Northern India.

A great portion of the modern Rajputana was still the home of aboriginal tribes in the time of Megasthenes, of men who lived in woods, among tigers, noted for their ferocity. He speaks of the tribes who lived in the fertile tracts surrounded by deserts, and of tribes who inhabited the hills (Aravalli), which ran in an unbroken chain parallel to the shores of the ocean. He also speaks of the tribes who lived enclosed by the loftiest mountain Capitalia which has been identified with Abu. He speaks further on of the Horatoe who were undoubtedly the Saurāṣṭras. They had a capital on the coast, which was a noble emporium of trade, and their king was the master of 1,600 elephants, 150,000 foot, and 5,000 horse.

"Next come the Pandoe, the only race in India ruled by women. They say that Hercules having but one daughter, who was on that account all the more beloved, endowed her with a noble kingdom. Her descendants rule over 300 cities and command an army of 150,000 foot and 500 elephants." The Pandoe are supposed to have occupied the basin of the Chambāl river, but we cannot identify the story given above with any Hindu tradition or myth relating to any tribe. A long list then follows of tribes dwelling in different parts of Rajputana.

But not only was the whole of India, except deserts and waste jungles, known, but the sea-coast line, too, was equally known at the time of Megasthenes. He puts down the distance from the mouth of the Ganges to Cape Calingon (Coringon at the mouth of the Godāvarī) at 625 miles, and to Tropina (Tripontari opposite Cochin) at 1,225 miles. Thence to the Cape of Perimula was 750 miles, and Perimula has been identified with the Island of Salsette or Bombay, It was even in the time of Megasthenes "the greatest emporium of trade in India." From Perimula to the Island of Palata, *i.e.,* the delta of the Indus, was 620 miles.

And lastly, the Island of Ceylon, too, was known in the time of Megasthenes. The island was called by the Greeks Taprobanê, a slightly altered form of the Pāli name Tambapannī, which corresponds to the Sanscrit Tāmraparṇi or the copperleaved. Megasthenes says that the island was separated from the mainland by a river, and that the country was productive of gold and large pearls and elephants much larger than the Indian breeds. AElian who wrote long after Megasthenes, but like most other Greek and Roman writers, got much of his information about India from the account of Megasthenes, says that Taprobane was a large mountainous island full of palm groves, that the inhabitants dwelt in huts of reeds and transported their elephants in boats which they constructed for the purpose, and sold them to the king of Kalingai.

Fortunately the people of Ceylon have preserved a chronology which is fairly reliable, and which points to a date approximately correct, when the island was first colonized by Hindus. The Dīpavaṁśa composed in the 4th century A. D., and the Mahāvaṁśa, composed somewhat later, are both based on an ancient commentary kept in the Mahāvihāra monastery, and are the national epics of Ceylon, and have a historical value. According to these works, the conquest of Ceylon is attributed to Vijaya in the year 543 B. C. The particular date was fixed upon to make the discovery of Ceylon correspond with the supposed date of Buddha's death; but even after some necessary adjustment, Ceylon may be supposed to have been conquered by Hindus in the 5th century B.C. Vijaya was the son of Sinhabāhu, the king of Sāla in Magadha, and was connected with the kings of Vanga and Kalinga. It is said that the young prince committed numberless acts of fraud and violence, for which the people demanded his execution, but his royal father sent him and his companions adrift on the ocean, and they discovered Ceylon.

We need not accept the story of Vijaya literally as true. But there can be no doubt that the existence of the island was known to the Hindus for centuries, that the maritime trade in which the people of Kalinga largely engaged in the Sūtra Period made the people better acquainted with the island, and that when the products of the island were found to be valuable, and a trade sprang up between the island and the mainland, some venturesome or exiled scion of a royal house was drawn towards the newly discovered land by the romance which always hangs round all new discoveries, and settled there, and made it into a Hindu kingdom. Over two hundred years after the discovery of the island, Devānāmpriya Tiṣya, the contemporary of Aśoka became the king of Ceylon, and adopted the Buddhist religion, and the Cingalese have been Buddhists ever since. It is owing to this fact, probably, that Ceylon has (unlike the Hindu kingdoms of India) a connected and fairly reliable history.

Indeed the only other country or province which has some authentic history of the Rationalistic Period is Magadha, and the existence of a historical account of this province is probably due to the same cause, *viz.*, that Magadha, like Ceylon, early embraced Buddhism.

Ajātaśatru was the king of Magadha in the 5th century B. C. when Gautama Buddha closed his long cāreer of piety (477 B. C.) He was a powerful king and beat back the Turanian Vajjians who were invading from the north, and extended the power and the limits of the rising kingdom of Magadha over the sites of the ancient kingdoms on the Ganges Valley. A century after Ajātaśatru, nine Nandas reigned in this kingdom, probably from 370 to 320 B. C. when the great Chandragupta, by the help of Chāṇakya, the Bismarck of the age, overturned that dynasty and ascended the throne. The monarch extended his conquests westwards, and was fairly the master of all Northern India; and Megasthenes probably did not exaggerate his prowess when he stated, that Chandragupta had an army of 600,000 foot, 30,000 horse and 9,000 elephants. Chandragupta was for a time a fugitive in the camp of Alexander the Great, and he began his rule in Magadha a few years after Alexander had left India.

Chandragupta's successor, Bindusāra, reigned from 291 to 263 B. C. and he was succeeded by Aśoka the Great, the greatest Emperor who has ever ruled in India in ancient or modern times. His fame, however, rests not on extending and consolidating the great empire which had been founded by Chandragupta, but in giving his imperial sanction to Buddha's religion of humanity, which, during the preceding two hundred years, had made but humble progress in India. Aśoka adopted it as the State religion, and proclaimed it through all the civilized world. He published his rock-cut edicts through the length and breadth of India, sent his missionaries to Macedon, Egypt, and Greece, and numbered Antiochus of Syria, and Antigonas of Macedon, Ptolemy of Egypt, and Magas of Cyrene, and Alexander of Epiros as his allies.

It was at a great council of Pāṭaliputra, in 242 B. C. that Aśoka had the Buddhist Scriptures finally settled before proclaiming them all over India and the then known world. At this date, therefore, the Rationalistic Period ends, and the Buddhist Age begins. The history of Aśoka belongs to the Buddhist Period, and will be told in our account of that period.

REFERENCES

1. Dr. Bühler points out that such marriages still prevail among the Desastha and Kurhāda Brāhmans of the Deccan.
2. Later superstition and degeneracy have fabricated a prohibition against going to sea for all Hindus.
3. Dr. Bühler would, on linguistic grounds, place Āpastamba in the 3rd century B. C. but on other grounds he would put back that Sūtrakāra by another 150 or 200 years, *i.e.,* to the 5th century B. C.
4. The wooden wall was still standing in the 5th century after Christ when the Chinese traveller Fa Hian saw it. Fa Hian writes : "The palaces of the king which are in the city have walls of which the stones have been collected by the genii. The carvings and the scuptures which ornament the windows are such as this age could not make; they still actually exist." The fall of Pāṭaliputra was accomplished shortly after Fa Hian's time, for when Houen Tsang visited the place in the 7th century after Christ, he found nothing but ruins, and a village with two or three hundred houses. In an excavation made in 1876 for the construction of a public tank, some remains were discovered of

what is supposed to have been the wooden wall spoken of by Magasthenes. In a part of Patna, half way between the railway station and the *chauk* or market place, the excavators discovered some 12 or 15 feet below the surface, a long brick wall running from N. W. to S, E. Parallel to this wall was found a line of palisades, the strong timber of whith it was composed, inclined slightly towards the wall. In one place there appeared to be an outlet or gate, two wooden pillars rising to a height of 8 or 9 feet with no palisades between them. A number of wells were also found covered with fragments of broken mud vessels, and one of the wells being cleared, yielded capital drinking water, while among the rubbish taken out were discovered several iron spear heads. See *MacCrindlis Megasthenes and Arrian,* p. 207, note, .

CHAPTER – 3

ADMINISTRATION

An account of the system of administration which prevailed in India over two thousand years ago will naturally interest our readers, and fortunately, both Hindu Sūtrakāras and Greek writers furnish us with reliable information on the subject. We will begin our account with some extracts from Sūtra works. The king is directed to build a royal town and a palace for himself, looking towards the south :

"3. The palace shall stand in the heart of the town.

"4. In front of that there shall be a hall. That is called the hall of invitation.

"5. At a little distance from the town to the south he shall cause to be built an assembly house with doors on the south and on the north sides, so that one can see what passes inside and outside."

Fires shall burn constantly and oblations offered in these fires, and—

"8. In the hall he shall put up his guests, at least those who are learnt in the Vedas.

"9. Rooms, a couch, meat and drink should be given to them according to their good qualities."

A table with dice should also be provided, and Brāhmaṇas, Vaiśyas and Śūdras may be allowed to play there. Assaults of arms, dancing, singing and music are allowed in the houses of the king's servants; and the king shall constantly take care of his subjects.

"15. That king only takes care of the welfare of his subjects in whose dominions, be it in villages or forests, there is no danger from thieves.'[1] *Āpastamba,* II, 10, 25.

Vasiṣṭha thus details the duties of the king :

"1. The particular duty of a king is to protect all beings; by fulfilling it he obtains success.

"3. Let him appoint a domestic priest to perform the rites obligatory on the order of householders.

"8. Let him punish those who stray from the path of duty.

"11. Let him not injure trees that bear fruit and flowers.

"12. He may injure them in order to extend cultivation.

"13. The measures and weights of objects necessary for households must be guarded (against falsification).

"14. Let him not take property of his own use from the inhabitants of his realm.

"15. The measures and price of such property shall only be liable to deductions in the shape of taxes." *Vasiṣṭha,* XIV.

Vasiṣṭha (1,42) and Baudhāyana (1,10,18,1) declare that the king is entitled to a sixth portion of the income of His subjects as taxes, but exempt many classes who are unable to pay. Gautama details the taxes thus :—

"24. Cultivators pay to the king a tax amounting to one-tenth, one-eighth or one-sixth (of the produce).

"25. Some declare that the tax on cattle and gold amounts to one-fiftieth (of the stock).

"26. In the case of merchandise, one-twentieth (must be paid by the seller) as duty.

"27. Of roots, fruits, flowers, medicinal herbs, honey, meat, grassland firewood, one-sixtieth.

"Each artizan shall monthly do one day's work (for the king),

"32. Hereby the taxes payable by those who support themselves by personal labour have been explained.

"33. And those payable by owners of ships and carts.

"34.He must feed these persons while they work for him." *Gautama,* X.

Megasthenes gives us a valuable account of the manner in which the work of administration was actually carried on, and the following passages will be read with interest:—

"Those who have charge of the city are divided! into six bodies of five each, The members of the first look after everything relating to the industrial arts. Those of the second attend to the entertainment of foreigners. To these they assign lodgings, and they keep watch over their modes of life by means of those persons whom they give to them for assistants. They escort them on the way when they leave the country, or in the event of their dying, forward their property to their relatives. They take care of them when they are sick, and if they die bury them. The third body consists of those who inquire when and how births and deaths occur, with the view not only of levying a tax, but also in order that births and death among both high and low may not escape the cognizance of Government. The fourth class superintend trade and commerce. Its members have charge of weights and measures, and see that the products in their season are sold by public notice. No one is allowed to deal in more than one kind of commodity unless he pays a double tax. The fifth class supervises, manufactured articles, which they sell by public notice.: What is new is sold separately from what is old, and there is a fine for mixing the two together. The sixth and last class consists of those who collect the tenths of the prices of the articles sold."

The military officers "also consist of six divisions with five members to each. One division is appointed to co-operate with the Admiral of the fleet; another with the Superintendent of the bullock trains which are used for transporting engines of war, food for the soldiers, provender for the cattle, and other military requisites. The third division has charge of the foot soldiers; the fourth of the horses; the fifth of the war chariots and the sixth of the elephants."

Besides the municipal officers and military officers, there was yet a third class of officers who superintended agriculture, irrigation, forests, and generally the work of administration in rural tracts. "Some superintend the rivers, measure the land, as is done in Egypt, and inspect the sluices by which water is let out from the main canals into their branches, so that every one may have an equal supply of it. The same persons have charge also of the huntsmen, and are entrusted with the power of rewarding or punishing them according to their deserts. They collect the taxes, and superintend the occupation connected with land as those of the wood-cutters, the carpenters, the blacksmiths, and the miners. They construct roads, and at every ten stadia set up a pillar to shew the by-roads and distances." *MacCrindle's Translation.*

It must not be supposed that the highly organized system of administration described by Megasthenes prevailed in all kingdoms, or that all kings observed the same uniform method. Megasthenes describes the system which prevailed under the powerful king Chandragupta of Magadha, in whose court he lived. But nevertheless his description gives us a general idea of the careful system of administration which prevailed under Hindu kings in the Rationalistic Period. We have only to add that villages in the old Hindu times were little self-governing communities, and paid their taxes to the king's officers through their headmen. Of such officers—*i.e.* lords of ten villages, of hundred villages, and so on, we have frequent mention in Manu and other metrical codes.

Of the personal habits and occupations of kings, Megasthenes has given us a picture which agrees in the main with the picture given in Paurāṇik literature. The care of the king's person was entrusted to female slaves who are said to have been bought from their parents, and the guards and the rest of the soldiery were stationed outside the gates. The king attended the court every day, and remained there during the day without allowing the business to be interrupted. The only other occasions on which he left the palace were when he performed sacrifices or went out for the chase. Crowds of women surrounded him when he went out for the chase, and outside this circle, the spearmen were ranged. Armed women attended the king in chariots, on horses or on elephants, when he hunted in the open grounds from the back of an elephant.

Sometimes he shot arrows from a platform inside an enclosure, and two or three armed women stood by him on the platform. These accounts shew that the sturdy and warlike manners of the Kurus and the Pāñcālas of the Epic Age had already been replaced by more luxurious and effeminate habits in the Rationalistic Age. The age of chivalry had gone, and that of sophism and luxury had come !

Arrian gives an account of the mode in which Hindus equipped themselves for war :—" The foot soldiers carry a bow made of equal length with the man who bears it. This they rest upon the ground, and pressing against it with their left foot, thus discharge the arrow having drawn the string far backwards : for the shaft they use is little short of being three yards long, and there is nothing which can resist an Indian archer's shot—neither shield nor breastplate, nor any stronger defence if such there be. In their left hand they carry bucklers made of undressed ox-hide, which are not so broad as those who carry them, but are about as long. Some are equipped with javelins instead of bows, but wear a sword, which is broad in the blade, but not longer than three cubits; and this, when they engage in close fight (which they do with reluctance), they wield with both hands to fetch down a lustier blow. The horsemen are equipped with two lances like the lances called *Saunia,* and with a shorter buckler than that carried by the foot soldiers. For they do not put saddles on their horses; nor do they curb them with bits in use among the Greeks or the Kelts, but they fit on round the extremity of the horse's mouth a circular piece of stitched raw ox-hide studded with pricks of iron or brass pointing inwards, but not very sharp; if a man is rich he uses pricks made of ivory."—*MacCrindle's Translation.*

The laws of war were more humane among Hindus than among other nations in the world. "The Āryans forbid the slaughter of those who have laid down their arms, of those who beg for mercy with flying hair or joined hands and of fugitives." *Āpastamba,* II, 5,10,11. "Let him not right with those who are in fear, intoxicated, insane or out of their minds, nor with those who have lost their armour, nor with women, infants, aged men and Brāhmans,' *Baudhāyana,* I, 10, 18, 11. "The wives (of slain soldiers) shall be provided for." *Vasiṣtha,* XIX, 20. And Megasthenes, too, vouches for the humane laws of war among Hindus. "For whereas among other nations it is usual in the contests of war to ravage the soil, and thus to reduce it to an uncultivated waste, among the Indians, on the contrary, by whom husbandmen are regarded as a class that is sacred and inviolable, the tillers of the soil, even when battle is raging in their neighbourhood, are undisturbed by any sense of danger; for the combatants on either side in waging the conflict make carnage of each other, but allow those engaged in husbandry to remain quite unmolested. Besides, they neither ravage an enemy's land with fire, nor cut down its trees."

Megasthenes tells us that the Indian tribes numbered 118 in all. On the north of India, and beyond the Himālaya, the country "is inhabited by those Scythians who are called the Śakai." Such is the brief mention made of that powerful tribe which hung like an ominous cloud on the northern slopes of the Himālaya in the fourth century before Christ, but which, in course of a few centuries, burst like a hurricane on the plains of Western India, and convulsed and shattered Hindu kingdoms.

Of the peaceful and law-abiding people in India, Megasthenes gives a pleasing and grateful account : "They live happily enough, being simple in their manners and frugal. They never drink wine, except at sacrifices. Their beverage is a liquor composed from rice instead of barley, and their food is principally a rice pottage. The simplicity of their laws and their contracts is proved by the fact that they seldom go to law. They have no suits about pledges and deposits, nor do they require either seals or witnessses, but make their deposits and confide in each other. Their houses and property they generally leave unguarded. These things indicate that they possess sober sense. ...... Truth and virtue they hold alike in esteem. Hence, they accord no special privileges to the old unless they possess superior wisdom." Megasthenes further states that the Indians did "not even use aliens as slaves, and much less a countryman of their own," that thefts were very rare among them, that their laws were administered from memory, and even that the Indians were ignorant of the art of writing. We have conclusive proofs that writing was known in India in the Rationalistic Period, and the statement of Megasthenes only shews that writing was in very little use, either in schools where boys received their learning and their religious lessons by rote, or even in Courts of *Justice* where laws, *i.e.,* the Dharma Sūtras were administered by learned Judges entirely from memory.

The Dharma Sūtras present us with a full account of the way in which criminal and civil law was administered and judicial trials were held.

"5. Men of learning and pure descent, who are aged, clever in reasoning, and careful in fulfilling their duties, shall be judges in law suits.

"6, In doubtful cases, (they shall give their decision) after having ascertained the truth by inference or deeds and the like means.

"7. A person who is possessed of good qualities (may be called as a witness,) shall answer the questions put to him according to the truth on an auspicious day in the morning, before a kindled fire, standing near water, in the presence of the king, and with the consent of all, after having been exhorted by the Judge to be fair to both sides.

"8. If he is found out speaking an untruth, the king shall punish him.

"9. Besides in that case after death, hell.

"10. If he speaks the truth, heaven, and the approbation of all created beings." *Āpastamba,* II, 11, 29.

Gautama says:—

"22. Having learned the affairs from those who have authority to speak, he, the king, shall give the legal decision.

"23, Reasoning is a means for arriving at the truth.

"24.Coming to a conclusion through that, he shall decide properly.

"25.If the evidence is conflicting, he shall learn the truth from those who are well versed in the threefold sacred lore, and give his decision.

"26.For thus, blessings will attend him." *Gautama,* XI.

The oath that was administered to a witness was of the most solemn character :—

"32.Depose, O witness! according to the truth; expecting thy answer thy ancestors hang in suspense; in accordance with its truth or falsehood they will rise to heaven or fall into hell.

"33.Naked and shorn, tormented with hunger and thirst, and deprived of sight shall the man who gives false evidence go with a potsherd to beg food at the door of his enemy.". *Vāsiṣṭha,* XVI.

"10. The merit which thou hast acquired in the interval between the night in which thou wert born and that in which thou wilt die—all that will go to the king if thou speakest an untruth." *Baudhāyana,* I, 10, 19 .

The literature of no nation contains more earnest injunctions to speak the truth than the Dharma Sūtras. Gautama says that to give false evidence is a mortal sin, *mahapātaka,* which involves loss of caste, (XXI, 10), and "to speak the truth before the Judge is more important than all duties" (XIII, 31). Baudhāyana declares that the perjured man shall go to hell, and also prescribes a penance for the sin (I, 10, 19, 15).[1] Megasthenes informs us that Hindus seldom went to law, that they made their pledges and deposits without witnesses, that they held truth in high esteem, and that a person who bore false witness in India, suffered the dreadful penalty of the mutilation of his extremities. By the unanimous testimony of the Greek and Chinese writers who travelled and lived in India, Hindus detested falsehood, and were truthful and honest as a nation. Writers therefore who have judged the nation not by the general spirit and tenor of their literature and laws but by a few solitary passages, and administrators, too, who have judged the people, not by their conduct and mutual transactions in towns and villages, but by the chicanery and falsehood witnessed in Law Courts, have unconsciously made themselves liable to the serve punishment spoken of by Megasthenes, or at least to the milder penance prescribed by Baudhāyana !

REFERENCE

1. *Viz.*, that he should live on hot scalding milk for twelve days and nights, or should offer oblations, reciting certain texts.

CHAPTER – 4

LAWS

The caste-system had been completely organized in the Rationalistic Period, and threw an indelible stain on the criminal law of India. There was one law for the Brāhman, another for the Śūdra; the former was treated with undue leniency, the latter with excessive and cruel severity. If a Brāhman committed one of the four or five heinous crimes enumerated in the law books, *i.e.,* if he slew a Brāhman, violated his guru's bed, stole the gold of a Brāhman or drank spirituous liquor, the king branded him on the forehead with a heated iron and banished him from his realm. If a man of a lower caste slew a Brāhman, he was punished with death and the confiscation of his property. If such a man slew a man of equal or lower caste, other suitable punishments were meted out to him. A fine of a thousand cows was the punishment for slaying a Kṣatriya, that of a hundred for killing a Vaiśya, and that of ten cows only for slaying a Śūdra! *Baudhāyana,* I, 10, 18 and 19.

Adultery has always been looked upon in India not only as a criminal offence, but as an offence of a heinous nature; but the punishment for this offence also was regulated by the caste of the offender. A man of the first three castes who committed adultery with a Śūdra woman was banished; but a Śūdra who committed adultery with a woman of the first three castes suffered capital punishment. And an opinion is also quoted that for a Brāhman who once committed adultery with a married woman of equal class, the penance was one-fourth of that prescribed for an outcaste. *Āpastamba,* II, 10, 27.

The same iniquitous distinction pervades the rules for minor offences. The tongue of a Śūdra who spoke evil of a virtuous person belonging to one of the first three castes was to be cut out, and a Śūdra who assumed an equal position with those castes was to be flogged. *Āpastamba,* II, 10, 27, Similarly Gautama declares that a Śūdra who reviled a twice-born man or assaulted him with blows should lose the limb with which he offended; that if he listened to a recitation of the Veda, his ears should be stopped with molten lac or tin; that if he recited the Veda, his tongue should be cut out; and if he remembered Vedic texts, his body should be split in twain! *Gautama* XII. It must not be supposed that these cruel laws against the Śūdras were ever enforced. On the contrary, the reader will easily perceive, the Brāhman composers of the Sūtras were anxious to emphasise the distinction between themselves and the other castes, and especially Śūdras, and have therefore represented the laws as ten times more iniquitous than they were, as actually administered by sensible kings and Kṣatriya officers, or even by Brāhman judges.

A Kṣatriya abusing a Brāhman pays 100 kārṣāpaṇas, and beating a Brāhman pays 200 kārṣāpaṇas. A Vaiśya abusing a Brāhman pays 150 kārṣāpaṇas, and we suppose pays 300 for beating him. But a Brāhman pays only 50 kārṣāpaṇas for abusing a Kṣatriya, 25 for abusing a Vaiśya, and for abusing a Śūdra,—nothing! *Gautama,* XII, 8 to 13.

Death or corporal punishment seems to have been the punishment for theft, at least in some cases; and the thief is directed to appear before the king with flying hair, holding a club in his hand and proclaiming his deed. If the king pardons him and does not slay him or strike him, the guilt falls on the king. *Gautama* XII, 45. The prerogative of mercy was the king's alone, but a guru, a priest, a learned householder or a prince, could intercede for an offender, except in the case of a capital offence. *Āpastamba,* II, 10, 27, 20.

Vasiṣṭha reserves the right of self-defence in the case of a person attacked by an *Ātatāyin,* and that term includes an incendiary, a poisoner, one ready to kill with weapon in his hand, a robber, a man who takes away another's land, or abducts another's wife. A man may slay an Ātatāyin who comes to slay, even if the latter "knows the whole of the Veda, together with the Upaniṣads." *Vasiṣṭha,* III, 15 to 18,

Agriculture and trade were the means of the people's subsistence, and crimes relating to a cultivator's land or to an artisan's trade were punished with the utmost severity. We have seen that defence of land was one of the cases in which the right of self-defence was allowed, and false evidence given about land was looked upon with the utmost detestation. By giving false evidence concerning small cattle, a witness commits the sin of killing ten men, by false evidence concerning cows, horses and men, he commits the sin of killing a hundred, a thousand, and ten thousand men respectively; but by false evidence concerning land, he commits the sin of killing the whole human race. "Hell is the punishment for a theft of land." *Gautama,* XIII, 14 to 17. Similarly with regard to artisans, Megasthenes informs us that he who caused an artisan to lose his eye or his hand was punished with death.

A severe penance is ordained for the man who attempts suicide, and the relations of a suicide are prohibited from performing funeral rites for him. *Vasiṣṭha,* XXIII, 14, etc.

Turning to civil law, we find a number of provisions which throw light on the system of agriculture in the Rationalistic Period. Lands were leased as in the present time, and,

"1. If a person who has taken a lease of land does not exert himself, and hence the land bears no crop, he shall, if he be rich, be made to pay the value of the crop that ought to have been grown,

"2. A servant in tillage who abandons his work shall be flogged.

"3. The same punishment shall be awarded to a herdsman who leaves his work.

"4. And the flock entrusted to him shall be taken away

5. If cattle, leaving their stable, eat crops, the owner of the crops may make them lean (by impounding them); but shall not exceed.

"6. If a herdsman who has taken cattle under his care, allows them to perish or loses them, he shall replace them to the owners.

"7. If (the king's forester) sees cattle that have been sent into the forest through negligence, he shall lead them back to the village and make them over to the owners." *Āpastamba,* II, 11, 28.

Again, Gautama says :—

"19. If damage is done by cattle, the responsibility falls on the owner.

"20. But if the cattle were attended by a herdsman, it falls on the latter.

"21. If the damage was done in an unenclosed field near the road, the responsibility falls on the herdsman and on the owner of the field." *Gautama,* XII.

As in the present day, unenclosed fields were used as common property for grazing cattle, and for obtaining firewood.

"He may take, as his own, grass for a cow, and fuel for his fire, as well as the flowers of creepers and trees and their fruit if they be unenclosed." *Gautama,* XII, 28.

Somā equitable provisions are laid down by Vasiṣṭha about the right of way, and about the evidence necessary in disputes about immoveable property.

"10. It is declared in the Smṛti that there are three kinds of proof which give a title to property, *viz.,* documents, witnesses and possession; thereby an owner may recover property which formerly belonged to him.

"11. From fields through which there is a right of way, a space sufficient for the road must be set apart, likewise a space for turning a cart.

"12. Near new built houses and other things of the same description, there shall be a passage three feet broad.

"13. In a dispute about a house or a field, reliance must be placed on the depositions of neighbours.

"14. If the statements of the neighbours disagree, documents may be taken as proof.

"15. If conflicting documents are produced, reliance must be placed on the statements of aged inhabitants of the village or town, and on those of guilds and corporations of artizans or traders." *Vasitṣtha,* XVI.

The law of acquiring property by usage is thus laid down :—

"16. Now they quote also the following verse : 'Property inherited from a father, a thing bought, a pledge, property given to a wife after marriage by her husband's family, a gift, property obtained for performing a sacrifice, the property of re-united co-parceners, and wages as the eighth.'

"17. Whatever belonging to these eight kinds of property has been enjoyed by another person for ten years continuously is lost to the owner.

"18. They quote also a verse on the other side : "A pledge, a boundary, and the property of minors, an (open) deposit, a sealed deposit, women, the property of a king, and the wealth of a Śrotriya are not lost by being enjoyed by others.'

"19. Property entirely given up by its owner goes to the king." *Vasiṣṭha* XVI.

Gautama has similar rules :—

"37. The property of a person who is neither an idiot nor a minor, having been used by strangers before his eyes for ten years, belongs to him who uses it.

"38. But not if it is used by Śrotriyas, ascetics or royal officials.

"39. Animals, land and females are not lost to the owner by another's possession." *Gautama* XII.

Women and females in the above extracts must mean female slaves. With regard to minors, widows, etc.' there are provisions to the effect that the king shall administer their property and shall restore it in the case of a minor when he comes of age. *Vasiṣṭha,* XVI, 8 & 9.

We have seen that the practice of money-lending prevailed in India from the early Ṛg Veda times; but it is in the Rationalistic Period that we find the rate of interest legally fixed.

"Hear the interest for a money-lender declared by the words of Vasiṣṭha, five *Māṣās* for twenty *(Kārṣāpaṇas* may be taken every month); thus the law is not violated," *Vasiṣṭha,* II, 51.

Similarly Gautama declares (XII, 29) : —

"The legal interest for money lent is at the rate of five *Māṣās* a month for twenty *(Kārṣāpaṇas)?*

The commentator Hara Datta reckons 20 Māṣās to the kārṣāpaṇas, so that the rate of interest comes to 1.25 per cent, per month, or 15 percent, per annum. Kṛṣṇā Pandita correctly states that this rate of interest applies to loans for which security is given. Manu specially mentions (VIII, 140) that this rate is prescribed by Vasiṣṭha. Gautama says that after the principal has been doubled interest ceases, and when the object pledged is an object used by the creditor, the money lent bears no interest at all (XII, 31 and 32).

Other articles might be lent at a much higher, percentage of interest, apparently when no security was given.

"44. Gold may be lent, taking double its value on repayment, and grain trebling the original price.

"45. The case of flavouring substances has been explained by the rule regarding grain.

"46. As well as the case of flowers, roots and fruit.

"47. He may end what is sold by weight taking eight times the original value on repayment."

Similarly Gautama says :—

The interest on products of animals, on wool on the produce of a field, and on beasts of burden, shall not increase more than five-fold the value of the object lent. *Gautama,* XII, 36.

Thus apart from the loan of money on security, articles and products were lent, apparently without security, at an enormous rate of interest. In the former case the interest was only 15 per cent, and the principal could only be doubled; in the latter case it could increase six or eight-fold.

Gautama names no less than six different forms of interest, *viz.*, compound interest, periodical interest, stipulated interest, corporal interest, daily interest and the use of a pledge. (XII, 34 & 35.) He lays down that the heirs shall pay the debts of a deceased person, but provides that money due by a surety, a commercial debt, a fee due to the parents of the bride, immoral debts and fines shall not devolve on the sons of the debtor. (XII, 40 & 41.) And this brings us to the most important portion of the Civil Law, *viz.*, the Law of Inheritance.

To leave male issue was considered a religious duty by the ancient Hindus, and their extreme desire for male issue, and their fear also of having to suffer the forments of hell if no male issue was left behind, led to the custom of appointing childless widows and even unmarried daughters to raise issue which sounds strange in modern ears. Gautama, who is the earliest of the Sūtrakāras, whose Dharma Sūtras are extant, recognises both these customs which had been handed down from before the Rationalistic Period.

"2. Let her (a wife) not violate her duty towards her husband.

"3. Let her restrain her tongue, eyes and action.

"4. A woman whose husband is dead, and who desires offspring, (may bear a son) to her brother-in-law.

"5. Let her obtain the permission of her Gurus, and let her have intercourse during the proper season only.

"6. (On the failure of a brother-in-law she may obtain offspring) by a Sapiṇḍa, Sagotra, a Samānapra-vara, or one who belongs to the same caste.

"7. Some declare she shall co-habit with nobody but a brother-in-law.

"8. She shall not bear more than two (sons).

"9. The child belongs to him who begot it.

"10. Except if an agreement to the contrary has been made." *Guatama,* XVIII.

Again,

"18. A father who has no (male) issue may appoint his daughter (to raise up a son for him), presenting burnt offerings to Agni and to Prajāpati, and addressing, 'for me be the offspring.'

"19. Some declare that a daughter becomes an appointed daughter solely by the intention (of the father)." *Gautama,* XXVIII.

We will make one more extract from Gautama which indicates the different kinds of sons who were considered by him to be heirs, and those who were only members of the family.

"32. A legitimate son *(Aurasa),* a son begotten on the wife (*Kṣetraja*) an adopted son *(Datta),* a son made (*Kritrima),* a son born secretly *(Gūḍhaja),* and a son abandoned *(Apaviddha),* inherit the estate.

"33. The son of an unmarried damsel (*Kānīnd*), the son of a pregnant bride (*Sahodha*), the son of a twice married woman (*Paunarbhava*) the son of an appointed daughter (*Putrikāputra*), a son self-given (*Svayamdatta*), and a son bought (*Krīta*), belong to the family. XXVIII.

Baudhāyana and Vasiṣṭha lived long after Gautama, and their opinions varied from that of Gautama as well as from each other in some respects.

"14. One must know a son begotten by the husband himself on a wedded wife of equal caste to be a legitimate son of the body, *Aurasa.* * *

"15, The male child born of a daughter after an agreement has been made, is the son of an appointed daughter, *Putrikāputra.* * *

"17. He who is begotten by another man on the wife of a deceased man, of a eunuch, or of one diseased, after permission, is called the son begotten on a wife, *Kṣetraja.*

"20. He is called an adopted son, *Datta,* who being given by his father and his mother, or by either of the two is received in the place of a child.

"21. He is called a son made, *Kritrima,* whom a man himself makes his son with the (adoptee's) consent only, and who belongs to the same caste.

"22. He is called a son born secretly,. *Gūḍhaja,* who is secretly born in the house, and whose origin is after wards recognized.

"23. He is called a son cast off, *Apaviddha,* who being cast off by his father and his mother, or by either, is received in the place of a child.

"24. If anybody approaches an unmarried girl without the permission (of her father or guardian), the son born by such a woman is called the son of an unmarried damsel (*Kānīna*).

"25. If one marries either knowingly or unknowingly a pregnant bride, the child which is born of her is called a son taken with the bride, *Sahodha.*

"26. He is called a son bought, *Kṛta* who being purchased from his father and his mother, or from either of them, is received in the place of a child.

27. He is called the son of a twice-married woman, *Paunarbhava,* who is born of a remarried female, *i, e.,* of one who having left an impotent man, has taken a second husband,

"28. He is called a self-given son, *Svāyamdatta,* who abandoned by his father and his mother, gives himself to a stranger.

"29. He who is begotten by a man of the first twice born caste, on a female of the Śūdra caste, is called a *Niṣāda.*

"30. (He who is begotten by the same parents through lust is called a *Pārasava.** * *Baudhāyana,* II, 2, 3.

Baudhāyana then quotes verses which declare that of the fourteen kinds of sons enumerated above, the first named seven, *i. e.,* the Aurasa, the Putrikāputra, the Kṣetraja, the Datta, the Kritrima, the Gūḍhaja, and the Apaviddha, were entitled to share the inheritance. The next six, *i.e.,* the Kānīna, the Sahodha, the

Krita, the Paunarbhava, the Svayamdatta, and the Niṣāda, were considered members of the family. The Pārasava was not even considered a member of the family.

Vasiṣṭha enumerates twelve kinds of sons like Gautama.

"12. Twelve kinds of sons only are noticed by the ancients.

"13. The first is begotten by the husband himself on his legally married wife *(Aurasa.)*

"14. The second is the son begotten on a wife (or widow) *(Kṣetraja),* duly; authorised thereto on the failure of the first kind of sons.

"15. The third is an appointed daughter *(Putrikā-putra).*

"16. It is declared in the Veda 'a maiden who has no brothers comes back to the male ancestors (of her own family); *returning she becomes their son'*[1]

"17. With reference to this, a verse (to be spoken by the father when appointing his daughter), 'I shall give thee a brotherless damsel, decked with ornaments, the son whom she may bear, shall be my son.'

"18. The fourth is the son of a remarried widow (*Paunarbhava*).

"19. She is called remarried, *Punarbhū* who leaving the husband of her youth, and having lived with others, re-enters his family.

"20. And she is called remarried who *leaving an impotent outcast or mad husband, or after the death of her husband takes another lord.*[2]

21. The fifth is the son of an unmarried damsel *(Kānīna).*

"24. A male child secretly born in the house is the sixth *(Gūḍhaja).*

"25. They declare that *these six are hheirs and kinsmen,* preservers from a great danger.

"26. Now among those sons *who are not heirs but kinsmen,* the first is he who is received with a pregnant bride (*Sahodha).*

"28. The second is the adopted son *(Datta)*.

"30. The son bought *(Krīta)* is the third.

"33. The fourth is the son self-given *(Svayamdatta)*.

"36. The son cast off is the fifth *(Apaviddha)*.

"38. They declare that the son of a woman of the Śūdra caste *(Niṣāda)* is the sixth."* * * *Vasiṣṭha,* XVII.

The last named six kinds of sons cannot inherit according to Vasiṣṭha, but he quotes a verse that they shall be allowed "to take the heritage of him who has no heir belonging to the first mentioned six classes."

The rules of Gautama, Vasiṣṭha and Baudhayana may be thus shewn in parallel columns :—

	Gautama	Vasiṣṭha	Baudhāyana
Kinsmen and heirs	1. Aurasa.	1. Aurasa.	1. Aurasa.
	2. Kṣetraja.	2. Kṣetraja.	2. Putrikāputra
	3. Datta.	3. Putrikāputra	3. Kṣetraja.
	4. Kritrima.	4. Paunarbhava.	4. Datta.
	5. Gūḍhaja.	5. Kānīna.	5. Kritrima.
	6. Apaviddha.	6. Gūḍhaja.	6. Gūḍhaja.
			7. Apaviddha.
Kinsmen not heirs	7. Kānīna.	7. Sahodha.	8. Kānīna.
	8. Sahodha.	8. Datta.	9. Sahodha.
	9. Paunarbhava.	9. Krīta.	10. Krīta.
	10. Putrikāputra.	10. Svayamdatta.	11. Paunarbhava
	11. Svayamdatta.	11. Apaviddha.	12. Svayamdatta.
	12. Krīta.	12. Niṣāda	13. Niṣāda.
Neither Kinsmen nor heirs)	,,	,,	14. Pārasava.

But a reaction appears to have set in early against the recognition of sons legitimate and illegitimate,— even to escape the torments of hell after death! Āpastamba, who lived a century or more after Baudhāyana, protests against the recognition of heirs and sons of various kinds, and explains away ancient customs by stating that what had been allowed in ancient times could not be permitted among sinful men of the present one.

"1. Sons begotten by a man who approaches in the proper season a woman of equal caste, who has not belonged to another man, and who has been married legally, have a right to follow the occupations (of their castes).

"2. And to inherit the estate.

"8. Transgression of the law and violence are found among the ancients.

"9. They committed no sin on account of the greatness of their lustre.

10. A man of later times who, seeing their deeds, follows them, falls.

11. The gift (or acceptance of a child) and the right to sell (or buy) a child are not recognized." *Āpastantba,* II, 6, 13.

Elsewhere Āpastamba says:

"2. (A husband) shall not make over his (wife,) who occupies the position of a 'gentilis,' to others than to his gentiles' in order to cause children to be begot for himself.

"3. For they declare that a bride is given to the family.

"4. That is (at present) forbidden on account of the weakness of men's senses.

"5. The hand of a 'gentilis ' is considered in law to be that of a stranger, as well as that of any other person except the husband.

"6. If the marriage vow is transgressed, both husband and wife certainly go to hell.

"7. The reward (in the next world) resulting from observing the restrictions of the law, is preferable to offspring obtained in this manner (by Niyoga)." *Āpastamba,* II, 10, 27.

Thus Āpastamba, makes a clear sweep not only of Niyoga or appointment of a wife to raise issue, but also of the adoption or the buying of a son. It must not be supposed, however, that the ancient customs fell into disuse at once. On the contrary, we find these customs alluded to in Manu and other metrical codes compiled after the close of the Rationalistic Period, and adoption survives to this day.

There is the same dissimilarity of opinion in respect of the partition of property among brothers. The law of primogeniture never obtained in India, but so long as the joint family system remained in vogue, the property of the father was inherited by the eldest son, who supported the rest as a father. It would seem, however, that to live in a joint family under the eldest brother was never the universal custom in India, and even Gautama, the earliest of the Sūtrakāras whose works are extant, considers a partition among brothers preferable, for "in partition there is an increase of spiritual merit." (XXVIII, 4.)

According to Guatama, the eldest son gets, as an additional share, a twentieth part of the estate, some animals and a carriage; the middlemost son gets some poor animals, and the youngest get sheep, grain, utensils, a house, a cart, and some animals; and then the remaining property is equally divided. Or he would allow the eldest two shares, and the remaining sons one share each; or he would allow them each to take one kind of property by choice according to seniority; or the special shares may be adjusted according to their mothers. (XXVIII, 5 to 17.)

Further on he says that the property of not reunited brothers, dying without issue, goes to the eldest brother; that the property of a reunited co-parcener goes to the co-parcener; that what a learned co-parcener has acquired by his own efforts he may withhold from his unlearned co-parceners, and that unlearned co-parceners should divide their acquisitions equally. (XXVIII, 27 to 31.)

And lastly, Gautama lays down that a Brāhman's son by a Kṣatriya wife, if the eldest, shares equally with a younger brother by a Brāhman wife, and the same rule holds good between the sons of a Kṣatriya by a Vaiśya wife as between those of a Brāhman by a Kṣatriya wife. The son by a Śūdra wife, if righteous, receives a provision by maintenance, while even the son of a wife of equal caste does not inherit if he be living unrighteously. (XXVIII, 35 to 40.)

Vasiṣṭha allows the eldest brother to take a double share and a little of the kine and horses; he allows the youngest to take the goats, sheep and house, while the middlemost gets utensils and furniture. And if a Brāhman has sons by Brāhman, Kṣatriya and Vaiśya wives, the first gets three shares, the second two shares, and the third, *i.e.*, the son by the Vaiśya wife, gets one share, (XVII, 42 to 50.)

Baudhāyana allows all the children to take equal shares, or the eldest son to take one-tenth in excess.. Where there are sons born of wives of different castes, the sons will take four, three, two and one shares, according to the order of the castes. (II, 2, 3, 2 to 10). Āpastamba differs in this respect also from his pre-decessors and protests against unequal division of property. He quotes the opinion giving a preference to the eldest son, examines the texts on which the opinion is based, argues that the texts make a statement of facts and is not a rule, and therefore declares the preference of the eldest son to be forbidden. All sons who are virtuous inherit, but he who spends money unrighteously shall be disinherited, though he be the eldest son. (II, 6, 14, 1 to 15.).

The separate property, *viz.*, the nuptial presents and ornaments of a wife, were inherited by her daughters *(Gautama,* XXVIII, 24; *Vasiṣṭha* XVII, 46; *Baudhdyāna,* II, 2, 3, 43.) Āpastamba says that on the failure of sons, the daughter may inherit (II, 6, 14, 4.)

Our account of the system of laws of the Rationalistic Period has been long, but our readers will not probably regret it. For the legal system, as well as the philosophy of this period, shews unmistakeably the vast distance of time between this and the Epic *Age,* and shews the culture, the training, and the practical method of dealing with intricate subjects which had been achieved during centuries of civilization. Everything that was confused during the Epic Period was brought to order and subjected to a severe method of reasoning; everything that was discursive was condensed; everything that was vague and uncertain was dealt with in a practical manner. The same religious acts, Śrauta and Gṛhya, were still performed, but the elaborate and endless discussions of the Brāhmaṇas had disappeared, and religious rites were performed under strict and carefully condensed rules. Criminal offences and civil cases were no longer dealt with according to the vague and varying opinions and feelings of learned men and priests, those opinions were arranged, condensed and codified into bodies of laws which learned men were called upon to administer. The caste system itself, which was still pliable in the Epic Period, was unfortunately made more rigid, more in accordance with the inviolable codified rules of the Rationalistic Period; and the whole social system of the Hindus underwent a similar rigid treatment. And lastly, the bold but vague speculations of the Upaniṣads were matured into closely-reasoned systems of philosophy; and grammar, and geometry, and other branches of learning received the same scientific treatment.

REFERENCES

1. "The curious fact that Vasiṣṭha here calls the appointed daughter a son may perhaps be explained by a custom which, though rarely practised, still occurs in Kashmir, and by which a brotherless maiden is given a male name. A historical instance of this kind is mentioned in the Rāja Taraṅginī, where it is stated that Kalyānadevī, princess of Gauda and wife of king Jayāpīḍa, was called by her father Kalyanamalla."— Dr. Bühler.
2. "The circumstances which allowed the second marriage of a woman have been enumerated in this verse. They are insanity, impotency, loss of caste, or death of her husband. The son of a woman thus married a second time is allowed by Vasiṣṭha to inherit.

CHAPTER – 5

CASTE

But the gain was not all on one side nor the loss on the other. Social manners, as we have stated, underwent the same rigid system of arrangement which pervades the literature and learning of the Ration alistic Period. The system of caste was still a pliable institution in the Epic Period; but the rules of caste were made more rigid and inflexible in the Rationalistic Period, no doubt in order to bring society into better order, and to secure immediate gain, but to the detriment of future progress. Sages and legislators are excellent judges of the laws and institutions which are most conducive to progress in their own times; but no laws and institutions can be made permanent and immutable without interfering with the natural progress of a society capable of advancement in successive ages. Rigid and inflexible social rules, therefore, which are further hallowed by the sanction of religion, serve only to hamper and restrain a nation in its onward march in civilization. But the grave error, the national misfortune, should in justice be attributed not to those, wise men who framed rules for their own guidance under the conditions of ancient society, but to those who, from want of religious energy and political life, have failed to modify the rules in accordance with the requirements of modern society. Nor would it be philosophical to blame the modern priestly caste for upholding its privileges and maintaining caste inequality. Priestly supremacy is inevitable when the people are superstitious, just as kingly despotism is inevitable when the people are politically lifeless. Nations are themselves to a great extent responsible for their fate; and the people of modern India are slowly awaking to the conviction that it rests with themselves to cast asunder the broken links of an ancient chain, and to rise to the dignity of free men and a united nation.

We have seen that in the Epic Age an inviolable line had not yet been drawn between members of different castes. According to one remarkable passage in the Aitariya Brāhmaṇa, the descendants of a member of one caste might enter another by following the profession of the latter; while, according to another equally remarkable passage in the Śatapatha Brāhmaṇa, a Brāhman was a Brāhman by knowledge of religion and not by birth. Numerous instances have also been cited to shew that men of low birth actually entered the priestly caste by their knowledge and virtues; that the priestly caste did not acquire a monopoly of religious learning; that they often came as humble pupils to Kṣatriya kings to acquire religious knowledge.

We lose sight of all this, or nearly all this, in the Rationalistic Period. The rules of caste became more rigid, and it was impossible for the members of a lower caste to enter within the pale of priesthood. A Kṣatriya or a Vaiśya might be a Brāhman in succeeding births, but neither he nor his descendants could ever enter the priestly caste. We should remember, however, that a great body of Hindus broke away altogether in this period from the caste rules and followed the leadership of Gautama Buddha. And this fact in itself explains to some extent the greater care and rigidity with which those who remained within the orthodox pale were guarded and chained.

While the caste rules were made more rigid and inviolable in the Rationalistic Period, the real origin of the system was forgotten. We have seen that in the Epic Period the priests and warriors formed castes of their own; that the mass of the Āryan people remained Vaiśyas; while the Hinduized non-Āryans were the Śūdras. New tribes of aborigines, as they entered the Hindu community, still followed their ancestral professions and formed different castes at the lowest end of the ladder; and we have found the names of some of these non-Āryan tribes or castes in the White Yajur Veda.

This intelligible and historical origin of the caste- system was entirely lost sight of or ignored in the Rationalistic Period, and a theory was sought for and obtained which made each caste distinct from the rest by its very origin and inherent formation! The strange fiction was then conceived, that the different castes were created by a sort of permutation and combination among the men and women of the few parent castes! A child of twelve would hardly accept it as true, if he was told, that the medical profession of Modern Europe for instance, has sprung from a valiant knight of the Middle Ages who once took a fancy to a barber's pretty maiden; or that modern novelists are descended from a monkish scribe who once upon a time left the convent, fascinated by the merry glances of a Troubadour's daughter! Strange, ridiculous, childish as such a theory is, it has been scrupulously adhered to in India by Manu and all the later legal writers, and obtains credence to the present day !

Vasiṣṭha says:—

"1. They declare that the offspring of a Śūdra and of a female of the Brāhman caste, becomes a Caṇḍāla.

"2. That of a Śūdra and of a female of the Kṣatriya caste, a Vaina.

"3, That of a Śūdra and of a female of the Vaiśya caste, an Antyavasāyin.

"4. They declare that the son begotten by a Vaiśya on a female of the Brāhman caste becomes a Rāmaka.

"5. The son begotten by the same on a female of the Kṣatriya caste, a Paulkasa.

"6. They declare that the son begotten by a Kṣatriya on a female of the Brāhman caste becomes a Sūta.

"8. Children begotten by Brāhmans, Kṣatriyas and Vaiśyas on females of the next lower, second lower and third lower castes become respectively Ambaṣṭhas, Ugras and Niṣādas.

"9. The son of a Brāhman and of a Śūdra woman is a Pārasava." *Vasiṣṭha,* XVIII.

Baudhāyana is somewhat different.

"6. Sons begotten on wives of equal *or of the next lower castes* are called *of equal caste.*

"7. Those born of wives of the second or third lower castes become Ambaṣṭhas, Ugras and Niṣādas.

"8. Of females wedded in the inverse order of the castes are born Āyogavas, Māgadhas, Vainas, Kṣattris, Paulkasas, Kukkutakas, Vaidehakas and Caṇḍālas." *Baudhāyana,* I, 9, 16.

Again,—

"3. A Brāhman begets on a female of the Kṣatriya caste a Brāhman, on a female of the Vaiśya caste an Ambaṣṭha, on a female of the Śūdra caste a Niṣāda.

"4. According to some, a Pārasava,

"5. A Kṣatriya begets on a female of the Vaiśya caste a Kṣatriya, on a female of the Śūdra caste an Ugra.

"6. A Vaiśya begets on a female of the Śūdra caste a Rathakāra.

"7. A Śūdra begets on a female of the Vaiśya caste a Māgadha, on a female of the Kṣatriya caste a Kṣattri, but on a female of the Brāhman caste a Caṇḍāla.

"8. A Vaiśya begets on a female of the Kṣatriya caste an Āyogava, on a female of the Brāhman caste a Sūta."

And so a Svapāka has an Ugra father and a Kṣattri mother; a Vaina has a Vaidehaka father and an Ambaṣṭha mother; a Paulkasa has a Niṣāda father and a Śūdra mother; a Kukkutaka has a Śūdra father and a Niṣāda mother; and "the wise declare those sprung by an intermixture of the castes to be Vrātyas." *Baudhāyana* I, 9, 17.

But the wise are surely mistaken, for the Vrātyas were Āryans like the best born Āryan Brāhmans and Kṣatriyas, but did not practise Brāhmanical ceremonies, as stated in Book II, Chapter VIII.

Gautama's enumeration is comprehensive as well as brief, and we will therefore extract it.

"16. Children born in the regular order of the wives of the next, second or third lower castes become Savarṇas, *i. e.*, of equal caste, Ambaṣṭhas, Ugras, Niṣādas, Dauṣyantas, and Pārasavas.

"17. Children born in the inverted order (of wives of higher castes) become Sūtas, Magadhas, Āyogavas, Kṣattris, Vaidehakas, or Caṇḍālas.

"18. Some declare that a woman of the Brāhman caste has borne successively to husbands of the four castes sons who are Brāhmans, Sūtas, Māgadhas or Caṇḍālas ;

"19. And that a woman of the Kṣatriya caste has borne to the same Murdhavasiktas, Kṣatriyas, Dhīvaras, Paulkasas.

"20. Further, a woman of the Vaiśya caste has borne to the same Bhṛgyakanthas, Māhiṣyas, Vaiśyas and Vaidehas.

"21. And a woman of the Śūdra caste to the same Pārasavas, Yavanas, Karanas and Śūdras." *Gautama,* IV.

Here we have an authoritative statement which may well stagger the most faithful believer! Māgadhas and Vaidehas, who were different races, Caṇḍālas and Paulkasas, who were undoubtedly non-Āryan tribes, and even Yavanas, who were Bactrian Greeks and foreigners, were all treated by the same general and rigid law which recognized no exception—and were all declared to be descended directly or indirectly from the parent castes! And as the Hindus came to know other foreign nations later on, the elastic theory was stretched, and Manu derived from the Scythians, the Persians and the Chinese from the same Hindu parent castes !

It is remarkable, however, that the castes or races named above, of whom such a strange origin has been expounded, are nearly all aboriginal tribes or foreigners, or Āryans who had incurred odium by their partiality for scepticism and Buddhism. We do not find names of respectable profession-castes, answering to the Kāyasthas, the Vaidyas, or even the goldsmiths, the blacksmiths, the potters, the weavers, and other artizans of Modern India. How were these professions classed in Ancient India, if they were not classed as separate castes ? The reply is plain, that the great and yet undivided Vaiśya caste of the Rationalistic Period still embraced all those different professions which in modern times have been divided and disunited into castes.[1] The Āryan Vaiśyas followed different trades and professions in Ancient India, without forming separate castes; they were scribes and physicians, goldsmiths and blacksmiths, potters and weavers, while still belonging to the same common Vaiśya caste. Thus the great body of the Āryan population was still united, and was still entitled to religious knowledge and learning, and the worst features of the modern caste system had not therefore yet manifested themselves in the Rationalistic Age.

The study of the Veda, the performance of sacrifices, and the gift of alms are prescribed for all twice born men, *i. e.,* for Brāhmans, Kṣatriyas and Vaiśyas. The special and additional occupations of a Brāhman are the performance of sacrifice for others, and the receiving of alms, and agriculture and trade were also allowed to him *provided he did not work himself. (Gautama,* X, 5.) The abuses begotten of the privileges of caste had already commenced as early as the Rationalistic Period, and Brāhmaṇas, relieved of manual labour, had already commenced to feed on the resources of the industrious classes, without acquiring that learning which would alone justify their exemption from labour. Vasiṣṭha felt the abuse and the injustice keenly, and protested against idlers being supported and fed, in language which could only be indited when Hinduism was still a living nation's religion.

"1. (Brāhmans) who neither study nor teach the Veda nor keep sacred fires *become equal to Śūdras.*

"4. The king shall punish that village where Brāhmans, unobservant of their sacred duties and ignorant of the Veda, subsist by begging, *for it feeds robbers.*

"6. The sin that *dunces, perplexed by ignorance,* and unacquainted with the sacred law, declare to be duty, shall fall, increased a hundred fold, on those who propound it.

"11. An elephant made of wood, an antelope made of leather, and a Brāhman ignorant of the Veda, those three have nothing but the name of their kind.

"12. Those kingdoms where ignorant men eat the food of the learned will be visited by drought; or some other great evil will befall them." *Vasiṣṭha,* III.

Vasiṣṭha could scarcely have foreseen how terribly his wise prophesy was to be fulfilled in time.

The additional occupations of the Kṣatriya were governing and fighting and making conquests, to learn the management of chariots and the use of the bow, and to stand firm in battle and not to turn back. *(Gautama,* X, 15 and 16.) The special occupations of Vaiśyas were trade, agriculture, tending cattle, lending money and labour for gain, (*Gautama,* X, 49) Śūdras were to serve the other three castes, but were also allowed to labour for gain (*Gautama* X, 42); and there can be no doubt they traded and earned money by independent work to a large extent in the Rationalistic Period as in all succeeding periods. Religious knowledge was however forbidden to Śūdras.

"To see ourselves as others see us" is always a gain, and hence although our account of the caste system derived from our ancient Sūtras has been long, we will now examine how that system was regarded by foreigners. It is quite evident that the seven castes spoken of by Megasthenes are virtually the four castes spoken of above. His philosophers and councillors were the Brāhmans, those who engaged themselves in religious study, and those who took employment under the State respectively. His husbandmen, shepherds and artizans were the Vaiśyas and Śūdras who engaged themselves in cultivation, in pasture and in manufacture. And his soldiers were the Kṣatriyas; while his overseers were only special servants, spies of the king.

Megasthenes further sub-divides the philosophers into Brāhmans or house-holders, and Srāmans or ascetics. Of the former he says that "the children are under the care of one person after another, and as they advance in age, each succeeding master is more accomplished than his predecessor. The philosophers have their abode in a grove in front of the city within a moderate sized enclosure. They live in a simple style, and lie on beds of rushes or (deer) skins. They abstain from animal food and sensual pleasures, and spend their time listening to religious discourse and in imparting their knowledge to such as will listen to them. After living in this manner for seven and thirty years each individual retires to his own property, where he lives for the rest of his days in ease and security. They then array themselves in fine muslin, and wear a few trinkets of gold in their fingers and in their ears. They eat flesh, but not that of animals employed in labour. They abstain from hot and highly seasoned food. They marry as many wives as they please, with a view to have numerous children, for by having many wives, greater advantages are enjoyed, and since they have no slaves, they have more need to have children around them to attend to their wants."

Of the Srāmans or ascetics, Megasthenes tells us that "they live in the wood, where they subsist on leaves of trees and wild fruits and wear garments made from the bark of trees..... They communicate the kings, who consult them by messengers, regarding the causes of things, and who through them worship and supplicate the deity." Of those who practised medicines, Megasthenes writes : "by their knowledge of pharmacy they can make marriages fruitful, and determine the sex of the offspring. They effect cures rather by regulating diet than by the use of medicines. The remedies most esteemed are ointments and plasters." We learn from this account, as we learn from other sources, that sects of ascetics subsisting on roots and wild fruits, lived in Ancient India and bore the name of Srāmans before and after the time of Gautama Buddha. And when that great reformer preached a holy life and retirement from the world, as the essence of his religion, his followers, who retired from the world, were called Śākyaputriya Srāmans, or ascetics who followed the Śākya—to distinguish them from other sects of ascetics.

Elsewhere Megasthenes says of the Philosopher-caste that they, "Being exempted from all public duties, are neither the masters nor the servants of others. They are, however, engaged by private persons to offer the sacrifices due in life-time, and to celebrate the obsequies of the dead. They forewarn assembled multitudes about droughts and wet weather, and also about propitious winds and diseases." We have thus a brief but intelligent sketch from the hand of an impartial foreigner of the life which the Brāhmans lived in the Rationalistic Period. They gave religious instruction to the young, they presided at sacrifices and funeral ceremonies, they advised villagers and cultivators about weather and harvests, and they also prescribed simple medicines for various diseases. Kings looked up to them for advice in emergencies, and the class of Brāhmans whom Megasthenes considers a separate caste and calls councillors, also advised the king in state affairs, were entrusted with the treasury, and were the judges in civil and criminal cases. The educated classes looked up to the Brāhmans for priestly advice and assistance at large sacrifices, while the humble cultivators consulted the wise men about the prospects of the year. With the gradual decline of the nation the caste so universally honored gradually came to abuse its privileges, and tried to strengthen by superstition that pre-eminence which was first acquired by sanctity and knowledge.

Of the military class, or the Kṣatriya caste, Megasthenes gives a very brief sketch. The soldiers were organized and equipped for war, but in times of peace gave themselves up to idleness and amusements.

"The entire force, men-at-arms, war-horses, war-elephants, and all are maintained at the king's expense." It was the duty of the overseers to inquire into all that went on in India and report them to the king.

Of the husbandmen, shepherds and artizans, who obviously were the Vaiśya and Śūdra castes, Megasthenes gives us a more interesting and life-like sketch. Being exempted from fighting and other public services, the husbandmen "devote the whole of their time to tillage; *nor would an enemy, coming upon a husbandman at work on his land, do him any harm,* for men of this class, being regarded as public benefactors, are protected from all injury. The land thus remaining unravaged, and producing heavy crops, supplies the inhabitants with all that is requisite to make life very enjoyable. They pay a land tribute to the king, because all India is the property of the Crown, and no private person is permitted to own land. Besides the land tribute, they pay into the royal treasury a fourth part of the produce of the soil,"[2]

"The shepherds neither settle in towns nor in villages but live in tents.[3] By hunting and trapping they clear the country of noxious birds and wild beasts. Of the artizans some are armourers, while others make the implements which husbandmen and others find useful in their different callings. This class is not only exempted from paying taxes, but even receives maintenance from the rcyal exchequer."

REFERENCES

1. One instance will suffice. The Vaidyas or physician caste of Bengal were unknown in the Rationalistic Period, but later tradition has applied to them the same fiction that was developed in the Rationalistic Period, and the Vaidyas are said to have descended from the union of men and women of different castes. And yet common sense would suggest that they are the descendants of a section of the Āryan people—the Vaiśyas,—who specially applied themselves to one particular science as soon as the science was sufficiently developed to call for special application, and thus in course of time formed a hereditary caste. This view receives a curious confermation from the name which the Bengal Vaidyas still bear. All Vaidyas are Guptas (Sena Gupta, Dasa Gupta, etc.) Now there are passages in the Sūtra literature which clearly lay down that all Brāhmans are Sarmans, all Kṣatriyas are Barmans, and *all Vaiśyas are Guptas*. We will quote such a passage further on in Chapter VIII of this Book.
2. Megasthenes must have made a mistake here, or is describing the exceptionally rigorous land tax imposed by Chandragupta. The land tax in India was one-sixth the produce, and there was no separate tribute beyond this.
3. This description must refer to some tribes of aborigines who were scarcely yet completely Hinduized.

CHAPTER – 6

AGRICULTURE AND ARTS

We learn from the Greek writers what we already know from the ancient literature of India, that the time-honored *dhuti* and *chaddar* (which latter served as a *pagri* also) formed the national dress in Ancient India. Arrian quotes a passage from Nearchus, and says that the Indians "wear an under-garment of cotton which reaches below the knee half way down to the ankles, and also an upper garment which they throw partly over their shoulders and partly twist in folds round their head. They wear shoes made of white leather, and these are elaborately trimmed, while the soles are variegated, and made of great thickness." And the great mass of the "people of India live upon grain and are tillers of the soil, but we must except the hillmen who eat the flesh of beasts of chase."

Our faithful guide Megasthenes also gives us an account of cultivation in Ancient India which, on the whole, corresponds with the system of cultivation at the present time, except that Megasthenes speaks of a double rainfall in the year, considering the winter showers as a regular rainfall. He speaks of "many vast plains of great fertility, more or less beautiful, but all alike intersected by a multitude of rivers. *The greater part of the soil, moreover, is under irrigation,* and consequently bears two crops in the course of the year. It teems at the same time with animals of all sorts, beasts of the field and fowls of the air, of all different degrees of strength and size. It is prolific, besides, in elephants, which are of monstrous bulk In addition to cereals, there grows through out India much millet, which is kept well watered by the profusion of river streams, and much pulse of different sorts, and rice also, and what is called *bosporum,* as well as many other plant useful for food, of which most grow spontaneously. The soil yields, moreover, not a few other edible products fit for the subsistence of animals about which it would be tedious to write. It is accordingly affirmed that *famine has never visited India, and that there has never been a general scarcity in the supply of nourishing food.* For since there is a double rainfall in the course of each year—one in the winter season when the sowing of wheat takes place as in other countries, and the second at the time of the summer solstice, which is the proper season for sowing rice and *bosporum,* as well as sesamum and millet—the inhabitants of India almost always gather in two harvests annually and even should one of the sowings prove more or less abortive, they are always sure of the other crop. The fruits, moreover, of spontaneous growth, and the esculent roots which grow in marshy places and are of varied sweetness, afford abundant sustenance for man. . .. But, further, there are usages observed by the Indians which contribute to prevent the occurrence of famine among them; for whereas among other nations, it is usual, in the contest of war, to ravage the soil, and thus to reduce it to an uncultivated waste, among the Indians, on the contrary, by whom husbandmen are regarded as a class that is sacred and inviolable, the tillers of the soil, even when battle is raging in their neighbourhood, are undisturbed by any sense of danger, for the combatants on either side in waging the conflict, make carnage of each other, but allow those engaged in husbandry to remain quite unmolested. "Besides, they neither ravage an enemy's land with fire, nor cut down its trees."

It is impossible for a Hindu in the modern day to read without a feeling of pride this impartial testimony of an intelligent and observant foreigner regarding the prosperous condition of India as administered by Hindus over two thousand years ago. An industrious and intelligent peasantry peopled their fair villages and cultivated and irrigated, carefully and laboriously, the endless expanse of fertile fields, while the artisans carried the various manufactures and arts of peace to a high state of excellence. It is impossible to suppose that these results were achieved without a careful and watchful system of administration, without a fair degree of security of life and property, and without the help of laws which were on the whole just and fair, although stained by invidious distinctions based on caste. And even when kings fell out among themselves, and riotous Kṣatriya chiefs were engaged in their frequent wars, a humane custom, unknown elsewhere in the ancient world, mitigated the horrors of war, and saved the peaceful villagers and industrious cultivators from disturbance and danger.

The excellent manufactures of India were known to the traders of Phoenicia and in the markets of Alexandria long before the Christian era. Megasthenes naively says that the Indians were "well skilled in the arts, as might be expected of men who inhale a pure air and drink the very finest water." The soil, too, has "under ground numerous veins of, all sorts of metals, for it contains much gold and silver, and copper and iron in no small quantity, and even tin and other metals, which are employed in making articles of use and ornament, as well as the implements and accoutrements of war."

We have elsewhere given an account of town architecture, and have only to add that the oldest *stone buildings,* the ruins of which still exist in India, belong to the Rationalistic Period. Such, for instance, are the *Baiṭhak* of *Jarāsandha,* and the walls of old Rājagṛha in Behar, which General Cunningham assigns to a period anterior to the 5th century before Christ; and such also are many of the Buddhist caves like those of Khaṇḍagiri and Udayagiri in Orissa which are anterior to the time of Alexander. We have also spoken of the arms and accoutrements of war in a previous section. But the most remarkable progress was made in finery and ornament such as Hindus have always been fond of. Megasthenes says that "in contrast to the general simplicity of their style, they love finery and ornament. Their robes are worked in gold and ornamented with precious stones, and they wear also flowered garments made of the finest muslin. Attendants walking behind hold up umbrellas over them : for they have a high regard for beauty, and avail themselves of every device to improve their looks."

Vasiṣṭha in his chapter on Purification speaks of objects of gold, silver and copper, of stones and gems, and conch shells and pearl shells like gems, as well as of things made of bone, wood, leather, cloth, etc. (III, 49 to 63). More striking, however, is a passage in which Strabo describes a gorgeous procession such as Megas thenes must have seen paraded in the streets of Pāṭaliputra.

"In processions at their festivals, many elephants are in the train, adorned with gold and silver; numerous carriages drawn by four horses, by several pairs of oxen; then follows a body of attendants in full dress bearing vessels of gold, large basins and goblets, an *orguia* in breadth, tables, chairs state, drinking cups and lavers of Indian copper, most; of which are set with precious stones, as emeralds, beryls, and Indian carbuncles; garments embroidered and interwoven with gold; wild beasts, as buffaloes, panthers, tame lions, and a multitude of birds of variegated plumage and of fine *song.*" *Bohn's Translation of Strabo,* III p. 117.

CHAPTER – 7

SOCIAL LIFE : THE POSITION OF WOMEN

"A father who has committed a crime, causing loss of caste, must be cast off. *But a mother does not become an outcast for her son.*

"Now they quote also (the following verses) : 'The teacher (Āchārya) is ten times more venerable than a sub-teacher (Upādhyāya),[1] the father a hundred times more than the teacher, *and the mother a thousand times more than the father!'* *Vasiṣṭha,* XIII, 47 & 48.

Such is the respect for a mother which the ancient religion of the Hindus enjoins, and every true Hindu cherishes and follows that maxim faithfully.

We saw in our account of the Epic Period that ladies sometimes devoted themselves to the pursuit of philosophy, that Gārgī Vāchaknavi distinguished herself among the learned men in the court of Janaka, and that Maitreyi learnt the secrets of the Upaniṣads from her husband Yājñavalkya, the priest of Janaka. Megasthenes is a witness to the fact that sacred learning and philosophy were not forbidden in the Rationalistic Period to such ladies as desired to devote themselves to such studies.

Polygamy was allowed in India, but was, as we have remarked before, probably confined to the wealthier classes. The religion of India did not encourage that unwholesome institution, but only permitted it to ensure male issue. Āpastamba distinctly declares—

"12. If he has a wife who is willing and able to perform her share of the religious duties, and who bears sons, *he shall not take a second.*

"13.If a wife is deficient in one of these two qualities, he shall take another, but before he kindles the fires (of the Agnihotra)." II, 5. II.

Insanity, impotency, loss of caste or death of a husband were the circumstances (*Vasiṣṭha,* XVII, 20), which justified a woman to marry again. The circumstances which justified a husband to abandon his wife are mentioned in an ancient and well-known passage which is quoted in Baudhāyana, and which we find in Manu.

"Let him abandon a barren wife in the tenth year, one who bears daughters only in the twelfth, one whose children all die in the fifteenth, but her who is quarrelsome without delay." *Baudhāyana,* II, 2, 4, 6. Leaving out the last clause, which was never seriously intended to be followed, it will pe observed that it was only the desire for male issue among the ancient Hindus which was the origin of this unjust law of abandonment of a wife. The abandonment probably only meant that the husband took another wife, but still maintained his first wife, as a member of the family, and this is the practice which is still sometimes observed. To send a virtuous wife adrift in the world, because she is incapable of bearing male issue, is a practice unknown in India, and would bring disgrace and dishonour on the family. To unjustly forsake a wife without an adequate reason was looked upon with horror in the Sūtra days, and a penance was prescribed for the sin which young India may remember with advantage. "He who has unjustly forsaken his wife shall put on an ass's skin, with the hair turned outside, and beg in seven houses, saying ' give alms to him who forsook his wife.' That shall be his livelihood for six months. *Āpastamba,* I, 10, 28, 19."

It is in the Sūtras that we first find mention of the different forms of marriage with which we are familiar from the codes of Manu, Viṣṇu, etc, Vasiṣṭha mentions only six forms, *viz.* :—

Brāhma marriage; the father pours out a libation of water and gives his daughter to a suitor, a student.

Daiva marriage; the father decks his daughter with ornaments and gives her to an officiating priest, when sacrifice is being performed.

Ārṣa marriage; the father gives his daughter for a cow or a bull.

Gāndharva marriage; when a lover takes a loving damsel.

Kṣātra (or *Rākṣasa)* marriage; when a bridegroom forcibly takes a damsel, destroying her relatives by strength of arms.

Mānuṣa (or *Āsura)* marriage; when a suitor purchases a damsel from her father.

Āpastamba, too, recognizes only these six forms of marriage, but calls the Kṣātra marriage by the name Rākṣasa and the Mānuṣa marriage by the name Āsura. Āpastamba further mentions the first three forms only, *viz.,* the Brāhma, the Daiva and the Ārṣa, as praiseworthy.

Gautama and Baudhāyana prescribe, however, eight forms of marriage, adding to the above six forms one rite, Prājāpatya, which was considered praiseworthy, and another form *Paisācha* which was sinful. In the Prājāpatya form the father simply gave away his daughter to the suitor, saying, "Fulfil ye the law conjointly." The Paisācha form was simply a form of rape, when a man embraced a woman deprived of consciousness. We must remember that Gautama and Baudhāyana are older authorities than Vasiṣṭha and Āpastamba, and the inference therefore is that two of the old forms were omitted by the later authorities, because they scarcely considered those forms to be marriage rites.

Marriages among kinsfolk were rigorously prohibited in the Rationalistic Period. Vasiṣṭha prohibits marriage between a man and a woman of the same *Gotra* or *Pravara,* or who are related within four degrees on the mother's side, or within six degrees on the father's side. (VIII, I and 2.) Āpastamba prohibits marriage between men and women of the same *Gotra,* or who are related (within six degrees) on the mother's or (father's) side. (II, 5, 11, 15 and 16.)But Baudhāyana allows a man to marry the daughter of a maternal uncle or a paternal aunt (I, 1, 2, 4.)

The marriage of girls at a tender age was probably unknown in the Vedic Period and even in the Epic Period. The custom gradually came into vogue in the Rationalistic Period, but was yet unsettled in that period as we may infer from contradictory rules on the subject. Vasiṣṭha says :—

"67. A maiden who has attained puberty *shall wait for three years.*

"68. After three years, she may take a husband of equal caste.

"69. Now they quote also (the following verses) : 'But if through a father's negligence a maiden is here given away after the suitable age has passed, she who was waiting destroys him who gives her away, just as the fee which is paid too late to the teacher (destroys the pupil).

"70. Out of fear of the appearance of the menses, let the father marry his daughter while she still runs about naked (*i. e.,* while she is still a child). ' For if she stays after the age of puberty, sin falls on the father.'

"74 If a damsel at the death of her husband had been merely wedded by sacred texts, and if the marriage had not been consummated, she may be married again.'" *Vasiṣṭha,* XVII.

Thus, though women were sometimes married in their childhood, yet child-widows were allowed to re-marry in the Rationalistic Period.

The above passage, however, indicates that the marriage of widows, which was a prevalent custom in the Vedic and Epic Periods, became gradually restricted in the Rationalistic Period, and except in the case of child-widows, was not looked upon with favour. The son of a widow married again, was, as will appear from passages quoted in a previous chapter, often classed with adopted sons, or sons by an appointed wife or daughter.

The rules about funeral ceremonies and mourning have been laid down in detail in the Sūtras, but we are unable to make room for many extracts. Vasiṣṭha says that after burning the body of the deceased, the relatives shall enter the water; pour out water facing the south, for the south is sacred to the manes; and that on their return home, they shall sit on mats, and fast or live on poor food for three days. *Sapiṇḍa* relationship extends to the seventh person in the ascending or descending line, and the impurity caused by death lasts for ten days in the case of Sapiṇḍas, (IV, 11 to 17.) At the *Śrāddha* or funeral sacrifice the bereaved will feed a small number of Brāhmans, or "even a single Brāhman who has studied the whole Veda, who is distinguished by learning and virtue, and is free from all evil marks." (XI, 29.) The performance of Śrāddhas could scarcely have been so advantageous to Brāhmins under the above rule as it is in modern times! And, lastly, in a remarkable verse, Vasiṣṭha says," The manes consider him to be their descendant who offers food at Gayā, and they grant him blessings, just as husbandmen or well ploughed fields." (XI, 42.) The passage appears to be a later interpolation.

Gautama says that Sapiṇḍa relationship ceases with the fifth or the seventh (ancestor), and lays down that Sapiṇḍas remain impure for ten days after the death, but that a Kṣatriya remains impure eleven days, a Vaiśya twelve days, and a Śūdra one month. On the failure of sons, Sapiṇḍas can offer the funeral oblation. He recommends the feeding of at least nine Brāhmans, but they must be Śrotriyas. (XIV, 1 to 5, 13, and XV, 7 to 9.)

Baudhāyana includes only the great-grandfather, the grandfather, the father, oneself, the brothers, the son, grandson and great-grandson among Sapiṇḍas. (I, 5, 11,9.) Āpastamba extends the Sapiṇḍa relationship to blood relations within six degrees. (II, 6, 15, 2.)

Such are some of the rules laid down in the Dharma Sūtras for marriages and funeral ceremonies. We will now briefly review the rules laid down in the same Sūtras regarding the conduct of a student and that of a householder.

The turning point of a young man's life seems to have been his initiation as a student. A Brāhman boy was initiated between 8 and 16, a Kṣatriya between 11 and 22, and a Vaiśya between 12 and 24. The initiated boy then lived as a religious student in the house of his teacher for 12, 24, 36 or 48 years, according as he wished to master one, two, three or the four Vedas. During this period of his life he avoided all spiced food, perfumes, and articles of luxury, he tied his hair in a knot, he bore a staff and girdle and a cloth of flax or hemp, or even only a skin. Avoiding all places of amusement and of pleasure, restraining his senses, modest and humble, the young student went out every morning with his staff to beg for food from charitable householders in the neighbouring villages, and all that he obtained in the course of the day, he placed before his teacher; and he only tasted food after his teacher had done with his meals. He went to the forest to fetch fuel, and evening and morning he fetched water for household use. Every morning he swept and cleaned the altar, kindled the fire and placed the sacred fuel on it, and every evening he washed his teacher's feet and rubbed him and put him to bed, before he retired to rest. Such was the humble, obedient and simple life which ancient Hindu students led, when they devoted all the energies of their mind to the acquisition of the sacred learning of their forefathers.

Instruction, it is needless to repeat, was imparted by rote. The student respectfully held the hand of his teacher and fixed his mind on the teacher and said "Venerable Sir, recite," and the Sāvitrī (the well-known Gāyatrī verse of the Ṛg Veda) was recited, and learnt as the introduction to the learning of the Vedas (*Gautama,* I, 55, 56). And from day to day new lessons were recited and learnt, the student dividing his day's work between minding his lessons and minding the household work of his teacher.

When after years of study, often under different teachers, the student at last returned to his home, he made a handsome gift to his instructors, married and settled down as a householder or *snātaka, i.e.*, a man who has bathed after his studentship is over. *Agnihotra,* or the morning and evening libations in the holy fire, and hospitality to strangers are enjoined on him as his principal duties (*Āpastamba,* I, 4, 14). The Sūtrakāras are never tired of impressing on every householder their paramount duty of courtesy and hospitality towards guests, for the reception of guests is an everlasting sacrifice offered by the householder to Prajāpati. *Āpastamba,* II, 3, 7, 1.

Besides the order of the student and that of the householder, there were two other orders of life, *viz.,* those of the ascetic (Bhikṣu), and that of the hermit (Vaikhānasa). We learn from later Sanscrit literature that a typical or perfect life was the life of a man who belonged to these four orders in successive periods of his life. Āpastamba, too, who is one of the latest of the Sūtrakāras, says that "if he lives in all these four (orders of life) ... he will obtain salvation." (II, 9, 21, 2.) But this was not probably the original idea, and in early times a man might have chosen to spend the whole of his life in one of these four orders. Thus, Vasiṣṭha says that a man after completing his education may, according to his choice, embrace one of the four orders for the rest of his life (VII, 3) and Baudhāyana, too, quotes a rule that a man on finishing his education may be an ascetic at once (II, 10, 17, 2). It is needless for our purpose to dwell on rules laid down for an ascetic and a hermit respectively. It will suffice to state, that an ascetic shaved his head, had no property or home, practised austerities, fasted or lived on alms, wore a single garment or a skin, slept on the bare ground, and wandered about from place to place, discontinued the performance of all religious ceremonies, but never discontinued the study of the Veda or the contemplation of the Universal Soul (*Vasiṣṭha,* X). A hermit, on the other hand, though living in woods, living on roots and fruits and leading a chaste. life, kindled the sacred fire and offered the morning and evening libations *(Vasiṣṭha,* IX).

Numerous are the sacraments which have been prescribed for householders who form the best of the four orders. For the householders, and not hermits and ascetics, formed the nation, and "as rivers, both great and small, find a resting place in the ocean, even so men of all orders find protection with householders" *(Vasiṣṭha,* VIII, 15).

No less than forty sacraments have been prescribed for the householder *(Gautama,* VIII, 14 to 20), and as we will describe some of these rites in the next chapter, it is necessary only to enumerate them here.

Domestic Ceremonies.—

(1) Garbhādhāna (ceremony to cause conception);
(2) Puṁsavana (ceremony to cause the birth of a male child);
(3) Sīmantonnayana (arranging the hair of the pregnant wife);
(4) Jātakarman (ceremony on birth of a child);
(5) ceremony of naming the child;
(6) the first feeding;
(7) the tonsure of the head;
(8) the initiation;
(9 to 12) the four vows for the study of the Veda;
(13) the bath or completion of studentship ;
(14) marriage, or, as it is called, the taking a helpmate for the performance of religious duties; and
(15 to 19) the five sacrifices to gods, manes, men, goblins, and the Brāhman or Universal Soul.

Gṛhya religious rites, also called *Pākayajñas.*—They have been already alluded to in Chapter I of this Book, but for facility of reference, we will again enumerate them here.

(1) Astakā, or rites performed in winter;
(2) Pārvana, or new and full moon rites;
(3) Śrāddha, or funeral sacrifices;
(4) Srāvanī, a rite performed on the full moon of Srāvana month;
(5) Āgrahāyanī, performed in the Agrahāyana month;
(6) Chaitrī performed in the month of Chaitra; and
(7) Āsvayugi, performed in the month of Āsvina.

Śrauta religious rites.—These are again divided into two classes, *viz., Haviryajña,* performed with offerings of rice, milk, butter, meat, etc; and the *Somayajña,* performed with libations of the soma juice. There were seven rites of each class, and they have been described before in Book II, Chapter VIII, of the present work. We will again name them here.

The Haviryajñas are—

(1) Agnyādhāna,	(2) Agnihotra,
(3) Darsapūrnamāsa,	(4) Āgrayana,
(5) Chāturmāsya,	(6) Nirūdhapasubandha, and
(7) Sautrāmanī.	

The Somayajñas are

(1) Agniṣṭoma,	(2) Atyagnīṣṭoma,
(3) Ukthya,	(4) Ṣoḍasin,
(5) Vājapeya,	(6) Atirātra, and
(7) Āptoryāma.	

Such were the forty sacraments prescribed for householders; but far above the performance of these sacrifices was esteemed the possession of virtue and goodness which alone led to heaven. A living nation could never forget that—however much sacrifice might be esteemed and rules for their performance might be multiplied—it was virtue which held society together and smoothed the path of progress. So long as society was progressive, it commended virtue more than the rites it enjoined, and punished vice more than the "breach of caste-rules or the omission of rites. Compassion, Forbearance, Freedom from anger, Purity, Gentleness, the Performance of good actions, Freedom from avarice, and Freedom from covetousness, are esteemed as the eight good qualities, and Gautama says :—

"He who is sanctified by these forty sacraments, but whose soul is destitute of the eight good qualities, will not be united with Brāhman, nor does he reach His Heaven.

"But he, forsooth, who is sanctified by a few only of these forty sacraments, and whose soul is endowed with the excellent qualities, will be united with Brāhman and will dwell in His Heaven." (VIII, 24 and 25.)

Further on Gautama concludes his account of the duties of a householder with these pregnant rules :—

"68. He shall always speak the truth.

"69. He shall conduct himself as becomes an Āryan.

"70. He shall instruct virtuous men.

"71. He shall follow the rules of purification.

"72. He shall take pleasure in the Veda.

"73. He shall never hurt any being, he shall be gentle, yet firm, ever restrain his senses, and be liberal.

"74. A *snātaka* who conducts himself in this manner will liberate his parents, his ancestors, and decend ants from evil, and never fall from Brāhman's heaven." (IX.)

Similarly Vasiṣṭha says :—

"3. The Vedas do not purify him who is deficient in good conduct, though he may have learnt them all together with the six Aṅgas; the sacred texts depart from such a man even as birds, when full fledged, leave their nests.

"4. As the beauty of a wife causes no joy to a blind man, even so all the four Vedas together, with the six Aṅgas and sacrifices, bring no blessing to him who is deficient in good conduct.

"5. The several texts do not save from sin the deceitful man who behaves deceitfully. But that Veda, two syllables of which are studied with due observances of rules of conduct, purifies, just as the clouds in the month of Āśvina." (VI.)

It was but one short step from this to Buddhism which eschewed all sacred texts and sacred rites, and was essentially *a religion of holy life* which could create for man a heaven in this earth.

Gautama's list of the sins which led to loss of caste confirms the same impression, that so long as Hinduism was the religion of a living nation, immorality was despised and punished more than breach of artificial rules. Murder, drinking spirituous liquor, violation of a guru's bed, incest, theft, atheism, a persistent repetition of sinful acts, harbouring criminals and abandoning blameless friends, instigating others to such sinful acts, and associating with outcasts, giving false evidence, bringing false charges, and similar acts, involved loss of caste. (XXI, 1 to 10.) Vasiṣṭha's list of *Mahāpātakas* is shorter, but equally points to the abhorrence for sin and immorality rather than the breach of artificial rules. The violation of a guru's bed, the drinking of spiritious liquor, murder and theft, and spiritual or matrimonial connexion with outcastes, were the five greatest of sins. (I, 19 to 21.)

It is permissible for a historian to turn from ancient customs to modern facts! Ancient Hinduism, which was a living religion, laid down rules for the conduct of Āryans, but detested crime and immorality far more than the breach of artificial rules. Long subjection and political lifelessness have made modern Hindus lose sight of the spirit of the ancient faith, and cling to dead forms, or fabricate new-fangled and hurtful rules. Immorality, the use of spirituous liquor, and even crime, do not involve loss of caste in modern society; that penalty is reserved for the re-marriage of widows which was permitted in ancient days, for intermarriage and social intercourse among people descended from the same old Vaiśya stock, for voyage and foreign travel which were permitted to Northern Hindus. Caste was a valuable institution when it repressed crime and ordained a pure life. Modern caste represses harmless or even meritorious acts, and has become valuable in its loss more than in its preservation !

The taking of food cooked by men of inferior castes, which is a principal reason of loss of caste in modern times, does not seem to have entailed the same consequences in the Rationalistic Period. On the contrary, there are directions for keeping Śūdra cooks, provided the cooks had cleanly habits *(Āpastamba, II,* 2, 3, 4 to 9), and the food thus prepared was considered fit even for religious rites. Thus the ancients allowed between Āryans and Śūdras a degree of social intercourse which the moderns will not permit among different professions descended from the same Vaiśya stock.

Elaborate rules have been laid down in the Sūtras on the subject of food, and animals and birds which may be used as food have been carefully distinguished from those which should not be so used. Beef was still used as an article of food, but was gradually falling into disuse on account of the growing disinclination to kill animals except at sacrifices. On this point Dr. Bühler has drawn attention to a remarkable passage from Manu's Dharma Sūtra, which has been quoted by Vasiṣṭha. Manu's Dharma Sūtra exists no longer, having been replaced by the later metrical code of Manu, which is no doubt based on the old Dharma Sūtra. The extract is therefore of the utmost interest to all Sanscrit scholars.

"5. The Mānava (Sūtra states), 'only when he worships the manes and the gods, or honours guests, he may certainly do injury to animals.'

"6. 'On offering a madhuparka (to a guest) at a sacrifice, and at the rites in honor of the manes, but on these occasions only may an animal be slain, that rule Manu proclaimed.'

"7. 'Meat can never be obtained without injuring living beings, and to injure living beings does not procure heavenly bliss; therefore the (sages declare) the slaughter at a sacrifice not to be slaughter.'

" 8. 'Now he may cook a full-grown ox or a full-grown he-goat for a Brāhman or Kṣatriya guest; in this manner they offer hospitality to such a man.'" *Vasiṣṭha, IV,*

With regard to the above four Sūtras 5 to 8 from Vasiṣṭha, Book IV, Dr. Bühler makes the following remarks, which are worth quoting: "The fact that Vasiṣṭha gives in IV, 5, a prose quotation from Manu, may therefore be considered as certain. Moreover, several of the best manuscripts shew by adding the particle 'iti' at the end of Sūtra 8, that the quotation from the Mānava is not finished with Sūtra 5, but includes the two verses given in Sūtras 6 and 7, and the second prose passage in Sūtra 8. Among the verses the first is found entire in the metrical

Manu Smriti, and the second has likewise a representative in that work, *though its concluding portion has been altered in such a manner that the permission to slaughter animals of sacrifices has been converted into an absolute prohibition to take animal life.* Sūtra 8, which again is in prose, has no counterpart in the metrical 'Manu Smriti' as might be expected *from its allowing a ' full-grown ox' or 'a full-grown he-goat' to be killed, in honor of a distinguished Brāhmaṇa or Kṣatriya guest"* The italics are our own, and they shew, if Dr. Bühler's supposition be correct, how the ancient and now lost Mānava Sūtra has been changed into the modern metrical Mānava Śāstra to suit the changes in the customs and manners of the Hindu nation.

Dr. Rajendra Lala Mitra has, in his paper on Beef in Ancient India, pointed out that in several religious rites the slaughter of animals formed a necessary part. One is called the *Śūlagava* or "spitted cow," *i. e.,* Roast Beef, and it was performed in the autumn or spring season. Another was called *Gavāmanayana* or the sacrifice of the cow, otherwise called, *Ekāṣṭakā,* Kātyāyana recommends the sacrifice of a barren cow to the Maruts and seventeen oxen to Prajāpati in connection with the *Atirātra* rite. Similarly the *Nirūdha Paśubandha* rite required the sacrifice of oxen. The *Madhuparka* or honey-meat of which mention is made before, and was offered to a respectable guest—a priest, king, bridegroom or Vedic student, a teacher, a father-in-law, an uncle or a man of rank—had to be accompanied with the sacrifice of a cow in honor of the guest. Dr. Mitra rightly thinks that the use of beef went out when sacrifices themselves fell into disuse, and was finally abandoned in consequence of the Buddhist appeal to humanity.

But though beef as well as the meat of varfous other animals was allowed in the Rationalistic Period, the use of spirituous liquor was most strictly prohibited, and was, as we have seen, a Mahāpātaka both according to Gautama and Vasiṣṭha. The penance was death—hot liquor of the same kind being poured into the sinner's mouth till he was scalded to death *(Gautama,* XXIII, I; *Baudhāyana,* II, I, I, 18). But as we have said before, these laws indicate the state of society which was aimed at by priests, and not the estate which was ever actually secured. But nevertheless it is something to know the good results which were aimed at by ancient rules and restrictions. For they have now been replaced by new rules and restrictions which aim at no good results, and reveal neither sense nor reason to the most solicitous inquirer!

REFERENCE

1. Elsewhere Vasiṣṭha defines an Āchārya and an Upādhyāya. He who initiates a pupil and teaches him the whole Veda is called Āchārya : but he who teaches a portion of the Veda only, or the Vedāṅgas, is called the Upādhyāya—III, 21 to 23.

CHAPTER – 8

DOMESTIC CEREMONIES AND GṚHYA RITES

We have seen that the forty sacraments prescribed by Gautama included Domestic ceremonies, Gṛhya rites, and Śrauta rites. The Śrauta rites are described in detail in the Yajur Veda and the Brāhmaṇas, and also in a condensed form in the Śrauta Sūtras, as we have stated before. These rites and sacrifices throw little light on the manners and customs of the people, and are therefore not of very great importance for our historical purpose. The Domestic ceremonies and Gṛhya rites on the other hand give us glimpses which are of inestimable value into the manners of the ancient Hindus, and indeed give us perfect pictures of the life that they lived and the habits and customs they followed. These ceremonies and rites form the subject of the Gṛhya Sūtras, and to them we must now turn.

We will first treat of the Domestic ceremonies, the *Saṁskāras,* as they are called, and afterwards speak of the Gṛhya religious rites, The most important of the Saṁskāras are Marriage, Ceremonies during pregnancy of wife, Birth of child, Annaprāsana or the first feeding of a child, Tonsure, Cutting of beard. Initiation, Return from school, and the Building of a house, and Funeral ceremonies. As we read accounts of these domestic ceremonies, we think we survey the whole life of our ancient ancestors; and the ceremonies are all the more interesting to us because we continue to practise many of them to the present day, after a lapse of over two thousand years.

Marriage

The bridegroom sends messengers to the house of the girl's father, reciting verse X, 85, 23, of the Ṛg Veda which we have translated before, If the proposal pleases both parties, the promise of marriage is ratified, and both parties touch a full vessel into which flowers, fried grain, barley and gold have been put, and recite a formula. The bridegroom then performs a sacrifice. On the appointed day, the bride's relations wash her with water fragrant with the choicest fruits and scents, make her put on a newly dyed garment, and cause her to sit down by a fire while the family Āchārya performs a sacrifice. The bridegroom who has also bathed and gone through auspicious ceremonies "is escorted by happy young women who are not widows to the girl's house." *Sāṅkhāyāna.*

The actual marriage ceremony, varied in detail in different localities, but agreed in the essential points. "Various indeed are the customs of the different countries, and the customs of the different villages. What, however, is commonly accepted, that we shall state." *Āśvalāyana.* The bridegroom holds the bride by the hand, and leads her three times round a fire, reciting some verses as "Come let us beget offspring. Loving, bright, with genial mind, may we live a hundred autumns." Each time he makes her tread a millstone, saying "Like a stone be firm." The bride's brother or guardian fills her hands with Ājya or fried grain, and she sacrifices it to the fire. The bridegroom then causes the bride to step forward seven steps, reciting some suitable words, as "For sap with one step, for juice with two steps, for thriving of wealth with three steps, for comfort with four steps, for offspring with five steps, for the seasons with six steps, be friend with seven steps. So be thou devoted to me. Let us acquire many sons who may reach old age." The going round the fire, sacrificing the fried grain to the fire, and stepping forward seven steps, constituted the principal forms of the marriage ceremony. "And she should dwell that night in the house of an old Brāhman woman whose husband is alive, and whose children are alive. When she sees the polar star, the star of Arundhati, and the Seven Ṛṣis (ursa major) let her break the silence, and say, May my husband live, and I get offspring," *Āśvalāyana*. Sāṅkhāyana says "Let them sit silent, when the sun has set, until the polar star appears. He shews her the polar star with the words—'Firm be thou, thriving with me.' Let her say, 'I see the polar star; may I obtain offspring.' Through a period of three nights let them refrain from conjugal intercourse." The last injunction leads to the supposition that girls were generally married after they had attained maturity, in spite of the rules to the contrary which in the Dharma Sūtras. Pūraskara says the prohibition against conjugal intercourse may extend to three nights, or to twelve nights, or to six months, or to a year.

Gobhila lays down a rule about the selection of a wife, which will sound strange in these modern days of courtship and free choice! Eight lumps of earth were to be taken from different places, from an altar, a ploughed field, a lake, a pasture field, a meeting of roads, etc, and a ninth was to be formed by mixing portions of the other eight. These nine were to be placed before the girl—and she was to be considered a suitable bride or otherwise according to her blind choice !

Pregnancy

Various were the rites performed during the pregnancy of a wife. in the first place there was the *Grabhalambhana* rite, which was supposed to secure conception. The *Puṁsavana* rite was supposed to determine the male sex of the child, and the *Anavalobhana* or *Garbharakṣaṇa* secured the child in the womb from dangers. The *Sīmantonnayana,* performed according to Āśvalayana in the fourth month, and according to Sāṅkhāyana in the seventh month of pregnancy, is a more interesting ceremony. Gobhila says it may be performed in the fourth, sixth, or eigth month, and it consisted in the husband affectionately parting his wife's hair with certain rites.

Birth of child

The rites performed on this occasion are called *Jātakarman,* or birth ceremony, *Medhājananam,* or the production of intelligence, and *Āyuṣya* or rite for prolonging life. On this occasion the father gives the child a secret name—of an even number of syllables if the child is male, and an uneven number if it is female, and only the father and mother know that name. On the tenth day when the mother gets up from childbed a name for common use is given to the child. "The name of a Brāhman should end in Sarman *(e.g.,* Viṣṇu Sarman), that of a Kṣatriya *in* Varman, *(e. g.,* Lakṣmī Varman), *that of a Vaiśya in Gupta (e. g., Chandra Gupta).Pāraskara,* I, 17, 4.

First feeding of the child with solid food

This is the well known *Annaprasana* ceremony, which is observed to the present day. Only the child seems to have been allowed a greater variety of food in the olden days. "Goat's flesh, if he is desirous of nourishment, flesh of partridge if desirous of holy lustre, boiled rice with ghee, if desirous of splendour, "Āśvalāyana and Sāṅkhāyana. "Flesh of the bird called Bhāradvājī if he wishes fluency of speech; Fish, if swiftness was desired, etc, etc. *Pāraskara.*

Tonsure of the child's head, called Kaula or Cūḍā Karaṇa

This was performed when the child was one year old according to Sāṅkhāyana and Pāraskara, or when the child was in his third year according to Āśvalāyana Gobhila. The child's head was shaved with a razor with certain mantras, (without mantras in the case of a girl,) and some hair was left and arranged according to the custom of the family.

Cutting of the beard

The ceremony called *Godāna Karman,* or *Keśānta,* was similar to the tonsure of the head, but was of course performed at a later period. Āśvalāyana says it was performed in the sixteenth year of the boy, Sāṅkhāyana says in the sixteenth or eighteenth year, and Gobhila says in the sixteenth year after initiation.

Initiation or Upaṇayana

This was an important ceremony, and was performed when a boy was made over by his father or guardian to the teacher for education. The age of initiation, as we have seen before, varied in the case of Brāhmans, Kṣatriyas and Vaiśyas, and the sacred thread was worn on this occasion by all the three castes. A garment, a girdle, and a staff of appropriate materials were then assumed by the student, and he approached the teacher.

"He (the teacher) fills the two hollows of his own and the student's joined hands with water, and then says to him (*i. e.*, to the student) : 'what is thy name'?

"'I am N. N., Sir,' says the other.

"'Descending from the same Ṛṣis,' says the teacher.

"'Descending from the same Ṛṣis, Sir,' says the other.

"'Declare that thou art a student, Sir.'

"'I am a student, Sir,' says the other.

"With the words 'Bhūr Bhuvaḥ Svaḥ' the teacher sprinkles thrice with his joined hands water on the joined hands of the student.

"And seizing the student's hands with his own hands, holding the right uppermost, he murmurs :—

"By the impulse of the god Savitri, with the arms of the two Aśvins, with Pūṣan's hands I initiate thee, N. N.

* * * * * * *

"After one year, the teacher recites the Sāvitrī (Ṛg Veda, III, 62),

"or after three nights,

"or immediately.

"Let him recite a Gāyatrī to a Brāhman,

"a Triṣṭubh to a Kṣatriya,

"a Jagatī to a Vaiśya.

"But let it anyhow be a verse sacred to Sāvitrī.

"They seat themselves to the north of the fire,

"the teacher with his face turned eastward, the other westward.

"After the student has said 'Recite, Sir,'

"the teacher having pronounced the word OM, then causes the other one to say 'Recite the Sāvitrī, Sir.'

"He then recites the Sāvitrī to him, the verse, 'That glorious splendour of Savitri' (Ṛg Veda, III, 62, 10) firstly pada by pada, then hemistich by hemistich, and finally without a stop." *Saṅkhāyana,* II, 2 and 5.

Such was the ceremony of the *Upaṇayana* in ancient times, the initiation into the life of a student, the commencement of the study of the Veda. How has the *Upaṇayana* custom degenerated in modern times. It no longer means the study of the Veda which is now forgotten, nor the performance of sacrifices which have now fallen into disuse, It now means the habitual assumption of a meaningless thread which was neither meaningless nor habitually worn in ancient days; and modern Brāhmans, who do not sacrifice or read the Veda, claim a monopoly of the sacrificial thread which the ancient Brāhmans used to wear along with; Kṣatriyas and Vaiśyas, who all sacrificed and learnt the Veda. Thus national degeneracy has converted significant rites into meaningless forms, all tending to the enforced ignorance of the people, and to the exclusive privileges of priests.

The building of the house

The student, after he had finished his education, returned to his home, and if he had no ancestral house to go to, had to build a house. This, too, was accompanied by a ceremony and by the utterance of the hymns of the Ṛg Veda (VII 54, 55.) to Vāstospati, the lord of dwelling-houses, as well as to other divinities. Gobhila, with a curious punctiliousness, lays down that Brāhmans should build their houses on white-grained soil (sand ?), Kṣatriyas on red-grained soil (gravel ?), and Vaiśyas on black-grained soil (fertile cultivable clay ?). Of course these rules only shew the rage for generalizing, and were never meant to be followed. Many sensible rules are, however, laid down for the selection of desirable places on sanitary grounds. Then followed the setting up of fires—the Agnyādhāna—which is a Śrauta rite, and which has been described in Chapter VIII of the last Book. The building of a house and the setting up of fires were unnecessary if the father of the young householder and husband was still living. *Gobhila,* I, 1, 12.

Funeral ceremony

Many eminent scholars have treated of the funeral rites of the Hindus according to the Gṛhya Sūtras, and we will only note a few important points. The relations of the deceased carried his sacred fires and sacrificial Vessels, and aged men and women carried the dead body. The Āhavanīya fire, the Gārhapatya fire, and the Dakṣiṇa fire were placed to the south-east, to the north-west, and to the southwest of the ground selected for cremation, and the widow was placed near the body of her dead husband until her brother-in-law, or a pupil, or an aged servant caused her to rise and go away with verse X, 18, 8, of the Ṛg Veda. A she-animal was sacrificed, and was placed limb by limb on the corresponding limbs of the deceased, and then the three fires mentioned above were lighted together. The relations then left the corpse and had their ablutions. Afterwards the bones were collected in an urn, and were buried in a pit 'at a place where the waters from the different sides do not flow together." *Āśvalāyana.*

Funeral oblations

The last of the important rites is the Śrāddha; it is considered as one of the Pākayajñas or Gṛhya rites, but an account of it comes in more suitably among the domestic ceremonies, and we will glean one or two passages here from Āśvalāyana. 'Brāhmans who are endowed with learning, moral character and correct conduct, were invited, and sat down "as representatives of the fathers" to whom the oblations were offered. The sacrificer then offered the Arghya water of the fathers with the words, "Father, this is thy Arghya; Grandfather, this is thy Arghya, Great-grandfather, this is thy Arghya." Gifts of perfumes, garlands, incense, lights and clothes were then offered to the Brāhmans. With the permission of the Brāhmans food of the *Sthālīpāka* prepared for the *Piṇḍapitriyajña* was smeared with ghee and sacrificed in the fire, or in the hands of the Brāhmans, together with other food. And when the sacrificer saw that the Brāhmans were satiated, he recited the verse (Ṛg Veda, I, 82, 2), "They have eaten, they have enjoyed themselves."

Our account of Domestic ceremonies, though condensed as far as possible, has occupied a considerable space; but no Hindu reader will regret it, as many of the ceremonies are still observed by us, and it is interesting and instructive to learn how they were observed by our forefathers. The same reason emboldens us to add here an account of the Pākayajñas or Gṛhya rites, many of which we still observe to the present day, though they have lost their original purpose and character and even their name.

Parvan

This was the rite observed on the new and full moon days, and consisted in fasting as well as in offering cooked oblations to the deities of the festivals of those days, with appropriate mantras. Orthodox Hindus still make it a point to fast on these days.

Śrāvaṇī

This was a rite observed on the full moon day of the month of Śrāvaṇa in the rainy season, and the idea was to propitiate serpents which multiply in India in the rains. The words uttered were sufficiently grotesque.

"6. With the words 'May the Lord of the celestial serpents wash himself! May the celestial serpents wash themselves !'—he pours water into it.

"7. With the words 'May the Lord of the celestial serpents comb himself! May the celestial serpents comb themselves !'—he makes movements with a comb.

"8. With the words 'May the Lord of the celestial serpents paint himself! May the celestial serpents paint themselves !'—he pours out portions of paint."

And similarly a desire was expressed that the celestial serpents might deck themselves with flowers, put on clothing, anoint their eyelashes, look at themselves in a looking glass, and then accept food, and appropriate offerings were made with each wish! The aereal serpents were then propitiated—and lastly terrestrial serpents. *Sāṅkhāyana,* IV, 15.

The worship of serpents as such has nearly disappeared from the upper classes of the people of India, and they will have some difficulty in recognizing the rite performed at the *Rākī Pūrṇimā* as the last trace of the *Śrāvaṇī* rite of the Rationalistic Period. The *Rakī* string bracelet which friends distribute to friends, and sisters affectionately send to their brothers, is a bracelet which is intended to save from harm and evil proceeding from serpents.[1]

Aśvayugī

This was a rite performed on the full moon day of Āśvayuga or Āśvina month.

"1. On the full moon day of Āśvayuga a milk-rice oblation to Indra.

"2. Having sacrificed Ājya with the words 'To the two Aśvins, svāhā! To the two Āśvayuj, svāhā! To the full moon of Āsvayuga, svāhā! To the autumn, svāha! To Prajāpati, svāhā! To the tawny one, svāhā !'

"3. He shall sacrifice a mixture of curds and butter with this hymn,'The cows come hither.' (Rg Veda, VI, 28,) verse by verse.

"4. That night they let the calves join their mother.

"5. Then feeding of the Brāhmans. "

This is all the account which Sāṅkhāyana gives of this rite, and it is impossible not to suspect, from the above account, that the rite is essentially agricultural. This suspicion is confirmed when Pāraskara tells us that the above rite was to be followed by a sacrifice to Sītā, *the goddess of the field furrow.*

"In whose substance dwells the prosperity of all Vedic and worldly works, *Indra's wife, Sītā,* I invoke. May she not abandon me in whatever work I do Svāhā !

"Her, who, rich in horses, rich in cows, rich in delight, indefatigably supports living beings, *Urvarā (the fertile), who is wreathed with threshing floor,* I invoke at this sacrifice, the firm one. May she not abandon me. Svāhā! "(II, 17, 9.)

The worship of Sītā or the furrow goddess, following the Āsvajugī rite, her description as the wife of Indra, the rain giver, and as Urvarā or the fertile, wreathed with threshing floors, all suggest that the Āsvajugī rite was an agricultural rite of thanksgiving on the reaping of the crop which was harvested in Āśvina. And if this rite of agricultural thanksgiving was already somewhat obscure in the Rationalistic Period, how has that rite been further obscured in the *Kojagara Lakṣmī Pūjā* of modern India.

Lakṣmī is a young goddess who was unknown in the Rationalistic Period, but is now the most cherished deity in the Hindu Pantheon. Sītā is remembered only as the heroine of the Rāmāyaṇa and as a pattern of female virtue and female self-abnegation; but Lakṣmī has taken her place as the goddess of crops and of rice. Is it a wonder, then, the worship of Sītā has been replaced by that of Lakṣmī on the full moon night of the autumnal harvest ?

And if Lakṣmī is a modern name of Sītā as the goddess of grain, is it an improbable conjecture which we have elsewhere made (Book II, Chapter III,) that Rāma himself is another name of Indra, the Vedic husband of Sītā?

We have seen that the Kojāgara Lakṣmī Pūjā is the modern form of the ancient Āśvajugī rite. Still more recent than the Lakṣmī Pūjā is the worship of Durgā, which has in Bengal assumed wonderful dimensions within recent times, owing, no doubt, to the gladness of the harvest season, and has thrown the Lakṣmī Pūjā into shade. How has the petty harvest festival—the milk-rice oblation to Indra and his consort Sītā—developed in modern times !

Āgrahāyanī

This rite was performed on the full moon day of Āgrahāyana month. This particular night was considered to be the consort of the year, or the image of the year, and adoration was offered to the year, to Saṁvatsara, Parivatsara, Idāvatsara, Idvatsara and to Vatsara, which terms designate the different years of the quinquennial period of Yuga. *Pāraskara,* III, 2, 2.

Aṣṭakā

So called because they were rites which were performed on the *eighth* day of the three or four successive dark fortnights after the full moon of Agrahāyana. Sāṅkhāyana and Pāraskara prescribe three Aṣṭakās, Āśvalayana prescribes four. Gobhila quotes older authorities and says, that Kautsa prescribed four, while Audgāhamāni, Gautama and Vārkakhandī prescribed three. The majority of opinions is therefore in favour of three Aṣṭakās, followed by three Anvaṣṭakās, and the three Aṣṭakās were performed on the eighth days of the dark fortnights in Agrahāyana, Pauṣa and Māgha respectively. According to Sāṅkhāyana oblations were made with vegetables, flesh and cakes respectively, according to the order of the three Aṣṭakās, but Pāraskara and Gobhila prescribe the oblation in a different order, beginning with cakes and ending with vegetables.

Gobhila quotes different opinions as to the object of these interesting rites, and says they may be for the gratification of Agni, or of the Fathers, or of Prajāpati, or of the Season Gods or of all the Gods (*Gobhila,* III, 2, 3). The intelligent reader will hardly fail to perceive, however, that the rites were suggested by the winter season, which is an enjoyable season in India, when the Amon rice is harvested and wheat and barley thrive, and when cakes and flesh and vegetables are not only acceptable to the "season gods," but are also highly gratifying to men! And the Hindu reader will, no doubt; at once perceive that a relic of this ancient rite still exists in Bengal in the *Pauṣa Pārvana,* when after the Amon has been harvested, our ladies delight in the preparation of delicious cakes of various kinds to the infinite joy of the young and old alike !

Modern Hindus will, however, scarcely wish to be reminded that, whereas our present *Pauṣa Pārvana* is performed with vegetables and cakes, our ancestors relished the flesh of cow in the middle or *Pauṣa Aṣṭakā (Sāṅkhāyana,* III, 14, 3; *Gobhila* III, 9, 14, etc.) For the rest, the Aṣṭakās came naturally to be regarded as goddesses, who had with motherly tenderness produced the good things of earth for thebenefit of men.

"She in whom Yama, the son of Vivasvat and all; gods are contained, the Aṣṭakā, whose face is turned to all sides, she has satiated my desires." *Sāṅkhāyna,* III, 12, 5.

Thirty sisters[2] go to the appointed place, putting on the same badge. They spread out the seasons, the knowing sages; having the metres in their midst, they walk around, the brilliant ones. Svāhā !

"The shining one clothes herself with clouds, with the ways of the sun, the divine night : manifold animals which are born look about in this mother's lap. Svāhā !" *Pāraskara*, III, 3, 5.

Chaitrī

The last rite in the year, was performed on the full moon day of Chaitra. According to Sāñkhāyana, Indra and Agni were worshipped, and balls were offered to Rudra, and the Nakṣatras or constellations were propitiated.

Such were the domestic ceremonies and Gṛhya rites in which Hindu ladies delighted in ancient times. And if some of these rites have since lost their original significance, and have even been replaced by modern and more degenerate forms, we can nevertheless trace most of them in the rites that we practice to this day, after a lapse of two thousand years and more. The conservative spirit of the Hindus and their loyalty to the past are pre-eminently conspicuous in their adherence to ancient ceremonies, which were generally conceived in a pure and healthy spirit. And the healthy joyousness which attended ancient Hindu celebrations has certainly lost nothing in the course of many centuries of foreign subjection and national decline.

REFERENCES

1. A new and aboriginal goddess, the *Manasā,* is now worshipped in Bengal to save men from snake bite, and the story of her admission into the Hindu Pantheon is dimly seen in the popular tale of *Manāsār Bhāsān.*
2. Apparently the days of the month.

CHAPTER – 9

GEOMETRY, GRAMMAR AND THE PROGRESS OF LEARNING

We have stated before that it was in the Rationalistic Age that all the learning and religious rites and laws of the previous ages received a philosophical treatment, and were condensed, arranged and codified. It was in this period that the contents of the verbose and somewhat chaotic Brāhmans were brought into order, that civil and criminal laws and the law of inheritance were codified, that the caste system and social laws were rigidly fixed, and the duties of men, both as citizens and as members of a family, defined. And it can well be imagined, therefore, that science and philosophy received a high degree of development in this age, and some departments of inquiry and thought received their last development in India in this period. If we were to seek a parallel to the epochs of Indian History in the annals of Greece, we would compare the Epic Age of India with the Homeric Age of Greece, and we would identify the Rationalistic Period of India with the age of Socrates, Plato and Aristotle. The Vedic Age in India has no parallel in Greek history, for all accounts of the first settlement of the Āryans in Greece are lost.

We do not know what progress was made in this period in Astronomy. No Sūtra work on Astronomy has come down to us, and there can be little doubt that the astronomical works of the Rationalistic Period have long since been replaced by the later and completer works of the Paurāṇik Period—by the wonderful discoveries of Āryabhaṭṭa and Varāha Mihira, of Brahmagupta and Bhāskarācārya. But there is one branch of mathematics which was carried to a high degree of excellence in the Rationalistic

Period. Dr. Thibaut has deserved the thanks of all oriental scholars by publishing the fact that Geometry, as a science, was first discovered in India. The Greeks of a later age cultivated the science with greater success, but it should never be forgotten that the world owes its first lessons in Geometry not to Greece, but to India.

Geometry like Astronomy owes its origin in India to religion, and Grammar and Philosophy, too, were similarly inspired by religion. As Dr. Thibaut remarks :—"The want of some rule by which to fix the right time for the sacrifices, gave the first impulse to astronomical observations; urged by this want, the priest remained watching night after night the advance of the moon through the circle of the nakṣatras, and day after day the alternate progress of the sun towards the north and the south. The laws of phonetics were investigated because the wrath of the gods followed the wrong pronunciation of a single letter of the sacrificial formulas; grammar and etymology had the task of securing the right understanding of the holy texts. The close connexion of philosophy and theology—so close that it is often impossible to decide where the one ends and the other begins—is too well known to require any comment." And the learned Doctor then lays down the principle, which should never be overlooked by Indian Historians, that whatever science "is closely connected with the Ancient Indian Religion must be considered as having sprung up among the Indians themselves," and not borrowed from other nations.[1]

Geometry was developed in India from the rules for the construction of altars. The Taittiriya Saṁhitā (V, 4, 11) enumerates the different shapes in which altars could be constructed, and Baudhāyana and Āpastamba furnish us with full particulars about the shape of these *chitis* and the bricks which had to be employed for their construction.

(1) The Chaturasrasyena is a falcon-shaped altar built of square bricks, and is the most ancient.

(2) The Syena Vakrapakṣavyastapuchchha is an altar of the shape of a falcon with curved wings and outspread tail

(3) The Kankachit is a heron-shaped altar with two feet, and

(4) The Alajachit is very similar to it.
(5) The Praugachit is of the shape of the fore part of the poles of a chariot, an equilateral triangle, and
(6) The Ubhayatah Praugachit is of the form of two such triangles joined with their bases. Then follow
(7) The Ratha Chakrachit and
(8) the Sāraratha Chakrachit of the shape of wheels, without and with spokes.
(9) The Ghaturasradronachit and
(10) the Parimaṇḍala-dronachit are of the shape of a drona or vessel, square or circular,
(11) The Parichāyyachit is also of a wheel-shape, and
(12) the Samuhyachit has likewise a circular shape.
(13) The Smasānachit is a sloping quadrilateral altar, wider at one base than at the other, and higher at the wider end. The last chiti mentioned is the Kurma or tortoise, which may be either
(14) Vak-rānga,curved, or
(15) angular, or
(16) Pari-maṇḍala, circular.

The area of the earliest Chaturasra Syena was to be 7.50 square puruṣas, which means 7.25 squares, the side of each square being equal to a puruṣa, *i.e.,* the height of a man with uplifted arms. When any other shape of altar was required, *the size or area did not change,* so that a wheel, an equilateral triangle, or a tortoise had to be constructed—all of the area of 7.5 puruṣas. Then, again, at the second construction of the altar, one square puruṣa had to be added to the area, and at the third construction, two square puruṣas had to be added *without changing the shape or the relative proportions of the figure.* All this could not be done without a considerable knowledge of Geometry, and the science of Geometry was thus invented. As Dr. Thibaut says, "squares had to be found which would be equal to two or more given squares, or equal to the difference of two given squares; oblongs had to be turned into squares and squares into oblongs; triangles had to be constructed equal to given squares or oblongs; and so on. The last task, and not the least, was that of finding a circle, the area of which might equal as closely as possible that of a given square."

The result of these operations was the compilation of a

series of Geometrical rules which are contained in the Śulva Sūtras, which form a portion of the Kalpa Sūtras as we have stated before. These Śulva Sūtras date from the eighth century before Christ. The Geometrical theorem that the square of the hypotenuse is equal to the squares of the other two sides of a Rectangular triangle, is ascribed by the Greeks to Pythagoras; but it was known in India at least two centuries before, and Pythagoras undoubtedly learnt this rule from India. The proposition referred to above is contained in two rules, *viz,*,

(1) The square of the diagonal of a square is twice as large as that square; and
(2) The square of the diagonal of an oblong is equal to the square of both its sides.

Our limits forbid us to follow Dr. Thibaut's remarks-contained in his most valuable and instructive paper, and all we can do is to briefly mention a few of the most important results achieved in the Śulva Sūtras. One remarkable result was to find the value of a diagonal in number in relation to the side of the square. The rule laid down is "Increase the measure by its third part, and this third by its own fourth, less the thirty-fourth part of that fourth." In other words, if 1 represents the side, the diagonal will be

$$1 + \frac{1}{3} + \frac{1}{3 \times 4} - \frac{1}{3 \times 4 \times 34} = 1414213$$

The real value of the diagonal is, we know, 2 = 1 414213... and we see, therefore, that the rule given in the Śulva Sūtras, is correct up to five places of the decimal.

Rules were framed for the formation of squares of three, four, five or any times the area of a given square; for combining two squares of different sizes; for deducting one square from another; for turning an oblong into a square or a square into an oblong; for turning square into a circle or a circle into a square. As an example we will quote the rule of describing a circle equal to a given square.

The rule is this : "If you wish to turn a square into a circle, draw half of the cord stretched in the diagonal from the centre towards the Prāchī line (*i. e.,* the line due east); describe the circle together with the third part of that piece of the cord which will lie outside the square."

The rule may be thus illustrated :—

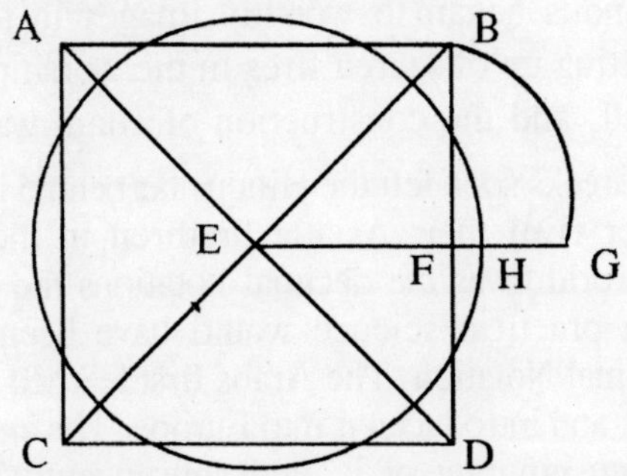

E B is half of the cord of the quare A B C D stretched in the diagonal C B. Keep the point E fixed, and draw the cord towards the Prāchī or eastern line E F. A part of the cord, *i. e.,* F G, will lie outside the square. Take a third part of it F H together with the part inside E F, and describe a circle with the radius E H.

It is needless to add that the result is only approximately correct.

Similarly; "If you wish to turn a circle into a square, divide the diameter into eight parts, and again one of these eight parts into twenty-nine parts; of these twenty-nine parts remove twenty-eight, and moreover. the sixth part (of the one left part) less the eighth part (of the sixth part)."

The meaning of the rule is this :—

$$\frac{7}{8} + \frac{1}{8 \times 29} - \frac{1}{8 \times 29 \times 6} + \frac{1}{8 \times 29 \times 6 \times 8}$$

of the diameter of a circle is the side of a square, the area of which is equal to the area of the circle.

Geometry is a lost science in India; for as soon as it was found that geometrical truths could be represented by algebra and arithmetic, geometry gradually fell out of use. The brilliant results achieved in arithmetic and algebra in the Paurāṇik Period probably led to the neglect of geometrical studies. And the practical necessity for geometrical studies no longer existed in India, when Hindus began to worship images in the Paurāṇik Age, and the setting up of sacred fires in the worshipper's house was discontinued, and the construction of altars was forgotten.

While the Greeks soon left the Hindus far behind in Geometry, they could never rival their Asiatic brethren in the science of Numbers. The world owes the decimal notations the Hindus, and Arithmetic as a practical science would have been impossible without the Decimal Notation. The Arabs first learned that notation from the Hindus, and introduced it into Europe. The ancient Greeks and Romans were ignorant of it, and consequently never made much progress in the numerical science.

There is, however, yet another science in which the Hindus were the first in the field, and achieved result in the Rationalistic Period which have never since been surpassed in the world. Professor Max Müller says that the Hindus and the Greeks are the only nations which have developed the science of Grammar; but the achievements of the Greeks in Grammar are poor indeed compared with the marvellous work of Pāṇinī—the greatest grammarian that the world has ever seen. We will not enter into the controversy on the age of Pāṇinī. Max Müller calls him the contemporary of Kātyāyana, and gives the fourth century before Christ as his probable date, while Goldstucker maintains that the grammarian lived in the ninth or eleventh century before Christ. Our own opinion is that he lived long before Katyayana, but after Yāska—and that the eighth century before Christ is not an improbable date. He undoubtedly belongs to the Rationalistic Period, the period when every department of thought received a philosophical treatment and generalization. But being born in Kandahar in the extreme west of India, he may not have been acquainted with, or may not have recognized the Brāhmaṇas and Upaniṣads, which, as we have seen before, were mostly produced among the nations of the

Gangetic Valley, who were widely separated by their learning, their customs, and even their form of religion from the Punjab Hindus.

It would be foreign to ourpurpose to attempt even a brief review of Pāṇinī's system of Grammar. The startling discovery has been made in Europe in the present century, that the tens of thousands of words in a language can be resolved to a small number of roots. This discovery was made in India three thousand years ago, before the time of Pāṇini, and the great grammarian resolves the Sanscrit language of his time to its simple roots. No grammarian of any other nation had the faintest suspicion of this fact, and no other language furnishes such clear evidence on this point as the Sanscrit.

It is the knowledge of Sanscrit which has enabled European scholars in the present century to discover the Science of Language or Philology; and Bopp and Grimm and Humboldt, and a host of other learned scholars, have resolved the Āryan languages to the same roots to which Pāṇinī resolved the Sanscrit language in the dawn of Āryan history, when Athens and Rome Were unknown !

REFERENCE

1. Journal Asiatic Society, Bengal, 1875. p. 227.

CHAPTER – 10

THE AGNOSTIC SĀṄKHYA AND THE THEISTIC YOGA PHILOSOPHY

But the glory of the Rationalistic Period consists in the philosophy of Kapila and the religion of Buddha. Kapila and Buddha are the Voltaire and Rousseau of Ancient India—the man of intellect and the man of feeling. Only the philosophy of Kapila was more clear and closely reasoned and consistent than anything that Voltaire wrote, and the morality and human sympathy of Buddha were loftier, purer and more comprehensive than that of Rousseau.

Kapila and Buddha worked to some extent on the same lines. They both started with the great object of affording humanity a relief from the suffering and pain which is the lot of all living-beings. They both rejected, with evident scorn, the remedies which the Vedic rites pretended to offer, and called those rites impure, because connected with the slaughter of living beings. They both declared knowledge and meditation to be the means of salvation (see Sāṅkhya Kārikā 1 and *2)*. They both adopted the doctrine of transmigration from the Upaniṣads (Sāṅkhya Kārikā 45), and declared that pious acts lead to higher states of life. And lastly, they both aimed at Nirvāṇa (Sāṅkhya Kārikā 67), and the creed of the philosopher as well as of the reformer is agnostic.

But here the parallel ends. Kapila, who probably lived a century or two before Buddha, started the system of philosophy, but meant it only as philosophy, addressed himself to high thinkers, and to speculative scholars. His philosophy knows nothing of sympathy with mankind in general, he did not go to the masses, founded no society or class. Buddha came after him, and was probably born in the very town sanctified by the memory of the great philosopher.[1] Certain it is that he was well versed in the philosophy of Kapila and obtained his principal tenets from that source. But he possessed, what his predecessor did not possess, a living, all-embracing sympathy, a feeling for the poor, a tear for the bereaved and the sufferer. This was the secret of Buddha's great success. For philosophy is barren if it is not true to its name, if it does not seek earnestly, and in a loving spirit, the good of fellow creatures, if it does not look with equal eye on the rich and the poor, on the Brāhman and the Śūdra. And the Śūdra and the poor came to Buddha one by one for his loving sympathy and meek beneficence. Good men admired his high-souled piety, just men yielded to his theory of the equality of men, and all the world admired his pure system of morality. The tide of the new religion rolled onwards, and swept away in its course the inequality of laws and the inequality of castes. Three centuries after his death, the Emperor of Pāṭaliputra, who ruled over the whole of Northern India, accepted the poor man's religion, and proclaimed it as the religion of all India. And a living nation accepted the faith of the equality of men, such as the Hindus have never done again since they have ceased to be a living nation.

These matters, however, will be treated in future chapters, and we return therefore to the philosophy of Kapila—"the first recorded system of philosophy" in the world, "the earliest attempt on record to give an answer from reason alone, to the mysterious questions which arise in every thoughtful mind about the origin of the world, the nature and relations of man and his future destiny."[2]

The original work composed by Kapila has been lost to us. The *Sāṅkhya Pravachana* or *Sāṅkhya Sūtra* is ascribed to Kapila himself, but has probably been compiled at a more recent age. An excellent edition of the work with commentaries and translation has been published by Dr. Ballantyne. The *Tattva Samāsa* is another authoritative work which is also incorrectly ascribed to Kapila. The *Sāṅkhya Sūtra* is composed by Vijñāna Bhikṣu, the commentator of Sāṅkhya Prava chana, and was probably composed in the sixteenth century; it is edited by Dr. FitzEdward Hall. And lastly, the *Sāṅkhya Kārikd* is an ancient and concise treatise on the subject in only 72 distichs, composed by Īśvara Kṛṣṇā, and commented on by Gaudapada and Vāchaspati. This small but excellent treatise has been translated into Latin by Lassen, into German by Windischmann and Lorinser, into French by Pantier and St. Hilaire, and into English by Colebrooke and Wilson, and recently by Davies. This small treatise will be our guide, specially as we have Mr, Davies's valuable notes to help us. We have only to add that it is impossible to give our readers the barest skeleton of Sāṅkhya Philosophy in a few pages, and that all we can do here is to notice a few essential principles of the system.

To relieve mankind from the three kinds of pain, *viz.*, (1) bodily and mental, (2) natural and extrinsic, (3) divine or supernatural, is the object of Kapila's philosophy. Vedic rites are inefficacious, because they are impure, and are tainted with the slaughter of living beings; the complete and final emancipation of the soul is secured by knowledge alone.

Nature and Soul are eternal and self-existent. From Nature *(Prakṛti)* is produced the *intellect*, the *consciousness,* the five *subtle elements,* the five *grosser elements*, the five *senses of perception,* the five *organs* of *action,* and the *mind.* Soul *(Ātman* or *Puruṣa)* produces nothing, but is only linked with Nature, with the corporeal body, until its final emancipation. Kapila does not accept the orthodox opinion of the Upaniṣads that all souls are portions of the Universal Soul. He asserts that each soul is separate, and has a separate existence after its emancipation from the bonds of Nature.

It will be seen that according to Kapila everything except Soul is derived from Nature or primodial matter and is therefore material. Not only the elements and the senses and the organs of action, but the mind, the consciousness, and the intellect, are results of matter, of "mind stuff, "as European philosophers call it. Kapila only differs from modern materialistic philosophers in asserting that there is a soul, independent of matter and eternal, though for a time linked with matter.

It is necessary to clearly understand the distinctions between the senses, the organs, the mind the consciousness, the intellect, the elements, and the soul, in order to grasp the mental philosophy of Kapila.

The five senses simply observe, *i. e.* receive impressions; the five organs of action, the voice, hands, feet, etc, act according to their functions. (S. K. 28). The mind *(manas)* is not what is implied by the English word, but is only a sense organ (S. K. 27), it is the *sensorium commune,* it simply arranges the impressions and presents them to ego or consciousness. Ego is self-consciousness (S. K, 24); it individualizes those impressions as "mine." And the intellect distinguishes and discriminates (S. K. 23), and forms them into ideas. It will thus be seen that the distinctions made between the senses, the *manas,* the consciousness and the intellect are real distinctions in the functions of the mind. In the language of European philosophy *manas* receives the sensations and makes them actual perceptions; consciousness, individualized them as "mine," and intellect turns these individualized perceptions into "concepts or judgments" in the language of Sir W. Hamilton,

Hindu commentators love to describe this mental operation in a poetic garb. "As the headmen of the village," says Vāchaspati, "collect the taxes from the villagers and pay them to the governor of the district; as the local governor pays the amount to the minister, and the minister receives it for the use of the king, so the *manas,* having received ideas from the external organs. transfers them to consciousness, and consciousness delivers them to the intellect, the general superintendent from *Prākṛti* as charge of them for the use of the (S.K. 15). Soul.' Such metaphorical descriptions nature not disguise from us the strictly scientific nature of the distinctions made, distinctions which are re-cognized by European philosophers as well as by Hindu thinkers. "Sensation proper," says Morell in his Elements of Psychology, "is not purely a passive state, but implies a certain amount of mental activity." A clock, for instance, may strike within our hearing, and yet we may be perfectly unconscious of the fact if we are absent-minded, i.*e.*, if our mind is not sufficiently active to catch the sensation; and this mental activity, which has no special name in European philosophy, is the *manas* of Kapila.

It shews no ordinary philosophic acumen in Kapila to have declared, at a time when the functions of the brain were still imperfectly understood, that the *manas,* the consciousness or *ahaṅkāra,* and even the intellect or buddhi, were material in their origin. More than this, Kapila declares that the subtle elements and the gross elements proceed from conciousness. Kapila herein seems to anticipate the philosophy of Berkeley and Hume and Mill, that objects are but permanent possibilities of sensations, and agrees with Kant that we have no knowledge of an external world except as by the action of our faculties it is represented to the soul, and take as granted the objective reality of our sense perceptions.

What again are the subtle principles of Kapila ? He is not content with enumerating the five gross elements, ether, air, earth, fire and water, but adds the five subtler principles, sound, tangibleness, odour, visibility, and taste. What are we to understand by the statement that these subtle principles have an independent existence? "The doctrine of Kapila seems to be, that in hearing, the ear has a relation not only to the ether, but to the subtler principle which underlies it, a dim apprehension of the truth that hearing depends not only on some channel of communication between the ear and the source of sound, but on sŏme modification of the material element through which the Kapila recognizes only three kinds of evidence Perception, Inference and Testimony. (S. K. 4.) The Nyāya or Logical school recognizes, four—dividing Kapila's Perception into *Anumāna* or perception, and *Upamāna* or analogy. The Vedāntic school adds a fifth, which is called *Arthāpatti,* an informal kind of information; as "Devadatta does not eat by day and yet is fat, it is presumed therefore that he eats by night."

Kapila will admit nothing which cannot be known by his three kinds of evidence. He rejects all inner ideas, and as neither Perception, nor Inference, nor reliable Testimony, presents to him the idea of an external Author of all things, the idea of a Supreme Deity is not admitted into his philosophy. This was the great want which made the Hindus as a body recoil from Kapila's system of philosophy, and other systems were started, as we will see further on, to meet the want. And this was the want also which probably finally sealed the fate of Buddhism in India, however excellent and righteous the religion may have been in other respects.

Kapila, however, believes in causation; *sat—karyam—asaṭ—akaranāt* what exists must have been caused, as there can be no existence without cause. (S. K. 9.) He also appeals to the observation of mankind that cause and effect imply each other, and ends by stating that an effect is identical with cause, or, as Sir William Hamilton puts it, "all that we at present come to know as an effect must have previously existed in its causes."

The three *guṇas,* or constituent elements of nature, *sattva* (goodness), *rajas* (passion), and *tamas* (darkness), form an important part of all Hindu philosophy, and find a place in Kapila (S.K. 11). The *guṇas* are only a hypothesis which accounts for the manifest differences in the conditions of all formal existences.

Kapila argues the production of all formal existences from *Prakṛti* or Nature on five different grounds (S. K. 15). Firstly, specific objects are finite in their nature and must have cause. Secondly, different things; have common properties and must be different species of the same primary genus. Thirdly, all things are in a constant state of progression, and shew an active energy of evolution which must have been derived from a primary source. Fourthly, the existing world is an effect, and there must be a primary cause. And fifthly, there is an undividedness, a real unity in the whole universe, which argues a common origin. It was this unity, this harmony in nature, which led some of the Ṛṣis of the Ṛg Veda to ascribe all created things to the One Unborn, and which led the sages of the Upaniṣads to postulate the existence of one Universal Soul. The agnostic Kapila noted the same uniformity and harmony, but his categories of evidence did not allow him to admit the idea of a Deity, and like the materialistic philosophers of the modern day, he referred all formal existences to primordial Matter.

All except Soul. And his reasons for the separate existence of soul also deserve mention. The first is the celebrated argument of design—but Kapila uses it differently from modern theologians. Matter has been apparently collected and arranged with a design—but this proves, according to Kapila, not a Designer, but the existence of Soul for which the things must have been arranged (S. K. 17). As a bed, argues Gaudapada, which is an assemblage of bedding, props, cotton, coverlet and pillows, is for another's use, not its own, even so this world, which is an assemblage of the five elements, is for the use of the Soul,

Secondly, Matter furnishes materials for pleasure and pain, hence sentient nature, which feels pleasure and pain, must be different from it. Thirdly, there must be a superintending force. Fourthly, there must be a nature that enjoys. And the fifth argument is Plato's argument quoted in Addison's Cato, that the yearning for a higher life points to the possibility of gaining it. These are Kapila's arguments for the existence of Soul independent of Matter, but he will not believe in one soul, but asserts and gives reasons for believing that the souls of different beings are different, not one (S. K. 18.) Here he goes counter to the Upaniṣads and to the Vedāntic school.

The vital actions of living systems are ascribed to certain subtle forces, and are generally described in Hindu philosophy as the five vital "airs" having some resemblance to the "vapours" of which the medical men of Europe spoke only a few generations ago. It was these subtle forces which were supposed to cause respiration, excretion, digestion, the circulation of blood, and the sensibility of the skin.

We have already said that Kapila borrowed the idea of transmigration of souls from the creed of the Upaniṣads. And having borrowed this idea, he had to suit it to his own system of philosophy. The soul, according to Kapila, is so passive that the individuality of a man is scarcely stamped on it. The Intellect, the Consciousness, the *manas,* all belong to the material part of a man. Hence Kapila was constrained by his own rigid reasoning to assume that something more than the soul migrated, that a subtle body, consisting of the Intellect, the Consciousness, and the *manas* and the subtle principles, migrated with the soul (S. K. 39 and 40.) And this idea of a subtle body, the *liṅga śarīra,* runs through the whole of Hindu philosophy; and Manu says (XII, 16) that a subtle body envelopes the souls of the wicked that they may suffer the torments of hell. The religious systems of all nations furnish something analogous to this idea, and the notion of a *liṅga śarīra* is accepted by Hindus as the doctrine of the resurrection of the body is accepted by all Christian nations. This *liṅga śarīra* forms the personality of an individual and ascends to a higher region or descends to a lower with the soul, according to the virtues or vices committed in this life (S. K, 44). The different regions are : (1) that of Pisāchas, (2) that of Rākṣasas, (3) that of Yakṣas, (4) that of Gandharvas, (5) that of Indra (sun), (6) that of Soma (moon), (7) that of the Prajāpatis, the abode of the Fathers and Ṛṣis, and (8) that of Brahmā, the highest heaven. Besides these eight superior orders of beings there are five inferior orders : (1) domestic quadrupeds, (2) wild quadrupeds, (3) birds, (4) reptiles, fishes and insects, and (5) vegetables and inorganic bodies. Man stands alone between the eight superior orders and the five inferior orders (S. K. 53), The quality of *sattva* prevails in the superior orders, of *rajas* in man, and of *tamas* in the lower orders (S. K. 54). A man, according to his actions, may descend or ascend to a lower or higher order, or be born again as man of some caste or other. When the soul is finally rid of the *liṅga śarīra,* it is finally emancipated.

It is the knowledge which the soul acquires through its union with nature that leads to its final emancipation. "As a dancer having exhibited herself on the stage ceases to dance, so does Nature *(Prakṛti)* cease when she has made herself manifest to soul." (S. K. 59.)

Even after the soul has obtained complete knowledge, it resides for a time in the body, as a potter's wheel continues to revolve from the force of the previous impulse." This is the *Nirvāṇa* of Buddha, a state of quietude, when perfect knowledge has been gained, when all passions have been restrained, all desires have been checked, and the enlightened soul awaits its final emancipation. That separation of soul and matter comes at last. Nature ceases to act, as her purpose has been accomplished and the soul, obtains an abstraction from matter, and both continue to exist eternally isolated from each other, and independent. (S. K. 68,)

Such is the barest outline of Sāṅkhya philosophy. The latest German philosophy, the system of Schopenhauer (1819) and Von Hartmann (1869), is "a reproduction of the philosophic system of Kapila in its materialistic part, presented in a more elaborate form, but on the same fundamental lines. In this respect the human intellect has gone over the same ground that it occupied more than two thousand years ago; but on a more important question it has taken a step in retreat. Kapila recognized fully the existence of a soul in man, forming indeed his proper nature—the absolute ego of Fichte—distinct from matter and immortal; but our latest philosophy, both here and in Germany, can see in man only a highly developed physical organization. 'All external things,' says Kapila, 'were formed that the soul might know itself and be free.' 'The study of psychology is vain,' says Schopenhauer, 'for there is no Psyche.'"[4]

The great want of Kapila's philosophy as a creed for the people was its agnosticism—and the Yoga system of philosophy sought to remove this want. It is ascribed to Patañjali who, according to Dr. Goldstucker, lived in the second century before Christ. All that we know of the life and history of Patañjali is that his mother was called Gonika, as he himself tells us; and that he resided for a certain time in Kashmir, a circumstance which may have led to his great grammatical commentary having been preserved by the kings of that country. Patañjali calls himself Gonardiya, or a native of Gonarda, a place in the eastern part of India.

We have seen before that Kātyāyana attacked Pāṇini's grammar about the 4th century B. C, and Patañjali's greatest work was his Mahābhāṣya or Great Commentary, in which he defended Pāṇini, and left a monument of his profound erudition and unrivalled critical acumen. The Yoga system of philosophy is also ascribed to him, and it is quite reasonable to suppose that the great defender of Pāṇini also sought to popularize Kapila among his countrymen, by adding to his cold and agnostic philosophy the doctrine of faith in a Supreme Deity, as well as some mystic practices and meditation by which beatitude (it was believed) could be obtained.

Patañjali's work, the *Yogasūtra* or *Yogānuśāsana,* has been edited and translated into English by Dr. Rajendra Lala Mitra, who also gives a brief abstract of its contents in his preface. As a system of philosophy the Yoga has no value whatever by the side of the Sāṅkhya, and our account of it will therefore be brief; and the learned translator of the Yoga Sūtra will be our guide in our brief account of the system.

The Yoga Sūtra comprises 194 aphorisms, divided into four chapters. The first chapter is called *Samādhi Pāda,* and contains 51 aphorisms treating of the nature of meditation. The second chapter consists of 55 aphorisms, and is called *Sādhana Pāda,* and treats of the practices and exercises required in meditation. The third chapter is called *Vibhūti Pāda,* and treats in 55 aphorism of the occult powers which may be recquired. The fourth chapter is called *Kaivalya Pāda* and treats in 33 aphorisms of the isolation and detachlment of the soul from all worldly ties, which is the ultimate object of meditation.

In the first chapter *Yoga* is derived from *Yuj,* "to join" or "to meditate," and this meditation is possible only by the suppression of the functions of the mind. By constant exercise and by dispassion the functions of the mind may be suppressed, and Yoga, conscious or unconscious, may be attained. The latter form of Yoga is higher than the former, and is devoid even of deliberation or joy, egoism, or the exercise of reason.

Devotion to God hastens the attainment of this coveted state of mind. The conception of God or Īśvara is that of a Soul untouched by affliction, works, deserts and desires. In Him "the seed of the Omniscient attains infinity," and He "is the instructor of even all early ones, for He is not limited by time" *(Yoga Sūtra,* I, 25 & 26), The sacred syllable *om* indicates the Deity.

Disease, doubt, worldly-mindedness, etc, are obstacles to the attainment of Yoga, but these may be overcome by concentration of the mind, by benevolence, by indifference to happiness or misery, and even by the regulation of the breath. The chapter ends with a description of various kinds of Yoga.

The second chapter details the exercises necessary for the performance of the Yoga. Asceticism, the muttering of a mantra, and devotion to God, are the earliest exercises. These overcome all afflictions like ignorance, egoism, desire, and aversion or ardent desire to live. These are the motives to work, and works must bear their fruits in subsequent births. We will see hereafter that this is the Buddhist theory of *Karma,* about which so much has been written. The object of Yoga is to devise means to abstain from works, and so preclude future births.

We have then the Sāṅkhya definition of the soul and the intellect; knowledge finally severs the connexion between the two, and thenceforward the soul is free, and an end is put to future births and suffering. Knowledge passes through seven stages before it is perfect, and eight means (which remind one of the eight-fold path of the Buddhists) are prescribed, by which this perfect knowledge can be obtained. The first means is abstaining from evil actions, slaughter, falsehood, theft, incontinence and avarice, and the second consists of an obligation to perform certain acts— purification, contentment, penance, study, and devotion to God. These two means are prescribed for all, householders and ascetics alike. Then come the duties special to Yogins. The third means is assuming special postures for meditation; the fourth is regulation of the breath; the fifth is the abstraction of the organs from their natural functions; and the sixth, seventh and eight are steadfastness *(Dhāraṇā),* contemplation *(Dhyāna),* and meditation *(Samādhi),* which three are the essential constituents of Yoga itself. When these three are united, *Saṁyama* follows, and results in the acquisition of occult powers.

The occult powers or *Siddhis* described in the third chapter are indeed wonderful! One may know the past and the future, make himself invisible to men, observe the details of what is passing in distant regions or in the stars, and planets, converse with spirits, travel in the air or through water, and acquire various super-human powers! The noble philosophy of Kapila was trailed through dirt and mire as soon as it was blended with popular superstitions !

But these occult powers are not the final objects which a Yogin seeks. The ultimate isolation of the soul is the final object of the Yogin, and this is discussed in the fourth and last chapter. We come back now to the theory that all works, all sensations and impressions on the mind, bear their fruit in future births. A discussion ensues regarding the nature of sensations and perceptions, of the intellect and the soul,—and the distinctions are much the same as in Sāṅkhya philosophy. Having explained these distinctions, Patañjali concludes by saying that perfect knowledge sweeps away all residue of former works (IV, 28 to 30), and the moment at last arrives when the three qualities become defunct, and the soul abides solely in its own essence. This emancipation of the soul is the object of the Yoga (IV, 33); it is absolute and eternal, and the soul which has attained it remains free for evermore.

It will thus be seen that as a system of philosophy, Yoga is valueless ; all its fundamental maxims about the soul and intellect and sensations, about the transmigration of souls, and their eternity and final emancipation by knowledge, are those of the Sāṅkhya Philosophy. In fact, Patañjali tried to blend the idea of a Supreme Deity with the philosophy of Kapila; but unfortunately he also mixed up with it much of the superstition and the mystic practices of the age! Or is it an untenable conjecture that the great Grammarian founded a pure theistic system of philosophy which has since been mixed up with much of popular superstitions and mystic rites, and the result is the *Yoga Sūtra* as we find it now. In still later times the philosophy of the Yoga system has been completely lost sight of, and the system has degenerated into cruel and indecent Tantrik rites, or into the impostures and superstitions of the so-called Yogins of the present day.

REFERENCES

1. Buddha was born in Kapila Vastu, which, according to the Pāli Dātha Vansa, was built by the sons of Ikṣvāku by the permission of the sage Kapila.
2. Davies's *Hindu Philosophy.*
3. Davies, p. 72.
4. *Davies Preface.*

CHAPTER – 11

NYĀYA OR LOGIC AND VAIŚEṢIKA OR ATOMIC PHILOSOPHY

Gautam or Gotama is the Aristotle of India, and his system of Nyāya is the Hindu Logic. His date is unknown, and he is said to have married Ahalyā. He lived, no doubt, in the Rationalistic Period, but probably a century or two after Kapila. The *Nyāya Sūtra,* which is ascribed to him, is divided into five books, each divided into two "days" or diurnal lessons, and these are again divided into articles, and each article consists of a number of Sūtras. Nyāya is still a favourite study in India, and we have seen students from Kashmir and Rajputana and Northern India attending the celebrated Nyāya schools in Navadvīpa in Bengal, living in the houses of their teachers, and pursuing their studies for years together, in the very same way in which students among the Magadhas and Aṅgas and Kosalas and Videhas pursued their studies when Gautama, the logician, lived and taught! Everything else has changed in India, but ancient traditional learning is still handed down in *tols* from generation to generation in the same ancient method. The spirit of the time, however, has told on these time-honored institutions, the mass of students turn away from these secluded seats of learning to schools and universities; the founders of *tols* get scarcely enough to subsist upon, and travel from place to place to seek the bounty of well-disposed men; and the number of students is getting fewer year by year. Nevertheless, with their wonderful loyalty to the past, Hindu pandits and Hindu students still adhere to this ancient system of teaching, of which we have given a brief account before from the Dharma Sūtra; and it is to be hoped this relic of the past will yet survive modern changes and innovations.

The Nyāya system starts with the subjects to be discussed. These are (1) *Pramāṇa,* proof, and (2) *Prameya,* or the thing to be proved. These are the principal subjects, while there are fourteen subsidiary subjects, *viz.,* (3) Doubt, (4) Motive, (5) Instance or Example, (6) Determined truth, (7) Argument or Syllogism, (8) Confutation, (9) Ascertainment, (10) Controversy, (11) Jangling, (12) Objection, (13) Fallacy, (14) Perversion, (15) Futility, and (16) Reasoning.

Proof, as we have said before, is of four kinds: Perception, Inference, Analogy, and Verbal Testimony. Cause *(Kāraṇa)* is that which necessarily precedes an effect, which could not be without the cause; and effect *(Kārya)* is that which necessarily ensues and otherwise could not be. For the relation of cause and effect, the connexions might be two-fold—simple conjunction *(Sanjoga),* and constant relation *(Sāmavāya).* Hence cause may be of three kinds:

(1) Immediate and direct, as the yarn is of cloth;
(2) Mediate or indirect, as the weaving is of cloth; and
(3) Instrumental, as the loom is of cloth,

The things to be proved, the objects of knowledge are (1) Soul, (2) Body, (3) the Senses, (4) the Objects of Sense, (5) Intellect, (6) *Manas,*(7) Production, (8) Fault, (9)Transmigration, (10) Fruit or Retribution, (11) Pain, (12) Emancipation.

The soul is different in each person, and is separate from the body *and the senses,* and is the seat of knowledge. Each individual soul is infinite, eternal, and transmigrates according to the works performed in life. So far we see an agreement with Kapila's philosophy. But the Nyāya adds that the Supreme Soul is one, the seat of eternal knowledge, and the maker or former of all things. The body is earthly, the five external senses are also material, and the *manas* is the organ of the senses. The reader will mark here in how far the Nyāya system, and indeed every system of Hindu philosophy, is indebted to the Sāṅkhya Philosophy, which may justly be called the first basis of Hindu Philosophy, as well as its highest development.

Intellect is two-fold, including *memory* and *concept.* A concept is true if derived from clear proof, and is wrong if not derived from proof. Similarly, memory may be right or wrong. The objects of sense are odour, taste colour, touch and sound.

Production or action is the cause of virtue or vice, of merit or demerit; and the only motive to action, as we are told by European philosophers also, is the desire to attain pleasure or to avoid pain.

Transmigration is the passing of the soul to succesive bodies. Pain is the primary evil, and there are twenty-one varieties of evil which are causes of pain. The soul attains its emancipation by knowledge and not by action.

It will be seen from the foregoing sketch that there is scarcely anything that is original in the Nyāya system as a system of mental philosophy. The speciality of Nyāya is its development of inference by the construction of a true syllogism, and, as Mr. Davies states, "the right methods of reasoning have been discussed with as much subtlety as by any of the Western logicians," We quote below an instance of Hindu syllogism :

1. The hill is fiery.
2. For it smokes.
3. Whatever smokes is fiery, as a kitchen.
4. The hill is smoking.
5. Therefore it is fiery.

The Hindu syllogism, therefore, consists of five parts, which are called (1) the proposition (*prātijñā),* (2) the reason *hetu* or a*padeśa,* (3) the instance (*udāharaṇa* or *nidarśana),* (4) the application of the reason *(upānayā),* and (5) the conclusion *(nigamana).* If the first two or the last two parts are omitted, it becomes a perfect syllogism of Aristotle.

Among the many technical terms in use in Hindu logic, *Vyāpti* and *Upādhi* are the most important. *Vyāpti* means invariable concomitance—the connection in the major premiss of Aristotle's syllogism. "Whatever smokes is fiery,"—this invariable concomitance is *Vyāpti.* As Sankara Misra argues, "It is not merely a relation of co-extension. Nor is it the relation of totality. For if you say that invariable concomitance: is the connexion of the middle term with the whole of the major term, such connexion does not exist in the case of smoke (for smoke does not always exist where there is fire). We proceed then to state that invariable concomitance is a connexion requiring no qualifying term or limitation. It is an extensiveness co-extensive with the predicate. In other words, invariable concomitance is invariable co-inherence of the predicate."[1]

On the other hand, the qualifying term or limitation is called *Upādhi.* Fire always underlies smoke, but smoke does not invariably accompany fire. The proposition, therefore, that smoke accompanies fire, requires a qualifying condition—a limitation—an *Upādhi, viz,* that there must be moist fuel.

We have no room to enter into the technicalities and the rigid and abstruse ratiocination of Hindu logic. Logic is a favourite study with learned Hindus, and neither the Ancient Greeks, nor the Medieval Arabs, or the European schoolmen of the middle ages, ever displayed more acuteness and subtlety in reasoning, or more rigid and scientific strictness in their discussions,, than is witnessed in the numerous works of the Hindus on Logic.

Kaṇāda's atomical philosophy is supplementary to Gautama's logic, as the Yoga philosophy is supplementary to Sāṅkhya and therefore need not detain us long. The cardinal principle of Kaṇāda is that all material substances are aggregates of atoms. The atoms are eternal, the aggregates only are perishable by disintegration.

The mote which is visible in the sunbeam is the smallest perceptible object. But being a substance and an effect, it must be composed of what is less than itself ; the ultimate atom only is not a compound, but is simple.

The first compound is of two atoms; the next consists of three double atoms, and so on. The mote visible in the sunbeam is thus a compound of six atoms. In this way two earthly atoms acting under an unseen law, *adṛṣṭa,* (and not under the will of God, which is unknown in Kaṇāda's philosophy,) constitute a double atom of earth; three binary atoms constitute a tertiary atom; four tertiary atoms make a quarternary atom; and so on to gross, grosser and grossest masses of earth. In this manner the great earth is produced, the great water is thus produced from aqueous atoms, great light from luminous atoms, and great air from aerial atoms.

Kaṇāda recognizes six categories or objects *(padārtha), viz.,*(1) Substances, (2) Quality, (3) Action, (4) Community, (5) Particularity, *(6)* Coherence, and (7) Non-existence.

Under the first of these categories, the nine substances of Kaṇāda are (1) Earth, (2) Water, (3) Light, and (4) Air, all eternal in atoms, but transient and perishable in aggregates. Next is (5) *Ākāśā* or Ether, which transmits sound, and which has no atoms but is infinite, one and eternal. As in Kapila's philosophy so in Kaṇāda's, we find a dim perception of the scientific truth, that what conveys sound is not the air, but a certain subtler cause which was called by the name of *Ākāśa.* (6) Time and (7) Space similarly are not material, and thereforeare not compounded of atoms. They are infinite, one and eternal. The last two in the category are (8) Soul and (9) *Manas* or the Internal Organ.

The second category, Quality, embraces 17 varieties or qualities of the nine substances enumerated above. The qualities are colour, savour, odour, tangibility, number, extension, individuality, conjunction, disjunction, priority, posteriority, intellections, pleasure, pain, desire, aversion and volition. *Light and heat are considered as only different forms of the same substances* Ākāśa or ether has the quality of sound; and Manas or the internal organ, is supposed to be extremely small, like an atom.

The third category, Action, is divided into five kinds, upward and downward movement, contraction, dilation, and general motion.

The fourth category, Community, is the source of our notion of genus. It denotes qualities common to many objects and also denotes species. These genera and species have a real and objective existence according to Kaṇāda, but not according to the Buddhas, who affirm that individuals only have existence, and that abstractions are false conceptions. "It is the quarrel revived in the Realist and Nominalist theories of the medieval schoolmen."[2]

The fifth category, Particularity, denotes simple objects, devoid of community. They are soul, mind, time, place, the ethereal element, and atoms.

The sixth category, Coherence (the *samavāya* of Gautama's philosophy), is connection between things which must be connected so long as they exist, as yarn and cloth.

The seventh category,. Non-existence, is either universal or mutual.

It will be seen from the above brief account that the Vaiśeṣika system of Kaṇāda, in so far as it is an original system, is physics more than philosophy. It was the first attempt made in India to inquire into the laws of matter and force of combination and disintegration.

In every system of Hindu Philosophy (except Vedānttism) matter is supposed to be eternal, and distinct from soul. The Vedantists alone.regard matter as the manifestation of the One Supreme Soul who comprises and is himself all. Of this system we will speak in the next chapter.

REFERENCES

1. Gough's Translation.
2. *Davies*, p. 131.

CHAPTER – 12

THE TWO MĪMĀṀSĀ SCHOOLS OR ORTHODOX PHILOSOPHY

We now come to the last two systems of the philosophy of the Hindus, the Pūrva Mīmāṁsā of Jaimini and the Uttara Mīmāṁsā of Badarāyana Vyāsa. As philosophy, the Mīmāṁsā schools have little that is new, but to the historian of India they are of the utmost importance and value. For the Mīmāṁsā schools represent the conservative phase of the Hindu mind at a time when philosophers and laymen were alike drifting towards agnostic and heterodox opinions. Sāṅkhya philosophy led away hosts of thinking men from the teachings of the Upaniṣads on the Universal Soul; and the Buddhist religion was embraced by masses of the lower classes as a relief from caste inequalities and elaborate Vedic rites. Against this general movement of the day, the Mīmāṁsā schools made a stand. The Pūrva Mīmāṃsā insisted on those Vedic rites and practices which modern philosophers had come to regard as useless or even as unholy; and the Uttara Mīmāṁsā proclaimed those theistic doctrines which the Upaniṣads had taught before.

The controversy, or rather the division in opinion, went on for centuries, but orthodoxy prevailed in India in the end. The great Kumārila Bhaṭṭa, who lived in the seventh century after Christ, wrote his celebrated Vārtika or commentary on the Pūrva Mīmāṁsā Sūtras, and was the most redoubted champion of the reviving Hinduism of his day, and the most uncompromising antagonist of decaying Buddhism. He not only vindicated the ancient rites of the Vedas, he not only proclaimed against the heterodox opinions of the Buddhists, but he denied them any consideration even when they happened to agree with the Veda.

The Uttara Mīmāṁsā, too, had its champion--and a greater man than Kumārila rose, two centuries later, in the celebrated Śaṅkarācārya. The Uttara Mīmāṁsā or Vedānta Sūtra is known as the Śārīraka Mīmāṁsā or Brahmā Sūtra, and Śaṅkara's great commentary is known as the Śārīraka Mīmāṁsā Bhāśya. Colebrooke, Wilson and Raja Ram Mohan Roy fixed the close of the eighth century, or the commencement of the ninth as the date when Sankara flourished. Later researches have confirmed this supposition, and it has been ascertained that Sankara was born in *788* A. D., and therefore wrote and preached in the first half of the ninth century;.

Thus both Kumārila and Śaṅkarācārya belong to the Paurāṇik Period, but they finally secured the triumph of that orthodox philosophy which took its rise in the Rationalistic Period. The history of philosophy in India is the history of the Hindu mind; and an account of the systems of philosophy which took their rise in the Rationalistic Period would not be intelligible, unless we indicated, however briefly, the bearings of these systems on the later history of the nations.

The Sūtras of the Pūrva Mīmāṁsā are ascribed to Jaimini, and are divided into twelve lectures, and subdivided into sixty chapters. The Sūtras have an old commentary by Sabara Svāmī Bhaṭṭa. Kumārila-Bhaṭṭa came later on the stage, and his commentary, as we have stated before, marks a new epoch in the History of this school, and has been respected by a most of succeeding commentators.

Jaimini's Sūtras, as stated before, are divided into twelve lectures. The first lecture treats of the authority of enjoined duty. The varieties of duty, supplemental duties, and the purpose of the performance of duties are treated in the second, third and fourth chapters. The order of their performance is considered in the fifth, and the qualification for their performance is treated in the sixth. This completes the first half of the Sūtras.

The subject of indirect precept is treated in chapters seventh and eighth, Inferrable changes are discussed in the ninth, and exceptions in the tenth chapter. Efficacy is considered in the eleventh chapter, and the work closes with a discussion of co-ordinate effect in the twelfth chapter.

These are the principal topics of the Pūrva Mīmāṁsā Sūtras, but a great many other matters are introduced, and we will briefly notice some of them which Colebrooke has presented at greater length to the English reader in his excellent analysis.

In the very first lecture we are told that the Vedas are eternal and revealed. It had no human origin, because no human author is remembered. This eternal and superhuman (i. *e.*, revealed) Veda consists of two parts, *Mantra* and *Brāhmaṇa*. Mantras are distinguished under three designations, *viz.*,(1) those in metre are Ṛik, (2) those chanted are Sāman, and (3) the rest are Yajus. Generally a Mantra is a prayer or invocation; a Brāhmaṇa is a precept directing religious observances, and the Brāhmaṇas include the Upaniṣads.

After the Veda, which is *Śruti,* comes the *Smṛti,* or works *composed by holy personages,* and possessing authority as grounded on the Veda. *Smṛti* includes the *Dharmaśāstras* (the Dharma Sūtras of the Rationalistic Period), comprising the institutes of civil and religious law.

Besides the Dharma Sūtras we are told of the *Kalpa Sūtras,* also composed by authors conversant with the Veda. The Kalpa Sūtras are not a part of the Veda, and have no authority except as is derived from the Veda. The reader will mark the broad line of demarcation which Hindus draw between the Brāhmaṇa literature, which is considered revealed and eternal, and the Sūtra literature, which is ascribed to human authors, and has no independent authority, The priority of the Brāhmaṇa literature 'may fairly be inferred from this.[1]

Sacrifice (*Yāga)* is the act of religion most inculcated in the Veda, and consequently most discussed in the Mīmāṁsā. Three ceremonies are mentioned as types of the rest: they are the setting up of the sacrificial fire, the presenting of an oblation, and the preparation of the Soma. Various curious questions are raised and discussed and answered with regard to sacrifices. One very remarkable example will suffice.

At certain sacrifices the votary is told to bestow all his property to the officiating priests. The question is raised, whether a king should give up all lands, including pasture lands, highways, and the sites of lakes and ponds. The answer is that *a king has no property in the land,* and cannot bestow it. His kingly power is for the government of the realm, but the right of property is not thereby vested in him, else he would have property in house and lands appertaining to his subjects. The lands of a kingdom cannot be given away by a king; but a house or field acquired by purchase, etc, may be given away.

Similarly, the question of self-immolation on fire, the question of performing sacrifices to injure others, and various similar questions are discussed with considerable acumen and closeness of reasoning. A complete *Adhikaraṇa* or argument according to the Mīmāṁsā consists of five members, *viz.*, (1) the subject, (2) the doubt, (3) the first side, (4) the answer, (5) the pertinence or relevency. Jaimini's aphorisms do not ordinarily exhibit all these five members; some are left to be surmised. But the disquisitions of the Mīmāṁsā resemble judicial disquisitions. As Colebrooke remarks, the logic of the Mīmāṁsā is the logic of the law, Each case is examined and determined upon general principles, and from the cases decided the principles may be collected. A well ordered arrangement of them would constitute the philosophy of the law; and this is in truth what has been attempted in the Mīmāṁsā."

To return to the subject of sacrifices, which is the all-pervading subject of the Pūrva Mīmāṁsā, we are told the full complement of persons officiating at a great ceremony is seventeen, *viz.*, the sacrificer and sixteen priests. On occasions of less solemnity four priests only are engaged.

The number of victims varies according to the nature of the sacrifice. At an *Aśvamehda* sacrifice there must be not fewer than 609 victims of all kinds, tame and wild, terrestrial and aquatic, walking, flying, swimming, and creeping things !

The cardinal idea of the Mīmāṁsā is to teach man his *Duty.* Jaimini commences his Mīmāṁsā with the enunciation of Duty, the only topic he has to propound. "Now then," he begins, "the study of Duty is to be commenced. Duty is a purpose which is inculcated by a command. Its reason must be inquired." But his idea of Duty is extremely orthodox, it consists in the proper performance of Vedic rites and practices! Pūrva Mīmāṁsā Philosophy is therefore a philosophy of Vedic rites.

In his anxiety to insist on ancient Vedic rites and practices Jaimini has forgotten to speak of Vedic faith and belief! As. Dr. Banerjea says in his Dialogues on Hindu Philosophy, Jaimini "urges the consideration of *duty* without caring for any to whom it may be *due*" While insisting on the eternity of the Veda, as Sabda or the Word, he has made no mention "of any co-eternal Intelligence uttering or revealing it."While enjoining the performance of the sacrifices inculcated in the Brāhmaṇas, he has nothing to say of the Universal Soul of the Upaniṣads. The Philosophy of Jaimini has therefore, although orthodox, been stigmatized as atheistical or at least agnostic in some of the Purāṇas; and even Śaṅkarācārya admits that God is not deducible from his philosophy.

A supplementary system of philosophy was therefore called for, and the Uttara Mīmāṁsā or Vedānta supplied this want. It is Vedānta which tells us of the Supreme Spirit, the Universal Soul, the Pervading Breath, as the Pūrva Mīmāṁsā speaks of rites and sacrifices. The Vedānta is the direct outcome of the Upaniṣads as the Pūrva Mīmāṁsā is the outcome of the Brāhmaṇas. The very first aphorism of the Vedānta substitutes Brahmā or God, for Dharma or Duty. The two schools of Mīmāṁsā, taken together, represent orthodox Vedic Hinduism—Hinduism in rites and observances, and Hinduism in its theistic belief. The two schools taken together are an answer to Buddhist heretics who ignored Vedic rites and ignored a Supreme Being. The two schools together are an answer also to the agnostic Sāṅkhya system of philosophy, and form the basis of modern Hinduism in its philosophical aspect.

The Śārīraka Mīmāṁsā Sūtra or Brahmā Sūtra is attributed to Bādarāyaṇa Vyāsa, who is said to be identical with Kṛṣṇa Dvaipayāna Vyāsa, the alleged compiler of the Vedas, although the Sūtra must have been compiled a thousand years after the Vedas were first compiled! The Brahmā Sūtra refers to the doctrines of Kapila, and the Yoga of Patañjali; and also to the Atomic theory of Kaṇāda, which is itself a sequel to the Nyāya of Gautama. There is reference also to Jaimini, and to the sects of Jainas, Buddhas, and Pāśupatas; and altogether the Brahmā Sūtra is undoubtedly the latest of the six schools of philosophy.

The Vedānta adopts the adhikaraṇa of the Pūrva Mīmāṁsā with its five members, and the syllogism of Nyāya with the obvious improvement of reducing its five members into three as in the syllogism of Aristotle. Colebrooke thinks this improvement was borrowed from the Greeks.

Bādarāyaṇa's Śārīraka Mīmāṁsā or Brahmā Sūtra is divided into four lectures, and each lecture is subdivided into four chapters. Anything like a complete analysis of this work is impossible within our limits, and we must therefore glean a few leading tenets from Colebrooke's excellent analysis, to which we refer those of our readers who wish to have an adequate idea of the subject.

The Uttara Mīmāṁsā opens precisely as the Pūrva Mīmāṁsā, announcing its purport in the very same terms, only substituting Brahmā or God for Dharma or Duty. The author then confutes the Sāṅkhya doctrine of Nature being the material cause of the universe, and declares a Sentient Rational Being to be the First Cause. That Supreme Being is the material as well as the efficient cause of the universe, and to Him meditation should be directed, and on Him the thoughts are to be fixed for obtaining final emancipation.

The second lecture continues the confutation of Kapila's Sāṅkhya philosophy as well of Patañjali's Yoga and Kaṇāda's Atomic theory. All the universe is rigidly assigned to Brahmā, who is the Cause and the Effect. The distinction between cause and effect, and between different effects, does not invalidate the unity of the whole. "The sea is one and not other than its waters; yet waves, foam, spray, drops, froth and other modifications of it differ from each other." (II, 1, 5). "As milk changes into curd, and water to ice, so is Brahmā variously transformed." (II, 1, 8).

Then follows a confutation of the doctrines of the Sāṅkhyas, the Vaiśeṣikas, the Bauddhas, the Jainas, the Pāsupatas and Pāñcharātras; the Nyāya is unnoticed.

The soul is active, not passive as the Sāṅkhyas maintain. Its activity is, however, adventitious. As the carpenter, having tools in hand, toils and suffers, and laying them aside, rests and is easy, so the soul in conjunction with the senses and organs is active, and quitting them, reposes (II, 3; 13). The soul is a portion, of the Supreme Ruler, as a spark is of fire (II, 3, 17.) As the sun's image reflected on water is tremulous, quaking with the undulations of the pool, without, however, affecting the images on other sheets of water, or the solar orb itself, so the sufferings of one individual affect not another, nor the Supreme Ruler. The corporeal organs and the vital actions are all modifications of Brahmā.

The third lecture treats of transmigration of souls, of the attainment of knowledge, of final emancipation, and of the attributes of the Supreme Being. The soul transmigrates, invested with a subtle frame, passing from one state to another. Departing from one body, it ascends the moon, experiences there the recompense of its works, and returns to occupy a new body with the resulting influence of its former deeds. Evil doers suffer in seven appointed regions of retribution. The returning soul passes through ether, air, vapour, mist, and cloud into rain, and thus finds its way into a plant, and thence through the medium of nourishment into an animal embryo (III, 1, 1 to 6).

The Supreme Being is unpassable, unaffected by worldly modifications, as the clear crystal seemingly coloured by the hibiscus flower is really pellucid. He is pure Sense, Intellect, Thought.

"Like the sun and other luminaries, seemingly multiplied by reflection though really single, and like space apparently subdivided in vessels containing it within limits, the Supreme Light is without difference or distinction." "There is none other but He" (III, 2). The reader will perceive that the Vedānta philosophy is a direct and legitimate result of the Upaniṣads, and the idea of Monoism is carried to the extreme limit in the Vedānta as in the Upaniṣads.

The last half of this lecture relates to devout exercises and pious meditation, which are necessary for the reception of divine knowledge.

The fourth and last lecture relates to the fruit of pious meditation properly conducted, and the attainment of divine knowledge. So soon as that knowledge is attained, past sins are annulled and future sins are precluded. In like manner the effects of merit and virtue are also annulled. And "having annulled by fruition other works which had begun to have effect, having enjoyed the recompense and suffered the pains of good and bad actions, the possessor of divine knowledge, on the demise of the body, proceeds to a reunion with Brahmā" (IV, I, 14). This is the final emancipation of the Vedāntists.

There are two other less perfect forms of emancipation : one which qualifies the soul for reception at Brahmā's abode, but not for immediate reunion and identity with his being; another, which is still less perfect, is called *Jīvan-mukti,* which can be acquired in lifetime by Yogis, and enables them to perform supernatural acts, as evoking the shades of forefathers, assuming different bodies, going immediately to any place at pleasure, etc. This is only a repetition of the superstition of the Yoga philosophy, described in a previous chapter.

The attributes of God according to the Vedānta philosophy have thus been recapitulated by Colebrooke : "God is the omnicient and omnipotent cause of the existence, continuance, and dissolution of the universe. Creation is an act of His will. He is both efficient and material cause of the world, creator and nature, framer and frame, doer and deed. At the consummation of all things, all are resolved into Him. The Supreme Being is one, sole existent, secondless, entire, without parts, sempiternal, infinite, ineffable, invariable, ruler of all, universal soul, truth, wisdom, intelligence, happiness."[2]

An idea has become current among later Vedāntists that all the universe, except Brahmā, is *Māyā, i. e.,* an illusion, a phantasy, an unreal appearance only. This notion is no part of the original Vedānta philosophy, and finds no sanction in ancient works. Ancient Vedantism declares the universe to be a portion of Brahmā, emanating from Brahmā, and resolving into Brahmā; but it does not declare that this emanation from Brahmā, this universe, is unreal or illusory.

Such are the six systems of philosophy which were developed in India in the Rationalistic Period; such are the answers which Hindu philosophers have given to questions which were started in the Upaniṣads, to questions which rise in the mind of every reflective man, which it is not given to him to answer satisfactorily, what is God, and what is the universe ?

For the rest the Rationalistic Period is rich in results of which every Hindu may be proud. It was probably in this period, that the great Epics of India received their epic form. It was in this period that the infant sciences of Geometry and of Grammar were first discovered by Hindus and proclaimed to the world. It was in this period that the first-recorded systems of Mental Philosophy and of Logic were conceived and perfected. It was in this period that

Laws and the rules of social life were codified and treated on a scientific basis. It was in this period that the whole of Northern India was first brought under one great and able ruler, and that an excellent and enlightened system of administration was finally perfected. And, lastly, it was in this period that the great saint and reformer Gautama Buddha proclaimed that religion of equality and brotherhood of man, which is at the present day the living faith of one-third of the human race. To that great revolution we now turn.

REFERENCES

1. See *ante,* Book II, Chapter I,
2. *The Philosophy of the Hindus. Vedānta* .

CHAPTER – 13

BUDDHIST SACRED LITERATURE

In the sixth century before Christ, India witnessed the commencement of a great revolution. Her ancient religion, which the Hindu Āryans had practised and proclaimed for fourteen centuries, had degenerated into forms. The gods of the Ṛg Veda whom the ancient Ṛṣis had invoked and worshipped, lovingly and fervently, had come to be regarded as so many names; and Indra and Uṣas raised no distinct ideas and no grateful emotions. The simple libations of the Soma juice, or offerings of milk, corn, or flesh, which the Ṛṣis of old had offered to their gods in the simplicity of their hearts, had developed into cumbrous ceremonials, elaborate rites, unmeaning forms. The descendants or successors of those Ṛṣis had now stepped forth as a powerful and hereditary caste, and claimed the right to perform elaborate religious rites and utter sacred prayers for the people. The people were taught to believe that they earned merit by having these rites performed and prayers uttered by hired priests. The religious instinct, the loving emotions which had inspired the composers of the Vedic hymns, were dead; vast ceremonials, dead forms, remained.

A reaction had taken place. About the eleventh century before Christ, *i.e.*, five centuries before the time of which we are now speaking, earnest and thoughtful Hindus had ventured to go beyond the wearisome rituals of the Brāhmaṇa literature, and had inquired into the mysteries of the soul and its Creator. composers of the Upaniṣads had dared to conceive the bold idea, that all animate and inanimate nature proceeded from One Universal Deity, and were portions of One Pervading Soul. Inquiries were made into the mysteries of death and the future world, conjectures were made about the transmigration of souls, and doctrines were started containing, in a crude form, the salient principles of Hindu philosophy.

But few could devote their lives to these abstruse speculations, and the abstruse philosophy which they led to. The mass of the Āryan householders—Brāhmans, Kṣatriyas, and Vaiśyas—contented themselves with performing the rites, unintelligible to them, which the Brāhmaṇas had laid down and the Sūtras had condensed. The rules of social and domestic life were similarly condensed for the people in the Sūtras, and all the learning and science known to the age were also codified in the Sūtra form.

Such was the state of things in India in the sixth century before Christ. Religion in its true sense had been replaced by forms. Excellent social and moral rules were disfigured by the unhealthy distinctions of caste, by exclusive privileges for Brāhmans, by cruel laws for Śūdras. Honor and reverence were paid those who lived piously and duteously, but in a higher degree to those who were born Brāhmans. Such exclusive caste privileges did not help to improve the Brāhmans themselves. As a community they became grasping and covetous, ignorant and pretentious, until Brāhman Sūtrakāras themselves had to censure the abuse in the strongest terms. For the Śūdras, who had come under the shelter of the Āryan religion, there was no religious instruction, no religious observance, no social respect. Despised and degraded in the community in which they lived, they sighed for a change. And the invidious distinction became unbearable as they increased in number, pursued various useful industries, owned lands and villages, and gained in influence and power. Thus society was still held in the cast-iron mould which it had long out-grown; and the social, religious, and legal literature of the day still proclaimed and upheld the cruel injustice against the Śūdra long after the Śūdra had become civilized and industrious, and a worthy member of society.

To an earnest and inquisitive mind, to a sympathetic and benevolent soul, there was something anomalous in all this. Gautama of the Śākya race was versed in the Hindu learning and religion of the age, but he pondered and asked if what he had learnt could be efficacious or true. His righteous soul rebelled against the unrighteous distinctions between man and man; and his benevolent heart hankered for a means to help the humble, the oppressed, and the lowly, The dead ceremonials and rites which householders practised appeared as vain and fruitless to him as the penances and mortifications which hermits voluntarily underwent in forests. The beauty of a holy life, of a sinless benevolent career, flashed before his mind's eye as the perfection of human destiny, as the heaven on earth; and with the earnest conviction of a prophet and a reformer, he proclaimed this as the essence of religion. His world-embracing sympathy led him to proclaim this method of self-culture and holy living to suffering humanity, and he invited the poor and the lowly to end their sufferings by cultivating virtue, by eschewing passions and desires, and by spreading brotherly love and universal peace. The Brāhman and the Śūdra, the high and the low, were the same in his eyes, all could equally effect their salvation by a holy life, and he invited all to embrace his catholic religion of love. Mankind responded to the touching appeal, and Buddhism in the course of a few centuries became the prevailing faith, not of a sect or a country, but of the continent of Asia.[1]

Nevertheless, it would be historically wrong to suppose that Gautama Buddha consciously set himself up as the founder of a new religion. On the contrary, he believed to the last that he was proclaiming only the ancient and pure form of religion which had prevailed among Hindus, among Brahmāns, Śrāmans and others, but which had been corrupted at a later day. As a matter of fact, Hinduism recognized wandering bodies of ascetics who renounced the world, performed no Vedic rites, and passed their days in contemplation (see *ante,* p. 284). Such bodies were known as Bhikṣus in the Hindu law books, and were generally known as Śrāmans. Gautama founded only one sect of Śrāmans among many sects which then existed, and his sect was known as that of the Śākyaputrīya Śrāmans to distinguish them from others. He taught them relinquishment of the world, a holy life, and pious meditation, such as all sects of Śrāmans recommended and practised.

What then is the distinguishing feature in Buddha's life-work which has made his tenets a religion—and the religion of a third of the human race ?

We answer, *his character.* Gautama's holy and pious life, his world-embracing sympathy, his unsurpassed moral precepts, his gentle and beautiful character, stamped themselves on his teachings which were not altogether new, gathered round him the meek and the lowly, the gentlest and the best of the Āryans, struck kings on their thrones and peasants in their cottages, and united sects and castes together as in a communion of love! And the sacred recollections of his life and doings remained after he had passed away, and held together the community which cherished his teachings, and in course of time gave those teachings the character of a distinct and noble religion.

Inspired by his love of purity, and a holy, gentle life, Gautama eschewed the rites of the Vedas and the penances of ascetics alike; he insisted only on self-culture, on benevolence, on pious resignation. He knew no difference between man and man except by their acts; he recognized no meritorious ceremonials and no meritorious penances, except the practice of virtue. This is what has made Buddhism a living and life-giving religion, when so many rival forms of ceticism have withered and died away.

It will be our endeavour to indicate the salient features of the Buddhist religion, and its far-reaching consequences on the people of India. Fortunately, we have no reason to complain of want of materials.

Indeed, so much has been written about Buddhism in recent years that it is almost difficult to imagine that Buddhist literature and religion were almost an unknown subject half a century ago. The distinguished missionary, Dr. Marshman, who lived and wrote in India for many years, could given better account of Buddha in 1824 than that his worship was probably connected with the

Egyptian Apis! And theories more wild and more imaginary were seriously recorded by other scholars.

Happily those days are past. Earnest enquirers and scholars have collected oriental manuscripts and works in different Buddhist countries, have studied, published, and translated many of them, and have thus formed a generally accurate idea of the religion as it was first preached by Gautama, and as it was subsequently modified in different times among different nations. It is not our purpose to record here a history of the researches into Buddhism during the last half century, but a few facts are so interesting that they cannot be passed over.

Mr. Hodgson was the English resident of Nepal from 1833 to 1843, and he was the first to collect original manuscripts on which a sober account of the religion could be based. He sent 85 bundles to the Asiatic Society of Bengal, 85 to the Royal Asiatic Society of London, 30 to the India Office Library, 7 to the Bodleian Library, Oxford, and 174 to the Societe Asiatique in Paris, or to M. Burnouf, personally. Mr. Hodgson also gave some account of these works and of the Buddhist religion in his essays.

The genius of Eugene Burnouf breathed life into these dead manuscripts, and his "Introduction to the History of Indian Buddhism," published in 1844, was the first rational, scientific, and comprehensive account of the Buddhist religion. The fame of the eminent scholar, and the great ability and philosophical acumen with which he treated the subject, attracted the attention of learned Europe to this wonderful religion, and the enquiry which Burnouf started has continued to the present day, and has been fruitful of great results.

What Hodgson did in Nepal, Alexander Csoma Korosi, a Hungarian scholar, did in Thibet. The annals of literary inquiry and research have few more wonderful stories to tell than that of the single-minded devotion of this simple Hungarian. He early made up his mind to devote himself to the study of eastern languages, and he set forth from Bucharest in 1820, without friends or money, and travelled on foot or by water on a raft till he came to Bagdad. He pushed on to Teharan, and thence started again with a caravan and came by Khorasan to Bokhara. In 1822 he came to Kabul and thence to Lahore, and from Lahore he travelled through Kashmir to Ladak where he finally settled. He sojourned and travelled long in these parts, and in 1831 he was at Simla "dressed in a coarse blue cloth loose gown, extending to his heels, and a small cloth cap of the same material. He wore a grizzly beard, shunned the society of Europeans, and passed his whole time in study."[2] In 1832, he came to Calcutta, where he was kindly received by Dr. Wilson and Mr. James Prinsep, and resided many years. In 1843, he left Calcutta again to go to Thibet, but died of fever on his way, at Darjeeiing, The Asiatic Society of Bengal has raised a monument on his grave in Darjeel ing. The present writer had the mournful satisfaction of paying a visit to this grave not many months ago.

About his work on the Thibetan Buddhist books, we find all necessary information in Vol. XX of the Asiatic Researches. Since Csoma's time other scholars have laboured in the same field of Thibetan Buddhist literature, and have added to our knowledge of the subject.

To the Rev. Samuel Beal is due the credit of procuring a complete collection of Chinese works on Buddhism. A request was made to this effect to the Japanese ambassador who visited England, and the ambassador at once acceded to the request, and on his return to Tokio, ordered the entire collection known as "The Sacred Teaching of the Three Treasures" to be sent to England. The collection contains over 2,000 volumes, and represents the entire series of sacred books taken during successive centuries from India to China, as also works and commentaries of native Chinese priests.

Buddhism and Buddhist scriptures were carried to Ceylon in the reign of Aśoka the Great, about 242 B. C. and the whole of the Buddhist scriptures, the "three baskets," exist to this day in Ceylon, as we will see further on, in the Pāli language, and in almost the identical shape in which they were taken there over two thousand years ago. A number of eminent scholars, Tumour, Fausboll, Oldenberg, Childers, Spence Hardy, Rhys Davids, Max Müller, Weber and others, have worked on these materials, and much of the Pāli scriptures has been published, and the most important portions of them have been translated.

Burma too has contributed to our knowledge of Buddhism, and a great deal of information on Burmese Buddhism is embodied in Bigandet's life of the Gaudama first published in 1868. All countries near and around India have furnished us with valuable records and contributions towards a scholar like knowledge of this great religion. India alone—the home of that religion—the country where It flourished more or less for nearly fifteen centuries—has kept no memorials worth the name of that noble faith! So complete has been the destruction of Buddhism, Buddhist monasteries, and Buddhist records in India !

Thanks to the researches of the scholars whom we have named above, the English-reading public have sufficient materials before them now for studying the developments of Buddhism in the different countries of the world, in China, Japan and Thibet, in Burma and Ceylon. English readers can thus study the progress of the religion in its various phases, at different ages, and among different conditions of life and civilization.

The historian of India must, however, forego that pleasant and most interesting task. The developments which Buddhism received in China, and Thibet and Burma, have no direct bearing on Indian history. It is his duty, therefore, to select from the materials before him those works only which illustrate the history of *Early Buddhism in India*. It is necessary for him to go to the fountain source of the information which is available, and to place his reliance on those works specially which illustrate the rise of Buddhism in India in the Rationalistic Period.

The form of Buddhism prevailing in Nepal and Thibet, China and Japan, is called Northern Buddhism, while the form prevailing in Ceylon and Burma is called Southern Buddhism. The Northern Buddhists furnish us with scanty materials directly illustrating the religion in its earliest from in India. The sacred books of the Northern Buddhists are not included in any comprehensive common name, and, as far as is known, none of them can be referred to the period immediately following on Gautama's death.

Kaniṣka, the King of Kashmir, convened a great council of Northern Buddhists in the first century after Christ, but the council, instead of collecting together the sacred works of the Northern Buddhists, wrote three great commentaries. The Lalita Vistāra, a most important work of the Northern Buddhists, is only a gorgeous poem; it is no more a biography of Gautama than the Paradise Lost is a biography of Jesus. It was composed probably in Nepal in the second or third or fourth century after Christ, although it contains passages—the Gathas—which are of a very much older date. In China, Buddhism was introduced from the first century after Christ, but did not become the State religion until the fourth century, and the works on Buddhism which were then carried by Chinese pilgrims from India from century to century, and translated into the Chinese language, do not illustrate the earliest phase of Buddhism in India. And lastly, Thibet has drifted still further away from primitive Buddhism in India, and has adopted forms and ceremonies which were unknown to Gautama and his followers in the fifth century before Christ.

On the other hand, the Southern Buddhists furnish us with the most valuable materials for our purpose. The sacred books of the Southern Buddhists are known by the inclusive name of the Three Piṭakas; and there is evidence to shew that these Piṭakas, now extant in Ceylon, are substantially identical with the canon as settled in the Council of Patna about 242 B. C. It is necessary that we should here briefly indicate the nature of this evidence.

The date of Buddha's death was for a long time believed to be 543 B. C.; but many facts ascertained within the last thirty years lead to the conclusion that the great reformer was born about 557 B. C, and died in 477 B. C. A Council of 500 monks was held in Rājagṛha, the capital of Magadha, immediately after his death, and they chanted the sacred laws together to fix them on their memory. A hundred years later, *i. e.*, in 377 B. C, a second Council was held in Vesāli, mainly for the discussion and settlement of ten questions on which difference of opinion had arisen. A hundred and eighteen years after this, *i. e.*, in 259 B. C, the great Aśoka was coronated king of the Magadhas, and a third Council was held by him in Patna about 242 B. C. to finally settle the religious works or Piṭakas.

It is well known that Aśoka was a most zealous Buddhist, and sent missionaries to foreign countries, and even to Syria, Macedon and Egypt, to preach the religion. He sent his own son Mahinda to Tissa, the king of Ceylon, about 242 B. C., and Mahinda took with him a number of Buddhist monks, and thus conveyed to Ceylon the Piṭakas as just settled in the Council of Patna.[3] It is needless to say that Tissa, the king of Ceylon, was glad to embrace the religion which Aśoka recommended and his son preached, and thus Ceylon embraced Buddhism in the third century B. C. About a hundred and fifty years after this, these Piṭakas were formally reduced to writing, and thus we have the most authentic account of the earliest form of Buddhism in Magadha in the Pāli Piṭakas of Ceylon.

These facts will shew that the Three Piṭakas of the Southern Buddhists can claim a date anterior to 242 B. C. For no work which could not claim a respectable antiquity was included as canon by the Council of Patna. Indeed, there is internal evidence in the Vinaya Piṭaka to lead to the supposition, that the main portions of that Piṭaka were settled before the Vesāli Council, *i. e.*, before 377 B. C. For in the main portions of the Vinaya Piṭaka there is no mention of the discussion on the ten questions alluded to above—questions which were "as important (or the history of Buddhism as the Arian controversy for that of Christianity,"and which agitated the whole of the Buddhist world to its very centre. The ten points in dispute were also matters of ecclesiastical law, and yet there is no decision in the main portions of the Vinaya Piṭaka on these points of law, no allusion to the great controversy which burst into flame in the 4th century B.C., and required the convocation of the Vesāli Council. The inference is irresistible that the main portion of the Vinaya Piṭaka is anterior to the date of the Council, *i. e.,* anterior to 377 B. C.

The same may be said of the main portions of the Sutta Piṭ aka. The third or Abhidamma Piṭaka gradually grew up later, and assumed its place by the side of Vinaya and Sutta, at the time of Aśoka or earlier.

We have thus found in the Scriptures of the Southern Buddhists reliable materials for the history of India for the centuries immediately before the time of Aśoka. For the contents of the Three Piṭakas were composed, settled and arranged in India during the hundred or two hundred years after the death of Gautama, just as the four Christian Gospels were composed and settled within a century or two after the death of Jesus. Hence the Three Piṭakas illustrate the manners and life of the Hindus and the history of Hindu kingdoms on the Gangetic valley. And, lastly, they give us a more consistent, and a less exaggerated account of the life and work and teachings of Buddha himself than anything which the Northern Buddhists can supply us with. Both as an index to the Hindu civilization of the period, and as an account of Gautama's life and work, the Three Piṭakas will be our guide. It is to these Pāli works that "we must go in preference to all other sources, if we desire to know whether any information is obtainable regarding Buddha and his life."[4]

The Three Piṭakas are known, as we have seen before, as the Sutta Piṭaka, the Vinaya Piṭaka, and the Abhid hamma Piṭaka. The works comprised in the Sutta Piṭaka profess to record the sayings and doings of Gautama Buddha himself. Gautama himself is the actor and the speaker in the earliest works of this Piṭaka, and his doctrines are conveyed in his own words. Occasionally one of his disciples is the instructor, and there are short introductions to indicate where and when Gautama or his disciple spoke. But all through the Sutta Piṭaka, Gautama's doctrines and moral precepts are preserved, professedly in Gautama's own words.

The Vinaya Piṭaka contain very minute rules, often on the most trivial subjects, for the conduct of monks and nuns—the Bhikkhus and the Bhikkhunis who had embraced the holy order. Gautama respected the lay disciple (Upāsaka), but he held that to embrace the Order was a quicker path to salvation. As the number of Bhikkhus and Bhikkhunis multiplied, it was necessary to fix elaborate rules, often on very minute subjects, for their proper conduct and behaviour in the Vihāra or monastery. As Gautama lived for nearly half a century after he had proclaimed his religion, there can be no doubt that he himself settled many of these rules. At the same time it is equally certain that many of the minute rules grew up after his death, but they are all attributed in the Vinaya Piṭaka to the direct order of the Blessed One himself.

And lastly, the Abhidamma Piṭaka contains disquisitions on various subjects, like the conditions of life in different worlds, on the explanations of personal qualities, on the elements, the causes of existence, etc. They have been miscalled metaphysics, for early Buddhism knows little of metaphysics. We now subjoin a list of works contained in the Three Piṭakas.

I. Sutta Piṭaka

1. Dīgha Nikāya or long treatises, being a collection of 34 Suttas. Seven of them with translations by Burnouf and Gogerly have been edited in Paris, and one other, the Mahā Parinibbāna Sutta has been translated by Rhys Davids in his "Buddhist Suttas."
2. Majjhima Nikāya or middling treatises, a collection of 152 Suttas of moderate size. They are being edited by Dr. Trenckner.
3. Saṁyutta Nikāya, or the connected treatises,
4. Aṅguttara Nikāya, treatises in divisions the length of which increases by one. They are being edited by Dr. Morris.
5. Khuddaka Nikāya or short treatises. It contains 15 works which should be mentioned in detail.[5]
   (1) Khuddaka Pāṭha or short passages, published with translation by Childers.
   (2) Dhammapada, published by Fausböll with Latin translation in 1855, and since translated into German by Weber (1860) and into English by Max Müller (1881).
   (3) Udāna, 82 short lyrics supposed to have been uttered by Gautama at different periods under strong emotion.
   (4) Itivuttika, 110 sayings of Buddha,
   (5) Sutta Nipāta, 70 didactic poems, thirty of them translated by Sir Coomara Swamy; the whole translated by Fausböll.
   (6) Vimāna Vatthu, stories of celestial mansions.
   (7) Peta Vatthu on departed spirits.

(8) Therā Gāthā, stanzas of monks.] Being edited for the
(9) Therī Gatha, stanzas of nuns.] [Pāli] Text Society.

(10) Jātaka, 550 stories of former births, text and commentary published by Fausboll and translated by Rhys Davids.

(11) Niddesa, explanations on the Sutta Nipāta (No. 5) by Sāriputta.

(12) Pati sambhidā, on intuitive insight.

(13) Apadāna, legends about Arhats or Saints.

(14) Buddha Vansa. Lives of 24 preceding Buddhas and of Gautama the historical Buddha. Being edited for the Pāli Text Society.

(15) Kariya Piṭaka, Gautama's virtuous acts in former births.

II. Vinaya Piṭaka, (Edited by Oldenberg,)

1. Vibhaṅga. Doctors Oldenberg and Rhys Davids consider it as only an extended reading of the Patimokkha, *i.e.*,as the Patimokkha with notes and commentary included. The Patimokkha is a formular of sins and their punishments recited every new moon and full moon day, and the members of the order who have committed any such sin are supposed to confess it and are disburdened of it. The Patimokkha is translated by Rhys Davids and Oldenberg.
2. Khaṇḍakas, *i.e.*, the Mahāvagga and the Chulla-vagga. Translated by Rhys Davids and Oldenberg.
3. Parivāra Pāṭha, admittedly an appendix and a later resume of the preceding portions of the Vinaya Piṭaka.[6]

III. Abhidhamma Piṭaka.

1. Dhamma Sangam. Conditions of life in different worlds. Edited for the Pāli Text Society.
2. Vibhaṅga, 18 books of disquisitions. 3. Kathā Vatthu, 1000 subjects for controversy.
4. Puggala Pannatti. On Personal Qualities.
5. Dhātu Katha. On the elements.
6. Yamaka, *i.e.*, pairs, *i.e.*, on apparent contradictions or contrasts.
7. Patthāna. On the causes of existence.

Such are the contents of the Three Piṭakas which have preserved to us the most reliable materials that are available for the history of Buddha's life and work, and the history of Buddhist India. Although writing was known when the Three Piṭakas were settled and compiled, yet for hundreds of years they were preserved solely by memory, even as the Vedas in India were preserved by memory.

"The text of the Three Piṭakas and the commentary too thereon.

"The wise Bhikkhus of former time had handed down by word of mouth.".

And it was in the first century before Christ, about B. C. that the sacred works were at last recorded to writing as we have seen before.

It is well known that Gautama, disregarding the precedent set by all classical writers and thinkers in India preached his doctrine and morality to the people of India in the language of the people, not in Sanscrit.. It is said in the Chullavagga (V, 33, I), that "There were, two brothers, Bhikkhus, by name Yamelu and Tekula, Brāhmans by birth, excelling in speech, excelling in pronunciation." And they went up to Gautama and said, "At the present time, Lord, Bhikkhus differing in name, differing in lineage, differing in birth, differing in family have gone forth. These corrupt the word of the Buddhas by their own dialect. Let us, Lord, put word of the Buddhas into Sanscrit Verse (Chandaso āropema)."

But Gautama would have none of this ; he worked for the humble and the lowly, his message was for the people and he wished it to be conveyed to them in their own tongue. "You are not, O Bhikkhus, to put the word of the Buddhas into (Sanscrit) verse. allow you, O Bhikkhus, to learn the word of the Buddhas *each in his own dialect*."

Generally we can apply to the Three Piṭakas the remarks which Doctors Rhys Davids and Oldenberg make in respect of the Vinaya Piṭaka. The text, as it lies before us, stands so well against all proofs, whether we compare its different parts one with another, or with the little that is yet known of its Northern counterparts, that we are justified in regarding these Pāli books as in fact the authentic mirror of the old Māgadhī text as fixed in the central schools of the most ancient Buddhist Church. That text in the dialect of Magadha may have been lost to us once for all; and we can scarcely hope, unless some isolated sentences may hereafter be found preserved here and there in inscriptions, that this loss will ever be even partially made good. But we may well be thankful that the faithful zeal and industry of these old monks has preserved for us a translation, in a dialect so nearly allied to the original, and in so perfect and trustworthy a state as the Pāli version of the Vinaya still undoubtedly presents."[8]

REFERENCES

1. The figures given below will shew approximately the proportion of Buddhists to the world's population ;—

Jews	7,000,000
Christians	328,000,000
Hindus	160,000,000
Mussulmans	155,000,000
Buddhists	500,000,000
Not included in the above	100,000,000
Population of the world ...	1,250,000,000

Between the fifth and tenth centuries after Christ, more than one-half of the human race were Buddhists.

2. Quoted in Beat's *Buddhism in China,* from Ralston's *Thibetan Tales.*
3. Dīpavaṁsa, XII. According to this historical epic of Ceylon, Mahinda was the son of Aśoka (born when Aśoka was a sub-king at Ujjayini, under his father who was king at Magadha), by the daughter of the Sethi or banker of Vidisa, *Dīpavaṁśa,* VI, 15 and 16.
4. Oldenberg's *Buddha,* (translation), p, 75.
5. The 15 works composing the fifth Nikāya are by some classed as Abhidhamma, and not in the Sutta Piṭaka.
6. But compiled before the time of Aśoka and carried to Ceylon by his son Mahinda according to the Dīpavaṁśa VII, 42. The works learnt and carried to Ceylon by Mahinda are thus described. The five Nikāyas Sutta Piṭaka), the seven sections (Abhidhamma), the two Vibhaṅgas, the Parivārar and the Khaṇḍaka (Vinaya).
7. Dīpavaṁśa XX, 20, 21.
8. Vinaya Texts, (translation), Part T, Introduction XXXVI.

CHAPTER – 14

LIFE OF GAUTAMA BUDDHA

In the sixth century before Christ, the kingdom of Magadha was rising to power and greatness. The kingdom, corresponding to modern South Behar, extended to the south of the Ganges, and on either side of the Son river. To the north of the Ganges it had a powerful rival in the haughty confederation of the Licchavis. Rājagṛha to the south of the Ganges was the capital of Bimbisāra, king of the Magadhas, and Vaisāli to the north of the Ganges was the capital of the Licchavis. To the east lay the kingdom of Aṅga of East Behar, which is spoken of in connection with Magadha, and Champā was the capital of Aṅga. Far to the north-west lay the ancient kingdom of the Kosalas, and the capital had been removed from Ayodhyā or Sāketa further northwards to the flourishing town of Śrāvasti, where Prasenajit reigned at the time of which we are speaking. The equally ancient country of the Kāsīs lying to the south seemed to be at this time subject to the king of Śrāvasti, and a viceroy of Prasenajit ruled at Benares.

A little to the east of the Kosala kingdom two kindred clans, the Śākyas and the Koliyans, lived on the opposite banks of the small stream Rohinī, and enjoyed a sort of precarious independence, more through the jealousies of the rival kings of Magadha and Kosala than by their own power. Kapilavastu was the capital of the Śākyas, who were then living in peace with the Koliyans, and Suddhodana, king of the Śākyas had married two daughters of the king of the Koliyans.

Neither queen bore any child to Śuddhodana for many years, and the hope of leaving an heir to the principality of the Śākyas was well nigh abandoned. At last, however, the elder queen promised her husband an heir and according to ancient custom left for her father's house in order to be confined. But before she reached the place she was confined in the pleasant grove of Lumbinī of a son. The mother and the child were carried back to Kapilavastu, where the former died seven days after, leaving the child to be nursed by his step-mother and maternal aunt, the younger queen.

The birth of Gautama is naturally the subject of many legends which have a most remarkable resemblance with the legends about the birth of Jesus Christ. One of them may be quoted here. The Ṛṣi Asita saw the gods delighted, and

"Seeing the gods with pleased minds, delighted, and shewing his respect, he said this on that occasion : 'Why is the assembly of the gods so exceedingly pleased, why do they take their clothes and wave them ?"

"The Bodhisatta, the excellent pearl, the incomparable is born for the good, and for a blessing in the world of men, in the town of the Śākyas in the country of Lumbinī. Therefore we are glad and exceedingly pleased."

Having obtained this reply, the Ṛṣi went to Śuddhodana's palace and asked "where is this Prince, I wish to see him."

"Then the Śākyas shewed to Asita the Child, the Prince, who was like shining gold, manufactured by a very skilful smith in the mouth of a forge, and beaming in glory and beautiful." And the Ṛṣi foretold that the boy would reach the summit of enlightenment and would establish righteousness, and that his religion would be widely spread. *Nālaka Sutta.*

The boy was named Siddhārtha, but Gautama was his family name. He belonged to the Śākya tribe, and is therefore often called Śākya Siṁha; and when he had proclaimed and preached a reformed religion, he was called Buddha or the "awakened" or "enlightened."

Little is known of the early life of young Gautama, except that he was married to his cousin Subhadrā or Yasodharā, daughter of the king of Koli, about the age of eighteen. It is said that Gautama neglected the manly exercises which all Kṣatriyas of his age delighted in, and that his relations complained of this, A day was accordingly fixed for the trial of his skill, and the young prince of the Śākyas proved his superiority to his kinsmen. It is not possible to decide what foundation this story has in truth.

Ten years after his marriage, Gautama resolved to quit his home and his wife for the study of philosophy and religion. The story which is told of the young prince abandoning his home and his position is well known. He must have for a long time pondered deeply and sorrowfully on the sins and sufferings of humanity, he must have been struck with the vanity of wealth and position. In the midst of his prosperity, position and wealth, he must have felt a secret yearning after something higher, which neither wealth nor position could satisfy; and a strong irresistible desire to seek for a remedy for the sufferings of men must have arisen in his heart even in the midst of the luxuries and comforts of his palace-home. It is said that the sight of a decrepit old man, of a sick man, of a decaying corpse, and of a dignified hermit led him to form his resolution to quit his home. The story has little foundation in truth, and only represents, in a concrete shape, the thoughts that must have arisen in his mind with regard to the woes of a worldly life, and the holy calm of a retired life.

At this time a son was born unto him. It is said that the news was announced to him in a garden on the river side, and the pensive young man only exclaimed "This is a new and strong tie I shall have to break.' The news gladdened the heart of the Śākyas, and Kapilavastu resounded with notes of joy at the birth of an heir to the throne. A perfect ovation awaited Gautama on his return to that town, and among the deafening cheers which arose, Gautama heard a young girl say "Happy the father, happy the mother, happy the wife of such a son and husband." Gautama understood the word "happy" in the sense of "emancipated" from sins and new births, and he took of his necklace of pearls and sent it to the girl. The girl believed the young prince was enamoured of her, and little knew the thoughts which were struggling within him.

That night he repaired to the threshhold of his wife's chamber—and there, by the light of the flickering lamp, he gazed on a scene of perfect bliss. His young wife lay surrounded by flowers, and with one hand on the infant's head. A yearning arose in his heart to take the babe in his arms for the last time before relinquishing all earthly bliss. But this he might not do. The mother might be awakened, and the importunities of the fond and loving soul might unnerve his heart and shake his resolution. Silently then he tore himself away from that blissful sight—that nest of all his joy and love and affection. In that one eventful moment, in the silent darkness of that night, he renounced for ever his wealth and position and power, his proud rank and his princely fame, and more than all this, the affection of a happy home, the love of a young wife and of a tender infant now lying unconscious in sleep. He renounced all this, and rode away that night to become a poor student and a homeless wanderer. His faithful servant Channa asked to be allowed to stay with him and become an ascetic, but Gautama sent him back, and repaired alone to Rājagṛha.

Rājagṛha as we have stated before, was the capital of Bimbisāra, king of the Magadhas, and was situated in a valley sorrounded by five hills. Some Brāhman ascetics lived in the caves of these hills, sufficiently far from the town for studies and contemplation, and yet sufficiently near to obtain supplies. Gautama attached himself first to one Alāra, and then to another Udraka, and learnt from them all that Hindu philosophy had to teach.

Not satisfied with this learning Gautama wished to see if penances would bring superhuman insight and power as they were reputed to do. He retired therefore into the jungles of Uruvelā, near the site of the present temple of Buddha Gayā, and for six years, attended by five disciples, he gave himself up to the severest penances and self-mortification, His fame spread all round, for the ignorant and the superstitious always admire self-inflicted pain; but Gautama did not obtain what he sought. At last one day he fell down from sheer weakness, and his disciples thought he was dead. But he recovered, and despairing of deriving any profit from penance, he abandoned it. His disciples, who did not understand his ohiect, lost all respect for him when he gave up his penances; they left him alone and went away to Benares.

Left alone in the world, Gautama wandered towards the banks of the Nirañjarā, received his morning meal from the hands of Sujātā, a villager's daughter, and sat himself down under the famous Bo-tree or the tree of wisdom. Many are the legends told of Māra, the evil spirit, having tempted him on this occasion, legends which have a curious resemblance with the legends of the temptation of Jesus Christ; but we have no space to narrate them here. For a long time he sat in contemplation, and the scenes of his past life came thronging into his mind. The learning he had acquired had produced no results, the penances he had undergone were vain his disciples had left him alone in the world. Would he now return to his happy home, to the arms of his loving, widowed wife, to his little child now a sweet boy of six years, to his affectionate father and his loyal people? This was possible; but where would be the satisfaction? What would become of the mission to which he had devoted himself. Long he sat in contemplation and in doubt, until the doubts cleared away like mists in the morning, and the daylight of Truth flashed before his eyes. What was this Truth which learning did not teach and penances did not impart ? He had made no new discovery, he had acquired no new knowledge, but his pious nature and his benevolent heart told him, that a holy calm life and love towards others were the panacea for all evils. Self-culture and universal love, this was his discovery —this is the essence of Buddhism.

The conflict in Gautama's mind which thus subsided in calm is described in Buddhist writings by marvellous incidents. Clouds and darkness prevailed, the earth and oceans quaked, rivers flowed back to their sources, and peaks of lofty mountains rolled down. Dr. Rhys Davids justly states that these legends have a deep meaning, and are "the first half-inarticulate efforts the Indian mind had made to describe the feelings of a strong man torn by contending passions."[1]

Gautama's old teacher Alāra was dead, and he went therefore to Benares to proclaim the truth to his five former disciples. On the way he met a man of the name of Upaka, belonging to the Ājīvaka sect of ascetics, who, looking at the composed and happy expression on Gautama's face, asked, "Your countenance, friend, is serene; your complexion is pure and bright. In whose name, friend, have you retired from the world ? Who is your teacher ? What doctrine do you profess ?" To this Gautama replied that he had no teacher, that he had obtained Nirvāṇa by the extinction of all passions, and added, "I go to the city of the Kāsīs to beat the drum of the immortal in the darkness of the world." Upaka did not understand him, and replied after a little conversation, "It may be so friend," shook his head, took another road and went away. *Mahāvagga,* I, 6,

At Benares, Gautama entered the Deer Park (Migadāya) in the cool of the evening, and met his former disciples. And he explained to them his new tenets.

"There are two extremes, O Bhikkhus, which the man who has given up the world ought not to follow— the habitual practice, on the one hand, of those things whose attraction depends upon the passions, and specially of sensuality, a low and pagan way, unworthy, unprofitable, and fit only for the worldly minded; and the habitual practice, on the otherof asceticism hand,which is painful, unworthy, and unprofitable,

"There is a middle path, O Bhikkhus, avoiding these two extremes, discovered by the Tathāgata (Buddha), a path which opens the eyes and bestovs understanding, which leads to peace of mind, to the higher wisdom, to full enlightenment, to Nirvāṇa!"

And then he explained to them the four truths concerning suffering, the cause of suffering, the destruction of suffering, and the way which leads to such destruction of suffering. And the way was described to be eight-fold, and consisted in correct beliefs, aims, speech and actions, in correct living and endeavour, mindfulness and meditation.[2] And this doctrine, Gautama rightly said "was not, O Bhikkhus, among the doctrines handed down." "In Benares, in the hermitage of Migadāya, the Supreme Wheel of the Empire of Truth has been set rolling by the Blessed

One—that wheel which not by any Śrāman or Brāhman, not by any god, not by any Brahmā or Māra, not by any one in the universe, can ever be turned back."—*Dhamma Chakka Ppavattana Sutta, Aṅguttara Nikāya.*

It is needless to say that the five former disciples were soon converted, and were the first members of the Order.

Yasa, son of the rich Sethi (banker) of Benares, was his first lay disciple, and the story of the conversion of this young man, nurtured in the lap of luxury and wealth, is worth repeating. "He had three palaces, one for winter, one for summer, one for the rainy season." One night he awoke from sleep and found the female musicians still sleeping in the room with their dress and hair and musical instruments in disorder. The young man who had apparently been satiated with a life of luxury, became disgusted with what he saw. and in a moment of deep thoughtfulness said : "Alas! what distress; alas! what danger! "And he left the house and went out.

It was dawn, and Gautama was walking up and down in the open air and heard the perplexed and torrowful young man exclaiming, "Alas! what distress; alas! what danger !" The sage replied, "Here is no distress, Yasa, here is no danger. Come . here, Yasa, sit down; I will teach you the Truth." And Yasa heard the Truth from the lips of the saintly Instructor, Yasa's father and mother and wife missed him and they all came to Gautama and listened to the holy truth. Yasa became a personal follower of Gautama, the other three remained his disciples.—*Mahāvagga I, 7 and 8.*

Within five months after his arrival at Benares, Gautama had sixty followers. And now he called them together and dismissed them in different directions to preach the Truth for the salvation of mankind. "Go ye now, O Bhikkhus, and wander, for the gain of the many, for the welfare of the many, out of compassion for the world, for the good, for the gain, for the welfare of gods and men. *Let not two of you go the same way.* Preach, O Bhikkhus, the doctrine which is glorious in the beginning, glorious in the middle, glorious in the end, in the spirit, and in the letter; proclaim a *consummate perfect and pure life of holiness." Mahāvagga J, II, I.* No missionaries of later days have evinced a holier zeal to proclaim the truth to the ends of the earth, than the followers of Gautama, acting on the sacred mandate quoted above. Gautama himself went to Uruvelā, and Yasa remained in Benares. At Uruvelā, Gautama achieved distinguished success by converting three brothers named Kāsyapa, who worshipped fire in the Vedic form, and had high reputation as hermits and philosophers. The eldest brother Uruvelā Kāsyapa and his pupils first "flung their hair, their braids, their provisions, and the things for the *agni-hotra* sacrifice into the river," and received the Pabbājja and Upasampadā ordination from the Blessed One. His brothers who lived by the Nadī (River Niranjarā) and at Gayā soon followed the example,—*Mahāvagga I, 15 to 20.*

The conversion of the Kāsyapas created a sensation, and Gautama with his new disciples and a thousand followers walked towards Rājagṛha, the capital of Magadha. News of the new prophet soon reached the king, and Seniya Bimbisāra, surrounded by numbers of Brāhmans and householders (Vaiśyas), went to vizit Gautama. Seeing the distinguished Uruvelā Kāsyapa there, the king could not make out if that great Brāhman had converted Gautama, or if Gautama had converted the Brāhman. Gautama understood the king's perplexity, and in order to enlighten him, asked Kāsyapa : What knowledge have you gained, O inhabitant of Uruvelā, that has induced you, who were renowned for your penances, to forsake your sacred fire." Kāsyapa replied that he had "seen the state of peace," and "took no more delight in sacrifices and offerings" The king was struck and pleased, and with his numerous attendants, declared himself an adherent of Gautama, and invited him to take his meal with him the next day.

The solitary wanderer accordingly went, an honored guest, to the palace of the king, and the entire population of the capital of Magadha turned out to see the great luminary of the religion of holiness and love who had suddenly appeared on the scene. The king then assigned a bamboo grove (Veluvana) close by for the residence of Gautama and his followers, and there Gautama rested for some time. Shortly after Gautama obtained two renowned converts, Sārīputra and Moggallānā. *Mahāvagga* I, *22 to 24.*

The daily life of Gautama has been well described by Dr. Oldenberg. "He, as well as his disciples, rises early, when the light of dawn appears in the sky, and spends the early moments in spiritual exercises or in converse with his disciples, and then he proceeds with his companions towards the town. In the days when his reputation stood at its highest point, and his name was named throughout India among the foremost names, one might day by day see that man before whom kings bowed themselves, alms-bowl in hand, through streets and alleys, from house to house, and without uttering any request, with down-cast look, stand silently waiting until a morsel of food was thrown into his bowl."

Such was the manner in which the greatest man of his age begged his food, day by day, from house to house, and preached his maxims of holiness and forgiveness to men and to women. For women were Gautama's listeners as well as men. "The seclusion of women from the outer world, which later custom has enjoined, was quite unheard of in ancient India; women took their share in the intellectual life of the people, and the most delicate and tenderest of the epic poems of the Indians shew us how well they could understand and appreciate true womanhood."[3]

The fame of Gautama had now travelled to his native town, and his old father expressed a desire to see him once before he died. Gautama accordingly went to Kapilavastu, but, according to custom, remained in the grove outside the town. His father and relations came to see him there; and the next day Gautama himself went into the town, begging alms from the people who once adored him as their beloved prince and master! The story goes on to say that the king rebuked Gautama for this act, but Gautama replied, it was the custom of his race. "But," retorted the king, "we are descended from an illustrious race of warriors, and not one of them has ever begged his bread." "You and your family," answered Gautama, "may claim descent from kings, my descent is from the prophets (Buddhas) of old."

The king took his son to the palace where all the *members of the family came* to greet him except his wife. The deserted Yasodharā, with a wife's grief and a wife's pride, exclaimed, "If I am of any value in his eyes, he will himself come, I can welcome him better here," Gautama understood this and went to her with only two disciples with him. And when Yasodharā saw her lord and prince enter—a recluse with shaven head and yellow robes—her heart failed her, she flung herself to the ground, held his feet, and burst into tears. Then, remembering the impassable gulf between them, she rose and stood aside. She listened to his new doctrines, and when, subsequently, Gautama was induced to establish an order of female mendicants— Bhikkhunīs— Yasodharā became one of the first Buddhist nuns. At the time of which we are now speaking, Yasodharā remained in her house, but Rāhula, Gautama's son, was converted.

Gautama's father was much aggrieved at this, and asked Gautama to establish a rule that no one should in future be admitted to the Order without his parents' consent. Gautama consented to this, and made a rule accordingly. *Jātāka 87—90. Mahāvagga I*, 54.

On his way back to Rājagṛha, Gautama stopped for some time at Anupiyā, "a town belonging to the Mallas." And while he was stopping here, he made many converts both from the Koliyan and from the Śākya tribe some of whom deserve special mention. Anuruddha, the Śākya, went to his mother and asked to be allowed to go into the houseless state. His mother did not know how to stop him and so told him "If, beloved Anuruddha, Bhaddya, the Śākya Rāja, will renounce the world, thou also mayest go forth into the houseless state."

Anuruddha accordingly went to Bhaddya, and it was decided that they would embrace the Order in seven days. "So Bhaddya the Śākya Rāja, and Anuruddha and Ānanda, and Bhagu and Kimbila, and Deyadatta, just as they had so often previously gone out to the pleasure ground with fourfold array, even so did they now go out with fourfold array, and Upāli the barber went with them, making seven in all.

"And when they had gone some distance, they sent their retinue back and crossed over to the neighbouring district, and took off their fine things, and wrapped them in their robes, and made a bundle of them, and said to Upāli the barber, 'Do you now, Upāli, turn back. These things will be sufficient for you to live upon.' "But Upāli was of a different mind and so all the seven went to Gautama and became converts. And when Bhaddya had retired into solitude he exclaimed over and over, "O happiness! O happiness !" and on being asked the cause said :

"Formerly, Lord, when I was a king, I had a guard completely provided both within and withont my private apartments, both within and without the town, and within the (borders of my) country. Yet though, Lord, I was thus guarded and protected I was fearful, anxious, distrustful and alarmed. But now, Lord, even when in the forest, at the foot of a tree, in solitude, I am without fear or anxiety, trustful and not alarmed; I dwell at ease, subdued, secure, with mind as peaceful as an antelope." *Chullavagga VII,* 1,

It is necessary to add here that of these converts, Ānanda became the most intimate friend and companion of Gautama, and after his death led the band of 500 monks in chanting the Dharma in the Council of Rājagṛha. Upāli, though a barber by birth, became an eminent member of the Order, and his name is often mentioned in connexion with the Vinaya Piṭaka. It is a striking proof how completely the caste system was ignored in the Order established by Gautama. Devadatta became subsequently the rival and opponent of Gautama, and is even said to have advised Ajātaśatru the prince of Magadha to kill his father Bimbisāra, and then attempted to kill Gautama himself, *Chullavagga VII,* 2 *to* 4. All the charges, however, which are heaped on Devadatta, who was a rival of Gautama, should not be accepted. And, lastly, Anuruddha lived to become the greatest master of Buddhist metaphysics.

After spending his second *vassa* or rainy season in Rājagṛha, Gautama repaired to Śrāvasti, the capital of the Kosalas, where, as we have seen before, Prasenajit reigned as king. A wood called Jetavana was presented to the Buddhists, and Gautama often repaired and preached there. Gautama's instructions were always delivered orally, and preserved in the memory of the people, like all the ancient books of India, although writing was known at his time.[4]

The third *vassa* was also paṣed in Rājagṛha, and in the fourth year (from the date of his proclaiming his creed) Gautama crossed the Ganges, went to Vaisāli and stopped in the Mahāvana grove. Thence he is said to have made a miraculous journey through the air to settle a dispute between the Śākyas and the Koliyans about the water of the boundary river Rohinī. In the following year he again repaired to Kapilavastu, and was present at the death of his father then ninety-seven years old.

His widowed step-mother Prajāpati Gautamī, and his no less widowed wife Yaśodharā had now no ties to bind them to the world, and insisted on joining the Order established by Gautama. The sage had not yet admitted women to the Order, and was naturally most reluctant to do so. But his mother was inexorable and followed him' to Vaisāli, and begged to be admitted.

Ānanda pleaded her cause, but Gautama still replied, "Enough Ānanda! Let it not please thee that women should be allowed to do so." But Ānanda persisted and asked—

"Are women, Lord, capable—when they have gone forth from the household life and entered the homeless state, under the doctrine and discipline proclaimed by the Blessed One—are they capable of realizing the fruit of conversion or of the second path, or of Arhatship ?"

There could be only one reply to this. Honor to women has ever been a part of religion in India, and salvation and heaven are not barred to the female sex by the Hindu religion. "They are capable, Ānanda," reluctantly replied the sage. And Prajāpati and the other ladies were admitted to the Order as Bhikkhunis under some rules making them strictly subordinate to the Bhikkhus. *Chullavaggā X,* 1. After this Gautama retired to Kosāmbī near Prayāga.

In the sixth year after spending the rains at Kosambī Gautama returned to Rājagṛha, and Kṣemā, the queen of Bimbisāra, was admitted to the Order. In the same year Gautama is said to have performed some miracles at Śrāvasti, and went to heaven to teach Dharma to his mother who had died seven days after his birth.

In the eleventh year Gautama converted the Brāhman Bhāradvāja by the parable of the sower which is so pretty that it deserves to bequoted.

Kāsī Bhāradvāja's five hundred ploughs were tied in the sowing season. He went to the place where his men were distributing food to the poor, and he saw Gautama standing there to get alms. On this he said :—

"I,O Śrāman, both plough and sow, and having ploughed and sown, I eat; thou also, O Śrāman, shouldst plough and sow, and having ploughed and sown, thou shouldst eat."

"I also, O Brāhman, both plough and sow and having ploughed and sown, I eat." So said Bhagavat.

"Yet we do not see the yoke or the plough, or the ploughshare, or the goad, or the oxen of the venerable Gautama."

Bhagavat answered—"Faith is the seed, penance the rain, understanding my yoke and plough, modesty the pole of the plough, mind the tie, thoughtfulness my ploughshare and goad.

"Exertion is my beast of burden; carrying me to Nibbāna, he goes without turning back to the place where, having gone, one does not grieve."

The Brāhman was abashed, and after further instructions joined the Order.— *Sutta Nipāta, Kāsī Bhāradvāja Sutta.*[5]

In the next year he undertook the longest journey he had ever made, and went to Mantala and returned by Benares, and then preached the famous Mahā Rāhula Sutta to his son Rāhula, then eighteen years old. Two years after, Rāhula, being twenty, was formally admitted in the Order, and the Rāhula Sutta was preached.

In the following year, *i. e.,* in the fifteenth year from the date of his proclaiming his creed, he visited Kapilavastu again, and addressed a discourse to his cousin Mahānāma who had succeeded Bhadraka, the successor of Suddhodana, as the king of the Śākyas. Gautama's father-in-law, Suprabuddha king of Koli, publicly abused Gautama for deserting Yasodharā, but is said to have been swallowed up by the earth shortly after.

In the seventeenth year he delivered a discourse on the death of Śrīmatī, a courtezan; in the next year he comforted a weaver who had accidentally killed his daughter; in the following year he released a deer caught in a snare and converted the angry hunter who had wanted to shoot him; and in the twentieth year he similarly converted the famous robber Aṅgulimāla of the Chaliya forest.

For twenty-five years more Gautama wandered through the Gangetic valley, preached piety and a holy life to the poor, the lowly and the misguided, made converts among the high and the low, the rich and the poor, and proclaimed his law through the length and breadth of the land. His pure life of benevolence and his pure religion of love were widely known and universally respected by his followers and the orthodox Hindus alike; nations and their kings honored the doctrines of the saintly reformer whose acts were those of kindness and benevolence; and when Gāutama died in the advanced age of eighty, Buddhism was already a power in the land, which, not by any Śrāman or Brahmān, "not by any god, not by any Brahmā or Māra, not by any one in the universe, could ever be turned back."

Gautama lived forty-five years from the date of his proclaiming his new religion; and accepting the year 477 B. C. as the year of his death, the main facts of his life may be thus arranged:—

Born near Kapilavastu	557 B. C
His marriage with Yaśodharā ...	538 B. C.
He left his home, wife and infant ...	528 B. C.
He became enlightened at Buddha Gayā.—and proclaimed his religion at Benares ...	522 B.C.

He revisted his home … …	521 B. C.
His father Suddhodana died, and	
his stepmother and wife joined the Order …	517 B. C.
His son Rāhula joined the Order …	508 B. C
Yaśodharā's father died … …	507 B. C
Gautama died … …	477 B. C.

Happily we have a fairly complete account of the events immediately before his death in the *Mahāparinibhāna Sutta* in the *Dīgha Nikāya,* and to these facts we now turn.

Gautama was now eighty years of age, and the generation among whom he had worked in his youth had passed away. Most of those men whom he had known in his early days were dead, and the aged saint preached to sons and grandsons the same holy law which he had proclaimed to their sires and grandsires before. Many of his intimate friends were dead, but the faithful Ānanda still accompanied him like his shadow, and ministered to his wants. The old king of Rājagṛha was no more; his warlike and ambitious son Ajātaśatru had ascended the throne of Magadha—it is said by murdering his father—and was now maturing schemes of conquest. It was no part of Ajātaśatru's policy to offend so popular and widely respected a person as Gautama, and outwardly at least, Ajātaśatru honored the reformer.

The powerful Vajjian clans who occupied the plains on the northern shores of the Ganges, opposite to Magadha. first attracted Ajātaśatru's attention. They were a Turanian tribe who had entered into India through the northern mountains and had established a republican form of government in the very centre of Hindu civilization, and were threatening the conquest of all Magadha. They were probably the same Yu-chi tribe[6] who conquered Kashmir and Western India four or five centuries later, and became, under Kaniṣka, the most powerful supporters of Buddhism.

Ajātaśatru Videhiputra[7] said to himself, "I will root out these Vajjians, mighty and powerful though they be, I will destroy these Vajjians, I will bring these Vajjians to utter ruin."

Gautama was then residing in the Vulture's Peak (Gridhrakūta), a cave on the side of the loftiest of the five hills overlooking the beautiful valley of Rājagṛha. Ajātaśatru, who was not without some kind of superstitious faith in prophecies, sent his prime minister Vassakāra to Gautama to enquire how his expedition against the Vajjians would end. Gautama was no re spector of kings, and replied that so long as the Vajjians remained united in their adherence to their ancient customs "we expect them not to decline, but to prosper."

From the Vulture's Peak Gautama wandered to neighbouring places—to Ambalathikā, to Nālanda and to Pāṭaligrāma, the site of the future capital of Magadha, Pāṭaliputra. At the time of Gautama it was an insignificant grāma or village, but "Sunīdha and Vassakāra, the chief ministers of Magadha, were building a fortress at Pāṭaligama to repel the Vajjians". Such was the origin of the town which became the capital of Chandragupta and Aśoka, and was the metropolis of India for nearly a thousand years. Gautama is said to have prophesied the greatness of the place and said to Ānanda :

"And among famous places of residence and haunts of busy men, this will become the chief, the city of Pāṭaliputra, a centre for the interchange of all kinds of wares" Modern readers who disbelieve in prophesies, will argue from this that the Mahāparinibbānam Sutta, or at least this passage was composed when Pāṭaliputra had already become the busy capital of Magadha. Gautama is said to have also foretold that "three dangers will hang over Pāṭaliputra,' that of fire, that of water and that of dissension,"—a very safe prophecy to make about any riverside capital town in India!

Vassakāra and Sunīdha, the ministers of Ajātaśatru, invited Gautama there and fed him with "sweet dishes of boiled rice and cakes," and after this Gautama left the place, and is said to have crossed the Ganges which was then "brimful and overflowing," by a miracle—passing over the water without a boat or a raft.

He then went to Kotigrāma, and then to Nādika where he rested in "brickhall," which was a resting place for travellers. There Gautama taught Ānanda the pregnant lesson that each disciple could ascertain for himself if he had attained salvation. If he was conscious, if he felt within himself, that he had faith in the Buddha, that he had faith in the Truth, that he had faith in the Order; then he was saved. Buddha, Dharma, and Saṅgha became the Trinity of the Buddhists.

From Nādika, Gautama came to Vaisāli, the capital of the powerful confideracy of the Licchavis to the north of the Ganges. Ambapāli, a courtezan, heard that the saint was stopping in her mango grove and came and invited him to a meal, and Gautama accepted the invitation.

"Now the Licchavis of Vaisāli heard that the Blessed One had arrived at Vaisāli and was staying at Ambapāli's grove. And ordering a number of magnificent carriages to be made ready, they mounted one of them and proceeded with their train to Vaisāli. Some of them were dark, dark in colour and wearing dark clothes and ornaments; some of them were fair, fair in colour and wearing light clothes and ornaments; some of them were red, ruddy in colour and wearing red clothes and ornaments; some of them were white, pale in colour and wearing white clothes and ornaments.

"And Ambapāli drove against the young Licchavis, axle to axle, wheel to wheel, and yoke to yoke; and the Licchavis said to Ambapāli the courtezan, How is it Ambapāli, that thou drivest up against us thus.

"My Lords, I have just invited the Blessed One and his brethren for their morrow's meal" said she.

"Ambapāli give us this meal for a hundred thousand, said they.

"My Lords, were you to offer all Vaisāli with its subject territory, I would not give up so honorable a feast.

"Then the Licchavis cast up their hands exclaiming, 'we are outdone by this mango-girl,[8] we are outreached by this mango-girl,' and they went on to Ambapālikā's grove."

There they saw Gautama and invited him to a meal on the morrow, but Gautama replied, "O Licchavis, I have promised to dine to-morrow with Ambapāli the courtezan." And Ambapāli fed Gautama and his brethren with "sweet rice and cakes" and "waited upon them till they refused any more." And then she was edified and instructed, and said, "Lord, I present this mansion to the order of mendicants, of which Buddha is the chief," and the gift was accepted.[9]

From Ambapāli's grove, Gautama went to Beluva. He felt his end approaching and said to the faithful Ānanda, "I am now grown old and full of years, my journey is drawing to its close, I have reached the sum of my days, I am turning eighty years of age. Therefore, O Ānanda! be ye lamps unto yourselves. Be ye a refuge to yourselves. Betake yourselves to no external refuge. Hold fast to the Truth as a lamp. Hold fast as a refuge to the Truth."

In Chāpāla Chetiya, Gautama delivered a discourse in which he enumerated four classes of men, *viz.*, the Nobles, the Brāhmans, the Householders and the Śrāmans ; and four classes of angels, *viz.*, the Angels, the Great Thirty-three,[10] Mara[11] and Brahmā.[12]

At Kūtāgāra Gautama once more proclaimed to his followers the substance and essence of his religion, and enjoined upon them to practice it, to meditate upon it, and to spread it abroad, "in order that pure religion may last long and be perpetuated, in order that it may continue to be for the good and the happiness of the great multitudes."

Having paid his last visit to Vaisāli, Gautama then wandered through villages, Bhandagrāma, Hastigrāma, Ambagrāma, Jambugrāma, and Bhoganagara, and then went to Pāvā. There Chunda, a goldsmith and ironsmith, invited him to a meal, and gave him "sweet rice and cakes and a quantity of dried boar's flesh." Gautama never refused the poor man's offering, but the boar's flesh did not agree with him. "Now when the Blessed One had eaten the food prepared by Chunda, the worker in metal, there fell upon him a dire sickness, the disease of dysentery, and sharp pain came upon him even unto death. But the Blessed One, mindful and self-possessed, bore it without complaint."

On his way from Pāvā to Kusinagara, Gautama converted a low caste man Pukkusa. At Kusinagara, eighty miles due east from Kapilavastu, Gautama felt that his death was nigh. With that loving anxiety which had characterised all his life, he tried on the eve of his death to impression his followers, that Chunda was not to blame for the food he had supplied, but that the humble smith's act, kindly meant, would redound to length of life, to good birth, and to good fortune.

It is said that just before his death the trees were in bloom out of season, and sprinkled flowers on him that heavenly flowers and sandalwood powder descended on him, and that music and heavenly songs were wafted from the sky. But the great Apostle of holy life said, "It is not thus, Ānanda, that the Tathagāta (Buddha) is rightly honoured, reverenced, venerated, held sacred or revered. But the brother or the sister, the devout man or the devout woman, who continually fulfils all the greater and the lesser duties, who is correct in life, walking according to precepts—it is he who rightly honours, reverences, venerates, holds sacred, and reveres the Tathāgata with the worthiest homage." Who is not reminded by these noble precepts of the holy precept in the Bible so happily rendered into verse by a Christian poet—

> But thou hast said, the flesh of goat,
> The blood of ram, I would not prize,
> A contrite heart, an humble thought,
> Are my accepted sacrifice."

On the night of Gautama's death, Subhadra, a Brāhman philosopher of Kusinagara, came to ask some questions, but Ananda, fearing that this might be wearisome to the dying sage, would not admit him, Gautama, however, had overheard their conversation, and he would not turn back a man who had come for instruction. He ordered the Brāhman to be admitted, and with his dying breath explained to him the Law and the Truth. Subhadra was the last disciple whom Gautama converted, and shortly after, at the last watch of the night, the great sage departed this life—with the exhortation to his brother men still on his lips, "Decay is inherent in all component things, work out your salvation with diligence."

The body of Gautama was cremated by the Mallas of Kusinagara who surrounded his bones "in their council-hall with a lattice work of spears and with a rampart of bows; and there, for seven days, they paid honour and reverence and respect and homage to them with dance and song and music, and with garlands and perfumes."

It is said that the remains of Gautama were divided into eight portions. Ajātaśatru of Magadha obtained one portion and erected a mound over it at Rājagriha. The Licchavis of Vaisāli obtained another portion and erected a mound at that town. Similarly the Śākyas of Kapilavastu, the Bulis of Allakappa, the Koliyas of Rāmagrāma, the Mallas of Pāvā, the Mallas of Kusinagara, and a Brāhman Vethadīpaka obtained portions of the relics and erected mounds over them. The Moriyans of Pipphalivana made a mound over the embers, and the Brāhman Dona made a mound over the vessel in which the body had been burnt.

This account of the division of relics is undoubtedly mythical, and was probably invented when Buddhists had adopted the custom of preserving relics, long after Gautama's death.

REFERENCES

1. *Buddhism.*—Dr. Rhys Davids quotes a passage from Milton's Paradise Regained, describing a similar disturbance of the elements on the *occasion* of Christ's temptation.
2. We shall have to dwell hereafter on these four truths and the eightfold path which are the cardinal principles of Buddhism. The above extracts will

shew that they were also the principles which Gautama proclaimed to the world at the very outset of his career.

3. Oldenberg's *Buddha*. (Translation), pp. 149 & 164.
4. "Brief written communications, brief written notifications, appear to have been common in India even at that time, *(i.e.,* Gautama Buddha's time) : books were not written but learnt by rote and taught from memory." Oldenberg's *Buddha,* (Translation), p. 177.
5. Compare Gospel of St. John, V. 17.
6. See Bears *Buddhism in China,* p. 43. *Vajji-Yuchi.*
7. This appellation shews that the king's mother was a lady of the ancient Videha tribe. Persons were frequently called in those days by their mother's name; and Upatissa, the distinguished disciple of Gautama was always better known as Sāriputra.
8. *Ambapālikā* means the grower of mangoes.
9. Bishop Bigandet says : "In recording the conversion of a courtezan, like Apapālika, her liberality and gifts to Buddha and his disciples, and the preference designedly given to her over princes and nobles, who, humanly speaking, seemed in every respect better entitled to attentions— one is almost reminded of the conversion of a woman that was a sinner, mentioned in the Gospels,"—*Life: or Legend of Gaudama.*
10. Vedic gods reduced to the position of beneficent spirits.
11. The tempter or evil spirit. "Mara est le demon del' amour, du peche et de la mort; ce la tentateur et l'ennemi de Buddha."—Burnouf.
12. The Universal Being of the Upaniṣads reduced to the position of a beneficent spirit.

CHAPTER – 15

DOCTRINES OF GAUTAMA BUDDHA

It is not possible that we should, within the limits of a single chapter, give our readers anything like a complete summary of the doctrines of a religion which now forms the subject of so much elaborate and learned inquiry by so many distinguished and able scholars. Our attempt will rather be to give here the substance of that lesson, and those ideas which Gautama preached and inculcated to his countrymen.

Buddhism is, in its essence, a system of self-culture and self-restraint. Doctrines and beliefs are of secondary importance in this system; the effort to end human suffering by living a holy life, free from passions and desires, is the cardinal idea with which Gautama was impressed on the day on which he was "enlightened" under the Bo-tree in Buddha Gayā, and it was the central idea which he preached to the last day of his life.

When he went from Buddha Gayā to Benares, and first preached his religion to his five old disciples, he explained to them the Four Truths and the Eightfold Path, which form the essence of Buddhism.

"This. O Bhikkhus, is the *Noble Truth of Suffering,* Birth is suffering, decay is suffering, illness is suffering, death is suffering. Presence of objects we hate is suffering, not to obtain what we desire is suffering. Briefly, the fivefold clinging to existence *(i. e.*, clinging to the five elements) is suffering.

This, O Bhikkhus, is the *Noble Truth of the Cause of Suffering*. Thirst, that leads to re-birth accompanied by pleasure and lust, finding its delight here and there. (This thirst is threefold), *viz.*, thirst for pleasure, thirst for existence, thirst for prosperity.

"This, O Bhikkhus, is the *Noble Truth of the Cessation of Suffering*. It ceases with the complete cassation of thirst—a cessation which consists in the absence of every passion, with the abandoning of this thirst, with the doing away with it, with the deliverance from it, with the destruction of desire.

"This, O Bhikkhus, is the *Noble Truth of the Path* which leads to the cessation of suffering. That holy Eightfold Path, *viz,*—

Right Belief,
Right Aspiration,
Right Speech,
Right Conduct,
Right Means of Livelihood,
Right Exertion,
Right Mindfulness.

Right Meditation."—*Mahāvagga I,* 6.

The substance of this teaching is that life is suffering, the thirst for life and its pleasures is the cause of suffering, the extinction of that thirst is the cessation of suffering, and that such extinction can be brought about by a holy life. It is impossible to convey in a few words all that is implied by the eight maxims into which a holy life has been analysed, but to Buddhists, trained in the traditions of the Law, these maxims speak volumes Correct views and beliefs must be learnt and entertained; high aims and aspirations must always remain present before the mind's eye; truthfulness and gentleness must characterise every word that is uttered; uprightness and absolute integrity must mark the conduct. A livelihood must be sought and adhered to which does no harm to living and sentient things; there must be a lifelong perseverance in doing good, in acts of kindness, gentleness and beneficence; the mind, the intellect, must be active and watchful; a calm and tranquill meditation shall fill the life with peace. This is the Eightfold Path for conquering desires and passions and thirst for life. A more beautiful picture of life was never conceived by poet or visionary; and a more perfect system of self-culture was never proclaimed by philosopher or saint.

The idea, of self-culture was no doubt developed during the long course of meditation and practical good work in which Gautama passed his life. On the eve of his death he called together his brethren, and appears to have recapitulated the entire system of self-culture under seven heads, and these are known as the Seven Jewels of the Buddhist Law.

"Which, then, O brethren, are the truths which, when I had perceived, I made known to you; which when you have mastered, it behoves you to practise, meditate upon, and spread abroad, in order that pure religion may last long and be perpetuated, in order that it may continue to be for the good and the happiness of the great multitudes, out of pity for the world, to the good and the gain and the weal of gods and men ? "They are these :—

The four earnest meditations,
The fourfold great struggle against sin,
The four roads to saintship,
The five moral powers,
The five organs of spiritual sense,
The seven kinds of wisdom, and
The Noble Eightfold Path."—*Mahāpārinibbānā Sutta, III,* 65.

Here, again, it is simply impossible to convey in a few words any adequate conception of all that is implied by these rules of discipline; a volume could be written on this most edifying subject.

The four earnest meditations alluded to are the meditations on the body, the sensations the ideas, and the reason. The fourfold struggle against sin is the struggle to prevent sinfulness, the struggle to put away sinful states which have arisen, the struggle to produce goodness, and the struggle to increase goodness. The fourfold struggle comprehends in fact a life-long, earnest, unceasing endeavour on the part of the sinner towards more and more of goodness and virtue. The fourfold roads to saintship are the four means—the will, the exertion, the preparation, the investigation—by which Iddhi is acquired. In later Buddhism Iddhi means supernatural powers, but what Gautama meant was probably the influence and power which the mind by long training and exercise can acquire over the body. The five moral powers, and the five organs of spiritual sense, are Faith, Energy, Thought, Contemplation, and Wisdom; and the seven kinds of wisdom are Energy, Thought, Contemplation, Investigation, Joy, Repose, Serenity. The Eightfold Path has already been described before.

It is by such prolonged self-culture, by the breaking of the ten fetters, doubt, sensuality, etc. that one can at last obtain Nirvāṇa.

"There is no suffering for him who has finished his journey, and abandoned grief, who has freed himself on all sides, and thrown off all fetters.

"They depart with their thoughts well collected, they are not happy within abode; like swans who have left their lake, they leave their house and home.

"Tranquil is his thought, tranquil are his word and deed, who has been freed by true knowledge, who has become a tranquil man." *Dhammapada, 90, 91, 96.*

It was generally believed that "Nirvāṇa" implied final extinction or death; and Professor Max Müller was the first to point out, what most scholars have now accepted, that Nirvāṇa does not mean death, but only the extinctions of that sinful condition of the mind, that thirst for life and its pleasures which brings on new births. What Gautama meant by Nirvāṇa is attainable in life; it is what he attained in life; it is the sinless calm state of mind, the freedom from desires and passions, the perfect peace, goodness and wisdom, which continuous self-culture can procure for man. As Rhys Davids puts it, "the Buddhist heaven is not death, and it is not on death but on a virtuous life here and now, that the Piṭakas lavish those terms of ecstatic description which they apply to Arhatship, the goal of the excellent way, and to Nirvāṇa as one aspect of it."

But is there no future bliss, no future heaven beyond "the virtuous life here and now" for those who have attained Nirvāṇa? This was a question which often puzzled Buddhists, and they often pressed their great Master for a categorical answer. Gautama was an agnostic—and there never was an honester religious teacher born than Gautama. He would not inspire in his followers a false hope which he did not feel in his own heart—and to all questions about a future life after the attainment of Nirvāṇa, his consistent reply was, "I do not know. It is not given to me to know."

Malūkyaputta pressed this question on Gautama, and desired to know definitively if the perfect Buddha did or did not live beyond the death. Gautama inquired Have I said, come, Malūkyaputta, and be my disciple; I shall teach thee whether the world is everlasting or not everlasting ? "That thou hast not said, sire," replied Malūkyaputta. "Then, said" Gautama, "do not press the inquiry." Gautama taught the lessons which contributed to peace and enlightenment and holiness in this life, and invited his brother men to accept these great lessons without inquiring after the unknown. If a man struck by a poisoned arrow, says to his physician, "I shall not allow my wound to be treated until I know who the man is by whom I have been wounded, whether he is a Kṣatriya, Brāhman, a Vaiśya or a Śūdra,"—what would be the end of him ? He would die of his wound. And so would the man perish who did not strive after enlightenment and a holy life, because he did not know what lay beyond. Therefore, Malūkyaputta, whatsoever has not been revealed by me, let that remain unrevealed, and what has been revealed, let it be revealed." *Kūla-Mālukya-Ovādā, Majjhima Nikāya.*

In the same manner we are told that King Prasenajit of Kosala, during a journey between his two chief towns, Sāketa and Srāvasti, fell in with the nun Khemā, renowned for her wisdom. The King paid his respects to her, and asked,—" Venerable lady, does the Perfect One exist after death ?" She replied,— ' The Exalted One, O great King, has not declared that the Perfect One exists after death." "Then, does the Perfect One not exist after death, Venerable lady ?" inquired the King. But Khemā still replied—"This also, O great King, the Exalted One has not declared, that the Perfect One does not exist after death." *Saṁyutta Nikāya.* These extracts will shew that Gautama's religion was a perfect and consistent agnosticism, which did not and could not look beyond the Nirvāṇa.[1] Gautama's aim was clear and well defined; he invited all men, by a strict self-culture, to end their sufferings, to avoid future states of suffering, to attain in this world to a state of holy bliss and perfect sinlessness, which is Nirvāṇa.

If a man does not attain to this state of Nirvāṇa in life, he is liable to future births. Gautama did not believe in the existence of a soul; but, nevertheless, the theory of transmigration of souls was too deeply implanted in the Hindu mind to be eradicated, and Gautama therefore adhered to the theory of transmigration without accepting the theory of soul! But if there is no soul, what is it that undergoes transmigration ? The reply is given in the Buddhist doctrine of Karma.

The doctrine is, that "Karma," or the "doing" of a man cannot die, but must necessarily lead to its legitimate result. And when a living being dies, a new being is produced according to the Karma of the being that is dead. Thus, though the pious Buddhist does not believe in a soul, he believes that his state of life is determined by his Karma in a previous birth. And Buddhist writers are fond of comparing the relation of one life to the next, as that of the flame of a lamp to the flame of another lighted by it. And if the innocent man suffers in this world, he argues, "it is the result of my own work, why should I complain ?" But wherein is the identity of the man who suffers with the man who is dead, if there is no soul ? The Buddhist answers,—"In that which alone remains when a man dies and is dissolved into atoms—in his action, thought and speech, in his Karma which cannot die."

The reasoning seems to us like arguing in a circle—but nevertheless there is one aspect of the theory the correctness of which will be admitted by modern social philosophers. The Buddhist believes, as well as the modern philosopher, that each generation is the heir to the consequences of the virtues and sins of the preceding generation, and that in this sense, a nation reaps as it sows. "The Buddhist saint does not mark the purity of his self-denial by lusting after positive happiness which he himself shall enjoy hereafter. His consciousness will cease to feel, but his virtue will live and work out its full effect in the decrease of the sum of the misery of sentient beings."[2]

But the theory of transmigration was not the only doctrine which Gautama accepted from ancient Hinduism and adopted in a modified form into his own religion. The whole of the Hindu Pantheon of the day was similarly accepted, and similarly modified to suit his cardinal idea, the supreme efficacy of a Holy Life:. The thirty-three gods of the Ṛg Veda were recognized— but they were not supreme. Brahmā, the Supreme Deity of the Upaniṣad, was recognized, but was not supreme. Holy Life: alone was supreme; they who had attained the Nirvāṇa or perfect bliss by holy life—the Buddhas—were supreme, higher than the 33 gods, higher than the angel hosts, higher than Brahmā. Never was there such a daring attempt made by man to elevate holiness and purity above the supernatural and the celestial; to raise goodness—attain-able by man—above the gods and the unknown powers of the universe !

In a passage to which we have already referred in the previous chapter, four kinds of celestial or supernatural beings are named, Brahmā, the thirty-three gods, angels and Māra, or the evil one. Except Māra all the rest are regarded as a kind of fairies, generally beneficent but more or less ignorant. They are not eternal, being liable like men to dissolution, and not entitled to worship; they are all subject to repeated births, and can only obtain the salvation of Nirvāṇa by walking along the Eightfold Path. Brahmā himself is no exception to the rule; he knows the superior greatness of Buddha, he assisted at his birth, induced him to proclaim the truth when he had discovered it under the Bo-tree, and gave utterance to the universal sorrow on Buddha's death. In a legend about an anterior birth of Gautama as a great king, we are told that Śakra (Indra) directed Viśvakarmā to build a palace for that king, and Viśvakarmā vanished from the heaven of the Great Thirty-three (gods), and appeared before the king to build the palace. *Mahāsudassanā Suttā, I*, 67, 68.

It is necessary, however, to remark that it is doubtful whether Gautama himself adopted such stories, or even recognized the Hindu Pantheon. It is not impossible that the Devas and Gandharvas and Brahmā lingered in the traditional language of the people who had adopted Buddhism. Gautama was probably indifferent towards such popular beliefs; his whole mind and heart were devoted to preaching a Holy Life:.

Similarly the popular beliefs about heaven and hell, were passively adopted without ever attaining to much importance in Gautama's religion. We are told in one place, that "evil-doers go to hell, righteous people go to heaven; those who are free from all worldly desires attain Nirvāṇa"—*Dhammapada,* 126. And in another place Gautama is said to have given an account of different hells,[3] and backbiters are sent to the very worst hell, Paduma. It is doubtful whether Gautama ever troubled himself about these categories of hells and heavens; they probably grew from popular beliefs.

Gautama respected a Brāhman as he respected a Buddhist Śrāman or Arhat; but he respecied him for his virtue and learning, not for his caste, which he in his soul ignored. When two Brāhman youths, Vasiṣṭha and Bhāradvāja, began to quarrel on the question, "How does one become a Brāhman ?" and came to Gautama for his opinion, Gautama delivered to them a discourse in which he emphatically ignored caste, and held that a man's distinguishing mark was his work, not his birth. The grass and the trees, he said, the worms, moths and ants, the quadrupeds, snakes, fishes and birds are all divided into species which are known by their distinguishing marks. Man, too, has his distinguishing mark, and that is his profession.

"For whoever amongst men lives by cow-keeping, know this, O Vasiṣṭha, he is a husbandman, not a Brāhman.

"And whoever amongst men lives by different mechanical arts * * is an artisan, not a Brāhman.

"And whoever amongst men lives by trade* * is a merchant, not a Brāhman?

"And whoever amongst men lives by serving others* * is a servant, not a Brāhman.

"And whoever amongst men lives by theft * * is a thief, not a Brāhman.

"And whoever amongst men lives by archery* * is a soldier, not a Brāhman.

And whoever amongst men lives by performing household ceremonials* * is a sacrificer, not a Brāhman.

"And whoever amongst men possesses villages * * is a king, not a Brāhman.

"And I do not call one a Brāhman on account of his birth, or of his origin from a particular mother— he may be called Bhupati, and he may be wealthy— but the one who is possessed of nothing and seizes upon nothing, him I call a Brāhman.

"The man who is free from anger, endowed with holy works, virtuous, without desires, subdued, and wearing his last body, him I call a Brāhman.

"The man who, like water on a lotus leaf, or a mustard seed on the point of a needle, does not cling to sensual pleasures, him I call a Brāhman. "*Vāsettha Sutta.*

Similarly in the Assalāyana Sutta of the Majjhima Nikāya, we are told that a distinguished Brāhman scholar, Assalāyana, came to controvert Gautama's opinion that all castes were equally pure. Gautama, who could meet a logician with his own weapons, asked if the wives of Brāhmans were not subject to all the disabilities of childbirth like other women. "Yes," replied Assalāyana. Were there not differences in colour among the people of adjacent countries like Bactria and Afganistan, asked Gautama, and yet could not slaves become masters, and masters slaves in those countries ? "Yes," replied Assalāyana. Then, asked Gautama, if a Brāhman "is a murderer, a thief, a liber tine, a liar, a slanderer, violent or frivolous in speech, covetous, malevolent, given to false doctrine," will he not after death be born to misery and woe, like any other caste ? "Yes," said Assalāyana, and it was also admitted that good works would lead to heaven irrespective of caste. Gautama proceeded further to argue that when a mare was united with an ass, the offspring was a mule, but the offspring of a Kṣatriya united to a Brāhman resembled its parents, and the obvious conclusion, therefore, was that there was really no difference between a Brāhman and a Kṣatriya! By such arguments Gautama drove the truth home to the young logician" mind, and he, "sat there silent, awkward, distressed looking downwards, reflecting, not able to answer,"—and then became a disciple of Gautama.

Elsewhere Gautama said of himself, to Bhāradvāja living by the Sundarikā river, "No Brāhman am I nor a king's son, nor any Vaiśya; having thoroughly observed the class of common people, I wander about the world.* * Do not ask about descent, but as about conduct." *Sundarikā Bhāradvāja Sutta.*

At another time Gautama explained to his followers "As the great streams, O disciples, however man they may be, the Gaṅgā, Yamunā, Asirāvatī, Sarabhi and Mahī, when they reach the great ocean lose the old name and their old descent, and bear only one name—the great ocean"—so also do Brāhmans, Kṣatriyas, Vaiśyas and Śūdras lose their distinctions when they join the Order. And we know that this theory was consistently carried out in practice, and Upāli, a barber, as we have seen before, joined the Order and became one of the most revered and learned of Buddhist monks. A touching story is also told in the *Theragāthā* which enables us to comprehend how Buddhism came like a salvation to the humble and the lowly in India, and how they eagerly embraced it as a refuge from caste-injustice. Sunita, the Thera or Elder says, "I have come of a humble family, I was poor and needy. The work which I performed was lowly—sweeping the withered flowers. I was despised of men, looked down upon and lightly esteemed. With submissive mien I shewed respect to many. Then I beheld Buddha with his band of monks as he passed, the great hero, into the most important town of Magadha. Then I cast away my burden and ran to bow myself in reverence before him. From pity for me he halted, that highest among men. Then I bowed myself at the Master's feet, stepped up to him and begged him, the highest among all beings, to accept me as a monk. Then said into me the gracious Master—'Come hither, O monk'—that was the initiation received." And the passage concludes with the is lesson which Gautama had so often preached, "By holy zeal and chaste living, by restraint and self-repression, hereby a man becomes a Brāhman; that is the highmost Brāhmanhood."

Who can read this touching story of humble Sunita's Conversion without realizing the loving spirit of equality which was the soul of early Buddhism, and which insured its success ? The great Master who regarded or wealth nor rank, nor caste, came to the poor and the despised as well as to the rich and the noble, and welcomed them to effect their own salvation by a pure fe and unstained conduct. A virtuous life opened wore path to the highest honour, to the low-born and the high-born alike—no other distinction was known or recognized in the Order. Thousands of men and women responded to this loving and rational appeal, and merged their caste inequalities in a common love for their Master and a common emulation of his virtues. And within three centuries from the date when Gautama proclaimed his message of equality and of love in Benares, the religion of equality and of love was the prevailing religion of India. Caste was unknown within the Order, and lost its sting among laymen outside the Order; for it was open to the lowest born among them to embrace the Order and thus win the highest honour.

393. "A man does not become a Brāhman by his platted hair, by his family, or by birth; in whom there is truth and righteousness, he is blessed, he is a Brāhman.

394. "What is the use of platted hair, O fool! What of the raiment of goat skins ? Within thee there is ravening, but the outside thou makest clean.[4]

422. "Him I call, indeed, a Brāhman, the manly, the noble, the hero, the great sage, the conqueror, the impassible, the accomplished, the awakened.

141. "Not nakedness, not platted hair, not dirt, not fasting or lying on earth, nor rubbing with dust, nor sitting motionless, can purify a mortal who has not overcome desires."[6] *Dhamapada.*

Accordingly, from the very commencement of his religious career, he expressed his pronounced disapprobation of the two *extremes:*

"A life given to pleasures, devoted to pleasures and lusts; this is degarding, sensual, vulgar, ignoble and profitless; and a life given to mortifications; this is painful, ignoble and profitless." *Mahāvagga,* I, 6, 17. The *middle path* is one of holy purity and calm sinless contemplation, and this is Gautama's Eightfold Path to salvation.

But Gautama not only expressed his pronounced disapprobation against the Hindu caste-system, and the ascetic practices sanctioned by Hinduism, he also exclaimed against the Vedic rites which were practised according to the injunctions of the Brāhmaṇas and the Sūtras. And the reasons are not far to seek. Gautama was not a thoughtless destroyer, nor a heedless and enthusiastic opponent of all that was orthodox and ancient. He did not raise his hand against a single ancient institution or belief which he did not consider positively mischievous, and a later corruption of the old religion. He denounced caste because he found it mischievous, and believed it to be a late and corrupted form of ancient Brāhmanism. He denounced asceticism because he found it harmful and misleading. And he proclaimed the fruitlessness of Vedic rites, because he found them, as then practised, to be silly, meaningless, dead forms, attended with needless cruelty to animals and loss of life.

It is possible to conceive that the utter lifelessness of these forms had something to do in first awakening the earnest mind of Gautama to a higher need. Did these forms and rites lead to any good ? Did they im prove the human heart, regulate the human conduct, alleviate human suffering? If not, are there no means to secure these objects, the only legitimate objects of Religion ? And when after long and fruitless penances, and long and fruitful contemplation, he did discover a system which would improve the human heart, alleviate human suffering, and regulate human conduct, he naturally proclaimed the uselessness of the rites and ceremonies which the people then called Religion.

A sinless, passionless state of the mind, a freedom from all desires of the senses, this is what Gautama aimed at; religious rites did not secure this end, retirement from the world and contemplation helped it.

"Having left son and wife, father and mother, wealth and corn and relatives, the different objects of desire, let one wander alone like a rhinoceros.

"This is a tie, in this there is little happiness, little enjoyment, but more of pain; this is a fish hook, so having understood, let a thoughtful man wander alone like a rhinoceros.

"Having torn the ties, having broken the net as a fish in the water, like a fire not returning to the burnt place, let one wander alone like a rhinoceros." *Khagga Visāna Sutta.*

And this brings us to the subject of retirement from the World, to that institution which, outwardly at least, most distinguishes Buddhism from Hinduism, *viz.,* the, Buddhist Monastic life.

It is a mistake to suppose that Gautama positively enjoined on all men to retire from the world and live the life of a recluse, of a Bhikkhu or a Bhikkhuni, *ie.,* a Buddhist monk or nun. To conquer the yearning thirst for life and its pleasures was the cardinal aim of the reformer, and he assigned no peculiar virtue to an outward act of renouncement of the world. But, nevertheless, as it is difficult to conquer that thirst so long as one is actually living in the midst of his family and enjoying the pleasures of life, Gautama recommended the life of a Bhikkhu as the more efficacious means for securing the great end. And so thousands retired from the world and became Bhikkhus, and thus the Buddhist Monastic system was formed.

But even now, when the Bhikkhus, and Bhikkhunīs have come to be regarded as the Priesthood of the Buddhists, there is no such line of demarcation as obtains in the Hindu world. Any lay disciple who desires to do so, may become a Bhikkhu by joining the fraternity, and any Bhikkhu who wishes to return to the world may leave the fraternity. Bhikkhus are supposed to live a holier life and claim superior wisdom, learning and sanctity; but to the present day the original idea of Gautama so far rules his followers, that the Bhikkhus living in Vihāras or monasteries all over the Buddhist world, are not priests in the ordinary sense of the 'word; they are not intercessors between the laymen and their gods; they are no more than travellers on the same road towards Nirvāṇa, by which the householders and laymen are also supposed to be travelling.

The peculiar rules relating to the Holy Order will be detailed in another chapter, as they do not come in among the essential doctrines of Gautama's religion. We will only quote here a beautiful Sūtra, giving a supposed conversation between Gautama and a herdsman relating to the comparative virtues of worldly security and religious bliss.

"I have boiled my rice, I have milked my cows"—so said the herdsman Dhaniya—"I am living together with my fellows near the banks of the Mahi river. My house is covered, the fire is kindled : therefore, if thou like rain, O Sky!"

2."I am free from anger, free from stubbornness"—so said Bhagavat—"I am abiding for one night near the banks of the Mahī river. My house is uncovered the fire (of passions) is extinguished: therefore, if thou like, rain, O Sky !"

3."Gad flies are not be found with me,"—so said the herdsman Dhaniya—"in meadows abounding with grass the cows are roaming, and they can endure the rain when it comes: therefore, if thou like, rain O Sky !"

4."By me is made a well-constructed raft"—so said Bhagavat—"I have passed over (to Nirvāṇa). I have reached the further bank, having overcome the torrent (of passions); there is no further use for a raft : therefore, if thou like, rain, O Sky !"

5. "My wife is obedient, not wanton"—so said the herdsman Dhaniya—"for a long time she has been living together with me. She is winning, and I hear nothing wicked of her : therefore, if thou like, rain, O Sky!"

6. "My mind is obedient and freed"—so said Bhagavat—"it has for a long time been highly cultivated and well subdued. There is no longer anything wicked in me: therefore, if thou like, rain, O Sky !"

7. "I support myself by my own earnings"—so said the herdsman Dhaniya,—"and my children are about me healthy. I hear nothing wicked of them : therefore, if thou like, rain, O Sky!"

8. "I am no one's servant"—so said Bhagavat— "with what I have gained, I wander about in all the world. There is no need for me to serve : therefore, if thou like, rain, O Sky !"

9. "I have cows, I have calves"—so said Dhaniya— "I have cows in calf and heifers. And I have also a bull as lord over the cows : therefore, if thou like, rain, O Sky !"

10. "I have no cows; I have no calves"—so said Bhagavat—"I have no cows in calf and no heifers. And I have no bull as a lord over the cows : therefore, if thou like, rain, O Sky !"

11. "The stakes are driven in, and cannot be shaken"—so said the herdsman Dhaniya—"the ropes are made of munja grass, new and well made, the cows will not be able to break them, therefore, if thou like, rain, O Sky!"

12. "Having, like a bull, rent the bonds; having, like an elephant, broken through the galuchchhi creeper, I shall not again enter into a womb: therefore, if thou like. rain, O Sky !"

Then at once a shower poured down, filling both sea and land. Hearing the sky raining, Dhaniya spoke thus:—

13. "No small gain indeed to us, since we have seen Bhagavat. We take refuge in thee, O thou endowed with the eye of wisdom! Be thou our master, O great Muni !" *Dhaniyasutta.*[6]

We have already said before that Gautama denied the existence of a soul. Man is supposed in the Buddhist philosophy to consist of an assemblage of *skandhas* or aggregates. These *skandhas* are :—

(1) The material properties like the elements, the organs of sense, etc.

(2) Sensations, divided into six classes, according as they are received through the six senses, including the mind.

(3) The abstract ideas belonging to six classes of sensations.

(4) Tendencies of the mind, divided into fifty-two divisions: Thought, Reflection, Memory, Effort, Pity, Envy, Pride, etc.

(5) Reason.

As the body is continuously changing, all its component parts are changing also, and man is never the same for two moments.

The denial of a soul is repeated throughout all Buddhist works, and this was a part of Gautama's own teachings. In the *Brahmājālā Sutta* of the *Dīgha Nikāya,* Gautama is supposed to discuss sixty-two different kinds of wrong belief, among which the belief that the soul and the world are eternal is a principal one. "Mendicants," concludes this sermon, "that which binds the Teacher (Buddha) to existence is cut off; but his body still remains. While his body shall remain, he will be seen by gods and men, but after the termination of life, upon the dissolution of the body, neither gods nor men will see him." "Would it be possible," asks Dr. Rhys Davids, "in a more complete and categorical way, to deny that there is any soul, any entity of any kind, which continues, to exist, in any manner after death ?"

The same writer quotes a passage from an ancient Ceylonese work giving a series of conversations between the Greek king Menander of Sagala in the Punjab, and Nāgārjuna or Nāgasena, the founder of the Madhyamika school of northern Buddhism.

Nāgasena— "Did your majesty come here on foot or in a chariot ?"

King—"In a chariot"

Nāgasena— "What is a chariot? Is the ornamental cover the chariot? Are the wheels, the spokes of the wheel, or the reins, the chariot ? Are all these parts together (in a heap) the chariot ? If you leave these out, does there remain anything which is the chariot ?."

King— "No."

Nāgasena—"Then I see no chariot, it is only a sound, a name. In saying that you came in a chariot, you have uttered an untruth. I appeal to the nobles, and ask them if it be proper that the great king of all Jambu-dvīpa (India) should utter an untruth."

King— "No untruth have I uttered, venerable monk. The cover, wheels, seat, and other parts all united form the chariot. They are the usual signs by which that which is called a chariot is known."

Nāgasena "And just so in the case of a man." And he quoted the words of the Teacher where he had said, "As the various parts of the chariot form, when united, the chariot, so the five skandhas, when united in one body, form a being, a living existence."[7]

Such is the Buddhist philosophy about the *skandhas* and the non-existence of the soul, which arose out of Gautama's teachings. It should be remembered, however, that the philosophy is of a later date than Gautama, and that the Reformer, though well versed in Hindu philosophy, discouraged philosophical discussions as useless for the great object he had in view. "When Mālunka asked the Buddha whether the existence of the world is eternal or not eternal, he made no reply; but the reason of this was that it was considered by the Teacher as an enquiry that tended to no profit."[8] And we are repeatedly told in the *Sutta Nipāta,* that one should not give himself up to philosophical disputations which lead to no good.

"Those wishing for dispute, having plunged into the assembly, brand each other as fools mutually; they go to others and pick a quarrel, wishing for praise, and calling themselves expert.* *

"These disputes have arisen amongst the Sāmans; in these disputes there is dealt blow and stroke; having seen this, let him leave off disputing, for there is no other advantage in trying to get praise." *Pasūra Sutta, Sutta Nipāta.*

"The opinions that have arisen amongst people, all these the wise man does not embrace; he is independent.

"A dogmatist is no leader to purity, being guided by prejudiced views, saying that good consists in what he is given to." *Mahāniyūhā Suttā. Sutta Nipāta.*

These are the leading doctrines of Gautama's religion, and a brief recapitulation of them will probably interest our readers. We have explained that Buddhism is in its essence a system of self-culture, an effort towards a holy life on this earth, and nothing more. We have seen that Gautama considered life to be suffering, the thirst after life to be the cause of suffering, the conquering of that thirst to be the cessation of suffering, and the Eightfold Path of self culture to be the means of conquering the thirst after life. Placing a holy life and sinless peace as the ideal of his religion and as the highest aim of human destiny, Gautama carefully elaborated the system of self-culture, the method of self-restraint in thought, word and speech, which he called the Noble Eightfold Path, or which is known as the Seven jewels of his Law.

And that holy peace, that sinless, tranquil life which is the object of so much self restraint and self culture, is attainable in this earth; it is the Buddhist's heaven, it is Nirvāṇa. Gautama's religion offers no glowing rewards in a world to come; virtue is its own reward; a virtuous life is the Buddhist's final aim; a virtuous peace on earth is the Buddhist's Nirvāṇa.

We have seen that Gautama nevertheless adopted the Hindu idea of transmigration in a modified form into his own religion. If Nirvāṇa is not attained in life, the Karma or actions of a living being lead to their legitimate results in re-births, until the discipline is complete and Nirvāṇa is attained. Gautama ignored the soul, but could not shake off the belief in transmigration, which was firmly implanted in the Hindu mind in his day.

In the same manner Gautama adopted, or permitted the adoption of, the popular beliefs of the day about the 33 gods of the Ṛg Veda, about Brahmā, about Gandharvas and angels, heaven and hell. But all this belief was modified so as to suit the cardinal idea of Buddhism, that a holy life was the supreme good; and gods, like men, were striving through repeated births after that Nirvāṇa which was the Buddhist's salvation.

But there were doctrines and customs of Hinduism which he could not accept. The caste system he eschewed, asceticism and penances he disapproved, the Vedic religious rites he declared to be fruitless. In place of such rites, he enjoined a benevolent life and the conquest of all passions and desires; and he recommended a retirement from the world as the most efficacious means for securing this end. The recommendation was followed, and led to the Buddhist monastic system—the earliest monastic fraternity known in the world.

And, lastly, we have seen that, although Gautama himself disapproved of philosophical discussion, a system of Buddhist philosophy soon arose on the lines laid down by him; that it ignored the existence of soul, and maintained living creatures to be only assemblages of *Skandhas,* or aggregates.

The great distinguishing feature of Buddhism then is, that it is a training towards a virtuous and holy life on this earth, and takes little thought of rewards and punishments in a future world. It appeals to the most disinterested feelings in man's nature, sets before him virtue as its own reward, and enjoins a life-long endeavour towards its attainment. It knows of no higher aim among gods or men than the attainment of a tranquil, sinless life; it speaks of no other salvation than virtuous peace, it knows of no other heaven than holiness.

"It swept away from the field of its vision the whole of the great soul-theory which had hitherto so completely filled and dominated the minds of the superstitious and of the thoughtful alike. For the first time in the history of the world, it proclaimed a salvation which each man could gain for himself, and by himself, in this world, during this life, without any, the least reference to God or to gods, either great or small."[9] It discards all the tempting pictures of joys and pleasures in heaven by which other religions lead men to virtuous deeds, it offers no glowing temptations, no imaginary rewards, it makes no appeal to man's selfish nature. Holding out no prospects of everlasting happiness, promising no happy heaven of gladness or bliss, Buddhism silently and sternly points to the path of virtue, and directs men to strive after a holy life,, because holiness is its own reward and its own heaven. Herein Buddhism stands alone among the great religions of the world.

On the other hand, this very feature of Buddhism is the subject of charges frequently brought against the religion. It is urged, and rightly urged, that it is an agnostic religion, that it knows of no God, no soul, no future world for those who have attained salvation. Dr. Rhys . Davids points out, however, that agnostic philosophy has come, not once or twice, but repeatedly to the forefront, when theology has failed to offer satisfactory replies to inquiries after the unknown, and men have sought for new solutions to old questions, "It is their place in the progress of thought that helps us to understand how it is that there is so much in common between the agnostic philosopher of India, the stoics of Greece and Rome, and some of the newest schools in France, in Germany, and among ourselves."[10]

But what was it that the agnostic Buddhists worshipped ? What was the concrete form which Gautama's religion took in the early age of which we are speaking; before vast monasteries and an unwieldy priesthood replaced the primitive faith ? What was the actual form of worship which drew and engaged the multitude who could not all have appreciated or worshipped the abstract idea of a holy life ? The reply is simple. For centuries the people worshipped holiness and virtue *as typified in the life of Gautama*. They revered the memories of the Great Teacher, they worshipped his invizible presence. The sculptures at Sanchi, at Amarāvatī, at Bharhut and other places, represent homage paid to tree, to serpent, to the wheel, or to the umbrella;

but in every case the object represents the presence or religion of Buddha, It was a worship "paid to the invisible presence of the Teacher, or to the power supposed to reside in his teaching (the wheel). It is a worship of association or of memory. The spots rendered famous by Buddha's presence during his life-time are consecrated in the mind of his disciple to sacred recollection, and worship is offered on those spots to the invisible object of faith."[11] Thus early Buddhism was the worship of holiness as typified in Buddha, and of his holy invisible presence.

REFERENCES

1. See the question fully and elaborately discussed by Dr. Oldenberg in his work on *Buddha, His life, His doctrine, His order.* The learned scholar has based his opinion on a careful examination of the entire body of the Buddhist canon.
2. Rhys Davids' *Buddhism,* p. 104.
3. Abbuda, Nirabbuda, Ababa, Ahaha, Atata, Kumuda, Sugandhika, Uppalika, Pundarika, and Paduma.
4. Compare Mathew XXIII, 27, Luke XI, 39.
5. Professor Max Müller has the following interesting note to the above verse :— "Walking naked and the other things mentioned in our verse, are outward signs of saintly life, and these Buddha rejects because they do not calm the passions. Nakedness he seems to have rejected on other grounds if we may judge from Sumāgadhā Avadāna. A number of naked friars were assembled in the house of the daughter of Anatha Pindika. She called her daughter-in-law Sumāgadā, and said,. 'Go and see those highly respectable persons.' Sumagādhā expecting to see some of the saints like Sāriputra, Maudgalāyana, and others, ran out full of joy. But when she saw these friars, with their hair like pigeon-wings, covered by noihing but dirr, offensive, and looking like demons, she became sad. 'Why are you sad ?' said her mother-in-law. Sumagādhā replied, 'O mother, if these are saints, what must sinners be like ?'"
6. Compare the parable in St. Luke XII, 16.
7. Rhys Davids' *Buddhism*, p, 97.
8. Spence Hardy's *Manual of Buddhism,* p. 375. See *ante,* p. 381.
9. Rhys Davids. Hibbert Lectures, 1881,
10. *Buddhist Sutta,* p. 145.
11. *Beal' s Buddhism in China,* p. 100.

CHAPTER – 16

MORAL PRECEPTS OF GAUTAMA BUDDHA

A religion, the great aim of which is the teaching of holy living in this world, must necessarily be rich in moral precepts, and such precepts are the peculiar beauty of Buddhism for which the religion is still held in honour all, over the civilized world. It will be our pleasant task in this chapter to glean some of these graceful precepts which will give our readers some idea of the essence of Gautama's moral teachings.

Gautama prescribed for lay disciples five prohibitory rules or Commandments, which were, no doubt, suggested by Vasiṣtha's five *Mahāpātakas* enumerated before, in chapter VII of this Book.

18. "A householder's work, I will also tell you, how a Sāvaka is to act to be a good one; for that complete Bhikkhu Dhamma cannot be carried out by one who is taken up by worldly occupations.

19. "Let him not kill or cause to be killed any living being, nor let him approve of others killing, after having refrained from hurting all creatures, both those that are strong and those that tremble in the world.

20. "Then let the Sāvaka abstain from taking anything, in any place that has not been given to him, knowing it to belong to another, let him not cause any one to take, nor approve of those that take. Let him avoid all theft.

21. "Let the wise man avoid an unchaste life as a burning heap of coals; not being able to live a life of chastity, let him not transgress with another man's wife.

22. "Let no one speak falsely to another in the hall of justice, or in the hall of the assembly; let him not cause any one to speak falsely, nor approve of those that speak falsely. Let him avoid all untruth.

23. "Let the householder, who approves of this Dhamma, not give himself to intoxicating drinks; let him not cause others to drink, nor approve of those that drink, knowing it to end in madness"—*Dhāmmika Sutta, Sutta Nipāta*.

These five precepts which are known as the Five Commandments, or the five rules of conduct (Pañca Śīla), are binding on all Buddhists, laymen and Bhikkhus. They are recapitulated thus :—

25. "Let not one kill any living being.

"Let not one take what is not given to him.

"Let not one speak falsely.

"Let not one drink intoxicating drinks.

"Let not one have unchaste sexual intercourse." *Ibid*.

Three other rules are laid down which are not considered obligatory, but which are recommended to pious lay disciples. They are—

25, 26. "Let him not at night eat untimely food.

Let him not wear wreaths or use perfumes.

"Let him lie on a bed spread on the earth."

Ibid. The pious householder is recommended to take a vow of all these eight precepts, which are known as the Eight Commandments, or the eight rules of conduct, (Aṣṭānga Śīla.)

To these eight rules two more are added, and they are: To abstain from dancing, music, singing and stage plays; and To obstain from the use of gold and silver. These ten Commandments (Dasa Śīla) are binding on Bhikkhus, as the Five Commandments are binding on all laymen and Bhikkhus.

To honour one's father and mother, though not included in the Commandments, is enjoined in the same Sutta on all householders.

"Let him dutifully maintain his parents, and practise an honourable trade. The householder who observes this strenuously, goes to the gods Sayampabhas *(Sanscrit* Svayambhū).

Buddhists had a weekly sabbath which was determined by the days of the moon. These Uposatha (*Sancrit* Upavāsa) days were four in the lunar month, *viz.,* when the moon was full or new, or half way between the two; and abstinence and the special observance of the moral precepts were enjoined on those days. The reader will perceive that the idea was taken from the Vedic Darsapūrṇamāsa ceremony which was held at the full moon and the new moon.

Again certain fortnights (Pātihāraka Pakkha) were set apart for the special and rigid observance of the moral precepts. And on the expiry of the Uposathas and Pātihāraka Pakkhas, the householder was recommended with a believing mind to "make distributions according to his ability."*—Dhāmmika Sutta, 28.*

A more exhaustive category of the duties of the householder is given in the well-known *Sigālovāda Sutta,* common both to the Northern and the Southern Buddhists, and which has been more than once translated into European languages. The enumeration of the duties gives us so clear an insight into the state of Hindu society and into the ideal of Hindu social life, that we feel no hesitation in quoting it.

1. Parents and Children

Parents should—

1. Restrain their children from vice.
2. Train them in virtue.
3. Have them taught in arts or sciences.
4. Provide them with suitable wives or husbands.
5. Give them their inheritance.

The child should say—

1. I will support them who supported me.
2. I will perform family duties incumbent on them.
3. I will guard their property.

4. I will make myself worthy to be their heir.
5. When they are gone, I will honour their memory.

2. Pupils and Teachers

The pupil should honour his teachers—

1. By rising in their presence.
2. By ministering to them.
3. By obeying them.
4. By supplying their wants.
5. By attending to instruction.

The teacher should shew his affection to his pupils—

1. By training them in all that is good.
2. By teaching them to hold knowledge fast.
3. By instruction in science and lore.
4. By speaking well of them to their friends and companions.
5. By guarding them from danger.

3. Husband and Wife

The husband should cherish his wife—

1. By treating her with respect.
2. By treating her with kindness.
3. By being faithful to her.
4. By causing her to be honoured by others.
5. By giving her suitable ornaments and clothes.

The wife should shew her affection for her husband—

1. She orders her household aright.
2. She is hospitable to kinsmen and friends.
3. She is a chaste wife.
4. She is a thrifty housekeeper.
5. She shews skill and diligence in all she has to do.

4. Friends and Companions

The honorable man should minister to his friends—

1. By giving presents.
2. By courteous speech.

3. By promoting their interest.
4. By treating them as his equals.
5. By sharing with them his prosperity.

They should shew their attention to him—

1. By watching over him when he is off his guard.
2. By guarding his property when he is careless.
3. By offering him a refuge in danger.
4. By adhering to him in misfortune.
5. By shewing kindness to his family.

5. Masters and Servants

The master should provide for the welfare of his dependants—

1. By apportioning work to them according to their strength.
2. By supplying suitable food and wages.
3. By tending them in sickness.
4. By sharing with them unusual delicacies.
5. By now and then granting them holidays.

They should shew their attachment to him as follows :—

1. They rise before him.
2. They retire later to rest.
3. They are content with what is given them.
4. They work cheerfully and thoroughly.
5. They speak well of him.

6. Laymen and those devoted to religion

The honourable man ministers to Bhikkhus and Brāhmans—

1. By affection in act.
2. By affection in words.
3. By affection on thoughts.
4. By giving them a ready welcome.
5. By supplying their temporal wants.

They should shew their affection to him—

1. By dissuading him from vice.
2. By exhorting him to virtue.

3. By feeling kindly towards him.
4. By instructing him in religion.
5. By clearing up his doubts.
6. By pointing the way to heaven.

The legend is that Gautam saw Sigāla, the householder, bowing to the four quarters of the heaven, and to the zenith and the nadir, to avert evils from these six directions. Gautama told him that the best way to avert evils from the six quarters was to perform good deeds towards his fellow-men, and so proclaimed the six categories of duties enumerated above. Sigāla was converted and became a lay-disciple.

What glimpses of pure Hindu life, of pleasant domestic and social feelings and duties, do we obtain from the above categories! The anxious care of parents to give children education and moral teaching and earthly comforts; the dutiful desire of children to support and respect their parents and honour their memory when dead; the respectful behaviour of the pupil towards the teacher, and the teachers anxious care and affection for the pupil; the respect, the kindness, the honourable and affectionate treatment which the Hindu religion, has ever enjoined on husbands towards their wives, and the faithfulness and scrupulous attention towards domestic duties for which Hindu wives have always been known; the kindly relations between friends and friends, between masters and servants, between laymen and spiritual instructors : these are among the noblest lessons that the Hindu religion has taught, and these are among the noblest traditions which Hindu literature has handed down for thousands of years. Buddhism accepted this noble heritage from the ancient Hindus, and embalmed it in its sacred literature. In Gautama's categories of duties we find all that is noblest and best in the Dharma Sūtras, and we do not find the moral precepts disfigured by those caste distinctions which we so much deplore in Hindu literature and religion.

We turn now from Gautama's categories of duties to those precepts and benevolent maxims to which Buddhism mainly owes its deserved fame in the modern world. Gautama's religion was a religion of benevolence and love; and five centuries before Jesus Christ was born, the Hindu Teacher had declared,

5. "Hatred does not cease by hatred at any time, hatred ceases by love : this is its nature."

197. "Let us live happily, not hating those who hate us. Among men who hate us, let us live free from hatred."

223. "Let one overcome anger by love, let him overcome evil by good. Let him overcome the greedy by liberality, the liar by truth."—*Dhammapada.*

Parables were told to impress this great lesson on the followers of the meek and gentle Gautama, and we will tell one of these stories as briefly as we can. Trying to heal contentions and differences among his followers, Gautama said :

"In former times, O Bhikkhus, there lived at Benares a king of the Kāsīs, Brahmādatta by name, wealthy, rich in treasures, rich in revenues, and rich in troops and vehicles, the lord over a great realm, with full treasuries and storehouses. And there was also a king of the Kosalas, Dīghīti by name, not wealthy, poor in treasures, poor in revenues, poor in troops and vehicles, the lord over a small realm, with empty treasuries and storehouses."

As often happens the rich king robbed the weak one of his realm and treasures, and Dīghīti with his queen fled to Benares, and dwelt there in a potter's house in the guise of an ascetic. There the exiled queen gave birth to a child who was called Dīghāvu, and in course of time the boy reached his years of discretion.

In the meantime king Brahmādatta heard that his former rival was living in the town in disguise with his wife, and he ordered them to be brought before him and had them cruelly executed.

Their son Dīghāvu was then living outside Benares, but happened to come to the town at the time of his father's execution. The dying king looked at his son, and with more than human forgiveness left his last injunctions on his son. "*Not by hatred, my dear Dīghāvu, is hatred appeased. By love, my dear Dīghāvu, hatred is appeased*"

"And young Dīghāvu, O Bhikkhus! went to the forest, there he cried and wept to his heart's content." He then returned to the town, after having formed his resolutions, and took employment under an elephant trainer in the royal stables.

Early in the dawn he arose and sang in a beautiful voice and played upon the lute. And the voice was so beautiful, that the king inquired who it was that had risen so early and had sung in the elephant stables in so beautiful a voice. And the young boy was taken to the king, pleased him, and was employed as his attendant.

And it so happened that on one occasion the king went out to hunt, taking young Dīghāvu with him. Dīghāvu's secret resentment was burning within him, and he so drove the royal chariot, that the hosts went one way, and the king's chariot went another way.

At last the king felt tired and lay down, laying his head on the lap of young Dīghāvu, and as he was tired, he fell asleep in a moment.

"And young Dīghāvu thought, O Bhikkhus, 'this king Brahmādatta, of Kāsī, has done much harm to us. By him we have been robbed of our troops and vehicles, our realm, our treasuries, and storehouses. And he has killed my father and mother. Now the time has come to me to satisfy my hatred'—and he unsheathed his sword."

But with the recollection of his father, the last words of his dying parent came to the recollection of the vengeful prince, "*Not my hatred, my dear Dīghāvu is hatred appeased; by love, my dear Dīghāvu, hatred is appeased*" "It would not become me to transgress my father's word," said the prince, and he put up his sword.

The king dreamt a frightful dream and arose terrified and alarmed. Dīghāvu told him the whole truth. The king was astonished, and exclaimed, "Grant me my life, my dear Dīghāvu! Grant me my life, my dear Dīghāvu !" The noble young prince forgave his father's murderer in carrying out his father's injunction, and granted Brahmādatta his life. And Brahmādatta gave him back his father's troops and vehicles, his realm, his treasuries and storehouses, and he gave him his daughter,